# Does God Make a Difference?

# Does God Make a Difference?

*Taking Religion Seriously in Our Schools and Universities*

WARREN A. NORD

OXFORD
UNIVERSITY PRESS
2010

# OXFORD
UNIVERSITY PRESS

Oxford University Press, Inc., publishes works that further
Oxford University's objective of excellence
in research, scholarship, and education.

Oxford   New York
Auckland   Cape Town   Dar es Salaam   Hong Kong   Karachi
Kuala Lumpur   Madrid   Melbourne   Mexico City   Nairobi
New Delhi   Shanghai   Taipei   Toronto

With offices in
Argentina   Austria   Brazil   Chile   Czech Republic   France   Greece
Guatemala   Hungary   Italy   Japan   Poland   Portugal   Singapore
South Korea   Switzerland   Thailand   Turkey   Ukraine   Vietnam

Published by Oxford University Press, Inc.
198 Madison Avenue, New York, New York 10016

www.oup.com

Oxford is a registered trademark of Oxford University Press

Library of Congress Cataloging-in-Publication Data
Nord, Warren A.
Does God make a difference? : taking religion seriously in our schools
and universities / Warren A. Nord.
   p. cm.
ISBN 978-0-19-976688-8
1. Education—Religious aspects. 2. Religion. I. Title.
LB1027.2.N67   2010
379.2′8—dc22   2010017036

9 8 7 6 5 4 3 2 1

Printed in the United States of America
on acid-free paper

*For my parents*

# Foreword

*Does God Make a Difference?* is the most important—and surely the most provocative—book ever written about the role of religion in American education. It is *not*, as the author underscores many times, a religious argument for taking religion seriously in schools and universities; it *is* an educational, moral, civic, and constitutional argument for providing students with the liberal education they need to be educated persons.

Sadly, Warren Nord did not live to see his extraordinary book published. On June 19, 2010, just eleven days after he sent his final edits to Oxford University Press, Warren passed away after a heroic nine-month battle with acute leukemia. Despite harrowing and lengthy stays in the hospital, round after round of chemo, a bone marrow transplant and considerable discomfort, Warren was determined to finish this book because he very much wanted to reach a wide audience with his ideas about the place of religion in education. Not only did he finish this book, he also managed to write *quickly* (as he put it) new essays that he had long hoped to write. In the spring of 2010, *Ten Essays on Good and Evil* was published by the Program in the Humanities and Human Values at the University of North Carolina-Chapel Hill, a program he directed for twenty-five years.

No one who knew Warren was surprised by his one-pointed determination to complete at least some of the many writing projects he planned to tackle in his "retirement." An outstanding philosopher and teacher with a keen intellect and compassionate heart, Warren had much of significance to say—and every word he left behind is worth reading.

In the pages that follow, Warren challenges the reader to rethink the curricula of public schools and universities (and of many private schools and universities as well) that virtually ignore religious ways of making sense of the world. Of course, some progress has been made on this front, at least in K–12 public schools. Twenty years ago, for example, social studies standards and textbooks were mostly silent about religion. Today there is more inclusion of study about religions in history textbooks and classrooms, but unfortunately much of it is superficial.

Warren argues persuasively that simply adding additional information about religion in history and elsewhere is not the solution to the problem as he defines it. He is not asking for more "mention" of religion; he is calling for a truly liberal education that exposes students to religious as well secular interpretations of the world. As he writes in the conclusion to this book: "An educational system that ignores the great existential questions—political, moral, spiritual, religious—is not worthy of respect, indeed, it shouldn't count as educational at all."

Needless to say, implementing Warren's vision would require a profound revolution in education—a revolution that, at present, has few advocates ready to mount the curriculum barricades of schools and universities that see nothing unjust or unconstitutional about leaving students ignorant of religion.

Is change possible? Over the years, Warren and I have alternated between optimism and pessimism about the possibilities for genuine reform in education that would cause schools and universities to take religion seriously. The publication of this book gives me new grounds for optimism. A good number of the recommendations made here are modest and practical (e.g., dramatically increase the number of public school electives in religious studies) and would make real improvements in study about religions in classrooms across the country. Other proposals (e.g., require courses in high school and college on morality and meaning that also take religion seriously) are more daunting. But if any book can inspire action, *Does God Make a Difference?* is that book.

I only wish that Warren had lived to see how you, his readers, will respond to the compelling, controversial, and sometimes contentious arguments he makes for taking religion seriously in American education. But I know that in his final months he was deeply gratified to have finished this book—and was satisfied, as he writes in the preface, that he had "gotten things about right."

He did indeed get it right. *Does God Make a Difference?* is a worthy capstone to the life and work of a wise and gentle man, one of the most empathic and thoughtful human beings I have ever known. I celebrate his legacy as found in the pages of his writings—and deeply mourn the loss of a great scholar and wonderful friend.

Charles C. Haynes
Freedom Forum First Amendment Center

# Preface

This is my third book on religion and education—the conclusion of a trilogy of sorts. My first book was primarily for scholars (much longer, more academic, many more quotes and notes), the second was for teachers (more practical), while this one is primarily for the general public (though I trust that there is a good deal in it for scholars, teachers, students, and the clergy). I have changed my mind about a few things over the twenty years I have been writing about religion and education, so I would like to think that I have now gotten things about right. In any case, this book is the place to start, though enthusiastic readers may find aspects of my first two books that complement this one and go into more detail on particular issues.

I would particularly like to thank a number of colleagues who read large parts or all of the manuscript: Bruce Grelle, Martha Dill, Kathy Wildman, Collins Kilburn, Weldon Thornton, and especially Charles Haynes, from whom I have learned more—much more—about religion and education than anyone else. I am truly grateful to Cynthia Read, my editor at Oxford University Press, for her encouragement, advice, and speeding the manuscript along. As always, I am immensely grateful to my wife, Nancy, for her love and support, and to our son, Jeremy, for the joy he has brought into our lives.

I dedicate the book to my parents, Delphie (1917–83) and Elmer Nord (1913–96). They would have appreciated the fact that I take religion seriously.

# Contents

# Does God Make a Difference?

# Introduction

## *An Overview of the Argument*

In its last issue of the twentieth century, *The Economist* printed an obituary for God. Almost a decade later, its editor and its Washington bureau chief coauthored a book titled *God Is Back: How the Global Revival of Faith Is Changing the World.*[1] Both stories were old news. Long before *The Economist*, *Time* magazine had pressed the issue in its Easter 1966 issue, with a cover that asked, in large capital letters, IS GOD DEAD? In fact, many scholars had been predicting the death of God for more than a century. And yet, most Americans denied that God had died, and the very public resurgence of religion in the United States in the 1970s and 1980s cinched it for many scholars who didn't need 9/11 to awaken them from their slumbers. God wasn't back; he hadn't even gone away.

No doubt, not all Americans believe in God. The number of people who identify themselves as atheists may be growing slowly, cheered on by a newly vocal, militant movement of atheist intellectuals (or "brights" as they sometimes call themselves). There are also more of the "merely secular," those folks uninterested in either religion or atheism.

Still, the vast majority of Americans, like the vast majority of people around the world, believe in God, and even if much of this belief is nominal, much of it is sincere. Conservative churches continue to thrive (although their growth spurt of the last few decades may have slowed), and if liberal churches continue to decline in membership, there is considerable evidence of a widespread, if amorphous, liberal spirituality in American popular culture. Of course, Americans are not just Christians; the United States has become home to a bustling mix of the world's religions.

It is true that many intellectuals are atheists, but it is also true that many intellectuals believe in God. Surveys show that even college professors (by reputation a godless lot) are more likely to believe in God than not. For several decades now there has been a lively discussion among scholars about the relationship of religion and science, much of it directed to integrating them rather than simply dismissing religion. In some scholarly quarters, postmodernism has undermined Enlightenment certainties—perhaps opening doors to religion in the process. Contemporary theologians, liberal and conservative, have created a rich scholarly literature on every moral and social issue.

In fact, religion makes a difference to most people—to the ways in which they find meaning in their lives, to their moral and political judgments, to how they make sense of the world. Not surprisingly, religious voices are prominent in our culture wars, in battles over abortion and homosexuality, war and peace, social justice and family values, the environment and the arts, and, of course, education.

So what do students learn about all of this?

Virtually nothing. It is true that over the last several decades a new national consensus has developed about the role of religion in public schools—one that legitimates a significant role for the study of religion—yet this agreement on principles has resulted in few changes in practice.[2] School textbooks still largely ignore religion except in the context of distant history. The national content standards for K–12 education essentially ignore religion (except, again, in the context of history). Courses in religion are not even elective possibilities in most public schools. And while departments of religious studies have become increasingly common in universities since the 1960s, the majority of public universities still lack such departments. And even where there are such departments, religion courses are electives taken by a minority of students. Needless to say, religious ways of making sense of the world are not likely to be taken seriously in other courses.

American education proceeds on the assumption that God is either dead or irrelevant. Irrelevant gods are not unknown: the ancient Epicureans believed that the gods kept to themselves in their heaven and took no interest in us mere mortals. Historically, this has not been the typical take on God, however. The more common view has been that if God exists there are implications. In the Western religious traditions it has been held that God created the world and that nature fulfills God's purposes, that we have souls and there is an afterlife, that we are obligated in our lives to serve God and do justice to humankind, that

God acts in history, and that truth is revealed in Scripture. These have not been understood to be minor matters of antiquarian interest, of concern only to the mindlessly devout.

And yet the conventional wisdom of educators is that students can learn everything they need to know about any subject in the curriculum (other than history and historical literature) without learning anything about religion. We systematically and uncritically teach students to make sense of the world in exclusively secular categories. Consequently, the great majority of students earn their high school diplomas and their undergraduate degrees without ever contending with a live religious idea.

I will argue that with regard to religion American education is superficial, illiberal, and unconstitutional. These are not insignificant claims. Indeed, this should be recognized for what it is, a scandal.

There are many reasons for taking religion seriously in public schools and universities. A liberal education requires it. Because religion continues to be such an influential force for good and for evil one simply can't be an educated person without understanding a fair amount about it. Even more important, because we disagree so deeply about the merits of various religious and secular ways of making sense of the world and our lives, students must be introduced to the religious as well as the secular alternatives if they are to think critically. It is not justifiable for public schools and universities to institutionalize secular interpretations of the various subjects of the curriculum and, in so doing, marginalize or discredit religion uncritically. This is profoundly illiberal and suggests an extraordinary degree of either hubris or thoughtlessness; indeed, as we shall see, it borders on secular indoctrination.[3]

There is a cluster of moral and civic reasons for taking religion seriously. It is an important task of education to locate students in the world morally and address important moral controversies (including the nature of morality itself). No doubt the relationship of morality and religion is deeply controversial, but religion must be part of the conversation; if it is not, it is, once again, illiberal. Education should address those "big questions" about the meaning of life that almost inevitably concern students (like all thoughtful human beings) and it is inconceivable to take on such questions without allowing religion a place at the table. Students must understand religion in order to be thoughtful voters. Justice requires that schools and universities take religion seriously. Political liberty is incompatible with secular indoctrination. And both the civility and respect for people's rights that are necessary in a democracy require that students learn about one another's religions as well as religious liberty.

There are, of course, constitutional considerations. There is widespread agreement that it is constitutionally permissible to teach about religion in public schools and universities (when done properly). I will argue for a stronger position, that on the U.S. Supreme Court's interpretation of the Establishment Clause, public schools and universities are obligated to take religion seriously. Of course, public schools and universities cannot privilege or promote religion—a particular religion or religion generally. Public schools and universities must be neutral in dealing with religion. But neutrality, as we shall see, requires fairness, and fairness requires that (various) religious as well as secular interpretations of the world, and of the subjects of the curriculum, be taken seriously.

All of these reasons for taking religion seriously must be spelled out in some detail if they are to be convincing, and occasional qualifications will be necessary. Still, if I am right, radical educational reforms are necessary in how we teach virtually every subject of the curriculum. Does God make a difference? Not now, according to the conventional wisdom. Should God make a difference? Of course.

This book is divided into three sections. In part 1, I will show just how secular education has become, and explain how this came to be and why this is a major problem. In part 2, I will explain why schools and universities must take religion seriously—and consider a number of objections to my position. In part 3, I will discuss how to take religion seriously, drawing out the implications of my position for the curricula of schools and universities, leading us to some rather far-reaching and provocative conclusions.

The problems and solutions that I will discuss cut across secondary and higher education, so I will discuss both. Most important, the study of religion is essential to liberal education, and both secondary and undergraduate education must be liberal (unlike elementary, graduate, and professional education). I will say a little, but not much, about prayer and the practice of religion, but my primary concern is with the curriculum and how teachers and textbooks address (or fail to address) religion in the classroom. I will focus much of my attention on public schools and universities, though much of what I say will be relevant to private schools and universities. The big question, after all, is about what it means to be well educated whatever the setting.[4]

Perhaps a confession is in order at this point. Some readers may already wonder if my position is beyond the pale, less then fully respectable. They may suspect that I am a political and religious conservative—maybe even (gasp) a fundamentalist. I am none of the above. I am a liberal in my politics and in my religion—though I hasten to add that it will not be my purpose to convince you that either my political or religious views are the right ones. In fact, I will try very hard to be neutral in matters of politics and religion. However, I *am* going to try to convince you that my views on education are the right ones.

In fact, I will argue for what I take to be a middle way in our culture wars over religion—though it is an indication of how far we have gone astray that efforts to point it out inevitably prove controversial. Although my primary concern is with what counts as a good education I also regard my proposal as "articles of peace" (to use John Courtney Murray's fine phrase) in our culture wars. Americans are deeply divided over religion, and the battles will continue so long as public education takes sides in matters of religion as is now the case. Peace requires, I suggest, that religion be taken seriously but not privileged. Of course, not everyone will agree.

Before jumping into the thick of things I need to say something about two words—*God* and *religion*—that appear in the title of this book and that will be of considerable importance to us. Both present problems. Let me explain.

## God

Different languages have different words for God—*Gott*, *Dieu*, or *Dios*, for example. Muslims believe that the Qur'an must be read in Arabic, the language of God's revelation to Muhammad; consequently, *Allah*'s name cannot be translated. Jews sometimes write *G-d*, indicating that God's name must not be written or spoken, just as YHWH (Yahweh) could not be spoken by anyone other than the High Priest, in the Holy of Holies, on the Day of Atonement. The name "God" isn't quite neutral among religious traditions.

There is a more fundamental problem. In the aftermath of 9/11 it was often said that Jews, Christians, and Muslims all worship the same God. After all, they are all monotheists who trace their religion back to Abraham and Abraham's God. But do they worship the same God? Christians believe that Jesus was God incarnate and Christianity is Trinitarian (God the Father, God the Son, and God the Holy Spirit). Judaism and Islam reject this conception of God. In fact, many people within each of these traditions believe that their conception of God is the correct one, not just one of several variations of the true God. The more liberal one is, the more plausible it will appear that different conceptions of God are all inadequate approximations to the true God. The more conservative one is, the more plausible it will be that the conception of God rooted in one's own tradition and language is the correct one—and that somewhat different conceptions of God in other traditions are inadequate so that people in those traditions worship a false God.

Of course, theists within the Western traditions don't agree on how to characterize God—on how literally to take scriptural God-language. Is God a supernatural being, distinct from his creation, or is God something more like the spirit or soul of the universe? They disagree about gender language (the masculine pronoun I just used, for example); indeed, some feminist theologians reject the word God as implicitly masculine.

The problem cuts even deeper when we consider other religious traditions, especially the more mystical Eastern traditions. In some traditions of Hinduism, for example, God is the One "before whom all words recoil"—as Shankara put it in his great prayer—except, of course, Shankara didn't use the English word God. The critical difference here is that within much Eastern religion (not all) and within Western mysticism (not all), God isn't personal; God isn't the kind of being whose nature can be put into language (much as we can describe persons within language). In the theistic traditions we talk of a God who is loving or judgmental, who created the world or who intervenes in history, but this makes no sense within mystical traditions. Does it then make sense to speak of the God of mysticism? Indeed, it may be best not to think of Brahman, Nirvana, or the Tao as a being at all, but rather as ultimate being itself.

The philosopher of religion John Hick has suggested that we use "the Real" as an umbrella term for what is ultimate in all the world's religions. We might think, he suggests, of the Real as "experienced by human beings in terms of one of two basic religious concepts. One is the concept of God, or the Real experienced as personal, which presides over the theistic forms of religion. The other is the concept of the Absolute, or the Real experienced as nonpersonal, which presides over the various nontheistic forms of religion."[5]

What's the point of all of this for us? Well, different conceptions of ultimate reality are found in different religious traditions, and some traditions will have trouble with the English word God or the Western conception of a personal God for this reality.

I have no intention of taking a position on the "correct" conception of God (Allah, G-d, YHWH, Nirvana, Braham, the Tao, the One, the Absolute, the Real). My goal is to be neutral—or at least as neutral as I practically can be. But I am writing primarily for an American, English-reading audience for whom God is the least confusing term, and it would be impossibly cumbersome to constantly use all of the various alternatives or the abstract and bloodless term, the Real. So I will settle on the word God. But I acknowledge that in doing so I fall short of my own ideal. Alas, this will not be the last time that neutrality proves hard to come by.

Religion

Like the word *God*, the word *religion* doesn't always translate well. The great
historian of religion Wilfred Cantwell Smith noted that there "have been in the
past relatively few languages into which one can translate the word 'religion'—
and particularly its plural, 'religions'—outside [modern] Western civilization."[6]
Most cultures have not divided the world up conceptually as we do, and, consequently, we need to be wary of the claim that religions have a conceptual
essence. The word may impose order where there is considerable disorder. As
we've just seen, even the claim that God is at the core of all religion is problematic; there are such radically different conceptions of God—of the Real—that
we quickly find ourselves in murky waters. Not only does much Eastern and
mystical religion not have a personal God, some strands of religion, of Buddhism, for example, are agnostic about any transcendent reality, yet Buddhism
has long been categorized as a religion.

   We might better think of religion as what the philosopher Ludwig Wittgen-
stein called a family-resemblance term. Like members of families, religions
appear to share a network of overlapping similarities and differences, but no
universally shared characteristic (even belief in God). On this way of thinking
there may even be secular religions. Some social scientists, for example, have
defined religion functionally or analogically so that if a tradition or ideology or
worldview shares most of the characteristics of the traditional great religions, if
it functions religiously in the lives of people and cultures, then we might best
think of it as religious even if it is secular.

   It has often been argued, for example, that atheistic communism has
functioned as a religion complete with a mythic framework for life, sacred
scriptures, saints, dogmas, an ecclesiastical hierarchy, an ethic, an iconography
(socialist realism), eschatology, and, of course, heresies and heretics.[7] (As communism was discredited, one widely read critique was titled *The God That
Failed*.) The influential sociologist of religion J. Milton Yinger has argued that
we should think of scientism as a religion when science becomes an
overarching worldview or way of life, rather than simply a methodology.[8] Will
Herberg talked about the American way of life as the true religion of the United
States—and he also argued that public schools taught the "substitute religion
of secularism," which he defined as "the theory and practice of human life con-
ceived as self-sufficient and unrelated to God."[9] Many scholars have claimed
that nationalism functions as a kind of religion.

   The U.S. Supreme Court has sometimes used an expansive notion of
religion. In a famous ruling, *Torcaso v. Watkins* (1961) Justice Hugo Black
wrote: "Among the religions in the country which do not teach what would

generally be considered a belief in the existence of God are Buddhism, Taoism, Ethical Culture, *Secular Humanism* and others."[10] In *United States v. Seeger* (1965), Justice Tom Clark noted: "over 250 sects inhabit our land. Some believe in a purely personal God, some in a supernatural deity; others think of religion as a way of life envisioning as its ultimate goal the day when all men can live together in perfect understanding and peace. There are those who think of God as the depth of our being; others, such as the Buddhists, strive for a state of lasting rest through self denial and inner purification." Given these differences, Clark argued, for constitutional purposes we should accept as religious any "sincere and meaningful belief which occupies in the life of its possessor a place parallel to that filled by the God in tradition religion."[11]

But if the word *religion* is sometimes expanded to include secular traditions, ideologies, or ways of life, it is also sometimes given a considerably narrower meaning. Many people nowadays will say that they are spiritual but not religious.[12] I'll have more to say about spirituality shortly; for now I'll just note that people have increasingly come to reject institutional religion (with its creeds, rituals, and traditions) for spirituality. If much religion has embraced spirituality, there are ways of being spiritual that are not religious.

It is also essential to remember that religions involve much more than belief in God. Ninian Smart has famously argued that we should think of religions as having a variety of dimensions—doctrines, myths or sacred narratives, ethical and legal teachings, rituals, religious experiences, social institutions, and art.[13] Different religions emphasize different dimensions. In all cases, however, religions have broad implications for how we make sense of the world. So, for example, belief in God may make sense from within a broadly religious worldview or way of life when it may not make sense from within a scientific worldview or secular way of life. Historically, religions have provided a richer set of categories for understanding our experiences and for grounding our beliefs and values than has modern science.

Moreover, all of the major religious traditions address profound existential concerns and profess powerful moral teachings that orient people in the world, give their lives meaning, promote (particular conceptions of) goodness and justice, and require people to overcome self-concern, setting themselves right with God or living in harmony with the moral structure of the universe. That is, religion isn't simply a matter of taking the question of God's existence seriously, of believing in God; it is also a matter of taking the moral and existential implications of God's existence seriously.

So where does this leave us? We need to keep in mind that in other times and places people have understood their own religions in very different ways from how we, in the modern West, understand ours. While I will be primarily concerned with the great world religions, there are also, arguably, secular religions, and it is often claimed that one can be spiritual (perhaps accepting God or the Real in some sense) apart from organized religions. Perhaps most important, we cannot forget that religion is about much more than the existence of God; it is also about how we make sense of the world and how we live our lives. Inevitably, we will have to come back to all these points.

God, Religion, and Our Culture Wars

Finally, in thinking about the role of God and religion in education we need to keep in mind three somewhat different sets of tensions and conflicts embodied in our culture wars.

During the seventeenth century the most important conflicts in America and Western Europe were between different religions—particularly between Catholics and Protestants (but also, in Eastern Europe, between Muslims and Christians). No doubt the hostility among Protestants could also be fairly intense: so, for example, the Massachusetts Puritans found it necessary, on occasion, to hang a few Quakers. This kind of religious conflict has not quite disappeared in the United States (though the hangings have), and it certainly hasn't disappeared in the rest of the world. Over the last decade or two there has been a good deal of talk about a *clash of civilizations* that is defined in large part by each civilization's religious traditions and values. Of course, even when religions and civilizations aren't at war with one another, there can be conflicts and tensions among religious traditions within our increasingly pluralistic cultures.

By the end of the eighteenth century the first skirmishes in a new culture war had been fought—primarily in Europe—between traditional religious thinkers and secular, sometimes atheistic, intellectuals committed to the Enlightenment and modern science. Over the course of the nineteenth century tensions between science and religion developed in Europe and the United States. A large part of my discussion in this book will focus on this culture war.

By the end of the nineteenth century deep divisions had appeared within Christianity and Judaism between conservatives who wished to maintain theological orthodoxies grounded in Scripture and tradition, and liberals who believed that religion could be progressive as theologians rethought and reformed their own traditions. E. J. Dionne captures this difference nicely in writing that "the conservative keeps the tradition alive by honoring it. The progressive [or liberal] keeps the tradition alive by adapting it."[14] James Davison

Hunter highlighted this third culture war in his seminal book *Culture Wars*, arguing that the deepest religious differences nowadays are between liberals and conservatives (or, as he calls them, progressives and the orthodox) within each tradition. Indeed, Hunter argues, liberal Jews, Catholics, and Protestants share ways of making sense of the world that differ strikingly from ways of making sense of the world shared (to some considerable extent) by conservative (or Orthodox) Jews, Protestants, and Catholics.

Though I will often contrast (all too simply) religious liberals and conservatives, I want to fine-tune my taxonomy by suggesting that we think in terms of four rather than two alternatives, adding "spirituality" to the left of religious liberalism, and "fundamentalism" to the right of religious conservatism.[15] While these distinctions have been worked out primarily in Christianity and Judaism, scholars have drawn roughly parallel distinctions within other religious traditions. No doubt many people, perhaps *most* people, fall betwixt and between the overly stark and simplistic positions that I will sketch.[16]

## 1. Religious Liberals

As the term suggests, liberals place a good deal of emphasis on the liberty to rethink their traditions. They are open to truths in other traditions (religious and secular—in modern science or feminism, for example). Liberals have tended to have a relatively optimistic view of human nature, reason, and social institutions. Scripture, while it is to be taken seriously, is not to be taken literally. While Scripture surely records people's experiences of God, we know, as a result of historical and textual biblical scholarship, that the Bible is filled with contradictions, changing conceptions of God, and the very fallible ideas of people living in ancient cultures. Liberals value scholarship and the critical study of contending traditions. They typically understand religion as progressive. The truth wasn't given once and for all in the past. Rather, there is moral and spiritual progress in history. Liberals often say that God works through people and social institutions (rather than through supernatural intervention) to bring about justice, the kingdom of God, or the liberation of the oppressed.

By the end of the nineteenth century, Reform Judaism and liberal Protestantism had acquired considerable influence in Europe and the United States. While World War I chastened liberal optimism for a generation or two, liberals recovered their courage in the 1960s, the decade of the civil rights movement and the decade when Pope John XXIII threw open the windows of the Vatican to the winds of change that blew through the Second Vatican Council—perhaps the most significant Christian event since the Protestant

Reformation. Liberal biblical scholarship flourished. Liberation theology, feminist theology, and ecotheology became major movements within liberal religion, putting poverty, the Third World, women, civil rights, the environment, and gay rights on the agenda of liberal causes within both Judaism and Christianity.[17]

## 2. Religious Conservatives

Generally speaking, conservatives believe that the Truth has been revealed in Scripture, or in Tradition, and, as a result, they have been wary of the idea of progress, reason, and scholarship, often believing that they are symptoms of pride (the original sin for many Christians). Orthodox Jews rejected Reform Judaism both in Europe, and then in the United States, at the end of the nineteenth century, while evangelical Protestants rejected religious liberalism (not least its biblical scholarship), emphasizing instead revivals and born-again religious experience. In 1909, long before the liberalism of Vatican II, Pope Pius X required all Catholic clergy and scholars to sign the Oath against Modernism rejecting the new biblical scholarship and asserting their allegiance to the papacy and traditional Catholicism.

After World War II, Billy Graham's crusades ushered a conservative neo-evangelicalism into U.S. homes via television. Perhaps most important, there was a powerful conservative reaction against the moral liberalism and counterculture of the 1960s, sparked, in part, by the Supreme Court's rulings on school prayer in 1962 and abortion in 1973. Pope Paul VI dampened enthusiasm over the reforms of Vatican II by reasserting the church's stand on birth control, and John Paul II, who was certainly not a conservative on all issues, tempered the theological liberalism of post-Vatican II Catholicism.

## 3. Fundamentalism

The line between conservative religion and fundamentalism isn't clear or sharp.[18] Fundamentalism takes its name from a series of essays called *The Fundamentals*, published in the United States between 1910 and 1915, the goal of which was to determine what was fundamental to Protestant Christianity. Lists differ, but the fundamentals were often taken to be the virgin birth of Jesus, his miracles, his atoning death, his Second Coming, and, perhaps most important at the time, the inerrancy of Scripture, a direct response to secular and liberal biblical scholarship. Opposition to evolution quickly became central to fundamentalism as well, resulting in antievolution laws in some southern states. On the usual telling of the story, fundamentalism went into retreat as a result of the public ridicule that followed in the wake of the 1925 Scopes Trial, resurfacing only in the 1970s, as part of the conservative backlash to the liberal 1960s, when Jerry Falwell created the Moral Majority, and he and his fellow clergy helped shape the new Religious Right that was eventually incorporated into the Reagan Revolution.

In spite of the Protestant origins of the term, in the 1980s and 1990s scholars began to talk about fundamentalisms in other religious traditions, and it has now become commonplace to talk about Jewish, Islamic, Hindu, Sikh, or Buddhist fundamentalisms. What unites these fundamentalisms, as most scholars use the term, is a militant (sometimes violent) rejection of modernity, though it is often pointed out that fundamentalists are often adept at using modern technology. Fundamentalists typically understand the world as being caught up in a cosmic war between the forces of good and evil (God and Satan in Christianity), which often leads them to demonize their enemies and resist compromise. Fundamentalists typically insist on reading Scripture literally, assert the authority of men over women, reject religious pluralism, and defend religious nationalism.

## 4. Spirituality

Back on the left, the line between liberal religion and spirituality is no easier to draw than that between conservatives and fundamentalists. Of course, all religions draw on spiritual experiences. Often, however, spirituality becomes submerged and lost in the doctrines and traditions, the moral rules and social bureaucracies, that shape and define religions. The fundamental idea of spirituality is to shuck the oppressive layers of institutional authority and seek one's own experience of God (or the Sacred, the Divine, the Real, of whatever most deeply moves us). The God of spirituality (if we wish to use such language) is more likely to be immanent, within us, than transcendent. Spirituality refuses to be confined within the structures and institutions of traditional religion—which are often viewed as stifling, bureaucratic, and authoritarian—and is, instead, deeply individualistic. Spirituality is also profoundly eclectic, drawing on a wide range of religious and secular resources in seeking new forms of meaning: Eastern religions, myth, meditation, humanistic, and Jungian psychology and various kinds of therapy, holistic healing, new developments in cosmology, deep ecology, left-right brain research, feminism and goddess religion, the self-help movement, and, on its ill-defined New Age borders, shamanism, astrology, channeling, reincarnation, witchcraft, and neopaganism.

Because spirituality is so eclectic and diffuse, so individualistic and so anti-institutional, there is no way to count its adherents—though a few surveys have claimed that as many as a third of Americans (and maybe more Europeans) prefer to think of themselves as spiritual rather than religious. It is clear that the language of spirituality has become increasingly common, infiltrating and influencing most domains of contemporary culture (health care, business, education, and, of course, religious communities). I suppose that we shouldn't be surprised that spirituality in the United States is changing as we move from being, in Robert Wuthnow's apt phrase, a nation of communities to a nation of commuters; increasingly, faith is no longer something people inherit but something that they seek.[19]

As we proceed we will see that education needs to be sensitive to the somewhat different roles religion plays in each of these three culture wars—among religions, between religious and secular ways of making sense of the world, and between liberals and conservatives within religious traditions.

Our next task, however, will be to remind ourselves just how important and pervasive religion is in the world today.

# PART I

# Problems

# I

# Does God Still Matter at the Beginning of the Twenty-First Century?

Several times at conferences Martin Marty, the distinguished historian of religion, has demonstrated the importance of religion in today's world by paging through an issue of *The New York Times* or *USA Today*, noting the (perhaps surprising) number of articles that address religion in some way. In this chapter I'm going to survey not the *Times*, but contemporary culture more generally, sometimes adding a little historical perspective, noting the importance and influence of religion on people's lives, our social institutions, and our intellectual life. I am not going to argue that people should believe in God. Rather, I am going to provide a good deal of evidence for two somewhat less controversial theses: that most people do believe in God, and that religion still matters in our world. As we will see in chapter 2, education utterly fails to acknowledge the importance of religion. Taken together, my first two chapters suggest an educational problem of some significance.

## Secularization

Historically, most people have believed in some kind of God or gods (or "the Real" by whatever name); they have made sense of the world and organized their lives in religious categories. Over the course of the nineteenth century some intellectuals (e.g., Comte, Feuerbach, Marx, Nietzsche, Freud, Durkheim, and Weber) came to believe that with science, enlightenment, and social progress, religion would wither away. During the twentieth century many scholars held what has come to be called "the secularization thesis," according to which secularization inevitably follows in the wake of modernity. And yet, at the beginning of the twenty-first century, religion hasn't disappeared. Far from it.

But just what is supposed to become more secular? There are at least three possibilities: first, people are increasingly less likely to believe in God; second, religious practice is declining; third, public life and institutions are becoming increasingly secular. So what are the facts? Let's start with belief and practice.

The numbers differ depending on the poll, but about 85 or 90 percent of Americans claim to believe in God (of some kind). While some believers have doubts, most are sure that God exists.[1] About 5 percent of Americans call themselves atheists or agnostics. The other 5 or 10 percent either claim not to know, refuse to answer, or are perhaps simply indifferent to both religion and atheism.[2] According to recent polls, 77 percent of Americans believe that the Bible is either the literal or inspired word of God, 63 percent are "absolutely sure" there is a heaven, and 57 percent say that religion is very important in their lives.[3]

About 80 percent of Americans identify with a particular religious tradition (down about 10 percent over the last twenty years). About 40 percent of Americans say that they attend religious services weekly (though many scholars are skeptical of this number). In 2005, Americans gave $93.2 billion to religious organizations (more than double the $36.6 billion given to educational organizations, the next highest category of giving).[4]

The percentage of Europeans who believe in God is significantly lower. According to a 2005 Eurobarometer survey, 52 percent of adults in the European Union "believe there is a God," 27 percent believe in "some sort of spirit or life force," and 18 percent believe in neither God nor spirit nor life force.[5] The results varied greatly by country, however; in Malta, 95 percent of people believe in God, compared to only 16 percent of Estonians. Church attendance is considerably lower than in the United States: in some countries fewer than 10 percent of people attend church regularly. (The usual observation is that the only people in European churches on Sunday are American tourists.) Here too, however, there are significant differences among countries.

Worldwide, about 85 percent of people identify with a religious tradition (a somewhat different measure from belief in God). This is probably down from 1900, but up from mid-century during communist rule. Over the last several decades there has been a remarkable growth of religion in the Third World, fueled in large part by converts to evangelical and Pentecostal Protestantism.

For advocates of the secularization thesis, Europe is the wave of the future. As societies modernize and become postindustrial, people become less religious—as in Europe. On this view the United States is something of an aberration. Critics of the secularization thesis believe that Europe is the aberration in a world that has always been, and continues to be, highly religious. One thing about which there is agreement: because religious societies have much higher birth rates than the more secular societies of Europe (some of which are failing to reproduce themselves) the world is becoming more religious in terms of absolute numbers.

Of course, even in Europe, most people continue to believe in God. But belief in God can be uncoupled from religious practices and commitment to religious institutions. Church attendance (a favorite sociological measure of secularization) and belief needn't go together. There are reasons for this that may be peculiar to Europe. Unlike the United States, Europe has a long history of anticlericalism stemming from the traditional hostility of established religions to social progress, which alienated in various ways and at various times, intellectuals, the working class, and the middle class. It has also often been argued that religious establishments in Europe undermined the individual initiative that has kept religion vital in the United States. On this "market" analysis countries with free enterprise in religion—like the United States—are much more religious than countries with (putatively lazy) state-supported religious establishments (though there are European exceptions to this rule like Poland).

There is another factor to consider. Individualism, which cuts across all modern societies, resists traditional institutions that define what one should believe and how one should live. As I've already noted, as more and more people find churches oppressive, they are inclined to say that they are spiritual but not religious. This is an increasing trend in the United States as well as in Europe. Consequently, people may continue to believe in God or in a higher spirit or life force but in their own way, apart from churches, dogma, and tradition.

We also need to remember our third type of secularization—the institutional secularization that takes place when social institutions and practices (law, government, welfare agencies, education, art, science) achieve autonomy from religious authority. In this case, religion need not disappear, but it is privatized. The United States is a very religious country in terms of belief in God, and it is comparatively religious in terms of commitment to religious institutions, but it is quite secular in terms of its public institutions—in part a consequence of our historic decision to separate church and state constitutionally. In fact, in this regard, the United States is more secular than many European countries with their established churches. With regard to public education, the

United States is also more secular (as many European countries provide tax support for religious schools). At the same time, American politics has a strong religious dimension, unlike most European countries.

Where does this leave us? With something of a paradox. On the one hand, while religious belief and practice has declined markedly in Europe, the United States and much of the rest of the world continue to be very religious. Though some religious belief is, no doubt, merely nominal, the majority of Americans—indeed, the majority of people in the world—make sense of their lives and the world to some considerable extent in religious categories. On the other hand, our public institutions, not least our educational institutions, are highly secular. Just how secular, we shall see.

## Intellectuals and Scholars

About a decade ago the distinguished sociologist Peter Berger, long an advocate of the secularization thesis, recanted, arguing that "the world today, with some exceptions . . . is as furiously religious as it ever was, and in some places more so than ever." The exceptions, Berger claimed, were intellectuals and Western Europe. The "'international subculture' of intellectuals . . . is indeed secularized. This subculture is the principal 'carrier' of progressive, Enlightened [i.e., secular] beliefs and values. While its members are relatively thin on the ground, they are very influential, as they control the institutions that provide the 'official' definitions of reality, notably the educational system, the media of mass communication, and the higher reaches of the legal system."[6]

There can be little doubt that intellectuals are less religious than the public generally and that our intellectual life, not least in universities, has become pervasively secular.

That said, it must also be acknowledged that many prominent intellectuals are religious, and while not all university faculty members are intellectuals, there are a good deal of survey data that show that they are almost as likely to believe in God as are other folks. A 2006 study found that well over half of American college faculty members believe in God or a higher power of some kind.[7] According to a 2004–5 UCLA study of more than 40,000 faculty members at 421 colleges and universities, 64 percent consider themselves to be religious (29 percent to some extent, 35 percent to a great extent).[8] Moreover, if we cast the net a little wider to the well-educated we find, according to a 2006 Gallup poll, that 77 percent of Americans with postgraduate degrees are certain or have little doubt that God exists.[9] While it is true that the more education people have, the less likely they are to believe in God or consider themselves religious, even they are more likely to believe in God, and consider themselves religious, than not.

One might conclude from such statistics that education doesn't appear to undermine religious belief—at least not much. But as we've seen, secularization is not just a matter of belief. I have distinguished between the secularization of belief and institutional secularization. It appears that scholars can hold personal religious views that are not reflected in the very secular world of universities and scholarship. This raises an important question to which we shall return: why is this? If they believe in God (or some kind of "higher power") are there no implications for how they think about their own field of study?

Of course, some scholars do draw out the implications of their religious beliefs in their scholarly work. We need to recognize that there is a thriving countercultural world of religious scholarship, much of it done by scholars in seminaries, religious colleges, and nonprofits, that is, to some considerable extent, segregated from research universities and mainstream journals of ideas. Simply casting our eye over the usual locales of our intellectual life may leave us blind to alternative kinds of ideas and scholarship.

So yes, intellectuals are more likely to be unbelievers than the public generally, but there is no consensus among them about God. In fact, religion continues to be a live option among intellectuals as well among the public more generally.


## Morality and the Meanings of Life

No doubt the ethos of modern, Western civilization has become highly secular. This has come about for two different kinds of reasons: first, it is the result of the large-scale social forces of modernity—the market, urbanization, technology, and the growing pluralism and individualism of modern culture; second, it has been encouraged by intellectuals—scientists and philosophers, psychologists and social scientists, who have replaced religious with secular ways of thinking about morality and society: morality is a matter of maximizing utility, of life-constituting existential choices, of enlightened self-interest, of social conventions, or of long-standing traditions. Moral behavior can be explained in terms of social conditioning, the unconscious mind, genetics and evolutionary biology, or neurology and brain chemistry. And yet, many people— indeed, many scholars—find it difficult to disentangle morality from its traditional religious contexts.

First, a historical point. In large part because of institutional secularization our actions are much less consciously governed by religious ideals and motivations than was the case for much of human history. Still, almost everyone agrees that historically, religions did a great deal to shape people's moral understanding of the world and their ways of finding meaning in their lives. Religions provided the overarching frameworks of interpretation, the worldviews, within which people lived and organized their lives. Indeed, our moral conceptions are what they are today in large part because of our religious past. The moral value we place on justice goes back to the great Hebrew prophets, on love to the teachings of Jesus, on conscience to the Protestant Reformation. No doubt these values have other roots as well (and have been re-thought along the way). Still we are who we are morally in large part because of our religious past.

Indeed, most people continue to shape their lives to some extent on their understanding of what God requires of them. Biblical teachings continue to be a moral touchstone for most Jews and Christians (with scriptural analogs in other religious traditions). Much discussion of the most controversial moral problems of our time—abortion, sexuality, homosexuality, euthanasia, capital punishment, stem-cell research, poverty, social justice, war and peace—hinges on religious beliefs and values. The great rights movements (civil rights, women's rights, and gay rights) have been promoted and resisted on religious grounds. The environmental movement has long had a spiritual dimension and is now a major concern of (conservative as well as liberal) theologians and religious institutions. And even if some people make sense of moral issues in fully secular terms, even those secular categories of thought have been influenced by deep currents in civilization that can be traced back to our religious past.

Of course, religious traditions take different positions on particular moral issues. Indeed, liberals and conservatives within the same traditions often take quite different positions. There is no single religious position on any issue (though many religious believers hold that there is a single right position on any given issue). After all, religious people draw on different sacred texts and traditions. Even within a tradition they often disagree about the nature of the relationship of morality and religion. Is morality grounded in God's commands, in reason and natural law, in divine grace, or in love? They disagree about whether we know what is required of us by reading our respective Holy Scriptures, by accepting the authority of our religious tradition (the church, the *umma*, rabbinic commentary), or by critical theological reflection. They disagree about God's relationship to the world: is God utterly transcendent and unchanging, or fully immanent, suffering with us? Is human nature fundamentally sinful, fundamentally good, or poised somewhere in between? Does God leave us on our own to do God's work, or is God the kind of being who intervenes (through miracles or in response to prayer) to ensure that his purposes are realized? Theologians (like ordinary folks) disagree.

But they also agree about some things that set them apart from their more secular counterparts. All religious traditions share the conviction that there is a right and wrong built into the structure of the universe and that we in some way have access to what is right and wrong through our religious traditions. In the Western traditions, God is our creator and we are God's creatures; we have obligations to God and to the rest of God's creation. In setting ourselves right with God we reorient our lives morally. Our lives have a spiritual purpose. Religious people are more apt than secular people to understand their moral lives in terms of concepts such as sin, grace, and redemption, and, arguably, emphasize certain traditionally religious values such as mercy, forgiveness, and self-sacrifice. All of the major religious traditions have some doctrine of the afterlife; this world is not all there is to reality, and we are grievously shortsighted if we fail to recognize this. This, together with the conviction that all things work toward that which is good, is, in part at least, a source of profound hope and life morale.

Hence, while religious and secular folks may often agree about the rights and wrongs of particular moral issues, there is still a deep tension between broadly religious ways of thinking about morality and the world and secular alternatives. Moreover, it is not uncommon for religious thinkers to argue that what is wrong with modern civilization is not so much particular policies or institutions, but the pervasively secular cultural commitments of modernity that, they claim, encourage self-interest, materialism, technocratic thinking, the manipulation of people, and the exploitation of the environment.

It is sometimes naively believed that religious morality hinges entirely on Scripture—and, as such, is hopelessly antiquated. It is true, of course, that all religious (if not all spiritual) people place considerable emphasis on Scripture, and some fundamentalists do wish to return their cultures to past centuries. But there is also an immense scholarly literature in moral theology created over the last century as theologians and religious scholars have confronted modernity—sometimes, as with liberals, accepting much of it, sometimes, as with conservatives, rejecting much of it. This literature is not an anti-intellectual exercise in simple devotionalism (yes, there is that too), but often a soul-searching, sophisticated, and critical exploration of modern and postmodern ideas and ideals written by religious intellectuals.

## Politics, War, and Peace

It has been the conventional wisdom for some time that red states and religion go hand in hand, but in the 2008 race for the White House most of the candidates for president (in both parties) testified that they had found God and they were happy (or at least willing) to talk about it. Of course, the story line has changed several times over the course of the last century. Since the 1960s, liberals have been wary of mixing religion and politics, and since the 1970s, with the rise of the Religious Right, conservatives have tried to suffuse politics with religion at every turn. If we look a little further in history, however, we find that Reform Judaism had long supported a liberal political agenda, and Protestant conceptions of the kingdom of God shaped progressive and liberal politics from the Social Gospel through the various rights movements of the second half of the century. At the same time, through much of the last century evangelicals believed that religion was about saving souls, not saving society. (This was, for example, Jerry Falwell's position for the first part of his career.)

While the term "values issues" has often been taken as code in contemporary politics for religiously conservative issues (abortion, gay marriage, stem-cell research, faith-based welfare programs), religious liberals also take moral positions on these issues (usually the opposite position) and add their own moral issues (poverty, economic justice, peace, capital punishment, the environment, and gay rights, for example) to the political agenda. It now appears that these sharp lines of demarcation may be breaking down at least a little, as evangelicals have become increasingly concerned about poverty, global warming, and AIDS.

Of course, much of the disagreement between liberals (secular and religious) and conservatives has been grounded in a long-running debate about the relationship between church and the state. Most conservatives trace their lineage back to John Winthrop and the Puritans, who believed themselves to be in a covenantal relationship with God; America is a Christian country. Liberals, by contrast, invoke Jefferson, of course, but also the great Puritan dissenter (and sometime Baptist) Roger Williams who, more than a century before Thomas Jefferson, argued for separating church and state (which got him kicked out of the Massachusetts Bay Colony). Needless to say, the Founding Fathers didn't all agree about religion, but they did agree to give us the religion clauses of the First Amendment, the interpretation of which continues to be a matter of some controversy. At the end of the nineteenth century the U.S. Supreme Court held in *The Church of the Holy Trinity v. United States* (1892) that our cultural and legal traditions make clear that "this is a Christian nation."[10] Conservatives applauded. But in 1947, in *Everson v. Board of Education*, the court, appealing to Jefferson, explained that the Establishment Clause required a wall of separation between church and state. Liberals applauded. (This is a little too simple: historically, some theological conservatives—Baptists, for example—were strong supporters of separating church and state; this tradition largely ended with the rise of the Religious Right in the wake of *Roe v. Wade* and Supreme Court rulings on school prayer and government regulation of religious schools.) Not surprisingly, appointments to the Supreme Court have become a major issue in the politics of religion in America. Of course, many of the nastiest battles in our culture wars have to do with religion and public education.

It is not only domestic politics that excite religious folk, so do international affairs. From the Puritans' conception of America as a "city on a hill," through Manifest Destiny (both in the conquest of the North American continent and expansion beyond our shores), America's cold war defense of religion against godless communism, the Vietnam War peace movement and the nuclear freeze movement, to President Bush's conviction that it is the United States' task to fight evil and promote every person's God-given right to liberty, and mainline religious opposition to the Iraq war and President Bush's national security policy, religious ideas and ideals have pervaded our understanding of the U.S. role in the world. Or think of the efforts on the part of religious leaders to shape foreign policy with regard to abortion, family planning, and AIDS.

Needless to say, we aren't the only country that has infused its foreign policy with religious ideas and ideals. All too often, true believers and institutional religions have ended up sanctioning, sometimes even promoting, violence and war. During World War I, the churches lined up behind their respective governments, sanctifying the slaughter in the trenches of Europe. During that war, Muslim Turks massacred more than a million Armenian Christians. With only a very few exceptions, both the Lutheran and Catholic churches gave legitimacy and support to Hitler and Nazism. Hindus and Muslims each killed more than a million of the other during the partition of Indian and Pakistan. Until fairly recently, Protestants and Catholics did the same (in thankfully lower numbers) in Northern Ireland. Serb Christians massacred Bosnian and Albanian Muslims, and religious violence continues with a desultory inevitability in parts of the Middle East and Africa.

In the 1990s, Samuel Huntington proposed (contrary to the spirit of the secularization thesis) that with the demise of the cold war and ideological conflict, the world is now caught up in a clash of civilizations, driven largely by religious differences that are not easily negotiated (*The Clash of Civilizations*, 1996) Huntington's thesis has been controversial, though many take the ongoing conflict between some of the Islamic world and the West as evidence in his favor. Other scholars have argued the problem is really religious fundamentalism, with its deep hostility to modernity. Yet others have claimed that violence is inherent in the nature of monotheism (which, the argument goes, justifies or even demands a kind of exclusivity that inevitably demonizes members of other religions).

Of course, religions are responsible for considerable oppression and injustice quite apart from warfare. We need only remember anti-Semitism, anti-Catholicism, and the complicity of white Christians in segregation (and earlier, of course, in slavery) in America. Religious conservatives would no doubt point to the complicity of liberal churches in abortion (which they sometimes liken to the Holocaust). Liberals would point to the complicity of religious conservatives in the oppression of women and gays.

Having mentioned the distressing frequency of religious war and oppression, I should also mention that religious violence pales by comparison with violence caused by entirely secular (sometimes militantly antireligious) movements of the last century—particularly communism and fascism. Moreover, some scholars note that in ostensibly religious conflicts, religion often serves only as a social marker for groups whose conflicts have largely secular causes. (One example: conflict between Israel and Palestine isn't about Judaism and Islam, but about rival claims to the land and past injustices.) Just War Theory, grounded in Western theology, has also provided a significant constraint on the use of violence.

In his book *The Ambivalence of the Sacred*, Scott Appleby reminds us that just as religion can give rise to violence, it is also a powerful source of nonviolence, and he walks us through many case studies of militant goodness in the world. Unfortunately, with the exception of a few notable religious advocates of peace and nonviolence—Gandhi, King, Bishop Tutu, the Dalai Lama—peace movements are never so well publicized as are wars and terrorism, but it is the everyday work of most religious organizations to promote peace. Indeed, humanitarian efforts are central to the role of religion in the world: soup kitchens, homeless shelters, hospitals, schools, relief and welfare programs, and emergency aid, are the heart and soul of much religious work both in the United States and around the world. Again we may know the names of a few religious humanitarians—Jane Addams, Mother Teresa, Albert Schweitzer, or Dorothy Day—but, as Appleby reminds us, "countless people, serving in the relative anonymity of religious orders and communities, perform difficult and dangerous socially constructive ministries of compassion and healing."[11] Perhaps the most impressive case of peacemaking in the last fifty years was brokered by the religiously inspired Truth and Reconciliation Commission in South Africa chaired by Archbishop Desmond Tutu.

## Economics

Religious people may disagree among themselves and form alliances with their secular counterparts on specific economic issues and policies—taxes, welfare, globalization, unions, or the minimum wage, for example—just as they do regarding political issues more generally. And, as with politics, theologians have usually taken the position that no sharp divorce of economics and religion is possible. Economics must be understood, at least in part, in religious categories.

Yet the economic domain of modern life is highly secular; indeed, capitalism and market economies have contributed to the secularization of public life in a variety of ways. First, market economies have undermined traditional communities with their religious values. In Joseph Schumpeter's classic formulation, creative destruction is the "essential fact" about capitalism.[12] The market requires ceaseless change, competition, technological advances, mobile labor, and the creation of new wants—all subversive of tradition, as people in the developing countries (not least Muslims) are particularly aware. Second, market economies have proved extraordinarily successful in creating consumer goods and raising standards of living. As a result, we (well, most of us) have been converted into consumers whose hearts and souls are in the material goods of this life rather than in (dare I say it?) higher goods. Third, it is important to remember that the freedom in "free enterprise" is freedom from religious as well as from governmental regulation. Within the new market economies of the West, usury, which had once been a sin, was rehabilitated as interest in order to facilitate the accumulation of capital; supply and demand replaced the conception of a just price; religious guilds collapsed before the need for free and mobile labor; charity and begging, once virtues and signs of saintliness, became vices; self-interest and acquisitiveness, once vices, became the governing virtues of the economic world; holy days (and the Sabbath) became business days; and intellectual authority shifted from theologians and philosophers to businessmen and the value-free calculus of that new (secular) specialty, economics.

According to neoclassical economic theory (the prevailing, though not unchallenged, orthodoxy of professional economists) economics is a value-free science, people are essentially self-interested utility maximizers, and moral judgments have been replaced by cost-benefit analyses. All religions, by contrast, share the idea that we are moral beings who exist in webs of obligation with other persons and God, and some practices and policies are right or wrong in and of themselves and not subject to cost-benefit analysis. No doubt people are, in fact, self-interested, but it is our responsibility (with God's help) to rise above our sinful natures, acting for the good of our fellow creatures and God. From within any religious tradition some of our wants are misguided or sinful, and the idea of an economy that thrives on feeding and nurturing indiscriminate wants is morally problematic to say the least. It has sometimes even been held (remarkable as it may seem) that we should be satisfied with what we have.

Central to Scripture and to the vast twentieth-century literature on economics and moral theology is the claim that we must employ moral and religious categories to understand economic issues, ideals, and institutions. As the American Catholic bishops put it in their 1986 statement on the economy, we must guard against a "tragic separation" between religion and our economic life. People cannot "immerse [them]selves in earthly activities as if [they] were utterly foreign to religion, and religion were nothing more than the fulfillment of acts of worship and the observance of a few moral obligations." Indeed, economists, like all of us, must realize that "human dignity, realized in community with others and with the whole of God's creation, is the norm against which every social institution is measured."[13]

So, for example, from within all religious traditions, work must be understood in moral and spiritual as well as in economic terms. There are moral rights that should protect workers from exploitation, and working conditions must respect the dignity of people. Whether this requires, in particular cases, unions, affirmative action programs, or worker participation in decision making may be debatable, but it is essential to ask these questions. Of course, some work, even if freely undertaken, is by its very nature degrading (its contribution to the gross national product notwithstanding). From within many religious traditions, work is regarded as a calling, as a way in which we fulfill our obligations to God by using our talents for the good of humanity.

Virtually every religious tradition has placed special emphasis on compassion and the duty to help the poor and oppressed: God has a special concern for the widow and orphan, for the "least" of those among us. Almsgiving is one of the Five Pillars of Islam. Compassion is the fundamental Buddhist virtue. Of course, churches, nongovernmental organizations, and religious organizations have created a variety of programs for the poor—schools, soup kitchens, settlement houses, hospitals, programs for migrant workers, prisoners, and victims of AIDS. They have also lobbied for legislation that addresses social justice, and theologians have created a rich literature on economics and moral theology.

At the end of the nineteenth century, American Reform rabbis declared in their *Pittsburgh Platform* that it was the task of Judaism to address the "great task of modern times," solving the problem of rich and poor on the basis of justice and righteousness. Jews, Catholics, and Protestants played important roles in labor unions. Pope Leo XIII defended the rights of workers in his great encyclical *Rerum Novarum* (1893), declaring a Catholic middle way between socialism and capitalism. In the United States, populism united evangelical religion with progressive politics, nowhere more so than in the campaigns of William Jennings Bryan. In the early twentieth century the Social Gospel was a powerful effort among mainline Protestants to address poverty and critique capitalism. In the years between the world wars, Reinhold Niebuhr argued influentially for an unsentimental commitment to social justice in the face of human sinfulness. Influenced by Niebuhr, Martin Luther King Jr. spoke out for social justice, not just for civil rights. Beginning in the 1970s, Latin American Catholic theologians developed a liberation theology that was adopted by mainline and liberal Protestant theologians. Such theology has been critical of capitalism, arguing that the great Christian task is liberating the oppressed. While Pope John Paul II was critical of liberation theology (for its use of Marxist theory) he was also critical of capitalism; in his important encyclical *Centesimus Annus* (1993) he maintained Catholicism's "middle course" between the Left and Right in matters of economics. More recently, Pope Benedict XVI has highlighted both the strengths and the weaknesses of capitalism in *Caritas in Veritate* (2009). While there is an evangelical Left (with Jim Wallis as its guru), and while there is a long-standing tension between cultural conservatism and capitalism, religious conservatives are often advocates of capitalism; Michael Novak has been particularly prominent in articulating a theological defense of capitalism.

The pervasive poverty of the Third World—and the wealth of the First World—creates a moral problem of profound importance. Many theologians (not least Pope John Paul II) have spoken out forcefully regarding justice and the obligations of wealthy nations to the Third World. The movement for Third World debt reduction at the turn of the century was, in large part, a response to the biblical idea of a Jubilee year, advocated by theologians and religious leaders. Of course, much Islamic thought has been highly critical not just of Western culture in general, but of capitalism in particular, as it subverts Islamic conceptions of community and justice.

While some religious traditions have found special virtue in monasticism and vows of poverty (Catholicism and Buddhism, for example) most have not condemned wealth per se, but rather the undue attachment to wealth that keeps us from God. But virtually all religious traditions condemn contemporary consumer culture for nurturing attachments to wealth and the material goods of this life. There have been and currently are religious movements that equate spiritual salvation with worldly wealth, but the religious mainstream is deeply wary of the effects of wealth and consumerism on our spiritual lives. Of course, should the rest of the world continue to aspire to our standards of life, the stress on natural resources and the environment will be catastrophic. We cannot all consume more and more. Consequently, it is not surprising that there has come to be a strong religious emphasis on practicing social justice, protecting the environment, and finding models of sustainable growth.

## God and Science

The once commonplace notion that religion and science have historically been locked in mortal combat (in an ongoing culture war) has fallen into disrepute among many scholars. After all, most of the towering figures of the Scientific Revolution—Newton, Descartes, Galileo, Kepler, Copernicus, Harvey, Boyle— were deeply religious, and until the latter part of the nineteenth century the view was widespread that science and religion complemented each other. God had revealed himself in two texts: in the Bible, of course, but also in the "text" of nature where, as Galileo put it, God wrote in the language of mathematics.

This isn't to say that there haven't been occasional conflicts, the two nastiest of which have been over whether the earth revolves around the sun (a conflict that we've gotten past) and evolution (a conflict that is still very much with us). Fundamentalists and many religious conservatives reject evolution because it conflicts with the book of Genesis, read literally. (Some have proposed creation-science as an alternative to evolution-science; the vast majority of scientists have not been amused.) Because religious liberals don't insist on reading the Bible literally, they have accepted evolution as God's ways of creating persons. But many liberals have their own problem with the neo-Darwinian mechanism of evolutionary theory. If evolution is the result of natural selection acting on the random mutation and recombination of genes (neo-Darwinism is the synthesis of genetics with Darwin's theory of natural selection) that would appear to make evolution a purposeless process, one that has no goal. Indeed, far from being the goal of evolution, human beings are, as the paleontologist Stephen Jay Gould once put it, only a minor species in the Age of Bacteria. Darwin himself was convinced that evolution has no goal or design.

Consequently, many scholars argue that the primary scientific challenge to religion isn't so much particular scientific discoveries or theories (heliocentrism or evolution), but the replacement of teleological by naturalistic categories for understanding nature. Traditionally, nature was understood as the handiwork of God; it embodied God's purposes; it had a *telos*, a goal, a design, a purpose. But scientific method (or methodological naturalism) prohibits any appeal to supernatural causes or to design, purpose, or value (to what ought to be) in scientific explanations.

Over the last several decades a new wave of interest in the relationship of science and religion has led to hundreds of books, thousands of articles, major interdisciplinary conferences, and new academic programs, many at major universities. Most of the participants in this new science/religion dialogue reject two ways of thinking about the relationship of science and religion: the idea of conflict or warfare (held by most biblical literalists and by most atheists), and the idea that the two don't have anything to do with each other. (This latter idea was, perhaps, the dominant view of scientists and mainline and liberal Protestant theologians through much of the twentieth century: science and religion are about two different "worlds" or ways of thinking about reality; science is about mechanics, religion is about meaning; science asks how, while religion asks why. That is, science and religion are conceptual apples and oranges.) A third view has become increasingly common. Science and religion each make claims about the same world—nature, the universe. Each has its own sources of knowledge, but each has only a partial understanding of reality so that it is essential to engage in interdisciplinary dialogue in order to develop a complete and integrated account of nature. Perhaps the fundamental problem is reconciling the religious idea of purpose and design in nature with the (purposeless) naturalism of modern science.[14]

I'll mention several critical areas of current controversy and discussion.

### Before the Big Bang

There is a good deal of highly theoretical speculation among cosmologists about what, if anything, came before the big bang. Perhaps there wasn't anything, or perhaps there was an infinite series of big bangs each followed by a big crunch, or perhaps our universe is but one of many in a multiverse. Could God have created the universe through the big bang? Pope Pius XII thought so. Many theologians argue, however, that God's creation is not in time; rather, God sustains the universe through all time, and continues to create (perhaps through evolution). Still, there is a fascinating question here with religious significance. Is there a beginning to things? Is the existence of the universe just a brute fact or is some kind of religious explanation required?

### Mathematics and the Laws of Nature

It is widely agreed that mathematics has provided the key to unlocking the "deep order" of the universe scientifically. But why should the structure of the universe be transparent to human minds? Indeed, why should nature obey laws at all? Some scientists and theologians argue that the intelligibility and beauty of the universe revealed mathematically give us reason to believe that both the human mind and universe have a common origin in the mind of God.

## Cosmological Fine-Tuning

Over the last several decades cosmologists have become aware of a variety of ways in which the physical constants and laws of nature appear to be fine-tuned to be exactly what they must be if there is to be life in the universe. Some cosmologists, philosophers, and theologians find in these remarkable coincidences an argument for God's existence, for fine-tuning would seem to require a fine-*tuner*. (Or at least this: if there is a God, we would expect the universe to be fine-tuned to produce life.) Perhaps the most common response of atheists is that if our universe is only one of perhaps an infinite number of universes (a multiverse), then it wouldn't be surprising for a universe to come along, once every gazillion years or so, that generates life quite by accident. So which is the more reasonable explanation: a fine-tuner, or an infinite number of universes? Scholars disagree.[15]

## The Origins of Life

There is still no adequate scientific theory for how life came to be out of non-living matter. (*Science* magazine recently declared this among its twenty-five great unsolved scientific problems.) Most scientists expect a good naturalistic theory (that is, one that doesn't appeal to design or supernatural explanations) to be found, but at least a few scientists believe that the complexity of life and the information-bearing character of DNA are so extraordinary that they can be explained only in terms of some kind of design.

## Biological Evolution

There are many religious positions on evolution in addition to fundamentalist creationism. Some theologians argue that God initially gave the universe its own freedom to work through chance and natural selection. Others believe that neo-Darwinism provides only a partial explanation of origins; there is purpose in evolution, but scientific method is too restrictive to allow scientists to consider all the relevant evidence. Catholic theology discerns a providential God behind the "secondary" causes of evolution, and claims that science cannot account for the development of animals into persons with souls. Process theologians argue for an immanent God embodied in the workings of nature, who guides evolution from within. And there are a few scientists who accept "intelligent design theory," holding that God is the best scientific explanation for complex interrelated characteristics of DNA and cellular biology. And there are yet other views.

## Consciousness and the Soul

It is often claimed by scientists and philosophers that consciousness will eventually be explained in terms of the physical structures of nervous systems, though this continues to be very controversial and how this might work is a complete mystery. (Just what could possibly be the causal relationship between a thought and a neuron?) Of course, traditional religion has held that we have immortal souls. Needless to say, immortality is something of a problem if we must understand the mind or soul in terms of brains that decompose on death.

## Free Will and Rationality

Modern science has been widely thought to require determinism: the causal laws of science (including those that explain how the brain works) leave no room for free will or rationality (believing and acting as we do because we ought to, not because we have to). But if we have no choice about how to act, what sense does it make to say that we are responsible for our actions? Many theologians and philosophers have rejected the reductionism of such science, arguing for a top-down causality in which the mind has its own structure, one that cannot be reduced to the naturalistic laws of science. Some scientists have argued that subatomic indeterminacy (as understood in quantum mechanics) provides an opening for free will. It has also been argued that indeterminacy together with chaos theory (in which major events can be explained by minuscule causes) allows room in the causal joints of the universe for God to act.

## Morality

It is often claimed that altruism and social behavior can be given a Darwinian explanation in terms of group, kin, or reciprocal selection mechanisms that make social behavior and altruism a by-product of genetic selfishness. But many philosophers and theologians argue that we cannot move from what is the case to what ought to be the case, we cannot move from any scientific theory to morality; this is to commit the naturalistic fallacy. Moreover, most philosophers and theologians believe that morality requires a measure of self-conscious, deliberative thought that cannot be programmed into our genetic constitution; morality depends on other kinds of abilities and knowledge than those discerned by science. The relationship of morality to our evolutionary past is complicated and controversial.

## The Environment

Over the last several decades theologians have begun to take the environmental crisis seriously, drawing on biblical texts that emphasize the sacred character of God's creation and the need for our stewardship of nature. More liberal theologians have reshaped traditional interpretations of God and nature, arguing for an immanent God who is embodied in, and works through, nature. Some theologians draw on Native American and Eastern religious traditions with their more spiritual understanding of nature and the need to live in harmony with it. All of these theologies are critical of the way in which value-free scientific (and economic) ways of thinking about nature allow for its exploitation.

## Other Issues

Discussions of the role of prayer, meditation, and spirituality in health and healing have called purely naturalistic conceptions of illness into question and contributed to more holistic conceptions of medicine. Embryonic stem-cell research, cloning, germ-line genetic engineering, robotics, and nanotechnology raise urgent moral and religious questions about technology and what it means to be human. And as the technological ethos of modernity becomes more influential we tend to reconceive the world and people as objects to be manipulated and our sense of the sacred withers. Not only is there no moral compass built into technology or the science that shapes it, but the omnipresent technological imperative demands that we think and act technologically, nurturing a faith in technological solutions to what may be moral and spiritual problems.

Several themes run through all of these controversies. Does science (or methodological naturalism) have limits? Are there aspects of nature (physical or human) that science cannot explain, perhaps even in principle? Are there moral or spiritual dangers that accompany scientific naturalism? Is it possible to have philosophical or theological knowledge of nature? Can we achieve a deeper understanding of reality through integrating religious, philosophical, and scientific claims and perspectives? Can we make sense of the idea of purpose in nature?

Clearly, the current science/religion dialogue among scholars extends far beyond the old cultural controversy over evolution. In fact, the dialogue is anything but passé. The relationship of science and religion is considerably more interesting, more complicated, and more important than is often realized.

## The Arts and Culture

For much of history, the glory of art was the glorification of God, although the great artists of the last millennium may not have been so uniformly religious as the great scientists (at least up to Darwin). Still, Bach and Mozart, Michelangelo and Rembrandt, Tolstoy and Dostoyevsky, Dante and Milton, make for a fairly distinguished group.

Of course, things changed. Writing at the midpoint of the twentieth century, William Barrett argued "The Western artist now finds his own inherited classical forms unconvincing and indeed almost intolerable." Why? Because "the final intelligibility of the world is no longer accepted." After all, "the central fact of modern history in the West . . . is unquestionably the decline of religion."[16] Writing at the end of the twentieth century, the cultural critic Andrew Delbanco claimed that "it is the central and irreversible fact of modern history that we no longer inhabit a world of transcendence." Delbanco notes that while many Americans have refused to give up their belief in God, they are not to be found among the writers and artists who have transformed America's cultural history. The literary culture of America has become a culture of irony in which all talk of God and morality appears to mask claims to power or privilege, for "in the ironist's eye every pretender to legitimate authority becomes a Wizard of Oz, and the point is to draw aside the curtain."[17] Clearly, a major theme of twentieth-century art and literature has been the loss of meaning (which is sometimes mourned, sometimes simply noted, occasionally celebrated) that has resulted from the growing conviction among writers and artists that we live in a world without transcendence, without God.

But we can overstate the case. Some of the great writers of the last century (T. S. Eliot, W. H. Auden, Graham Greene, William Faulkner, Walker Percy, Flannery O'Connor, John Updike, Saul Bellow, Elie Wiesel, Alexandr Solzhenitsyn, Marilynne Robinson) were religious or at least continued to grapple with their religious traditions in an effort to wrest some sense of meaning from them. Religious conservatives are likely to reassert the authority of traditional orthodoxies. Religious liberals tend to search for new and deeper levels of meaning, resymbolizing God (or the sacred) in ways that speak to our times; they often find traditional religious symbols, narratives, and motifs naive, sentimental, and irrelevant. In either case, however, writers and artists typically war against the pervasive literalism of a scientific age; art points us toward meaning and truth by way of symbolism, myth, metaphor, and narrative.

Of course, many religious conservatives reject much of modern art and literature as unscriptural and irreligious, even sacrilegious. In fact, the conservative reaction against much modern art has resulted in occasional calls for censorship in America—and, in parts of the Muslim world, for death to some artists. (Think of the controversies over Andres Serrano's *Piss Christ* and Martin Scorsese's *The Last Temptation of Christ*, or the controversy over the publication of Danish cartoons of Muhammad and the fatwa calling for the death of Salman Rushdie.) The crassness, vulgarity, and sacrilege of much youth culture—movies, music, video games, Internet Web sites—has aroused the outrage of conservative religious parents (and sometimes of liberal parents as well).

Of course, much popular art is religious. There is Christian fiction, religious cable TV, and religious pop music. While *Newsweek* picked Picasso's *Les Demoiselles D'Avignon* (a painting of five naked, if highly abstract, prostitutes) as the "most influential work of [high] art of the last 100 years," Warner Sallman's *Head of Christ* sold much better (indeed, in terms of reproductions, it was the most popular painting of the twentieth century). Spiritual themes shape immensely popular movies like *Star Wars* (the most popular six-part movie series of all time) and *The Matrix*. The three mega best sellers of the first decade of the twenty-first century each have religious significance, albeit in different ways: *The Da Vinci Code*, the *Left Behind* series, and the Harry Potter series (which, after provoking a fair amount of controversy among fundamentalists for its celebration of magic, concluded with a distinctly religious ending).[18]

## Conclusions

It may be that religious belief among Americans is declining (while atheism, agnosticism, and secular indifference may be growing) but the vast majority of Americans continue to believe in God. Religious ways of making sense of the world—of morality, of politics, of economics, of nature, and of the arts—if controversial, are also influential. There continue to be religious intellectuals even if their numbers and influence have waned over the last century. Religious ideas and ideals continue to shape politics and world events (sometimes with a vengeance). Religion hasn't withered away, but continues to possess considerable vitality.

The vitality of religion at the beginning of the twenty-first century is remarkable not just because some social scientists thought it would disappear, but because governments, ideologies, and various intellectual movements have actively, even bitterly, fought religion. The greatest assault on religion came from Marxist governments in the Soviet Union, the Soviet satellites, and China, which murdered clergy, oppressed religious organizations, and indoctrinated children against religion. Some of the dominant schools of thought of the last century have been dismissive or actively hostile to religion, including psychoanalytic theory, behavioral social science, existentialism, postmodernism—and, of course, Marxism. (I suppose I should say that there are notable exceptions within each of these movements.) Many scientists believe that modern science has discredited any claims of God's existence. Much popular and consumer culture is hostile to traditional religious beliefs and values. Market economies, globalization, the World Bank, the Internet, and consumerism have been powerfully disruptive of traditional communities, cultures, beliefs, and values. And there is now a small, but highly vocal movement of atheists.

While particular religions were often oppressed in the past, there is no equivalent in history to this kind of general assault—sometimes intended, sometimes not—on religion. And yet, most people believe in God and religion continues to shape their lives and the world. Given its vitality, and given the importance of the claims that religion makes, one might think that students should be educated about it.

# 2

# Does God Measure Up to American Standards?

What do students learn about God and religion in American schools and universities? The answer: not much.

Happily, there is a fairly straightforward way of determining whether God measures up to American standards in public schools, for there have been for more than a decade now national content standards for K–12 education. During the 1980s a consensus emerged among educators, business leaders, and politicians, that we—like the countries whose students appear to outperform ours—needed national standards. President George H. W. Bush and state governors said this at their 1989 Education Summit and before long the U.S. Congress called for "all students [to] leave grades 4, 8, and 12 having demonstrated competency over challenging subject matter including English, mathematics, science, foreign languages, civics and government, economics, arts, history, and geography."[1] Consequently, during the 1990s, content standards were written for twelve areas of the curriculum.

For all the initial enthusiasm, the idea of national standards was quickly caught up in a withering cross fire of criticism, with the fiercest fire coming from those who feared greater federal control over education. As a result, the momentum shifted, in time, to the states, most of which have now developed their own standards. Nonetheless, the national standards are helpful for my purposes because they are the work of thousands of scholars, teachers, and representatives of professional associations who, over a decade and many drafts, refined what they took to be most important for students to learn about their respective fields. To some considerable extent, they continue to reflect the conventional wisdom of American education. I've also (for the third time) reviewed high school textbooks for their treatment of religion.[2] Here we can put our hands on what students put their hands on (and perhaps even read). Not surprisingly, the textbooks sometimes give us more, sometimes less, than what the standards require.

It is easy to be cynical about textbooks. After all, who remembers anything they learned from textbooks? In her study of textbooks, Francis FitzGerald suggested that often what "sticks to the memory" is "not any particular series of facts but an atmosphere, an impression, a tone. And this impression may be all the more influential just because one cannot remember the facts and arguments that created it." The responsibility of textbook authors and publishers, Fitzgerald suggests, is "awesome, for, as is not true of trade publishers, the audiences for their products are huge, impressionable, and captive."[3] Almost inevitably, textbooks give students some sense of what it is important and what is reasonable—and what isn't.

I am aware that neither the standards nor the textbooks determine what goes on in the classroom. Good teachers will often supplement (even correct) bad textbooks and inadequate standards. Of course. Still, looking at the standards and texts will give us some idea of what students are taught, and of widely shared ideals of what they should be taught.

I will address high school standards and textbooks in three major areas of the curriculum—history, economics, and science—and I'll say just a little about the rest of the curriculum. I'll also mention public school religion courses; there aren't many, so not much need be said.

I'll conclude with an assessment of the role of religion in the undergraduate curriculum. There are no national standards there; nor are there any obviously relevant textbooks to look at. Still, we are not without evidence—though my assessment will inevitably be somewhat more impressionistic.


History

I reviewed the national standards for both world and U.S. history (detailed documents that run, respectively, 284 and 245 pages) and eight widely used world history and American history textbooks (which average a little more than a thousand pages and seven pounds).

The standards are presented in the form of chronological outlines. Within each historical period there will be several general standards, with more specific "elaborated standards" and "illustrations" falling under them. Though any estimate will be rough at best, religion comes into play (in some way) in about 10 percent of the world history standards, and something under 5 percent of the American history standards.

The history texts also say a good deal about religion. Moreover, they're getting somewhat better. I remember a text from the 1980s that was so skittish about religion that in reprinting the Mayflower Compact it replaced all references to God with ellipses marks. Some of this progress has been, I suspect, a response to several highly publicized reviews that pointed out their shortcomings with regard to religion. Still, none of the high school textbooks I've reviewed have measured up to what the standards require. A part of the reason is that the standards are so comprehensive that no textbook could possibly satisfy them. Indeed, the authors of the standards recognize this, arguing that more time and courses must be devoted to the study of history. (I agree.)

My primary conclusion, however, is that both the standards and the texts fall well short of the ideal when it comes to religion. How so?

(1) Given everything that must be crammed into the texts, there simply isn't space to make religion intelligible. World history texts typically devote about three pages (including pictures and charts) to explaining the origins, basic teachings, and early development of each of the great world religions. Three pages won't do it. Unless students come to history classes already knowing a good deal about various religions, they will not learn enough to actually make any sense of them.

(2) The standards and the textbooks understate the importance of religion in the modern world. Religion largely, though not entirely, disappears from both the world and the American history standards and texts as we page past the seventeenth century. No doubt the modern world is more secular than the premodern world, though students might well conclude from the texts that the world has became almost completely secular. One reason for this is that the texts focus largely on military, political, and social history, all of which became considerably more secular after the seventeenth century. In discussing the nineteenth and twentieth centuries all the texts have occasional chapters on culture (both high and popular), but religion does not usually figure into these chapters either, and there are no parallel chapters addressing religion specifically. Rather, with very few exceptions, religious movements and issues are given only a paragraph or two here and there.

Roughly 5 percent of the American and world history standards for the twentieth century address religion in some way (though few focus exclusively or even primarily on religion). In her thorough study of *state* history and social studies standards Susan L. Douglass concludes that "with some exceptions, very little content on religion is written into state world history standards for the period after 1800 in European history, and after 1500 in non-Western cultures. All students will have been exposed to information about the role of religion in American history before 1800, but they will receive little additional information during their studies of 19<sup>th</sup> and 20<sup>th</sup> century US history."[4] If we exclude the Holocaust, which is typically discussed in some depth, the texts devote, on average, between 1 percent and 2 percent of their space to religion in covering the nineteenth and twentieth centuries. Again excluding the Holocaust, one American history text devotes more pages to railroads in the nineteenth century than to religion in all of the twentieth century; another gives more pages to consumerism in the 1950s than to all of religion in the twentieth century; yet another devotes twice as much space to popular culture at the beginning of the twentieth century (baseball, vaudeville, shopping) as it does to religion for the whole century.

(3) Perhaps because of the frequent focus on military and political history, when religion is mentioned it is typically for its contribution to violence or conflict. In order of the space given them in the texts here are the ten most commonly discussed topics relating to religion in the twentieth century: the Holocaust, the Iranian revolution, religious conflict in the partition of India, Islamic fundamentalism and terrorism (9/11, Al Qaeda, the Taliban), anti-Semitism in turn-of-the-century Europe (the Dreyfus affair, pogroms), Malcolm X and the Nation of Islam, the creation of Israel and religious conflict in the Middle East, the rise of the New Religious Right in the United States, the Scopes Trial, and evangelical revivalism in the early twentieth-century United States (Dwight Moody, Billy Sunday). True, other topics are mentioned, but they receive only the usual paragraph or two (or sentence or two) here and there.

In her (more general) review of history textbooks Diane Ravitch notes that the discussion of religion is often unduly favorable, and in several reviews of history textbooks Gilbert Seawell has argued that the treatment of Islam is uncritically sympathetic (Seawell has been challenged, in turn, by the Council for Islamic Education).[5] In fact, several of the texts I read appeared wary of discussing any relationship between Islam and terrorism. Of course, what counts as a fair or objective treatment of religion is controversial, even among scholars. But the problem is made much more difficult in light of the intense pressure of religious groups for favorable treatment in textbooks on profit-conscious publishers and politically sensitive boards of education. (This isn't always bad: sometimes mistakes and stereotypes surface in the process.) And we cannot forget that the pervasive ethos of multiculturalism makes it politically incorrect to say anything critical of almost any group. Having acknowledged all of this, it is still true that the texts encourage students to think of religion in the twentieth century largely in the context of war and they typically fail to give religion its due as a cause of peace and justice. For example, in addressing civil rights the texts say little about the black church and religion. They typically attribute Martin Luther King Jr.'s views on nonviolence to his study of Thoreau and Gandhi, and say nothing of his grounding in Christian theology. Indeed, two texts don't mention that he was a minister or make any reference to his religious beliefs; one of them identifies him as *Dr.* King five times, but never as Rev. King.

(4) There is virtually no discussion of the intellectual or theological dimensions of religion in the twentieth century (and little before that). It is true that the world history standards note that "the major religions have continued to grow and change dynamically. Spiritual quests and ethical questionings have been a vital part of the cultural history of the past [i.e., twentieth] century."[6] Still, the texts and the standards largely freeze the theological development of Christianity in the Reformation, while other religions are frozen much earlier in their classical shapes. As a result, students are given little sense of how religious traditions have responded intellectually to modernity and, inevitably, they appear to be fossilized remnants of the past.

An exception to this generalization is that both the standards and the texts discuss (if only briefly) the resistance of fundamentalism to modernity in the twentieth century. In the only explicit reference to the tension between modernity and religion in the U.S. standards, students are required to understand Christian fundamentalism and the "clash between traditional moral values and changing ideas as exemplified in the controversy over Prohibition and the Scopes Trial" (two of the less successful religious responses to modernity). This is also the theme of the textbook accounts of the Scopes Trial (found in all four American histories). Liberal responses to modernity are considerably less common. The Social Gospel movement in the early twentieth century receives a standard two paragraphs in each of the American histories. Liberation theology is mentioned in two of the eight texts, and one text mentions the rise of spirituality and New Age religion. Two of the eight texts mention modern biblical scholarship. Astonishingly, only two of the eight texts mention the Second Vatican Council, arguably the most important Christian event since the Reformation—it is given a single sentence in one text, a paragraph in the second—and it is not mentioned in either the world or the U.S. history standards.

Theologians are conspicuous by their absence from the standards and texts. Karl Barth, the most influential Christian theologian of the twentieth century, is mentioned in only one of the eight texts (a short paragraph).

Reinhold Niebuhr, the most influential American theologian of the twentieth century is not mentioned in either the texts or standards (though the rabble-rousing Father Coughlin is mentioned in all four American histories). Paul Tillich is mentioned only as an émigré from Nazi Germany. Other than a single passing reference to John XXIII, no pope is mentioned other than John Paul II, who is mentioned for his influence on politics. There is no discussion of the new science/religion dialogue, ecotheology, or feminist theology. Though the rise of the Religious Right in the 1970s is discussed in the American histories, it is for its influence on politics; conservative and evangelical theology is not discussed. There is no mention of Martin Buber, Abraham Heschel, or any Jewish theologian.

(5) It goes without saying that the standards and the texts assume that history is a secular discipline and that history should be interpreted in secular categories. In addressing "thinking skills" the standards are sensitive to the fact that there are multiple interpretations of history. They rightly require that students appreciate the "interpretative nature" of history as a discipline, and are able to compare "alternative historical narratives written by historians who have given different weight to the political, economic, social, and/or technological causes of events and who have developed competing interpretations of the significance of those events."[7] What students are not required to do is consider historical narratives written by scholars who interpret history in religious categories. Judaism, Christianity, and Islam (unlike Eastern religions) have each held that God acts in history, that history has a religious plotline. Whether or not one interprets such talk literally (as religious conservatives do) or mythically (as religious liberals are apt to do) there is a religious meaning to history that cannot be conveyed in secular categories. The standards make no note of this fact so central to understanding Western religion.

Of course the chronological periodization of history is secular. Each of the four world history texts explains the source of our dating system—what B.C. and A.D. (or B.C.E. and C.E.) mean, always in a single sentence, mentioning that the birth of Jesus was traditionally ascribed to the year 1—but that's it. So what is the significance of this? For Christians, Jesus is God incarnate—no small matter. Indeed, God's incarnation into this world is *the* turning point in the unfolding drama of human history. (Interestingly, none of the world histories that I've reviewed mention this claim about Jesus—that Christians believe that he was God.) Nor does the birth of Jesus make any difference at all in the way the texts divide history up into periods. The omnipresent time lines in the texts suggest that nothing hinges on the break between B.C. and A.D. That is, students are taught to conceive of the shape of history in secular rather than sacred categories. Of course, one could make parallel arguments regarding the calendars and theology of Judaism and Islam.

While it is widely acknowledged that students must learn something about religion in the course of studying history, we typically take this to mean that some mention of religious leaders, movements, and institutions should be incorporated into our historical narratives, but of course those narratives must be secular narratives. Indeed, our standards of historical evidence, our conceptions of historical causation, our interpretations of the meaning of history are, like historical periodization, entirely secular. So while students will learn something about religion in the course of studying history, we teach them how to think about religion in secular historical terms; we don't teach them how to think about history religiously.

(6) The world history standards require students to understand eleven "long-term changes and recurring patterns in world history," all of which are drawn from social, technological, and political history (e.g., population changes from paleolithic times to the present, the origins and development of capitalism, the origins and development of the nation-state); none are religious. Three of the eight texts end with discussions of broad historical themes; only one includes a religious theme—a worldwide return to traditional religious beliefs and rituals that sometimes takes the form of fundamentalism. It would appear that the long-term historical significance of religion is marginal at best.

In sum, then, if students take a course in world history they will learn a good deal about religion in premodern history, though far less than what they need to know to actually make sense of it. (It is worth keeping in mind that not all states require high school students to take world history.) Students will learn a little about religion over the last two centuries, usually in the context of understanding conflict, violence, and war, but they will learn nothing at all about theology or the intellectual development of religion. And they will learn to interpret history in secular categories. When educators have attempted to take religion more seriously, it has typically resulted in mentioning it a little more often; they have not recognized the importance of enabling students to understand the events and themes of history from religious perspectives.

## Economics

The sole reference to religion in the forty-seven pages of the *National Content Standards in Economics* refers to religious organizations as one among several types of nonprofit organizations. There are three references to religion in the four economics texts I reviewed most recently: the first, a quotation from Isaiah ("They will beat their swords into plowshares, and their spears into pruning hooks") appears in a one-paragraph box on eco hotels; the second is a three-paragraph description of President Bush's faith-based initiative on welfare programs; the third is a reference to "religious beliefs" along with rituals, habits, and laws in shaping traditional economies. That's it. If I throw in the ten economics texts that I reviewed in the 1990s, the cumulative references to religion total less than three out of 6,700 pages. In these fourteen economic texts the only reference to religion after the Protestant Reformation is the three-paragraph account of President Bush's faith-based initiative.

## Morality

Even more striking is the fact that the standards never make moral judgments or discuss morality. They make no reference to unions, social classes, the environment, materialism, poverty, justice, rights, codes of ethics, or the dignity of human beings. In fact, the standards are ahistorical, apolitical, and amoral.

The texts rarely consider morality explicitly. I'll mention all the references. Three of the texts have boxes that briefly discuss codes of ethics (in two cases a part of the argument is that such codes make good business sense). One text calls on consumers to act ethically by respecting the rights of sellers. Another defines "moral suasion" as the unofficial pressure that the Federal Reserve places on the banking system. Yet another discusses the "moral hazard" of behaving irresponsibly when one has insurance.

Occasionally, the texts appear to make implicit moral judgments. For example, two texts have boxes that feature Oprah Winfrey, both emphasizing her generosity to the needy. Two of the texts mention humanitarian motives for foreign aid—albeit, in passing. Three of the texts have a short historical section that describes the horrible working conditions that gave rise to the union movement in the United States. Another notes that "*as a society*, we recognize some responsibilities to the very young, the very old, the sick, the poor, and the disabled" in the context of a discussion of welfare programs.[8] The texts will sometimes refer to the fact that Americans value economic freedom or economic efficiency, or fairness, or equal pay for equal work. But there is never any effort to explain or to morally justify such empirical generalizations, or to consider whether people are reasonable to have such values.

The texts address at some length morally loaded issues such as taxes and poverty. For example, each of the texts distinguishes three types of taxes: flat, progressive, and regressive. Only one of the texts provides any context for thinking about which is fairer, however, devoting several paragraphs to the difference between the "benefits-received" and the "ability to pay" principles that underlie different theories of taxation. Unfortunately, these principles remain abstractions; the discussion is brief and leaves the principles floating free of any kind of moral, political, or religious context or theory. Or, to take another example, the texts all discuss poverty, presenting considerable information (often by way of graphs and charts) documenting the extent and causes of poverty and inequality. But again, the texts provide no moral, political, or religious context for thinking about poverty as a moral or spiritual problem about which something ought to be done.

## Neo-Classical Theory

So why is this? The problem is that the disciplinary framework that shapes the standards and the texts is neoclassical economic theory, according to which economics is a value-free science, people are essentially self-interested utility maximizers, and values are personal preferences. Economics is one thing, while religion and morality are something else.

The commitment to neoclassical theory is explicit in the standards. In the texts, it is more implicit, though the texts typically make it clear that economics is a social science and, as such, it is value-free. As one text puts it, "Learning about economics will help you predict what may happen if certain events occur or certain policies are followed. But economics will not tell you whether the results will be good or bad. Judgments about results depend on a person's values."[9] Nowhere do the standards or the texts suggest that people can have right or wrong values. Values are subjective preferences.

Ever since Adam Smith, economists have believed that self-interest makes the economic world go round, and Smith's "invisible hand" is still to be seen (in a manner of speaking) in the standards and the texts. According to the standards, people "usually pursue their self-interest."[10] The texts typically introduce the idea of self-interest (and the profit motive) in the context of discussing Smith. One text notes that the discipline of economics simplifies behavior, and it will assume that people act out of self-interest and make informed decisions. While neither the standards nor the texts insist that all action is self-interested, they show no interest whatever in altruism or compassion. When is it good to overcome self-interest? They aren't interested. (Studies by economists show that students who study neoclassical theory become more self-interested as a result of their coursework.[11])

Needless to say, it is all but impossible to maintain some sense of justice or right and wrong when all preferences are merely subjective (and assumed to be self-interested) and we think about everything in cost-benefit terms. In theory (and, as a result, almost inevitably in practice) the Bible and pornography become interchangeable consumer goods. The Sabbath and religious holidays cannot be kept holy, for there is no such thing as sacred time. Advertising plays on themes of sexuality, power, and greed in ways that corrupt human dignity and the sacredness of life. All religions, by contrast, hold that preferences may be intrinsically bad, and that we have duties that are not subject to the kind of weighing that is integral to cost-benefit analysis.

So should we teach students about alternatives to neoclassical theory? The standards provide a clear answer: students should be taught only the "majority paradigm" or "neo-classical model" of economic behavior, for to include "strongly held minority views of economic processes risks confusing and frustrating teachers and students who are then left with the responsibility of sorting the qualifications and alternatives without a sufficient foundation to do so."[12] We certainly don't want to confuse teachers or students with alternatives.

The texts are somewhat less narrow in this regard than the standards. For example, they each have short sections on Marxism and socialism, contrasting centrally planned with market economies; one even discusses Swedish socialism. One wonders why they can't also have short sections on religious ways of thinking about economics, or on philosophical theories of morality and justice. One response, from Robert Duvall, president of the National Council on Economic Education (which issued the standards), is that parents and educators fear that the study of economics might be politicized and will prove controversial; hence he has reassured us that the study of economics need have no ideological content.[13] So neoclassical theory isn't controversial?

*Other Issues*

There are a number of issues that are of particular concern to people within religious traditions that are either ignored, slighted, or discussed only in the narrow amoral categories of neoclassical theory. As I noted in the last chapter, every religious tradition has placed special emphasis on compassion, justice, and the duty to help the poor and oppressed. Neither the standards nor the texts give any weight to the needs of the poor or discuss poverty as a moral or spiritual problem; nor do they discuss economic or social justice. While three of the texts have substantial sections, running from thirty pages to several chapters, on personal finances (getting a job, writing checks, saving money, buying a car, renting an apartment, paying taxes, buying insurance, etc.) there is no mention in any of the texts (or in the standards) of charitable giving.

Virtually all religious traditions condemn contemporary consumer culture for nurturing attachments to wealth and the material goods of this life. Of course the economic system thrives by nurturing our acquisitiveness, creating stronger (and new) desires for consumer goods, requiring that we devote ever more time and energy to economic pursuits. Needless to say, the texts and the standards are silent about these concerns. One text has a box asking "Does Money Buy Happiness?" Students are told that surveys suggest that if everything is held equal, the more money one has the happier one is (a dubious proposition according to much other research). It also tells students that a "stable marriage" is worth approximately $100,000 in terms of "equivalent reported satisfaction."[14] (Hmm.)

It is now widely held that the effects of economic growth on the environment have become catastrophic—an increasing concern of our religious traditions. The texts and the standards ignore the implications of economic growth on nature and say nothing about the moral problem of sustainable growth.

From within all religious traditions, work must be understood in moral and spiritual as well as in economic terms, but the standards say nothing about this. While the texts do say something about inhumane conditions of work historically (albeit briefly) in discussing the rise of unions, they have nothing to say about contemporary concerns about the meaningfulness and dignity of work, or about thinking of vocations as callings.

I want to be clear that the problem isn't necessarily that theologians and economists take different positions on any particular issue. Nor is it a matter of Left-Right politics. If the standards are fairly uncritical of market economies, the texts often provide information that is grist for criticism (at least for those who have eyes to see). Rather, the problem is that economics texts and courses teach students to conceive all of economics in entirely secular, nonmoral categories. They don't do anything to help students think in an informed and critical way about the moral and spiritual dimensions of the economic domain of life. They do nothing to locate students in moral, political, or religious traditions that might guide their value judgments, and they totally ignore the rich literature of the last hundred years on economics and moral theology. In fact, as things now stand, schools don't teach the subject of economics, for subjects are open to various interpretations. Rather, they teach economics as a discipline, a particular way of thinking—that found in neoclassical economic theory—and they do so completely uncritically, without informing students that there are alternatives.

It is hard to reconcile the interpretation of human nature, values, and economics found in the texts and the national standards with that of any religious tradition, and there can be little doubt that the way we conceive of economics contributes to the growing secularization and demoralization of our economic life. We should not be surprised when the sociologist Robert Wuthnow reports that when "asked if their religious beliefs had influenced their choice of a career, most of the people I have interviewed in recent years—Christians and non-Christians alike—said no. Asked if they thought of their work as a calling, most said no. Asked if they understood the concept of stewardship, most said no. Asked how religion did influence their work lives or thoughts about money, most said the two were completely separate."[15]

## Science

There is no discussion of the relationship of science and religion in the 262 pages of the *National Science Education Standards*, although the standards do say that "explanations on [sic] how the natural world changes based on myths, personal beliefs, religious values, mystical inspiration, superstition, or authority may be personally useful and socially relevant, but they are not scientific."[16] The standards also acknowledge that "science is only one way of answering questions and explaining the natural world"—but they don't say anything about any alternatives.[17]

Each of the eight textbooks I reviewed most recently (four in biology, four in physics) has a short opening chapter on scientific method. Each of these chapters is depressingly perfunctory. The longest discussion of the relationship of science and religion is two short paragraphs in a physics textbook, which claims that science and religion have different domains: the domain of science is the natural order; the domain of religion is nature's purpose. Although it appears contradictory to claim that light is both a wave and a particle, physicists know that waves and particles complement each other. Similarly, although "science and religion are as different as apples and oranges" they "complement rather than contradict each other."[18] A second (biology) text notes that because science requires natural causes all appeals to supernatural causes are out of bounds. A third acknowledges that science cannot disprove the existence of unobservable or supernatural forces. A fourth text simply says that "some questions are simply not in the realm of science. Such questions may involve decisions regarding good versus evil, ugly versus beautiful, or similar judgments."[19] That's it.

There is not a hint in any of the eight texts or the standards of the existence of the new science/religion dialogue of the last few decades.

## Evolution

Each of the biology texts discusses Darwinian evolution at length, running through the major scientific arguments for evolution. None discusses the historical conflict over design in evolution. One does note in passing that "Darwin's book raised a storm of controversy in both religion and science, some of which still lingers."[20] No text says anything about the absence of design in neo-Darwinism, although one acknowledges that "modern evolutionary theory now recognizes that evolution does not move toward more 'perfect' states, not even necessarily toward greater complexity."[21] None of the texts discusses the relationship of religion and evolution.

While the national standards are clear that evolution is the "central unifying theory" of modern biology, the state standards (forty-nine of fifty states haves science standards) are not always so clear. According to Edward Larson, "By 2000, every state (except Iowa) had adopted some form of science standards that at least addressed the topic of biological evolution (though a few avoid using the word itself)."[22] In its study of state biology standards, the Thomas B. Fordham Foundation noted that some states downplay the centrality of evolution as a unifying explanatory theory, others fail to give adequate attention to geological evolution, and most state standards don't mention the place of human beings in biological evolution. As a result, it gave eleven states failing grades, and found that only about two-thirds of the states have adequate standards.[23] Several states have recently considered changing their science standards to acknowledge criticisms of evolution, Kansas, most prominently. (The Fordham study gave Kansas an F- for its efforts.) No doubt evolution continues to be controversial. At the same time, no state requires any discussion of creationism, Intelligent Design theory, theistic evolution, or any religious interpretation of nature.

## Other Issues

The big bang is discussed in three of the four physics texts, but none of them says anything about philosophical or religious arguments regarding it (though one does discuss the idea of an eternally oscillating universe). None of the texts mentions the evidence for cosmological fine-tuning.

All four of the biology texts acknowledge that scientists do not yet understand the origins of life, though none of them makes anything philosophically or religiously of this. Each suggests at least implicitly that a scientific explanation is forthcoming. One text does include a box that briefly describes four theories about the origins of life, one of them being divine origins: "Many of the world's major religions teach that life was created on Earth by a supreme being. The followers of these religions believe that life could only have arisen through the direct action of a divine force. A variation of this belief is that organisms are too complex to have developed only evolution. Instead, some people believe that the complex structures and processes of life could not have formed without some guiding intelligence."[24] This is the only reference to Intelligent Design (or design of any kind) in any of the texts.

Although each of the biology texts has several chapters on the development of the nervous system and brain, none says anything about the philosophical or theological problems relating to the development of consciousness or mind. Interesting, in the last chapter (titled "Frontiers") of a physics text the authors note that "the most amazing thing in the history of universe, at least from our perspective" is when life and people come to be, and "the characteristic of human beings that seems most different from inanimate matter includes consciousness and the realization of emotion, including love. Perhaps the reductionist view does not apply to systems as complex as living creatures. If not, why not? Whatever the ultimate answer, it will be fascinating to discover."[25] Yes, this is an interesting question. Unfortunately, we learn nothing more about the dangers of reductionism or the origins of love.

Three of four biology texts have short sections (from several paragraphs to two pages) relating to the development of altruism in animals, explaining it in terms of kin or reciprocal selection. None addresses morality or altruism (or love) in human beings.

None of the texts addresses the question of free will and determinism.

Although all of the biology texts have several chapters on the environment and ecology, none addresses the extensive literature on spirituality, religion, and ecology.

All of the references to religion added together come to less than 1 page out of 7,356 in the eight science texts. The texts certainly don't attack religion; indeed, they often pull their punches, probably to avoid controversy. They betray no doubt that science will solve currently unsolved problems (such as the origins of life). They ignore the Big Questions science raises and the immense literature on the relationship of science and religion of the last several decades. One reason this is possible is that although the texts occasionally provide a little historical or biographical context in discussing great scientists or changing formulations of important theories, the texts don't teach science historically. The assumption clearly is that the purpose of science education is to teach students what contemporary scientists believe to be good science, not to teach science in historical, cultural, or philosophical context.

## Other Subjects

### Literature

The *National Standards for the English Language Arts* bury three essentially incidental and passing references to religion and religious literature in an extended and largely indiscriminate discussion of lab manuals, reference materials, journals, computer software, databases, films, television, newspapers, speeches, editorials, advertisements, letters, bulletin board notices, and signs.[26] In fact, only two of twelve standards deal with literature. The second of these emphasizes the importance of literature in illuminating the ethical and philosophical dimensions of experience; this might be taken to provide an opening for religious literature, but the standards let the opportunity slip by. The standards show no overt hostility to religion or religious literature; they just ignore it.

Happily, the textbooks aren't so indifferent to religious literature.[27] Needless to say, the use of primary sources in literature anthologies has the potential of giving students greater insight into religion than the dry prose and endless facts of narrative history textbooks. Also, high school anthologies that organize world literature, British literature, and American literature by historical periods typically include a fair amount of religious literature—at least up to the nineteenth century when, after Romanticism and Transcendentalism, they pretty much lose sight of religion. Most literature anthologies for younger students are not organized historically, however, but by themes or genres, and anthologize literature drawn primarily from the nineteenth and twentieth centuries that is almost always secular.

While the world literature anthologies include selections from the sacred scriptures of many religious traditions, the selections are invariably short, taken out of context, and are chosen more for their literary than theological significance. The standard selections from the Bible are the creation narratives in Genesis, the story of Noah, the book of Ruth, several psalms, and one or two parables of Jesus. Altogether the biblical selections total about twenty pages of text (with pictures)—about half of the forty pages typically given to Homer's *Iliad* (in textbooks that run between 1,200 and 1,400 pages). Excerpts from the Qur'an total two pages on average. More pages are devoted to Asian religious texts, although again, the individual selections are always brief (typically a page or two). The British literature texts also include two pages or so of excerpts from the King James Bible.

Of course, many of the selections from premodern times address religious themes, and selections from the nineteenth and twentieth centuries will sometimes use religious imagery and grapple with existential, even spiritual, themes (albeit not usually in overtly religious categories). So, for example, the world literature texts all include (the same) four cantos from Dante's *Inferno*, and the British literature anthologies give a relatively generous ten pages, on average, to Milton's *Paradise Lost*. Jonathan Edwards's sermon "Sinners in the Hands of an Angry God" is in all the American literature textbooks—as is King's "Letter from a Birmingham Jail" (usually edited down). Two of the American literature texts included Arthur Miller's *The Crucible* (about an episode that is not one of the high points of the Christian tradition) in its entirety. The world and the American texts typically include some Holocaust literature (usually fairly brief excerpts from Elie Wiesel's *Night* or Primo Levi's *Survival in Auschwitz*).

Still, there are, I suggest, three major problems for our purposes. First, the selections are too brief for students to make much sense of them or of the religious traditions within which the texts are written. Second, students will learn little about religion over the last century or two. Third, most teachers will be unable to provide religious (as opposed to more narrowly secular literary) contexts for, and interpretations of, the selections they assign.

## Civics

The *National Standards for Civics and Government* are the most sensitive of all the content standards for religion in the contemporary world. They require, for example, that students understand different conceptions of the relationship of God to law (theories of natural rights, for example), the importance of religious liberty and the meaning of the religion clauses of the First Amendment, the impact of religious pluralism on American politics, the role of religion in creating conflict in the United States and in the rest of the world, and ways in which religion can challenge allegiances to the nation. Unfortunately, like the history standards, the civics standards are so comprehensive that their emphasis on religion is almost inevitably lost as textbook authors and teachers decide what to discuss in the limited time and space they have.

In fact, the four civics texts I reviewed fell far short of the standards in spite of their length (on average over five hundred pages). Three devoted several paragraphs to discussing religion and religious liberty in the colonies. While each quoted the passage from the Declaration of Independence saying that we are "endowed by our Creator with certain inalienable rights," none saw fit to comment on the significance of this reference to a Creator, and none discussed the religious background of conceptions of natural law or natural rights. Each discussed the religion clauses of the First Amendment, three utterly superficially, one in some detail. And each had a paragraph or two on some contemporary issue having to do with religion in American public life (religious schools, faith-based social services, or the correlation of religion with voting and political parties). The four texts gave, on average, less than 1 percent of their space to religion.[28]

### Courses on/in Ethics, Morality, and Religion

In spite of the importance we attach to morality, there are no (or very, very few) high school courses in ethics or morality. There are character education programs in many schools—usually in the lower grades—most of which ignore religion as too controversial. (I'll say more about character education in chapter 12.)

According to one recent survey, about 8 percent of high schools offer courses in the Bible, but they are always elective courses, and few students take them. I don't know the number of schools that offer courses in world religions, but my impression is that they are less common than Bible courses (and, with only one exception that I know of, they too are always electives).[29] I suspect that at most, 1 percent of public high school students take a course in religion. I'll have much more to say about Bible and world religions courses in chapter 10.

### Higher Education

It is difficult to say with any precision how God fares in higher education. There are no national standards at that level; nor have there been any studies of how religion is treated in college textbooks. There are, however, four reasons to think the situation may not be as bleak as in public schools.

First, university faculty members are not bound by state-adopted curricula and textbooks written by educators and policy makers who are tone deaf to religion; nor do they usually need to worry about how controversial it might be to include religion in the discussion. To some considerable extent they are collectively free to define their own curricula, and individually free, because of academic freedom, to shape their own courses and choose their own texts. Second, there are at most colleges and universities a scattering of courses that address religion in some depth: courses in the philosophy of religion or the sociology of religion, for example, and courses in classics, history, literature, and political science may also address religious issues, traditions, and movements. Third, many colleges and universities have departments of religious studies, which enable students to study various religions in some depth. Fourth, when students do take courses in which they study religion, they are more likely to read primary sources written from within religious traditions—this is not usually the case in high schools apart from literature courses—and this, as we shall see, is critical if religion is to be taken seriously.

This said, we still can't be too sanguine. Why?

I don't doubt that there are some undergraduate courses (apart from religion courses) in which students take religion seriously, but I suspect there aren't many. In my undergraduate philosophy of religion course I have often asked my students, usually juniors and seniors, a series of questions. How many of you have had a psychology course? Most hands go up. Did any of your professors ever discuss the soul or sin? No hands. How many of you have had a biology class? Most hands go up. Did any of your professors discuss the possibility of purpose in nature? No hands. How many of you have had a business or economics course? Most hands go up. Did any of your professors ever discuss the importance of love or religious conceptions of justice? No hands. How many of you have had a history course? All hands go up. Did any of your professors ever discuss the possibility that there is a religious meaning to history? No hands. I'll say a good deal in chapters to come about why religion comes up so rarely; here I simply note this no doubt unsurprising fact.[30]

What about courses in the philosophy, sociology, or psychology of religion? First, they are relatively rare; second, they are always electives; and third, very few students take them. Moreover, such courses are often reductionistic in the sense that they interpret or explain religion in terms of the host discipline (psychology, sociology, anthropology, or philosophy), which always employs secular categories to make sense of its subject matter. Consequently, students are less likely to learn how to make sense of the world religiously than they will be to learn how to make sense of religion psychologically or anthropologically (or whatever).

But don't departments of religious studies ensure that students at least have the opportunity to study religion in depth? In some places, yes; in others, no. In fact, departments of religious studies are still the exception rather than the rule in public universities. According to a 2000 survey of undergraduate departments of religious studies and theology conducted by the American Academy of Religion (AAR), about 40 percent of colleges and universities have such departments (about half of which are "combined" departments, often with philosophy).[31] Unfortunately, the study doesn't break down the numbers by public/private, but it is safe to say smaller, private, religiously affiliated schools are more likely to have such departments, while public colleges and universities (which enroll more than three-quarters of all undergraduates) are less likely to.[32] It is true that in the wake of 9/11, some universities—including several large public universities—have added departments of religion. So at the outside, perhaps 40 percent of public universities now have some kind of curriculum in, or department of, religious studies. We need to keep in mind, of course, that coursework in religious studies in public universities is virtually always elective.[33] I don't know of any statistics regarding what percentage of undergraduates will take an elective course in religious studies; I'll (generously) guess that half do. So (roughly) 20 percent of undergraduates at public universities will take a single course in religious studies.

But there's a further consideration. Some of these courses will be highly specialized, and many of them will address religion in narrowly historical contexts, more or less as historical or sociological artifacts. Sometimes what students learn from a course in religious studies is that scholars can make sense of religion in secular categories (be they historical, psychological, anthropological, or sociological), not that religious ways of making sense of the world should be taken seriously here and now. In such cases, religion is kept at arm's length. Not always by any means, but often.

Where does this leave us? I will suggest that about 10 percent of undergraduates in public universities take a course in which religious ways of making sense of the world are taken seriously. It is true that in courses in religious studies, and occasionally in courses in other disciplines, students will read primary sources and or scholarly texts written by theologians or religious writers who take religion seriously. But the great majority of undergraduates will never be required to read such a book.[34]

Might students encounter religion in ethics courses? Such courses are typically electives, though some universities now require a course in ethics or moral reasoning. In public universities ethics courses are almost always taught in philosophy departments, however, and my review of ethics anthologies reveals little religious literature. While Augustine or Aquinas may appear in anthologies in the history of ethics, it is unlikely that theologians or religious ethicists of the last two hundred years will appear. It is true that anthologies in applied ethics may use a religious text or two in surveying positions dealing with abortion, but this is rare in dealing with other issues.

We shouldn't be surprised when Alan Wolfe, director of the Boisi Center for Religion and Public Life at Boston College, notes that "universities, shaped by faculty priorities, are hands down the most secular institutions in American Society."[35]

## Conclusions

There are, of course, private schools and religiously affiliated colleges where students are required to study religion in some depth, but most students do not attend them. So what do most students learn about religion in schools and universities? Does God measure up to American standards?

There is no overt hostility to religion in the standards or in the high school textbooks. Indeed, the history standards and texts include a good deal about religion in the context of history. But the texts and standards also demonstrate that students need to understand virtually nothing about religion to make sense of the world here and now.

Not surprisingly, there are no national religion standards; nor are there required courses in religion in public schools and universities. Indeed, in most schools, and in the majority of public universities, there are no religion courses whatsoever.

I suspect that for the great majority of American students in secondary schools and universities, less than 1 percent of the content of their education will deal with religion. Most of what they learn about religion will be in the context of distant times and places. They will learn nothing about modern theology or the place of religion in contemporary intellectual life. They will not be taught that God doesn't exist, but they will inevitably learn to interpret whatever they study in secular categories. They will not unreasonably conclude that God is irrelevant to the subjects they study, to how they understand the world, and to how they live their lives. They will certainly not learn to take religion seriously.

So it would appear that God doesn't measure up to American standards.

We will see how this came to be in chapter 3.

# 3

# The Secularization of American Education

The New England Puritans were particularly zealous advocates of education, for it was by reading the Scriptures that false religion could be avoided and true religion secured, but one would have found variations on this theme in traveling from colony to colony over the next 150 years. Through most of the enlightened eighteenth century the most commonly used schoolbook was the *New England Primer,* which taught students the Lord's Prayer, the Apostles' Creed, the Ten Commandments, the "Duty of Children Towards Their Parents," the books of the Bible, and the Westminster Assembly's Shorter Catechism (which at forty pages was not so short).

The *McGuffey Readers* were to nineteenth-century America what the *Primer* had been to colonial America. The readers were filled with stories from the Bible; indeed, the index to *The Annotated McGuffey* contains more references to God than any other subject.[1] In her study of more than one thousand nineteenth-century schoolbooks, Ruth Miller Elson documented the continuing importance of religion in explaining nature, history, and morality, concluding that their most fundamental assumption was "the moral character of the universe." The values taught in the books were "absolute, unchanging, and they come from God."[2]

Higher education was no less religious. The primary purpose of establishing Harvard College in 1638 was to guarantee the supply of ministers, and both Harvard and Yale (America's second college) had formal goals of ensuring that students know God and Jesus Christ.

As at Oxford and Cambridge, the curriculum of the colonial colleges centered on ancient languages and the classics. Ancient languages were important so that ministers could read the Bible in the original languages. Saturdays and Sundays were devoted to theology and, of course, church.

While truth was to be found in Scripture, because God created the world all knowledge must be harmonious. Through the middle of the nineteenth century most scholars and college professors accepted the idea of the *unity of truth* that, as Julie Reuben explains in her superb history of American higher education, "entailed two important propositions. First, it supposed that all truths agreed and ultimately could be related to one another in a single system. Second, it assumed that knowledge had a moral dimension. To know the 'true,' according to the ideal, was to know the 'good.'"[3] The unity of truth made sense because everyone believed that the world was God's creation, and that God's world is a moral world, one in which the truths of science, human nature, and moral philosophy all cohere. Nature reveals the intricacy of God's handiwork, and history reveals God's plan for humankind. By the end of the eighteenth century, and for most of the next hundred years, most colleges required a senior capstone course in moral philosophy, typically taught by the minister-president of the college. The course in moral philosophy would draw out the implications of the curriculum for virtue and help students orient their lives in terms of their Christian vocation.

There were, to be sure, intermittent battles over orthodoxy and heresy. Still, these were essentially family squabbles among Protestants. Religious qualifications for faculty positions were a fact of life in state as well as in private colleges through much of the nineteenth century. As late as 1860, 262 of 288 college presidents were members of the clergy and more than a third of the faculty were ministers.[4] Indeed, "prior to 1870," Jon H. Roberts and James Turner write, "colleges typically functioned as the intellectual arm of American Protestantism" as they taught a "variety of courses that sought to integrate knowledge on Christian foundations."[5]

Through the mid-nineteenth century then, it appears that God did measure up to American standards. Our question now is what happened?

## Public Schools

### Politics and Pluralism

Control over schooling remained in local hands through the early years of the nineteenth century and, as a result, schooling remained religious. But when the movement for tax-supported state systems of public, or common, schools began in the 1830s in Massachusetts, schools were to be officially nonsectarian. Horace Mann, who led the movement, argued that because religious establishments have always led to persecution and tyranny, public schools must embrace a different principle: "that government should do all that it can to facilitate the acquisition of religious truth, but shall leave the decision of the question, what religious truth is, to the arbitrament, without human appeal, of each man's reason and conscience."[6]

Mann wanted no theology or religious indoctrination in his schools, but he did want Bible reading. Like most everyone, he believed that morality required a religious foundation: the Bible. But the Bible should "speak for itself." Teachers were to provide no divisive doctrinal gloss. Students should be free to interpret it as they will. In time this became the orthodox position of the public school movement. In 1869 the National Teachers Association resolved that the Bible should be "devotionally read, and its precepts inculcated in all the common schools of the land." It also held that the teaching of "partisan or sectarian principles in our public schools is a violation of the fundamental principles of our American system of education."[7]

The claim that public schools were "nonsectarian" was disingenuous. Even if there was no denominational catechism, the Bible that was read was the Protestant, not the Catholic or Jewish, Bible. Even among Protestants there was considerable suspicion, at least at first, of such nonsectarian teaching. After all, Mann and many of his fellow reformers in Massachusetts were Unitarians, committed to a liberal religion of moral duty and enlightenment; their foe was traditional, revealed religion, which they took to be divisive and socially dangerous.[8]

Of course, the idea of reading the Bible without the authoritative interpretation of the church was a distinctly Protestant idea, and in the long run the greatest opposition to common schools came from Catholics who, over the course of the nineteenth century, developed their own parochial school system. When they pressed for tax support (after all, Protestant common schools were tax supported) a number of states passed constitutional amendments banning tax support for "sectarian"—that is, Catholic—schools. After 1876 the U.S. Congress required that all states admitted to the union adopt constitutional provisions (often called Blaine Amendments) for prohibiting the use of tax revenues for sectarian purposes. As Douglas Laycock has noted, the motivation behind this movement was "not pretty" for it traced "not to any careful deliberation about constitution principles of the proper relations of church and state" but to "vigorous nineteenth century anti-Catholicism and the nativist reaction to Catholic immigration."[9]

For much of the nineteenth century Protestantism was the common coin of the realm, but if common schools were rather less nonsectarian than they claimed to be, the logic of secularization was clearly at work, at least in the long run. In a religiously pluralistic culture, peace is achieved by eliminating what is divisive from public institutions, and religion was clearly divisive. But the goal wasn't simply eliminating what was divisive, it was teaching what we had in common; and in an increasingly pluralistic and individualistic frontier society the need for a shared ideology was deeply felt. In a world swept by nationalism after the French Revolution, it is not surprising that Americanism became that ideology. According to Elson, the "first duty" of nineteenth-century textbook authors "was to attach the child's loyalty to the state and nation. . . . Every book contains many pieces sustaining the doctrine that one's loyalty to country must be paramount to all other loyalties."[10] The title page of a Noah Webster *Reader* set an ambitious goal for parents: "Begin with the infant in his cradle. Let the first word he lisps be Washington."[11]

Americanism took on new educational importance with the growing waves of immigrants during the twenty years on either side of the year 1900. In 1909, 58 percent of children in public schools in the thirty-seven largest American cities had foreign-born parents.[12] Public schools became the cultural factories of Americanization, transforming the raw material of foreign cultures into good American citizens. As Sidney Hook described it, public schools provided the common institutional ground for those "shared human values which must underlie all differences within a democratic culture if it is to survive. Where churches and sects and nations divide . . . the schools can unite by becoming the temples and laboratories of a common democratic faith."[13]

As Elson tells the story, after the 1830s, readers for the first time anthologized more nonbiblical than biblical stories. Gradually, more purely scientific accounts of nature made their way into textbooks. Theology disappeared from the later books though God often maintained a presence as the guarantor of virtue; indeed, religion became largely a matter of ethics. By the second half of the century, the virtues most often praised were the economic virtues of industry and frugality, and they often connected virtue with success. The anti-Catholicism of schoolbooks (once a major theme) declined over the course of the century, and religion played a smaller role in history. In his study of high school American history textbooks C. Kenneth Shannon has claimed that between 1860 and 1938 they underwent a significant philosophical transformation. The earlier texts typically assume a Christian point of view and credit Divine Providence with a role in our history while in the later texts "faith in the ideals of the democratic nation replaces faith in God."[14] Frances FitzGerald suggests that religion had virtually disappeared from textbooks by the 1890s. Until this time most authors were ministers or teachers in religious schools who understood the United States as an "arm of Christian civilization." By the turn of the century, however, social scientists, not clergymen, were writing the texts, and, not surprisingly, the "texts of the eighteen-nineties are silent of religious matters . . . and highly articulate on the subject of the nation-state."[15]

So gradually, over the course of the nineteenth century, Protestant private schools gave way to officially "nonsectarian" (if still largely Protestant) common schools that, in time, adopted Americanism as their ideology. In the twentieth century, devotional Bible reading and prayer became less and less common as the schools attempted to become truly common schools, acceptable to all religious communities. Eventually, the U.S. Supreme Court declared prayer and devotional Bible reading unconstitutional, though not until the 1960s.

## Economics and the Market

In his presidential farewell address, Ronald Reagan fretted that he had never adequately conveyed his understanding of that City on a Hill that he had so often mentioned in describing his vision of America. The phrase, he noted, came from John Winthrop, "an early Freedom Man." "In my mind," the president said, "it was a tall proud city built on rocks stronger than oceans, windswept, God-blessed, and teeming with people of all kinds living in harmony and peace—a city with free ports that hummed with commerce and creativity, and if there had to be city walls, the walls had doors and the doors were open to anyone with the will and the heart to get here."[16]

A striking vision—but it certainly wasn't Winthrop's or the Puritans', for neither put any stock in freedom other than their own, of course; they saw religious toleration as an unmitigated evil and required religious orthodoxy of those who would live among them. Nor did they take kindly to free ports that hummed with commerce and creativity; indeed, the Puritan City on a Hill did not long survive the influence of Yankee commerce. Already, at the middle of the seventeenth century, Captain Edward Johnson would claim, "An overeager desire after the world hath so seized on the spirits of many that the end of our coming hither is forgotten; and notwithstanding all of the powerful means used, we stand at a stay, as if the Lord had no farther work for his people to do but every bird to feather its own nest."[17] Commerce led to mobility and freedom, growth and acquisitiveness, consumer goods and the enjoyment of life. In fact, the merchants of the seventeenth and eighteenth centuries were often the most vocal advocates of tolerance, for they recognized that orthodoxy isn't good for trade.

American education was inevitably caught up in the economic revolution that played a major role in secularizing culture more generally. In fact, American education has long had a utilitarian bent. According to Elson, in nineteenth-century textbooks, the word *knowledge* was almost inevitably preceded by the word *useful* and neither a classical nor a religious education was considered particularly useful in frontier America.[18] The creation of high schools at the end of the nineteenth century was necessitated, in part, by the fact that business required an educated workforce. Indeed, there was growing concern about American competitiveness in world markets as several national reports made clear. During this time, the National Education Association dropped its support of general education (often viewed as "bookish") for comprehensive high schools that would allow specialization. In 1917 Congress responded with the Smith-Hughes Act, the first of a series of acts that encouraged and funded the development of vocational education. The goal, in the language of the time, was "social efficiency." According to FitzGerald, "Administrators and teachers put increasing faith in the notion that vocational training was the democratic alternative to the academic elitism of the European secondary schools." This ideology "reflected the fact that the community at large had no interest in providing intellectual training for the mass of high-school students; its concern was to train skilled workers for industry."[19]

In our own time the economic purposes of schooling have been paramount— for students, their parents, policymakers, and the educational establishment. Most of the major reform reports since the 1980s have emphasized the implications for education of the needs of our increasingly competitive, high-tech economy. Not surprisingly, these reform reports have said nothing about religion.

## Science

By the early decades of the twentieth century the dominant paradigm of education was Progressivism—which combined individualism, a practical or utilitarian orientation, and modern science and social science. Scientific testing, educational psychology, classroom management, and scientific administration quickly became integral parts of education, and as public education was professionalized it was reconceived in scientific categories. As David Tyack and Elizabeth Hansot note, "Whereas the educational evangelists of the mid-nineteenth century aroused the citizenry against evils, the administrative progressives [of the early twentieth century] talked increasingly of problems to be solved by experts. . . . Professional management would replace politics, science would replace religion and custom as sources of authority, and experts would adapt education to the transformed conditions of modern corporate life."[20] In 1876, 43 percent of articles in the *Journal of Education* included references to religion or God; by 1886 this had dropped to 13 percent, by 1891 it was 9 percent, and soon thereafter it dropped to nearly 0.[21] The basic categories for thinking about the purposes and the profession of education had changed radically.

Already, by the last decade of the nineteenth century, a largely secular form of character education had replaced the traditional reliance on the Bible. In its 1902 Declaration of Principles, the National Education Association held that the Bible—which through much of the nineteenth century served as the basis for moral education—was eminently worthy of study as literature, but only as literature, "side by side with the poetry and prose which it has inspired and in large part informed."[22] William Torrey Harris, the U.S. Commissioner of Education at the turn of the twentieth century, argued, "The principle of religious instruction is authority; that of secular instruction is demonstration and verification. It is obvious that these two principles should not be brought into the same school but separated as widely as possible."[23] The educational progressives went even further. As B. Edward McClellan notes in his helpful history of moral education, a "new order offered hope of an unprecedented period of social and moral progress if only Americans would abandon the tyranny of tradition and strive for a just, productive, and democratic society through the application of science and reason to the complex problems of the day."[24] On this view, which soon became the conventional wisdom, social efficiency replaced character education, child-centeredness replaced rote learning, pragmatism and critical thinking replaced tradition, and psychology and social science replaced the Bible as a source of authority.[25] The old religious consensus had completely fallen apart.

Students were also learning to think differently about nature. Before the Civil War, Elson tells us, elementary schoolbooks "accept without question the biblical history of the world and the creation of man. The Garden of Eden and its inhabitants are as real as the Appalachians."[26] When evolution did appear in textbooks in the second half of the century, it was not purposeless natural selection, but teleological evolution "instituted by God to perfect man's world."[27] Lessons on nature were still lessons in religion. By the end of the century, however, creation was being pushed further and further back in time to accommodate fossils and the "new geography," and "expository descriptions of the natural world, devoid of moral and supernatural meaning, increase significantly."[28]

By the 1880s, most American scientists had accepted evolution, and they began to incorporate it into high school textbooks (initially in zoology and botany, then into the new field of biology). According to Edward Larson, turn-of-the-century textbooks completely omitted any mention of God, "which represented a total reversal from both the pre-Darwinian creationist texts and the transitional theistic evolutionary works."[29] These texts discussed natural selection and described the "savage competition going on among living things" and the "fact of the struggle for existence."[30] The first generation of high school biology texts (including George W. Hunter's 1914 *Civic Biology*, the text at issue in the Scopes Trial) "far from not stressing evolution and almost in defiance of Christianity, exalted Darwinism as having supreme influence on modern thought, providing the base for future progress, and representing the greatest ever advance in understanding the laws of life."[31]

At this point in the story of secularization I need to acknowledge a twist in the plotline. In the 1920s, fundamentalist opposition to evolution led to the passage of laws prohibiting the teaching of evolution in some southern states. While the 1925 Scopes Trial was widely perceived as a cultural victory for science and Enlightenment, the trial together with antievolution laws (in at least a few states) convinced textbook publishers that evolution was controversial (a major problem if one's goal is to sell textbooks). While evolution didn't completely disappear from all biology texts, it did disappear from some and was more generally downplayed.[32] Still, public support for science continued to grow over the following decades along with federal financial support for scientific research, and when the Soviets launched *Sputnik* in 1957, beating the United States into space, it was widely perceived as demonstrating the shortcoming of American science education. As Larson puts it, "Fear of Soviet science drove the American public to heed scientific opinion in reforming domestic science education."[33] This led quickly, in the early 1960s, to a new generation of biology texts that embraced evolution. (Needless to say, opposition to evolution didn't disappear.)

The influence of modern science was felt far beyond the science curriculum. To some considerable extent, modern science increasingly came to provide the standards of intelligibility—the worldview—that shaped the content of the curriculum more generally. This becomes especially clear when we look at higher education—to which I now turn. It is important to remember that the agenda for K–12 textbooks and curricula is largely determined by the academic disciplines as they are understood by scholars in colleges and universities. And, as I've noted, by the end of the nineteenth century, public school textbooks were being written by scientists and university professors rather than by clergymen.

## Higher Education

According to George Marsden, "The Protestant colleges of the mid-nineteenth century would have been readily recognizable to the founders of Harvard two centuries earlier." Attendance at chapel services was typically required of students (at state universities as well as private colleges). The curriculum was still largely classical. Most presidents, and much of the faculty, were clergy. And yet, "despite these striking continuities," Marsden argues, "American education had also evolved in substantial, though subtle, ways." The most obvious change was that the education of clergy had been relegated to separate divinity schools or seminaries (the earliest professional education in America) as most college students were now preparing for professions other than the clergy. While theology remained a "point of intellectual reference" at most colleges the "distinctly Christian aspects of the intellectual enterprise" were disappearing. These more subtle changes in American higher education, Marsden claims, were the result of an "accommodation to the demands either of Enlightenment thought or of the culture of the first modern nation."[34]

## Science and the Enlightenment

If Christian theology had been exiled to divinity schools, a common conviction of the unity of truth survived into the second half of the nineteenth century. Science could hardly be a threat because science and religion must be harmonious. In fact, science and religion were often taught together in courses in natural theology in which the intricacies of nature were taken to provide evidence of design, of God's benevolence.

After 1870 the picture changed markedly; the ideal of the unity of truth broke apart, natural theology was discredited, and science began to be seen as undermining religion. Why? One reason was that the United States couldn't remain aloof from European currents of thought. Study in German research universities was commonplace for American scholars through much of the nineteenth century, and in Germany they were likely to encounter a quite different intellectual world. There, science had become a research specialty, freed from the theological constraints of an underlying religious worldview. German universities held a conception of academic freedom to pursue research that was foreign to American colleges where the ideal was to pass on the truths of the past. Moreover, German thought was attuned to the idea of historical development rather than the idea of timeless (biblical or self-evident) truths commonly accepted in the United States.

But it was Darwin who, in the words of Roberts and Turner, "cut the Gordian knot between science and supernaturalism and triggered the establishment of 'methodological naturalism' as the norm of scientific discourse."[35] Darwin was himself quite clear that it was illegitimate to appeal to supernatural causes in explaining evolution, and scientists increasingly accepted this constraint on science; indeed, the "very idea of what counted as an 'explanation' had changed." Supernatural causes "short-circuited" science, and "the appropriate response to the inability to account for natural phenomena naturalistically was to solicit further scientific inquiry, not posit the supernatural."[36] Scientific method made it illegitimate to appeal to God's purposes, or to design, in explaining nature. Natural theology was no longer respectable.

Darwin helped undermine another important aspect of traditional science stemming from Francis Bacon and Scottish Common Sense philosophy—the idea that science is simply the accumulation and ordering of facts. (It is still sometimes claimed by religious conservatives that evolution isn't scientific, because it doesn't stick to the facts.) Darwin made clear the extent to which the new science was deeply and profoundly theoretical. He showed how important it is to question traditional science; good science is open, tentative, questioning, self-corrective, progressive, often revolutionary. It cannot be constrained by dogmatic or commonsense convictions, religious or otherwise. In light of the immense successes of modern science, by the end of the nineteenth century scientists had developed confidence that they would be able to explain all of nature with no help from religion, thank you.

In tandem with this growing conviction of scientific progress the focus of education shifted from acquiring a body of classical or theological knowledge to thinking scientifically. As John Dewey put it, "The future of our civilization depends upon the widening spread and deepening hold of the scientific habit of mind." The educational "problem of problems" is therefore "to discover how to mature and make effective this scientific habit."[37] Inevitably, scientific method was applied to other disciplines, particularly in the new social sciences that developed in the second half of the nineteenth century.[38]

The Victorians, according to James Turner, created social science "as a consciously ethical assault on social problems; they aimed to unleash science on obstacles to moral improvement, and 'social scientists' roosted in settlement houses as comfortably as in universities."[39] In the United States, there was, for a while, an alliance between economists, sociologists, and liberal theologians who together advocated the Social Gospel. But by the first decades of the twentieth century the alliance had fallen apart as social science became more naturalistic and critical of traditional religion, which was increasingly seen as deeply oppressive. Even in the last decades of the nineteenth century anthropologists were explaining religion away as a survival of primitive societies. Early in the twentieth century Freud wrote: "The scientific spirit brings about a particular attitude towards worldly matters; before religious matters it pauses for a little, hesitates, and finally there too crosses the threshold. In this process there is no stopping."[40] Religion is a neurosis. Robert Bellah has noted that by early in the twentieth century the "best minds" in social science were "deeply alienated from the Western religious tradition." Indeed, "none of them were believers in the ordinary sense of the word. All of them believed themselves to be in possession of a truth superior to that of religion."[41] In his famous survey, James Leuba found, in 1916, that "nearly 90 percent of sociologists, biologists, and psychologists doubted the existence of God."[42]

In this intellectual context explaining human behavior is a matter of setting it in the context of a network of causes and developing social or psychological or physiological laws that then allow us to predict (and perhaps control) future behavior. Moral and religious experiences don't provide knowledge of reality, but are purely "subjective." Only sense perception is "objective" and grounds justifiable knowledge claims. By the 1920s, social science, like natural science, had come to accept the fact/value distinction; it can tell us what *is* the case (and how it came to be in terms of naturalistic causes), but it cannot tell us what *ought* to be the case. As Turner puts it, the social scientists of the twentieth century have "labored to squeeze their work dry of moral intent."[43] Social science that had begun, in part, as a moral critique of society, was now committed to naturalism.

## Specialization

Of course science requires specialization; American scholars learned this while studying in Germany. But more than that, specialization seemed to be a requirement of modernity. In his inaugural address as president of Harvard in 1869 Charles Eliot said, "The principle of divided and subordinate responsibilities, which rules in government bureaus, in manufactories, and all great companies, which makes a modern army a possibility, must be applied in the University" and he declared himself an apostle of the expert.[44] Traditional classical education was hopelessly backward looking, saddled with the heavy weight of amateurism. Scholars must have postgraduate training; they must be specialists.

This turn to specialization—and with it the autonomy of the disciplines— was the death knell of the traditional ideal of the unity of knowledge, and it severed the connection between religion and the developing scholarly disciplines. As Marsden puts it, scientists were to leave their religious beliefs behind when they passed through the laboratory door. And so did scholars in other disciplines when they passed through their respective departmental doors. They were to be free to define their own disciplines, apart from the imperialistic influence of religion. (This is what Marsden calls methodological secularization.) Roberts and Turner conclude that "there were many sources of secularization in higher education, and disciplinary specialization was only one. But together with the spread of naturalism, it was the main methodological or epistemological manifestation of secularization."[45]

It also marked the end of the unified college curriculum. The traditional curriculum emphasized general education, a shared conception of what an educated person should know and the classical literature that all students should master. By the end of the century Harvard and most progressive colleges and universities had all but eliminated required courses, making the curriculum almost entirely elective. Not only scholars would specialize; so would students. It was now possible to completely avoid religion.

## Economics

Already by the end of the eighteenth century the great majority of college students were headed not for the ministry but for a variety of secular pursuits. This provided added reason to do away with the classical curriculum and move to a more practical curriculum. Of course, science often served the purposes of business; it provided useful knowledge. Theology, by contrast, was irrelevant to the needs of business and the economy.

In 1862 Congress passed the Morrill Act, making federal aid available to states that supported colleges in which agricultural and mechanical instruction was given. Such aid provided a significant motivation for legislators who wished to influence the direction of higher education toward more practical concerns and occupations—extending even to carpentry and blacksmithing on occasion. Financial carrots were dangled in front of private institutions by major donors. As Frederick Rudolph put it in his history of the curriculum in American higher education, "When a generation of self-made manufacturers, engineers, and merchants were ready to attach their names and their fortunes to the development of schools of applied science, the classical colleges were standing in line with their hands out."[46] Andrew D. White, the first president of Cornell, declared: "Four years of good study in one direction are held equal to four years of good study in another."[47] Midwestern universities, much influenced by Cornell, lined up behind the battle flag of utility. Increasingly, the values of pragmatic legislators, wealthy donors, businessmen, and industrialists on boards of trustees dictated college policy. Capitalism, Christian Smith concludes "undercut the justification for the scholarly task of a college system that privileged religious knowledge in its education, bolstering instead a rationale for a kind of technical, instrumental scholarship that was at the very least indifferent to religious concerns and interests."[48]

By the end of the nineteenth century, scientists and educational reformers were working hard to free higher education from any remaining theological entanglements and the authority of the church. The vocation of teacher and scholar had to be separated from the vocation of minister. Convinced of this, the Carnegie Pension Fund was established in 1906 to wean universities from the church by establishing generous pensions for teachers at colleges and universities free from sectarian control—and many private religious schools severed their denominational ties as a result. In our time it is not uncommon to hear from business, governmental, and educational leaders alike, that the business of higher education is business.

## Politics and Morality

In the wake of the American Revolution, preparing students for their obligations as citizens suggested a stronger emphasis on moral and political philosophy, and relatively less emphasis on theology. In time, the commitment to liberty and individualism complemented the argument for electives grounded in economics and specialization, undermining the traditional, uniform curriculum ground in the classics and theology. The ideal of liberty was also seen, in time, to have implications for academic freedom—which was, in large part, freedom from religious authority. This recognition was hastened by scholars studying in Germany, where academic freedom was well established. American scholars were also exposed in Germany to European anticlericalism and to the historical and textual criticism of the Bible and theological liberalism that were commonplace there—and would become common, if never commonplace, in American universities at the end of the nineteenth century. Again, the old idea of tradition and sacred truths fell victim to historical consciousness and the idea of progress.

The trends of the times can be read into the demise, by the end of the nineteenth century, of the required senior year capstone course in moral philosophy, typically taught by the college president, usually a minister. The moral philosophy course had been an effort to convey the unity of knowledge to undergraduate students, drawing out both the moral and Christian implications of their studies. By the second half of the nineteenth century, it could no longer hold in check the forces of specialization and intellectual fragmentation. In the colleges of the early nineteenth century, Frederick Rudolph writes, the study of society still belonged "to the benign amateurs who were not intimidated by cosmic questions or their own ignorance." But the "narrow competence and specialization of the economists, historians, political scientists, and others who took their place deflected the classroom from advocacy and conspicuous moral judgment to a style that bore the approved description—'scientific,' a style that was objective, cautious, and wary of judgment. . . . [Scholars] were developing an academic style that was . . . removed from moral judgment, and . . . unrelated to the traditional social purposes of higher education."[49]

Like public schools, universities had secularized moral education largely by the end of the nineteenth century. Instead of grounding moral education in theology, or in moral philosophy (which still, in the nineteenth century, paid homage to religion), scholars looked to a variety of sources. There was, for a while, some enthusiasm for an "ethic of science" that emphasized values such as veracity, patience, open-mindedness, tolerance, love of truth, humility, and imagination.[50] Science was democratic (rather than authoritarian) and it was the engine of progress. Moreover, as I have noted, there was hope for a while that the new social sciences would provide moral and social guidance, but when their commitment to value-free methodologies demonstrated their impotence in matters of morality, the university turned to the humanities—particularly to the study of literature and, in time, history and Western civilization—for moral education.[51] But in neither context was religion likely to be more than a historical artifact. In his recent historical study of the humanities, Anthony T. Kronman has labeled this period one of secular humanism.[52]

## Religious Complicity

Several scholars, Marsden most prominently, have argued that liberal Protestantism played a major role in secularizing higher education at the end of the nineteenth century. Influenced by the Enlightenment and the idea of moral and spiritual progress, theological liberals identified true Christianity with science and the scholarly search for truth. Marsden comments that ironically this "contributed to establishing the sanctity of the scientific method and hence its autonomy. Science did not have to be conducted with any reference to theological formulae, not even with reference to the crucial doctrine of the previous era, that God had created the universe and its laws. . . . Science was part of a more general spiritual progress, an expression of God's ongoing creativity."[53] Secularization was also eased by the fact that religious liberals tended to place morality, rather than theology, at the center of their understanding of salvation. Hence, they were less likely to see a conflict between science and true religion.

Moreover, the openness and universalism of liberal Protestantism made it difficult to justify Protestant hegemony in the face of cultural pluralism. When Catholics, Jews, and secularists eventually pressed the argument for truly nonsectarian universities, liberal Protestants found it "awkward," as Marsden put it, "to take any decisive stand against the secularizing trends."[54] Liberals believed that religion should be voluntary in any case, not required. Hence it was easy to end compulsory chapel and other aspects of their control over the life of students and the curriculum." The liberal solution to the religion problem was, then, to grant autonomy to the disciplines, academic freedom to scholars, electives to students, and to make chapel voluntary (it was soon abolished altogether at state universities) while encouraging (or at least allowing) religion on the periphery of campuses by way of religious student organizations (campus Ys) and denominational organizations (such as Newman Centers and Wesley Foundations).

It is perhaps not surprising that many scholars began their careers as ardent liberal Protestants, but came in time to find their religious commitments largely irrelevant to their scholarship—and perhaps even their own beliefs. The celebrated sociologist (and onetime Episcopal priest) William Graham Sumner once remarked that in doing sociology he had put his religious beliefs in his desk drawer, only to discover, when he checked twenty years later, that they were gone.[55]

Religious conservatives are not without responsibility in secularizing education. As James Prothero has recently put it, for nineteenth-century evangelicals, the "road to hell" was paved "with logic and learning; the path to salvation ran through the heart."[56] Unlike for seventeenth-century Calvinists, for evangelicals theological learning was not necessary for salvation and religion was largely irrelevant to education. Douglas Sloan has argued that because of the sharp split between technical and utilitarian reasoning, on the one hand, and conversion experiences and the reasons of the heart on the other (the split between reason and faith in one of its guises), nineteenth-century evangelicals were wary of classical learning and "might even tend to favor the new utilitarian emphases of the state universities over the older liberal arts colleges."[57] Moreover, according to Franklin Littell, "the pious were determined that their sons and daughters would receive the technical training they needed in order to make their way in the world. . . . So the state colleges were voted massive subventions by the Federal Congress and state legislatures controlled by Methodists and Baptists and Disciples and others who wanted their children to have training in agricultural science, mechanical engineering and other 'useful' skills without the dangers of exposure to Greek philosophy . . . and other classical pursuits."[58] No doubt many religious conservatives were just as happy that their sons and daughters didn't have the opportunity to study religion when it would most likely be taught by liberals. Better to leave it to home and church.

## Secularization and Secularism

Religious conservatives have often blamed both the Supreme Court and a conspiracy of secular humanists for secularizing public education, tracing their malign influence to the 1960s. Though the Supreme Court did outlaw prayer and devotional Bible reading in the 1960s, public education had become essentially secular in purpose and content long before that—indeed, long before the court addressed the role of religion in public schools for the first time in 1948 (in *McCollum v. Board of Education*) and before the cultural turbulence and the rise of secular humanism in the 1960s. I don't want to get into the quagmire of defining secular humanism here (I have sunk knee-deep in several efforts to do so elsewhere[59]) but I do want to say something about secularism more generally.

We need to distinguish between secularization and secularism. *Secularization* is the multifaceted process by which people and institutions become secular. *Secularism* is an ideological or philosophical position; secularists favor secularization. But secularization may result from causes other than the actions and arguments of secularists. Advocates of the secularization thesis, as I noted in chapter 1, have argued that secularization is an inevitable outcome of the historical forces of modernity, independent to some considerable extent of the conscious intentions of individuals. Certainly much of the secularization of education was the result not of any hostility to religion, but, rather, a cultural shift from religious to more practical, utilitarian interests. For most people, after all, the primary purpose of education is to secure the credentials necessary for a good and materially rewarding job, not to study theology. No doubt our cultural commitments to consumerism, technology, individualism, liberty, and specialization have all contributed, often unintentionally, to the secularization of education. In this respect, education largely mirrors the secularization of our culture.

Of course, historical and sociological forces are always transmitted through the actions and intentions of individuals, and it is also clear that many scholars and educators fully intended that public education become secular, as Christian Smith argues in *The Secular Revolution*. He argues, as his title suggests, that "the secularization of American public life was in fact something much more like a contested revolutionary struggle than a natural evolutionary progression."[60] This revolution, which took place between 1870 and 1920, was fought especially over education, both K–12 and higher. "The rebel insurgency," he argues, "consisted of waves of networks of activists who were largely skeptical, freethinking, agnostic, atheist, or theologically liberal; who were well educated and socially located mainly in knowledge-production occupations; and who generally espoused materialism, naturalism, positivism, and the privatization or extinction of religion."[61] In one of the book's case studies, Smith shows how his own discipline of sociology became deeply hostile to religion for a variety of reasons, including the influence of Enlightenment skepticism, modern science, and historical positivism, all refracted through the ideology of German universities where most of the founders of American sociology studied.

Smith is no doubt right, but here we need to go back to a distinction I drew in chapter 1 among three types of secularization. While Americans (like most people) continue to believe in God and participate in religious services and activities, religion has been largely privatized, exiled to the margins of our public life, as a result of our institutional secularization.

We must distinguish in turn between two types of secularists. Some secularists hold that belief in God is a mistake and commitment to religious institutions is foolish (if not immoral). They are atheists (or agnostics, freethinkers, materialists, positivists, or naturalists). I will call them hard secularists. Other secularists believe only that public institutions (including the laws and public education) should be secular. These secularists may be deeply religious, but they believe that religion is best kept private. I will call them soft secularists.

Most of the American Founding Fathers were religious in one way or another, but they agreed that our new federal government must be secular as they made clear in both the U.S. Constitution and the religion clauses of the First Amendment. In part this was because they believed, reflecting on the last several hundred years of European wars, that in a religiously pluralistic culture any religious establishment would be controversial and conducive to conflict. Similarly, many nineteenth-century educators were deeply religious, but they believed that in a pluralistic culture public schools—*common* schools—must be secular if they are not to create public controversy and conflict (which, of course, Protestant schools did create). We've also seen how the secularization of higher education was presided over by (typically) liberal Protestants who, for what they took to be good educational and religious reasons, transformed colleges and universities into secular institutions.

It is also true that hard secularists played a role in the process. No doubt a major task of intellectuals over the last 150 years has been to work out the implications of the modern scientific worldview for all aspects of culture, education included. This has been very much the task of the social sciences (which were deeply hostile to religion, almost from the beginning). The debates about the irrelevance of religion in K–12 education were less frank, still we can see among the intellectuals of the Progressive movement, a self-conscious shift away from religion and to science in defining both reality and education.

What can we conclude? The secularization of public education in the United States is partly the unintended result of the secularization of the larger culture; it was also, in part, secularized by scholars and professional educators who adopted variations on both soft and hard secularism. My guess is that today the vast majority of educators in our public school system are soft secularists; in higher education a bracing dose of hard secularism is also common.

## Qualifications and Conclusions

I have focused primarily on the nineteenth century because the secularization of education—at least with regard to purposes of education and the curriculum—was accomplished largely by the end of that century, certainly by the 1920s. There are, however, three ways that the influence of religion in education lingered well into the twentieth century.

First, devotional religious exercises didn't disappear. In many public schools official prayers, devotional Bible reading, and the celebration of religious holidays continued well into the twentieth century, though these practices declined significantly after the Supreme Court's rulings on prayer and Bible reading in 1962 and 1963.[62] At public universities chapel services sometimes continued into the twentieth century, though universities soon stopped requiring attendance and chapel was abandoned altogether before long.[63] Ceremonial prayer has had a longer life. But for most of the twentieth century the practice of religion has existed only on the periphery of most state universities and private research universities, in religiously affiliated campus ministries. I should also note the some universities had religious quotas for students and faculty until the middle of the century.

Second, religious conservatives (and occasionally religious liberals and representatives of minority religious traditions) have used their political clout to influence the selection of, and sometimes censor, textbooks, occasionally with considerable success. I have already mentioned the most striking instance of this: from the 1920s through the 1960s (and sometimes even later) religious conservatives were often successful in blocking the teaching of evolution. While evolution was restored to (most) biology textbooks in the 1960s, it continues to be controversial and is downplayed in some state standards and sometimes ignored by individual, religiously zealous biology teachers.

Third, some schools and universities offer religion courses. A small minority of public schools offer Bible courses or world religions courses. Much more significant, many public universities (though not a majority of them) have created curricula in, or departments of, religious studies, most since the

1960s. I want to be clear (once again) that departments of religious studies are not divinity schools; they do not teach theology (except, perhaps, the history of theology). It is their task to use the fully secular methodologies of the humanities and social sciences to understand religions as historical, cultural, and sociological phenomena. Moreover, as I noted in the last chapter, most students don't take (or even have the opportunity to take) courses in religious studies. Still, the existence of such departments is important, and I will say a good deal more about religious studies in chapters to come.

These qualifications are significant. Still my main point holds: textbooks, the official curriculum, and the governing purposes of public education have become almost completely secular. Theology was exiled to professional divinity schools and seminaries during the nineteenth century, and courses in natural theology and moral philosophy, which had been taught from a religious point of view, were gone by the end of that century. Why? In the critical nineteenth century religion became controversial as the United States became religiously pluralistic. Americanism replaced "nonsectarian" Protestantism in providing the common values that bind us together. Industrialization and market economies uprooted traditional communities, created a consumer society, and refocused education on more practical matters. Darwin removed the last vestiges of divine purpose from nature. The social sciences made God irrelevant to our understanding of psychology, society, and morality. Specialization encouraged scholars to pursue their work free from encumbering religious beliefs. By the early decades of the twentieth century the cultural and intellectual authority of science was so great that the disciplines of learning were largely redefined in naturalistic categories—and religion was inevitably discredited in the process. That is, the basic categories in terms of which scholars think about reality had changed radically. Of course, this development and redefinition of the disciplines had an enormous impact on public schools, for it was passed on to teachers and educators as part of their educations.

What may be most striking about all of this is the vast indifference of educators, parents, and mainline religious leaders to the secularization of education. For all our supposed religiosity, we have, most of us, become settled, perhaps naively, in our secularity.

# 4

# Problems

In this chapter I argue that there are three related potential problems with how religion is treated in the curricula of public schools and universities. Whether these are real problems—and how critical they are—must ultimately be determined against the background of some conception of what education should be, and that will be our theme in chapters 5–7.

So what are the problems? First, education leaves students religiously ignorant. No doubt this is already obvious from chapter 2; here I will distinguish between two kinds of ignorance. Most important, I claim that very few students encounter religion as a live option for making sense of the world or living their lives. Second, public schools and universities are not religiously neutral; rather, they take sides, privileging secular over religious ways of making sense of the world and living our lives. This will turn out to be important given the U.S. Supreme Court's interpretation of the First Amendment. Third, public education borders on secular indoctrination. It will take a little philosophical work to make this last claim plausible, but a part of my argument is that we teach students to accept secular ways of making sense of the world largely as a matter of faith rather than reason—so I will conclude the chapter by saying a little about the thorny distinction between faith and reason.

## Religious Ignorance

It should be obvious by now that most students acquire their high school diplomas and college degrees having learned next to nothing about religion.

But ignorance comes in various shapes and sizes. There is what I will call religious illiteracy—ignorance of simple and straightforward religious facts, symbols, stories, and history. No doubt most students will learn a little about various religions in the course of studying history and historical literature, but they won't learn much. True, a small minority of high school students will take a religion course, but the vast majority won't. A larger minority of undergraduates will take a religion course, still most won't. And even if a student does take a course in religion, it may well deal with only one religious tradition and only a small historical or sociological segment of it at that. Consequently, the vast majority of students will not acquire a basic religious literacy.

In his book *Religious Literacy*, Stephen Prothero reports that most students flunked a religious literacy test he gave his students at Boston University.[1] (Name the four Gospels. Name a sacred text of Hinduism. What is the name of the holy book of Islam? Where according to the Bible was Jesus born? And so on.) I've given my undergraduate students (mostly seniors) a thirty-question religious literacy test several times (to four classes in 1988–89, and to four classes in 2006–8). Of about 240 students, not one scored a passing grade of 70 percent, and the average score was about 25 percent. Here are a few examples. Only 30 percent could name Exodus as the second book of the Bible; only a quarter knew that the New Testament was written in Greek; 10 percent could name Saul as the first king of Israel; not one could name Pope John XXIII as the pope who called the Second Vatican Council. About half could identify Passover; half knew that almsgiving and pilgrimage to Mecca are among the five Pillars of Islam; 30 percent could identify the law of karma; 10 percent could name the first Noble Truth of Buddhism. Four times as many students could identify the *Left Behind* series (40 percent) as Augustine's *City of God* (10 percent). Interestingly, the average scores dropped by about 5 percent over the eighteen years, so students may be getting more religiously illiterate.

But even if students acquire a basic religious literacy as a result of their courses in history and literature, they are unlikely to develop any significant religious *understanding*—the kind of understanding that people within a religious tradition have of their own tradition and of the world as it appears from the vantage point of their tradition.[2] It is one thing to collect a few facts, to locate a religion within a secular historical or literary narrative, to look at a religion from the outside using the secular categories of academic study. It is another thing to use the categories of a religious tradition to make sense of the world and of one's own tradition from inside that religion. This distinction between religious and secular ways of making sense of the world cuts deeply; indeed, we might say that it involves a difference of worldview, and employs a different set of categories, a different way of interpreting reality. (I will say much more about worldviews shortly.)

This kind of *inside understanding* requires that religion be studied in some depth, using primary sources that enable students to get inside the hearts and minds of people within a religious tradition. Apart from a few high school and undergraduate courses in religion students have little opportunity to acquire such understanding. Yet such understanding, I suggest, is necessary if students are to appreciate religions as live options for making sense of the world.[3] It is possible, of course, for students to acquire an inside understanding of a religion in a historical context—ancient Greek religion, for example, or the Puritans in colonial America—while failing to appreciate religion as a live option for making sense of the world and their lives here and now. In fact, when students study religion it is almost always as a historical or sociological artifact that makes no claim to truth, to be a live option for them, now.

Of course, one might argue that religion only comes alive when one encounters God in the practice of religion, and this is impossible in public schools and universities. As we shall see, however, there are fully constitutional ways in which students can acquire an inside understanding of a religious tradition using primary sources, not least art and imaginative literature. For now, I'll simply suggest that a course presents a religion as a live option if students study it in sufficient depth to make some sense of it from the inside and if they acquire some sense of the implications of that religion for how to make sense of the world here and now. A course presents religion—not just *a* religion—as a live option if it does all of this with regard to several different religious traditions. As we shall see in chapter 5, treating religions as live options is essential to taking religion seriously. For now my point is simply that we leave students religiously ignorant not just with regard to the facts, but, much more important, with regard to understanding.

Neutrality

The fact that most students graduate from public schools and universities religiously ignorant is strong but not compelling evidence for thinking that they aren't religiously neutral. The fact that the curriculum leaves students ignorant of farming and agriculture doesn't necessarily mean that education is not neutral regarding them. Why? Because the core idea of neutrality is that of not taking sides when we disagree, and there are no disagreements about farming on which schools or universities take sides. There are such disagreements, many of them, with regard to religion.

Of course one could respond that in a farming community it is hardly neutral to exclude the subject of farming from the curriculum; there may well be strong feelings (and some disagreement) about importance or value of farming, even of alternative ways of farming. Similarly, one could say that it is anything but neutral to exclude the subject of religion from the curriculum in religious communities. Of course, there is this difference: all communities are at least somewhat religious. But the argument regarding religion is considerably stronger than this. There are not agricultural interpretations of history, art, morality, nature, or psychology, but there are religious interpretations of all of those subjects. We disagree about how to make sense of them, and to ignore the religious interpretations is to take sides.

The critical consideration here is that neutrality requires fairness when we disagree; neutrality requires including both (or all major) points of view in the curriculum as live options. One cannot be neutral when there is a disagreement if one takes seriously only one point of view. Because schools and universities allow students to remain ignorant of religion while dealing with matters of religious controversy they inevitably fall short of neutrality. One might argue that it is impossible to avoid taking sides, to be truly fair, hence neutrality can't be required. No doubt fairness is an elusive virtue, but surely we can approximate it more or less.

## Two Kinds of Neutrality

We need to distinguish, as does the Supreme Court, between two kinds of neutrality: neutrality among religions, and neutrality between religion and nonreligion. The absence of either kind of neutrality is potentially a problem.

Regarding neutrality among religions it is clear that even if education has little to say about religion, it says considerably more about Christianity than it does about other religions. (There is much more about Christianity than Buddhism in history textbooks, and there are many more courses on the Bible than the Qur'an.) Moreover, Protestantism gets considerably more attention than Catholicism or Orthodox Christianity. There are, no doubt, reasons why Protestant Christianity has been privileged over other religions—most obviously, it has always been the dominant religion in America. This is a powerful, if ultimately inadequate response. I will discuss how to deal with neutrality among religions in upcoming chapters. Here I am going to focus on the second kind of neutrality.

With regard to religion and nonreligion—or let us say, religious and secular ways of making sense of the world and our lives—the situation is complicated. First, we need to be clear that secular ways of thinking and living need not be hostile to religion. In ordinary usage, the word *secular* doesn't mean antireligious, it means nonreligious. Indeed, one may even favor secular policies or institutions for religious reasons. As we saw in the last chapter, it was religious liberals who often took the lead in secularizing schools and universities in the nineteenth century, and as we shall see in chapter 7, evangelicals were largely responsible for disestablishing religion constitutionally, secularizing the federal government at the end of the eighteenth century.

No doubt much of secular life and thought *is* religiously neutral but it is also true that secularity is no guarantee of neutrality. Sometimes secular ways of thinking and living do conflict or stand in tension with religious alternatives— at least some religious alternatives—and, needless to say, much of what is taught in public schools and universities is not neutral with regard to the beliefs and commitments of some (and occasionally many) religious traditions. The idea of evolution conflicts with some religious traditions; so do certain kinds of sex education, particular interpretations of history, and certain stories in literature anthologies. Obviously, there could be no required curriculum at all if everything had to be neutral with regard to every religious tradition (and, as we shall see, the courts have been clear that religious groups don't get a veto over the curriculum).

But the problem cuts deeper than the violation of neutrality with regard to particular issues, texts, courses, or religious traditions. The more basic problem is that schools and universities systematically privilege secular over religious ways of making sense of the world. After all, in dealing with religiously contested questions, public schools and universities: (1) never require students to study contending religious ways of making sense of what is at issue (from the inside, in any depth, as live options), (2) often do not even give students the opportunity to learn about religious ways of making sense of what is at issue (by way of elective courses, for example), and (3) usually do not even tell students that there is a controversy. To leave religion—as a live option—out of the curriculum cripples the ability of students to understand what is at issue; it makes secular ways of thinking the victor by default. It implicitly suggests that religion is a dead option, that students need not understand religion to understand their various subjects, that it is irrelevant to being an educated person. This is to take sides.

It is sometimes thought that by not saying anything one can maintain neutrality: to ignore a point of view is not to take sides against it. True, it is not to take sides *explicitly,* but the discrimination is only a little more subtle. Consider an analogy. For most of our history, schools and universities did not include women's or minority voices in the curriculum. In fact, they didn't even make students aware of those voices and the traditions they were part of. Was this a benign neutrality (regarding gender, race, and ethnicity) or did it privilege male and culturally dominant voices and perhaps even contribute to the continuing oppression of women and minorities? No one, nowadays, would be so naive as to hold that such education was neutral (or fair) with regard to the interests, experiences, and perspectives of women and members of minority groups. So it is with religion. Indeed, some would argue that the conflicts between religious and secular ways of making sense of the world are both more basic and more important than the conflicts between men and women, or between different racial or ethnic groups or cultures.

Let me clear about three things I am *not* saying.

First, I am not saying that schools or universities fall short of neutrality because they issue a formal verdict regarding the truth or value of religion. Public schoolteachers are clearly required by law to refrain from any such verdicts and the vast majority of them do. But I trust no one is so naive as to believe that neutrality hinges on formal verdicts or overt hostility. The absence of an explicit verdict is not convincing evidence that sides haven't been taken for the simple reason that neutrality requires fairness; it requires that contending views (ideas, beliefs, theories, traditions) be taken seriously lest an implicit verdict is issued. If only one side in a controversy is given voice, then surely the teacher (or the text or the school or university) is implicitly taking sides.

Second, I am not saying that teachers or administrators or textbook authors *intend* to take sides. I don't doubt that most public schoolteachers intend to be neutral in matters of religion. But one needn't intend to take sides to actually take sides (just as there need be no formal verdict). Taking sides is often thoughtless. Schools of education pay no attention to this problem so it is not surprising that most schoolteachers and administrators aren't thoughtful about neutrality. In fact, knowing what is neutral in any particular case may require a great deal of sophistication. Academic freedom, specialization, and the secular norms of scholarship ensure that most university professors rarely consider religious neutrality in their courses or in the curriculum. But the victim will be just as dead whether murdered (i.e., killed intentionally with malice aforethought) or killed as a matter of negligence or reckless behavior (manslaughter). Neutrality can be violated with no intention or malice aforethought—in which case religion becomes, in effect, a dead option (so far as education is concerned).

Third, I am not saying that neutrality requires equal time for religion, in any particular course or in the curriculum generally. Neutrality requires that religion be given adequate time, that religious ideas and points of view be fairly included in the discussion as live options. This is a different idea from equal time. I'll address a number of specific cases in part 3.

So public education leaves students religiously ignorant *and* is not religiously neutral. But there is a (potentially) greater problem: public education is little more than secular indoctrination. I have to lay a little groundwork to make this claim clear and plausible.

## Subjects and Disciplines

There is an important difference between subjects and disciplines. A subject such as history or economics or psychology is open to various interpretations, religious and secular. A discipline, by contrast, provides a particular interpretive framework—or perhaps a set of related frameworks—for interpreting a subject. (If interpretations are not closely related, we may talk about a field rather than a discipline; some scholars argue, for example, that religious studies or environmental studies or American studies should be thought of as fields because the range of available interpretations is so great.)

Generally, students are taught disciplines at least as much as they are taught subjects; we teach them to interpret their subjects *in particular ways*. Textbooks are not just collections of factual statements about a subject. Depending on their interpretive framework, authors of history textbooks, for example, will pick out different historical events for inclusion, they will interpret their significance in different ways, they will find different forces at work in the world, they will have different heroes and villains, and they will organize history into different periods—and these differences may be substantial. (Think of the difference between Marxist, Christian, and progressive interpretations of history; or think of how history is refracted through the nationalistic ideologies of different countries.) Textbooks make certain kinds of arguments; they conceptualize the world in particular ways; they have a methodological, even a philosophical, stance. They teach students to think in certain ways about their respective subjects.

But there is a potential problem with disciplines. The astronomer Arthur Eddington once told a parable about a fisherman who used a net with a three-inch mesh. After never catching a fish shorter than three inches the fisherman concluded—mistakenly, of course—that there *were* no fish shorter than three inches. The moral is that one's net determines what size fish one catches. Similarly, Eddington argued, our conceptual nets will determine what aspects of reality we catch.

Needless to say, the kind of conceptual net that a discipline uses determines what it is able to catch—and, if we follow the logic of the parable, it also determines what slips through the mesh of their net. All disciplines abstract from the richness, messiness, and complexity of reality; their conceptual nets inevitably simplify the world. Arguably, the humanities catch the most of reality's richness because they are the least abstract, the most descriptive. And, arguably, because the sciences and hard social sciences are the most abstract (and theoretical) in defining their interpretive framework, they let more of reality slip through the mesh.

So, for example, the scientific conceptual net (methodological naturalism) can't catch obligations. It can tell us what *is* the case in the world, it can catch facts, but it can't tell us what ought to be the case in the world, or what we should do. Oughts (if there are such things) slip through the net. Similarly, design (if there is such a thing) can't be caught—for design involves the claim that something is as it is because it ought to be that way to fulfill a purpose. Scientific method rules out of bounds from the beginning oughts, design, and spiritual or supernatural causes (a God who might, for example, design the world). Nor can the scientific conceptual net catch beauty, miracles, or souls; it even has some difficulty with minds. Correlatively, we might ask what sense can we make of quarks or photons or quantum fields within a religious conceptual net—that of Christian theology, perhaps? This isn't to say that they are incompatible, only that to make sense of quarks and quantum fluctuations we need the framework of modern physics.

There are two related conclusions we might draw from this. First, we can only make sense of certain things (souls or quarks) from within hospitable frameworks of thought. Religious beliefs, values, and practices presuppose a religious worldview from within which it is legitimate to appeal to Scripture, to moral and religious experience, to revelatory patterns in history, to design in nature, or to existential wonder and mystery. Second, disciplines limit what can be discovered or even discussed meaningfully. They provide what the philosopher Stephen Toulmin once described as "professional blinders" that direct the attention of scholars "to certain narrowly defined considerations, and often prevent them from looking at their work in broad human perspective."[4] No doubt disciplines are necessary for scholarship to be productive (after all, scholars can't consider everything) but the risk is always that "rigor might degenerate into rigidity"[5] and that narrowness of vision will supplant breadth of vision.

According to Eric Weislogel, "Our disciplinary practices inevitably give rise to the fragmentation of knowledge. This fragmentation of knowledge leads to the fragmentation of the university. . . . The fragmented university leads— consciously or unconsciously—to training students (and faculty, too) to com- partmentalize their thinking, their reality, and hence their lives."[6]

## Worldviews

So what is a worldview? Consider reincarnation. The philosopher John Hick has suggested that the "idea that we have lived many times before and must live many times again in this world seems as self-evident to most people in the hindu and buddhist east as the contrary idea that we came into existence at conception or birth, and shall see the last of this world at death, seems self-evident to almost everyone in the Christian and post-Christian west. . . . Western religious thinkers have seen . . . little reason to provide arguments for their own assumption that a new human soul is created, or emerges, for every new baby born. That this must be what happened has usually seemed so evident to orthodox Christian theolo- gians that they have not stopped to examine or defend its plausibility." Of course, from the perspective of much Eastern religion, our Western assumptions seem "utterly unreasonable, implausible and unattractive."[7]

One might think that such beliefs are simply matters of blind faith, accepted without evidence. But surely this is wrong, for what makes our respective interpretations of identity and the afterlife so plausible to us is that they are embedded within a particular worldview. Reincarnation is woven into the stories and epic narratives of Indian tradition, the rituals and moral codes, the memories and dreams, the theological and philosophical reflection, the hopes and expectations of people. It is nestled within a worldview that makes sense of it—and so it is with Western views of personal identity.

A worldview provides a comprehensive interpretation of the world, of reality—and its categories provide a contrasting view to that of other worldviews. A worldview isn't simply a collection of beliefs; it is more or less systematically structured. It possesses a measure of coherence; its elements are mutually reinforcing. Worldviews hang together intellectually, culturally, institutionally, and emotionally. They are entangled with how we experience the world and how we make sense of our lives. They orient us in life. They make sense of the world for us. They tell us who we are; they give us an identity.

That is, a worldview provides the most basic framework—the concepts or categories—in terms of which people interpret reality. Often what defines a worldview is so basic that it goes without saying. It is simply assumed; it is an implicit or tacit way of making sense of the world. That's just the way it is, we say.[8] Worldviews are often embedded within cultural traditions. Often their basic outlines are conveyed in myths, or in cultural narratives. (In fact, I will use these three terms—"worldview," "tradition," and "narrative"—as overlapping ways of saying much the same thing.) But if worldviews are sometimes tacit or implicit within a cultural tradition or narrative, they may also be formally articulated and systematized—the Christian worldview, the Marxist worldview, or the modern scientific worldview, for example. (Needless to say, there are contending versions of each worldview.)

Now, to go back to souls, scientists take a rather different view from that found in either Eastern or Western religions. Souls are inherently problematic, for unlike brains, they aren't accessible to sense perception or scientific measurement (given the constraints of methodological naturalism). Scientists are apt to insist that consciousness is dependent on the brain, which disintegrates with death. That is, from within the categories of modern science—the modern scientific worldview—the concept of a soul (and reincarnation and immortality) makes no sense.

So who gets it right? Obviously, each worldview can provide various kinds of evidence and reasoned support for its own fundamental beliefs. Of course what counts as evidence and as rational depends on the worldview. Some scholars have argued that this leaves us with a conceptual relativism. We are all captives of our own worldviews and it makes no sense to try to step outside them to evaluate their truth or how reasonable they might be. Other scholars (I count myself among them) argue that some worldviews are more reasonable (or more true) than others. But even on this latter view, there is a problem, for worldviews can't in any straightforward way be verified or falsified. Any worldview that has come of age will have developed conceptual resources to handle difficulties and will possess resilience in the face of potentially falsifying evidence and arguments. Of course, for most adherents, their own worldview will define common sense and reality with such self-evident force that it is often hard to imagine what might shake their confidence. Attempts to criticize or falsify other worldviews will often appear to be question begging. Claims made within rival worldviews, perhaps only dimly understood, will seem implausible if not nonsense.

## Indoctrination

Our question now is what happens when students are provided by the academic disciplines with a set of secular conceptual nets that let all things religious (if there are such fish) slip through the mesh. Arguably, the cumulative effect of employing secular frameworks in every discipline is that education nurtures in students a secular mentality that marginalizes and at least implicitly discredits contending religious interpretations of the various subjects of the curriculum. When we teach students to think in entirely secular (often scientific) ways about history, nature, psychology, morality, and society, it should come as no surprise that after twelve (or sixteen) years of study they conclude either that there are no religious fish to find in the sea or that if there are, one must accept their presence as a matter of faith. We teach them to interpret (to see, to feel, to experience) the world from a broadly secular worldview. Is this indoctrination?

We can draw a fairly sharp distinction between education, on the one hand, and, on the other, training, socialization, and indoctrination. Education, I suggest, requires that students acquire critical distance on what they are learning, some ability to compare contending ways of understanding a subject, while training, socialization, and indoctrination do not. We toilet train small children; we don't educate them about contending theories of toiletry. We train children in their multiplication tables. We train soldiers to march. In these cases learning is more a matter of drill and habit than of critical thinking. We also talk about training accountants, doctors, and lawyers, and to the extent that there is a single right way of practicing a profession, a more or less closed system within which alternative practices are ignored, students in professional schools are trained rather than educated. (Of course, students in professional schools are trained regarding some things, and educated about others.) Training can require a good deal of intellectual sophistication; it just doesn't require critical thinking about the basic categories or assumptions of the profession.

We often say that children are trained or socialized to behave in certain ways, to accept basic moral values, for example. We don't encourage small children to think critically about whether or not to be honest; rather, we bring them up within a family, a community, a religious tradition, in which they have to be honest. Thinking critically about why one should be honest may have its time and place, but it is not for small children to do. In matters of politics and religion we often use the term "indoctrination" rather than "training" or "socialization" because doctrines are at issue, but the idea is the same: in indoctrinating children (or adults) we train or socialize them to accept certain traditions or values or doctrines; we discourage, or don't allow, open and critical thinking about contending alternatives.

Consider a Christian academy that requires students to study fundamentalist religion for twelve years but requires no coursework in science (though scientific beliefs and movements are occasionally mentioned in history textbooks that are, of course, written by fundamentalist theologians). The universe begins by divine fiat, biology recapitulates the first chapter of Genesis, people have souls, history begins with Adam and Eve and has a religious meaning that takes its decisive turn with the Incarnation, and morality is essentially a matter of the Ten Commandments and other biblical texts. The academy's teachers are not themselves required to have done any coursework in science—and few have. Would students in such an academy be indoctrinated? Yes. Would it make any difference if the teachers believe sincerely they are simply teaching their students the truth? No. Would it make any difference if parents supplemented their children's education by teaching them science or having them watch *Nova* on television? No. I take it that the academy cannot be acquitted of the charge of indoctrination because the teachers are sincere and the parents compensate for its shortcomings.

Now consider a public school that requires students to study secular ways of making sense of the world for twelve years but requires no coursework in religion (though religious beliefs and movements are occasionally mentioned in history textbooks that are, of course, written by secular historians). The universe begins with the big bang, neo-Darwinian accounts of evolution are taught in biology classes, Adam and Eve have been replaced in the cast of characters by various prehistoric primates, the soul is replaced by the self of modern psychology, history has no religious meaning and the Incarnation is never mentioned, God and religious texts and principles are absent from all discussions of morality, and students learn that persons are self-interested utility maximizers. The school's teachers are not required to have done any coursework in religion—and few have.

Would students in such a school be indoctrinated? Yes. Would it make a difference if the teachers sincerely believe they are teaching their students the truth? No. Would it make a difference if parents supplemented their children's schooling by taking them to church or synagogue? No.

Students are indoctrinated when they are systematically and uncritically taught to accept one basic framework for interpreting reality over other major, live alternatives. Occasional or unsystematic privileging of one interpretation over another, in some courses but not others, doesn't rise to the level of indoctrination, which must be systematic, across the curriculum. The privileged framework must be taught uncritically, without making students aware of, and informed about, alternative live options. The interpretations must be basic or foundational, so that they structure some broad range of ways in which students understand the world, as worldviews do. Hence, we don't indoctrinate students against alchemy or flat-earth geography, neither of which provides a philosophically basic view of the world (as religions do) or is a major, live alternative.

We sometimes think that indoctrination must be intended, or that it must be a matter of imposing a particularly narrow or obviously irrational way of thinking on students. We might think of communist brainwashing or fundamentalist parochial education, both of which have sometimes involved intentional efforts to indoctrinate students in a particularly narrow and (many would say) irrational way of making sense of the world. But the effect is the same even if there is no intention to indoctrinate. No doubt most teachers simply aim to teach students the truth, even to think critically about what is true. But they may fail utterly, as they do when they systematically fail to recognize the relevance of religion to thinking critically about the subjects that they teach. The point is that indoctrination, whether intended or not, crowds out critical thinking about the most basic ways of interpreting the subjects they study.[9]

Certainly, most educators don't think that they have a worldview problem. No doubt they encourage critical thinking and it is true that students are exposed to somewhat different conceptual nets in their courses in literature, history, and science. I would contend that there are deep and significant differences between the disciplines of the humanities and the sciences. But the disciplines of the humanities and the sciences are (typically) alike in employing secular methodologies, secular ways of interpreting their subject matters, that allow no conceptual room for religious ways of making sense of the world but are taken to define what is reasonable. The cumulative effect of these secular interpretations in all disciplines—this serial socialization—approximates indoctrination.

Allan Bloom once wrote that true freedom of the mind requires "the presence of alternative thoughts. The most successful tyranny is not one that uses force to assure uniformity but the one that removes the awareness of other possibilities, that makes it seem inconceivable that other ways are viable."[10] Public education does not indoctrinate students by overtly attacking religion or promoting a militant ideological secularism. Rather, it uncritically nurtures a secular mentality, an implicitly secular worldview. It not only leaves students unaware of religious possibilities, it makes religious accounts of the world seem implausible, irrational, perhaps even inconceivable. It fails to provide students the conceptual and imaginative resources that would enable them to take religion seriously and think critically about their secular studies.

Think again about women's and minority studies. It is now widely recognized that the problem wasn't just that women's history and African American literature were ignored, that such education wasn't neutral; the problem was that students were implicitly and uncritically taught to think like Western, white males. Similarly, we teach students implicitly and uncritically to make sense of the world and their lives in secular categories.

Having made a very general argument, let me qualify it—at least a little—in two ways. First, religious ways of making sense of the world are not totally excluded from public schools or universities. Indeed, some universities—those with departments of religious studies—may give students the opportunity to take religion seriously, even if such study is never required. (And some Christian academies take seriously modern science and secular ways of making sense of the world.) Second, schools and universities typically articulate the ideal of critical thinking and encourage it in some contexts; they just fall far short of taking it seriously in other contexts—in matters of religion in particular.

My qualified conclusion is that most public schools and universities border on secular indoctrination (and many cross the line). In doing so, they encourage (secular) faith and undermine critical reason.


Faith and Reason

Philosophers and theologians have used the terms "reason" and "faith" in many ways. I am going to single out several uses of each term that will, I think, be helpful for our purposes.

The philosopher Karl Popper wrote about the *attitude of reasonableness* (which he traced back to the Greeks, especially to Socrates), which may be characterized in this way: "I think I am right, but I may be wrong and you may be right, and in any case let us discuss it, for in this way we are likely to get nearer to a true understanding than if we each merely insist that we are right."[11] I want to distinguish this conversational or dialogical understanding of reason from a common alternative, that of following rules or a methodology within a discipline (or tradition or worldview). We might call these two conceptions reason$_1$ and reason$_2$ or, a little more elegantly, if somewhat arbitrarily, being reasonable and being rational.[12]

Scholars typically reason within a particular disciplinary framework. Euclidean geometry defines a way of reasoning deductively to theorems from self-evident axioms. For scientists, scientific method (methodological naturalism) provides rules for verifying and falsifying scientific claims. One can reason as a Marxist or neoclassical economist, though the background assumptions and the rules of evidence and argument will be considerably different. Religious fundamentalists are typically highly rationalistic: they verify and falsify particular moral and theological claims reasoning from biblical proof-texts (that function something like axioms in Euclidean geometry). I mentioned above that much training in professional schools requires sophisticated uses of reason, but within a particular professional or disciplinary framework. I will call such reasoning within such a conceptual framework or rules a matter of being rational.

We usually have a fairly clear idea of what it means to be rational within a disciplinary framework—following the internal structure of rules, argument, and evidence. But we might also ask whether that framework is true of the world, whether it captures or fails to capture what is real, whether it is a more reasonable framework than alternatives. With the discovery of non-Euclidean geometries in the nineteenth century it made sense to ask which geometry is true of physical space. (In the wake of relativity theory it turned out that space is not Euclidean.) Is it more reasonable to be a capitalist or a communist? Or, focusing on education, we can ask, why use one disciplinary conceptual net to understand a subject (or the world) rather than another? Are some frameworks more reasonable than others? Or might all frameworks provide only partial interpretations of reality? What is most reasonable all things considered?

It has become commonplace for postmodern scholars to reject the claim that we can reason about alternative ways of being rational. Needless to say, the term "postmodern" means different things to different scholars. All too briefly, I here take (what is sometimes called deconstructive) postmodernism to be the view that there are a variety of interpretative frameworks for making sense of the world, none more reasonable (or true) than the others. We are all constrained by the particularities of our cultures and subcultures; we inevitably interpret the world in terms of our own time and language, our own class, race, and gender. There is no way of stepping outside our cultural skins, outside the traditions and social locations that shape our ways of making sense of the world, to discover what is objectively true or reasonable. Rather, "truth," "reason," and "objectivity" are always internal to a cultural tradition, a language-game, a narrative, an ideology, a worldview. A part of what makes this view *postmodern* is that it rejects the claim that science (the dominant approach to knowledge within modernity) has any special standing in providing us with knowledge of the world; rather, science simply provides one narrative among many for interpreting the world, no more reasonable than any other. The result has often been a conceptual relativism and a hermeneutic of suspicion directed at all claims to truth or objectivity. In my terms, for postmodernists, being rational makes sense; being reasonable doesn't.

Of course, if we are caught up in some such relativism, then, as George Marsden has famously argued, it makes no sense to prefer science or secular scholarship over religion and religious scholarship as a matter of reason—in which case education becomes an arena for academic and cultural politics rather than critical thinking.[13] But while postmodernism has had a good deal of influence, particularly within the humanities, most scholars (and certainly most scientists) reject postmodernist relativism, believing that some conceptual frameworks are more reasonable than others, at least for understanding certain subjects, enabling us to at least approximate truth.

Still, there is a problem (a familiar problem at this point). Once we step outside a disciplinary framework how do we know what is reasonable? This is akin to the problem of assessing worldviews. Philosophers and theologians and scientists have given a variety of answers to this question. Needless to say, they don't agree. Perhaps we can at least say this: being reasonable is inevitably less a matter of being rigorously logical or methodological or rule following, than it is of being open to new patterns of meaning, of being deliberative, even creative. It requires an analytical sensitivity to the basic assumptions of a point of view, but it also requires empathy, being able to think (and feel) oneself into different ways of making sense of the world. It may require the ability to see or to experience the world differently, drawing on aesthetic or symbolic forms of expression for insight into reality. It is multicultural, interdisciplinary, and comparative. Perhaps most to the point here, it proceeds by way of interdisciplinary conversation and exploration. We might even say that it aspires to a transdisciplinary understanding of the world—one that recognizes the limitations of all of the disciplines and searches for new syntheses. Of course there are no knockdown arguments, no proofs, when it comes to such matters; perhaps the most that can be hoped for is some measure of plausibility.[14]

Our question is this: is it sufficient for schools and universities to teach students how to be rational within the conceptual frameworks of the secular disciplines, or do they also have an obligation to encourage and enable students to be reasonable as well, exploring alternative religious interpretations? I will say more about this in the next chapter.

## Faith

The word *faith* has many meanings, not least in religious contexts. Faith is often taken to mean "belief." Sometimes people talk about faith as a completely unreasonable leap in the dark—perhaps even believing something when, as Mark Twain once put it, one knows it ain't so. But few people make such blind leaps, believing for no reason at all. Theologians are more likely to understand faith as a gift of God, a deep and abiding assurance of God's presence in the world or in the truth of Scripture. Such belief is nonrational; it is not the consequence of arguments or evidence, though having such faith may make sense within a certain kind of religious worldview. Another sense of faith likens it less to belief than to perception: to have religious faith is to experience the world as good, as suffused with God's grace. (Think of the difference between experiencing the injured person by the side of the road morally, requiring one's help, and experiencing her scientifically, as a physical object. We might also experience her religiously as a creature of God, whose life is sacred.)

There is yet another sense of faith, the one on which I wish to focus—faith as trust. This use of faith is at home in secular as well as religious contexts. People might have faith in their friends or their country, in which case they trust that their friends or their country will do the right thing. There is a parallel religious meaning of faith. To have faith in God is not to believe in God, but to trust God. (God is faithful; after all, didn't God bring us out of bondage in Egypt? God will keep his covenant with us; he is trustworthy and we must be faithful to him.) Perhaps most people have religious faith as a matter of trust in their parents, their religious community and its leaders, their scriptures. Such faith is often grounded (at least implicitly) in evidence and is not immune to reasoned criticism; moreover, it is compatible with doubt.[15] Sometimes trust in a friend or one's country will prove to have been a mistake. Sometimes further experience will confirm one's faith so that our trust proves reasonable. Often we can't be sure.

Given the cultural authority of schools and universities in our culture, it is natural for students to have faith in their textbooks and their teachers, to trust that what they are taught is true and reasonable. As they pursue their studies they may well attribute greater authority to their teachers and the intellectual traditions they study, for what they learn will often make sense to them; it will be confirmed in various ways. No doubt from the vantage points of their disciplines it will be *rational* for them to trust their teachers.

But, of course, we can ask whether it is *reasonable* for them to have such trust because, after all, different disciplines interpret the world in different, sometimes conflicting, ways. Even within a discipline there will be disagreements, and schools of interpretation will develop and change over time. No doubt students (indeed, teachers) may believe that what they find rational within their respective disciplines will prove reasonable if they (or someone) think through it. Indeed, they may well trust those scholars within their discipline who have made the effort to determine whether their disciplinary frameworks are reasonable. (There always are some.) But short of undertaking such study themselves, their trust might be understood as a matter of faith.

Almost always, we teach students to reason in subtle and sophisticated ways within the interpretive frameworks of their various academic disciplines— that is, we teach them to be rational in highly sophisticated ways—but we allow them to accept those frameworks largely on faith because we do not require them to confront questions about the relationship of disciplines (and the worldviews within which they are embedded) to each other. This is even the case in science, as we shall see in chapter 11. We don't require them to think critically about what is most reasonable.

## Conclusions

In chapter 1 I noted that according to surveys the more educated one is, the less religious one is (though even well-educated people tend to be religious, just not as religious as those who are less educated). Why? One might take my arguments in this chapter to show that education prejudices students against religion. Though suggestive, this is not compelling. There are also powerful psychological and cultural drives for autonomy that, quite apart from formal education, make escape from religious traditions (with their burdensome and oppressive rules and rituals) seem desirable, particularly to adolescents and young people. The relentlessly secular nature of youth culture is a powerful secular influence. Indeed, one might argue that students become less religious not because of any kind of educational prejudice against religion, but simply because a good education rightly convinces students of the reasonableness of secular ways of thinking and living.

Perhaps what's more remarkable is that students survive their secular educations with so little damage to their core religious beliefs—after all, most of them still believe in God. How can it be that students continue to believe in God after twelve or sixteen years of (borderline) secular indoctrination? Again, there are many aspects of culture that influence students' beliefs. Whether students continue to believe in God will depend on a great deal besides their formal educations, so we perhaps shouldn't expect a dramatic decline in such religious belief from a totally secular education.

I suspect that a great deal of the staying power of religious belief can be attributed to the conventional, if shallow, view, at least implicitly encouraged by schools and universities, that religion and education are properly compartmentalized. Students learn (again, at least implicitly) that education and religion have nothing to do with each other. Religious ways of making sense of the world are irrelevant to being educated. The moral of the story is not so much that God doesn't exist but that belief in God plays no role in the reasoned pursuit of knowledge and is, consequently, properly a matter of blind faith. That is, education encourages the kind of compartmentalization that goes with the idea of secularization-as-privatization, even if it doesn't have a dramatic impact on belief. Religious belief is properly a private matter with no relevance to anything in the curriculum. It is perfectly reasonable to think in entirely secular ways about everything students study.

I have no doubt that education inhibits informed and critical thinking about the merits of religious and secular ways of making sense of the world. If this is the case, it is unfortunate indeed. But, in a sense, my argument doesn't hinge on evidence for this claim, for my primary concern is not so much about the consequences of not taking religion seriously, but about the principles governing a sound education. The question is this: are we giving students a good education?

I acknowledge once again that not all public schools and universities are alike. Some universities have departments of religious studies; some public schools offer Bible or world religions courses. Some schools and universities offer courses in other disciplines that enable students to study religion. But I believe the following rough generalizations are justifiable: public education leaves students religiously illiterate, it falls far short of religious neutrality, and it borders on secular indoctrination (if only unintended). In fact, on one meaning of a very tricky word, schools and universities teach students to accept secular ways of making sense of the world as a matter of faith. Not surprisingly, all of these potential problems are actual problems. Whatever their effect on students' beliefs, they all violate the principles of sound education as we shall see in part 2.

# PART II

# Solutions

# 5

# Liberal Education

In this and the next two chapters I will argue that public schools and universities must take religion seriously for a number of reasons. I'll begin this chapter by saying something about what it means to take religion seriously, distinguishing among a variety of ways in which students might learn about religion. I'll say a little about the importance of a basic religious literacy for understanding particular subjects in the curriculum, but my primary focus will be on liberal education and its role in facilitating critical thinking or what, in the last chapter, I called being reasonable.

As we shall see, a liberal education requires that students be initiated into an ongoing conversation about how to make sense of the world—one in which religious voices must be included as live options. I will explain why, if we take religion seriously, we need not take *everything* seriously—and I'll attempt to short-circuit the arguments of those who think that religion needn't be taken seriously because it is not intellectually respectable. I'll conclude with a few comments about the underappreciated virtue of humility in education.

Over the course of the chapter we'll see that two of the potential problems discussed in the last chapter (religious ignorance and secular indoctrination) are real problems given the fact that education must be liberal. The other potential problem (religious neutrality) must await treatment in chapter 7.

## Taking Religion Seriously

Schools and universities might ignore religion. Many do. But if they are going to address religion they have options. I am going to try to keep this simple but even my simple version requires a number of distinctions (five) and may get a little technical.

### 1. Religious Literacy

In an elementary school social studies course students may learn a little about religious holidays and symbols, perhaps even some religious history. High school history courses will likely provide more substantive descriptive or factual accounts of religious movements and leaders, beliefs and practices, and their influence (though, as we saw in chapter 2, we shouldn't expect too much). A literature course may discuss poems or novels that have religious themes or that employ biblical symbolism that needs to be unpacked. While such relatively straightforward approaches to religion may not be free of interpretive assumptions, they are often uncontroversial. In such cases, no deep understanding of religion may be provided, and no judgments regarding the truth of religious claims are made.

### 2. Religious Understanding

A course in religious studies might require students to get inside a religion by using sacred or theological texts that employ that religion's own categories for making sense of the world. In such a course, students might be asked to bracket their own assumptions in order to make sense of the world as people within that religion do. A high school or college literature course might enable students to get inside a religion imaginatively by way of literary texts (*Paradise Lost* or a novel like *The Chosen*) that give them some vicarious sense of what it is to experience the world from within a tradition at a particular time and place. Such a course does more than simply provide information about a religion; it nurtures inside, empathetic understanding— the ability to see and feel the world, no doubt in modest ways, as people within a religious tradition do. For a still deeper understanding students will need to study the religion more systematically, thinking and feeling themselves into the religious worldview within which beliefs, values, experiences, and rituals make sense.

It may be the case that a course will help students understand a religion, from the inside, in historical context—at the time of its founding, or when its sacred scriptures were written. Of course, some religions die, while others change over time and receive new theological articulations and defenses in response to cultural and intellectual developments. Hence, students might also come to understand contemporary religions, from the inside, as live options for making sense of the world here and now.

### 3. Comparative Perspective

A course in religious studies might ask students to compare how different religions make sense of the world generally or of a particular subject such as salvation. The idea here is to both get inside each religious tradition (using its categories for making sense of the world) and then step outside each to con-trast them. Of course we need to recognize that it is impossible to step outside all points of view, achieving some kind of pristine objectivity. Still, students may find similarities and differences that prove enlightening and acquire a measure of critical distance on their own beliefs and values in the process.

We might also compare religious with various secular ways of making sense of the world generally, or a particular subject such as the self, in evolu-tionary biology or neoclassical economics or Freudian psychology. In such comparative study religion isn't compartmentalized and rendered irrelevant as a possible way of making sense of the world. Rather, religion is engaged—and the similarities and differences that students discover may (again) prove enlightening and give them a critical distance on their own beliefs and values.

As I am going to use the phrase, "taking religion seriously" requires basic religious literacy, of course, but it also requires that students acquire inside (or empathetic) understanding of several religious traditions (otherwise we would just be taking a religion seriously) and it requires that students acquire compar-ative perspective on various live religious and secular traditions. The idea is that we don't take *a* point of view—a religious or secular perspective—truly seriously if we marginalize it, if we don't let it contend with alternatives ways of making sense of the world (or a particular subject) for our reasoned support.

While I'll say much more about neutrality in chapters to come, here I'll just note that taking religion seriously can be done without promoting religion or abandoning neutrality. Consider a philosophy course in which Buddhist, Chris-tian, Marxist, and Darwinian ways of making sense of ethics are all taken seriously—that is, students study each tradition in some depth, acquiring inside understanding of each live alternative (using primary sources written from within that tradition), and read (or hear) how advocates of each position respond to the alternatives, engaging, as it were, in a critical conversation with each other. So long as this is done fairly and the teacher doesn't pass judgment, such a course would be religiously neutral. Needless to say, this approach need not be limited to philosophy courses.

### 4. Teaching Religion

A teacher, text, or course might argue that a particular religion is true, or simply adopt its categories for assessing the truth of rival religious or secular frameworks of interpretation, as may happen in religious academies and colleges. This is a quite different approach to religion—one in which there is no pretense to neutrality.

### 5. Explaining Religion(s)

Yet another approach is that of taking religion as an object of scholarly study to be explained. In explaining religion the scholar or teacher tries to make sense of religions in terms of some broader or more fundamental categories. Here there would seem to be two possibilities. (This is my last distinction.)

5a. Some scholars have attempted to explain particular religious traditions in terms of more general religious categories. In this case, traditional religions may be taken to provide different but inevitably inadequate ways of getting at God (or the Real), but God (or the Real) exists and is an unreducible aspect of reality. I am thinking here of scholars such as William James, Mircea Eliade, Rudolf Otto, Wilfred Cantwell Smith, or John Hick.

5b. Other scholars have attempted to explain religions in secular categories. A course in the psychology, anthropology, or sociology of religion will typically take religion as an object of study in need of explanation in the categories of the host discipline. While some explanatory theories may be religiously neutral—as I've noted, "secular" means nonreligious not antireligious—many are reductionistic. They claim to show that religion is not what it appears to be when viewed from the inside; they reduce it to a more basic reality that can be fully understood in secular categories. In effect, they take a position on religion, arguing that its basic claims are false or at least misleading. Here I have in mind scholars working in the traditions of Freud, Durkheim, Marx, evolutionary biology, or neuroscience, who explain religion as, for example, a neurotic symptom of unconscious wishes, or in terms of neural mechanisms that can, in turn, be explained in terms of natural selection.

Of course, such theories can be discussed neutrally (just as the religious texts, theologies, and religious traditions can be discussed neutrally) but if such theories are endorsed or advocated then religious neutrality has been violated just as if a particular religious view or theology were endorsed or advocated.

No doubt advocates of reductionistic theories take religion seriously in this sense: they believe it sufficiently important to develop (secular) theories that try to explain it (away). But clearly this is not what I mean by taking religion seriously. We take religion seriously in my sense when a course (or the curriculum) takes religious ways of making sense of the world seriously as live options in critical, comparative conversations.


## The Argument for Religious Literacy

Before I explain why schools and universities must take religion seriously, I need to say something about the most common argument for learning about religion. It is often argued that students can't understand literature or history without learning something about religion. A 2007 *Time* magazine cover story on high school Bible courses noted that there are more than 1,300 references to the Bible in Shakespeare and that Christ's passion is a key to understanding *The Old Man and the Sea*. John Winthrop's "City on a Hill," Lincoln's second inaugural, and Martin Luther King Jr.'s rhetoric all draw on the Bible.[1] Or one could try to understand art apart from the Bible. I read once of an undergraduate who complained about the pervasive sexism in medieval and Renaissance art: in all of those paintings of mothers and child, the children were always little boys.

No doubt similar cases could be made for literacy regarding other religious texts, figures, events, and movements, including those from religions other than just Christianity. In our post-9/11 world the idea that students need to understand something about Islam if they are to understand politics and world affairs strikes most people as reasonable. (Not that we should need 9/11 to make us aware of the importance of Islam in history and culture.) In fact, in all cultures and for most of history religion pervaded all of life, shaping and informing people's understanding of politics, war, economics, justice, literature, art, philosophy, science, psychology, and morality, as well as their hopes for a world to come. It shouldn't be surprising that students need to know something of religion to understand their coursework in history, literature, art, politics, and perhaps other subjects of the curriculum.

This is the first—and I think completely uncontroversial—argument for requiring a basic religious literacy. Students can't understand the subject matter of at least some of their courses without knowing something about religion. In this case, the relevance of religion to the curriculum is derivative or secondary. This is an argument for religion in a supporting role. Religion isn't important in and of itself, only for understanding something else.

Does this argument require that students actually understand religion (from the inside) or take it seriously as a live option? No doubt in many contexts relatively uncontroversial factual information about religion will suffice, and advocates of cultural literacy typically stop short of requiring any deep understanding of religion. Hence, I am calling this the argument from mere religious literacy. As we shall eventually see, however, a deep understanding of history, literature, and politics does require that students actually understand religion, not just a few facts about it.

## Liberal Education

First, let me clear that in speaking of liberal education I do not mean an education that is politically liberal. In fact, a liberal education may have either a politically liberal or conservative bent to it (and I will say something good about both in due time). Second, I am not going to offer a full-blown theory of liberal education. Instead, I'll propose several relatively uncontroversial characteristics of a liberal education that should be compatible with various theories. My goal is to show that liberal education requires schools and universities to take religion seriously.

In his very helpful book *Orators and Philosophers: A History of the Idea of Liberal Education* Bruce Kimball charts the history of two quite different, sometimes competing ideals of liberal education.[2] The first—which he calls the *artes liberales,* or "liberal arts" ideal—is grounded in the classical canon. It assumes that moral truths and ideals of civic virtue are to be found in classical literature, and it is largely a literary education. It forms character, and is meant to be the ideal education for public leaders—historically, for men of leisure, of liberty (hence, liberal arts). Such an education binds students to the past, to tradition (and as such is typically conservative). While Kimball traces the liberal arts conception back to the Greek rhetorician Isocrates, Cicero is its patron saint. It was the educational ideal of late Greece and Rome, the early Middle Ages (where it took on Christian hues), the Renaissance, and early America.

The second conception of liberal education—which Kimball calls the liberal-free ideal—takes as its patron saint the philosopher Socrates, and is moved by the continuing search for truth. It values free, critical inquiry and tolerance; it is skeptical. It inclines toward egalitarianism and individualism rather than elitism and tradition. It pays scant attention to the classics but is concerned with philosophical inquiry and scientific experiment. It assumes no truth from the past, but is critical, constantly looking for new truths; it underwrites the idea of progress. It liberates students, rather than binds them to tradition (and is more liberal in a political sense). The liberal-free ideal was foreshadowed in Greek philosophy and in the philosophy of the High Middle Ages, but it came into its own only with the scientific revolution, the Enlightenment, and nineteenth-century research universities. Arguably, it had become the dominant conception of liberal education in American universities by the end of the nineteenth century.

Of course, much education nowadays is only marginally liberal in either sense, fixated as it often is on narrowly practical knowledge and vocationalism. Be that as it may, I am going to suggest a number of characteristics of liberal education that combine Kimball's two emphases and that cut across secondary and undergraduate education. My proposal is that we think of liberal education as having four dimensions related to one another by way fifth, of a structured, coherent conversation.

(1) I suspect that the most common conception of a liberal education is that of a broad education. A liberal education is not narrow, specialized, or merely vocational. It introduces students to other cultures and to a variety of subjects and disciplines.

There are several reasons for requiring such breadth. It has often been argued that a liberal education enriches the lives of students, and this is good in and of itself. In the next chapter I will say something about moral reasons for liberal education. Here I want to focus on the idea that a broad education is necessary for critical thinking (or what I call being reasonable). No doubt critical thinking involves more than breadth; it requires logical rigor and the reasoned assessment of evidence and arguments. But if education is to go beyond training, socialization, or indoctrination students must have critical distance on what they learn. They must be open to, and informed about, alternative ways of making sense of the world and their lives.[3] What do they know of England who only England know?

The idea of breadth often translates into acquiring an understanding of different subjects—history, literature, science, and art. But, as I argued in the last chapter, while we talk about studying subjects we always study them in terms of frameworks of interpretation provided by the various disciplines, and so it is not surprising that educators typically think of breadth in terms of disciplinary approaches to knowledge. In universities students are typically required to take several courses in the natural sciences, the social sciences, the humanities, and, perhaps, in the arts. What is important is not so much subject matter—in fact, there may not be any required subject matter—but how to think about subjects. Secondary schools are apt to place more emphasis on subject matter (in part because it can be more easily tested), though always as interpreted through the lens of the host disciplines. The essential point is that if students are to think critically, they must have some understanding of the major ways that humankind has devised for making sense of the world.

(2) If students are to understand different cultures, intellectual traditions, and academic disciplines they must be able to get inside them. They must acquire some sense of how their members or advocates understand them, not how we understand them given our preconceptions and values. If we screen alternative traditions through our own conceptual filters, assuming that we know how to interpret the world, we will gain no critical perspective on our own assumptions. It is hard to improve here on John Stuart Mill, who wrote that students must hear arguments "from persons who actually believe them . . . in their most plausible and persuasive form. . . . Ninety-nine in a hundred of what are called educated men . . . have never thrown themselves into the mental position of those who think differently from them . . . and consequently they do not, in any proper sense of the word, know the doctrine which they themselves profane."[4]

Such perspective is often difficult to acquire, particularly when the culture or tradition is very different from ours. At the least this requires imagination (much education fails for want of imagination), intensive study, and especially the use of primary sources. Here the humanities do most of the heavy lifting. I will call this dimension of a liberal education "inside understanding."

(3) If the ideal is to promote critical thinking and inside understanding, the next question is, about what? The answer: about the things that matter most. A liberal education is not superficial. It has often been argued that a liberal education should address those existential Big Questions regarding justice and suffering, love and death, beauty and the meaning of life, which any thoughtful human being must confront. A liberal education orients students in life; it gives them some sense of what is meaningful—all of which is of momentous importance. I will have a good deal more to say about the moral and existential nature of education in the next chapter. For now I simply note that a liberal education inevitably and properly orients students in the world; it gives them implicitly (if not always explicitly) some sense of what is important, of how to make sense of the world, and of how to live their lives. It provides a context in terms of which students can think critically about their vocational goals, their future education, their civic and moral obligations, and what makes life meaningful. The third dimension of a liberal education, then, is existential depth.

(4) Not all cultures, intellectual traditions, or academic disciplines are compatible with one another; there are tensions and conflicts, as well as continuities and complementarities, among them. (Think of cultures that are patriarchal and those that promote gender equality, of democratic and totali-

tarian ideologies; or of evolutionist and creationist theories.) It is not enough, if our goal is critical thinking, simply to introduce students to various cultures, disciplines, and intellectual traditions, in turn, like items on an academic cafeteria line. A good liberal education will initiate students into an ongoing conversation about how to sort out the contending views. This is the Socratic nature of a liberal education: we seek truth through conversation.

No doubt students may be exposed to contending cultures and theories within a particular course, but the disciplinary structure of education makes interdisciplinary or transdisciplinary discussion of contending intellectual traditions all but impossible. High school education is frozen into the traditional categories of social studies, language arts, math, and the sciences, and never the quatrain shall meet (except for math and science). University students are free to choose among a dizzying array of narrowly focused, highly specialized courses that are unlikely to relate to one another in any meaningful way (and cumulatively may leave them largely culturally illiterate). Textbooks rarely acknowledge that their subject matters may be interpreted in fundamentally different ways. And in spite of a widespread acknowledgment of the value of interdisciplinary studies, students are all too rarely required to participate in interdisciplinary conversations. As the literary critic Gerald Graff has put it, college curricula (and we might add high school curricula) are typically separatist "with each subject and course being an island with little regular connection to other subjects and courses."[5]

As we actually practice it, education is essentially a sequence of monologues, something closer to serial socialization than to a conversation and, as such, it is more a matter of training students than educating them. (I am reminded of the good soul who, when asked for an opinion of Dr. Johnson's new dictionary, replied that it is "most instructive, though I did seem to notice a trifling want of connection."[6]) Graff's proposal, one that I endorse, is to "teach the conflicts"—indeed, to use this as an organizing and connecting principle for a liberal education.[7] Alasdair MacIntyre has argued for a similar conception of the university as "a place of constrained disagreement, of imposed participation in conflict, in which a central responsibility of higher education would be to initiate students into conflict" in which, among other things, "the most fundamental type of moral and theological disagreement was accorded recognition."[8]

I suggest we put this a little more positively. A liberal education must be a conversation in which students come to understand the relationship of cultures, traditions, and disciplines to one another. Are they complementary, do they conflict, are they in tension with one another—and what are the implications for how we make sense of the world?

(5) Finally, a liberal education must have a historical dimension. (We might think of this as temporal breadth.) One can't understand one's own time without historical perspective. One can't understand race relations in the United States without understanding the history of slavery, Jim Crow, and the civil rights movement. History is a record of the cultural experiments of humankind from which we must learn to live responsibly. It is commonplace to quote George Santayana: "Those who cannot remember the past are condemned to repeat it." The point, of course, is that our lives might well be changed by the lessons of history—and Santayana's use of the word *condemn* points to the gravity of the lessons.

But, of course, we aren't simply external observers of history, self-contained, morally unencumbered individuals or social atoms. We are caught up in history, we live in communities of memory (to use Robert Bellah's fine phrase) that give shape and substance to our identities. We inherit roles in stories (or, as scholars would say, in narratives). We are historical beings, enmeshed in webs of influence and obligation that tie us not just to other people in our own time, but the past and the future. Indeed, all thinking takes place within cultural and intellectual traditions (embodying narratives or worldviews) that constrain and guide it, that make sense of it. (This is a more conservative complement to the somewhat more liberal emphasis on breadth and critical thinking.) Needless to say, traditions aren't static; they change in response to political, cultural, technological, and intellectual developments. Our traditions are caught up in cultural and intercultural debates—in culture wars—and to some considerable extent, it is in response to these challenges that progress takes place.

If we think of a liberal education as a conversation, it is clearly a historical, ongoing conversation, and just as we cannot understand any conversation if we walk into the middle of it, so students cannot understand the curricular conversation unless they understand something of its history.

A liberal education has, then, four dimensions—breadth inside understanding, existential depth, and historical perspective—all connected, fifth, by way of an ongoing critical conversation.

Now, what are the implications of all of this for taking religion seriously? First, in terms of breadth, what is obviously missing in both public schools and universities is any requirement that students study religious ways of making sense of the world. Second, if religious perspectives are to be included, students must be given an inside understanding of them—or they fail to serve their critical purpose. Third, the relevance of religion is even more pronounced if education should address the moral and existential Big Questions (which I will take up in the next chapter). Fourth, given the historical influence of religion it is clear that religious perspectives must have an important role in the ongoing conversation. Finally, religious perspectives must be allowed to contend with other perspectives in the critical conversation that a liberal education should nurture; religion can't be compartmentalized, rendered irrelevant to the rest of education, if education is to serve the purposes of critical thinking.

It would seem, then, that barring any special reasons for excluding religion from the conversation (I'll consider several possibilities in due course) a liberal education must take religions seriously, nurturing an inside understanding of religions, as live options, as part of a critical conversation. The study of religion is important not just derivatively, for what it can contribute to the study of other subjects; if students are to be liberally educated they must understand religious perspectives on the world (and their subjects) not just a few domesticated facts about religion swaddled in the secular categories of history, literature, politics, and science. To leave religion out of the conversation is clearly and utterly illiberal.

## Reason Again

I have focused here on the fact that a liberal education is necessary if students are to think critically. Short of this, what we call education is nothing more than training, socialization, or indoctrination. The problem is that almost always, critical thinking is pursued only within disciplines. I don't mean to condemn disciplines. Scholars make progress by narrowing their focus, by working within methodologies that are fruitful and that give them rules for adjudicating disputes. But if disciplines are necessary for intellectual progress, they aren't sufficient for the purposes of a liberal education because they fail to address critically important interdisciplinary and transdisciplinary disputes regarding the relationships and limitations of the disciplines. As I suggested in the last chapter, too often disciplines function as intellectual blinders that keep scholars from seeing the whole of reality.

In terms of the two conceptions of reason I distinguished in the last chapter, a liberal education requires more than simply teaching students to be rational (or to think critically) within a particular framework of thought (an academic discipline, an intellectual tradition, a narrative, a worldview). A liberal education requires that students are encouraged and enabled to be reasonable about contending ways of being rational. Students must acquire critical perspective on the disciplines; they must be initiated into conversations in which they learn to assess the assumptions and claims of contending disciplines and the traditions and worldviews within which they are embedded. Short of this, education, while teaching students to be rational in a variety of ways, ends up a matter of serial socialization in one discipline after another.

I might put a little meat on these bones by way of an example of what's at issue. As we have seen, economics texts and courses are typically framed in terms of neoclassical economic theory (which is part and parcel of the modern worldview shaped by modern science and social science). From the commitment of the discipline of economics to value-free social science, a whole series of claims follow about human nature, morality (or values), decision making, and what it is important to understand in order to study economics. Neoclassical economic theory may, in the end, be the most reasonable way of thinking about the economic domain of life, but it is deeply controversial when viewed from the vantage point of alternative disciplines, worldviews, and cultures. While the basic assumptions (and the underlying worldview) of neoclassical theory may be articulated in textbooks or courses, alternative assumptions about economics, human nature, and morality—grounded in different disciplines and worldviews—are not apt to be. As a result, while students will learn to think critically (or rationally) about economic problems in terms of neoclassical theory, it will be all but impossible for them to think critically or reasonably about neoclassical economic theory itself.

Economists may respond that the proof is in the pudding of predictive reliability (a foul-tasting pudding these days). But this is only one possible measure for thinking about the adequacy of an economic theory. One might reasonably wonder, for example, whether neoclassical theory is compatible with what we know about human nature from philosophy, history, or literature, or whether neoclassical economics gives us adequate resources to understand justice and human flourishing. We might also wonder if neoclassical theory is compatible with a religious understanding of the world. But these questions and controversies are rarely raised—and never in the introductory textbooks I've reviewed.

Students must be taught neoclassical economics. After all, most (but not all) economists accept neoclassical theory. But students must also be exposed to other ways of making sense of economics or the whole idea of critical thinking about the subject of economics will come to naught. If students don't engage in informed, critical conversation about the alternatives we will be training or indoctrinating rather than (liberally) educating them. I will say more about how this should happen in chapter 10.

There are, of course, religious as well as secular ways of making sense of human nature, value judgments, and the economic domain of life. Indeed, there are religious ways of making sense of virtually every subject in the curriculum. But it is virtually never explained to students that these religious alternatives exist. Consequently, as we saw in the last chapter, both secondary and higher education unrelentingly and uncritically nurture across the curriculum a secular mentality that borders on indoctrination. Let me acknowledge again that much secular and scientific scholarship is compatible with much, perhaps most, religion. The problem is that we don't just teach discrete scientific facts and secular theories. Instead we teach students to interpret all of their subjects in secular categories—categories that often conflict with and marginalize religious categories (as is the case with economic theory).

Critical thinking, learning to be reasonable, is not an optional philosophical frill that educators have the freedom to take or leave at their pleasure. It is at the heart of what a liberal education is about. Short of this, schools and universities should stop talking about educating students and retreat to talk of training or indoctrination. And, of course, talk of exploring alternative ways of making sense of the world is thin gruel if religious alternatives are not among them.

## Must All Alternatives Be Taken Seriously?

If schools and universities must take religions seriously, must they also take alchemy, flat-earth geography, astrology, Fascism, or Marxism seriously? Must they be considered as live options? Are some ways of making sense of a subject or the world beyond the pale? And how might we set priorities among legitimate alternatives?

First, only live traditions need be taken seriously as live options, though there may be very good reasons for studying dead traditions in the context of history. There are no (or very few) defenders of alchemy or a flat earth nowadays. Marxism is trickier because there are still Marxists. Obviously, not all religions—for example, Greek, Roman, and Norse religion—are live alternatives that need be taken seriously.

Second, among living traditions, we may justifiably give priority to those that are most influential. There are only so many pages in the textbooks and hours in a course, and this imposes a major practical constraint on the range of alternatives that can be considered. While the thrust of a liberal education is always toward broadening the range of alternatives to be considered, there is inevitably a trade-off between breadth and depth of understanding; the more alternatives, the more superficial the treatment. Compromises are necessary. Minor intellectual, political, and religious movements do not have the claim on us that influential movements do.

Third, it is justifiable to give some priority to traditions depending on prox-imity: it is more important for students to learn about their own states than other states, their own country than other countries, Western civilization than other civilizations. It may be more important to take seriously a local religious tradition with little influence on the world stage than a major religious tradition whose influence is more distant. True, the purpose of a liberal education is to broaden the conversation, the range of (live, influential) traditions considered; but, again, there are trade-offs given the time (and textbook pages) that is avail-able. This is not an argument for excluding distant traditions, only for giving them somewhat less priority.

Fourth, we have already seen that a liberal education addresses questions of existential depth, and this provides a criterion for choosing among contend-ing alternatives. Some traditions are more important in people's lives than others, and if there is not time for all, then those of more importance to more people should be given priority. Even though polls show that perhaps a quarter of Americans believe in astrology (including a recent president and first lady) it just doesn't have anything like the importance for most people that, say, religion has.

Fifth, it is justifiable to discriminate on the grounds of what is intellectually serious; after all, the purpose of a liberal education is to put students into a position where they can be reasonable. Of course, what counts as intellectually serious is controversial and changes from time to time. A reason that astrology need not be taken seriously is that there is now, as opposed to several centuries ago, only a superficial intellectual tradition connected with it. (Perhaps not everyone will agree.) When voices speak out of the context of a rich and reflec-tive intellectual background there is reason to take them more seriously than if they express (relatively) superficial ideas or ideals—no matter how common, relevant, and influential.[9] Perhaps I should say that the phrase *intellectually* se-rious shouldn't be taken too narrowly; certainly much art, for example, is intel-lectually serious; artistic traditions provide live, influential, and important ways of finding meaning in the world.

Sixth, while it is important to learn about, and even to understand from the inside, live traditions that most Americans would consider evil or deeply misguided (communism or religious terrorism) I don't see that they need to be taken seriously as live options; indeed, it may be justifiable to condemn them on moral grounds. Needless to say, where we draw the lines will be controversial.

I don't think these criteria should be particularly controversial in principle (though they may be in particular cases); in fact, we use most of them routinely. In any case, the world's major religious traditions are live, influential, intellectually rich traditions that address matters of great existential significance to people in ways that are not (typically) beyond the moral pale. In taking them seriously we are not committed to opening the floodgates to everything.

## Is Religion Intellectually Respectable?

I said above that religion must be taken seriously if there are no special reasons for excluding it from the conversation. In chapter 7 I will consider the claim that there are constitutional problems with taking religion seriously, and in chapter 8 I will consider several practical and political reasons for not taking it seriously. Here I want to discuss what is probably the most influential argument among scholars for not taking religion seriously: religion is not intellectually respectable.

In arguing several years ago against a faculty task force recommendation that Harvard introduce a "faith and reason" general education requirement for undergraduates, the psychologist Steven Pinker claimed this would give religion "far too much prominence. It [religion] is an *American anachronism* in an era in which the rest of the West is moving beyond it."[10] In response, Mark Edington, Pinker's Harvard colleague, pointed out that this is "more than a little like standing at the water's edge and commanding the tide not to rise."[11] As I noted in chapter 1, the secularization thesis, much loved by social scientists, has come in for a great deal of criticism lately. Religion hasn't disappeared; indeed, much of the world is becoming more religious. As a result, it might even seem that religion deserves *more* prominence in the curriculum. (The Harvard faculty ended up rejecting the recommendation, proposing instead that students be required to take a course in "culture and belief.")

Of course Pinker doesn't want to count noses in deciding what to let into the curriculum. His real problem is that religion isn't intellectually respectable. What is really important, he argued, is that students learn to make sense of the world scientifically. Needless to say, science has many "cascading effects" on how we "view ourselves and the world in which we live" including "that our planet is an undistinguished speck in an inconceivably vast cosmos; . . . that humans are primates; that the mind is the activity of an organ that runs by physiological processes; [and] that precious and widely held beliefs [religious beliefs, no doubt], when subjected to empirical tests, are often cruelly falsified." He concludes that "a person for whom scientific understanding is not second-nature cannot be said to be educated."[12]

The intellectual historian David Hollinger puts this kind of argument into historical context, claiming that while "Christianity marched into the modern era as the strongest, most institutionally endowed cultural program in the Western world" it is no longer plausible "within disciplinary communities in the social sciences and humanities." While some scholars argue for a greater pluralism of views in the academy, one that includes religious voices, Hollinger responds that no such pluralism is required, for things have been settled as a result of the Enlightenment and modern science. Universities "should not surrender back to Christianity the ground they have won for a more independent, cosmopolitan life of the mind." Christianity had its chance and failed. In effect, the price of admission to the academy is a principled rejection of Christianity and those religious views whose advocates refuse to play by the rules of the prevailing secular "epistemic communities" of the academy.[13]

No doubt most scholars acknowledge that there is value in studying religion historically or sociologically for its influence on culture. But, like Pinker and Hollinger, many scholars believe that religion no longer warrants being taken seriously in the academy (any more than alchemy or astrology). Indeed, to include religious voices may corrupt the conversation with appeals to holy books and uncritical faith.

There are several problems with this position.

The appeal to science as the arbiter of intellectual respectability is a nonstarter. After all, universities don't impose scientific standards of respectability on philosophy, ethics, politics, literature, or art. I have noted the remarkable new dialogue among some theologians and scientists over the last several decades that has undercut much of the traditional antagonism between science and at least some kinds of religion. Postmodernists have told us that all efforts to establish metanarratives, including the scientific metanarrative, are misguided, and if this is the case then surely the fact that religion isn't scientifically respectable doesn't settle anything. What must be avoided is granting modern science the authority to define what is reasonable and respectable across the curriculum. In fact, what most people (including scientists in their off-hours) find most meaningful in life—love, morality, beauty, the spiritual—slips right through the conceptual net of science. Indeed, many atheists have taken the position that scientific naturalism isn't a reasonable position.

Hollinger's claim that religion is no longer respectable "within disciplinary communities in the social sciences and humanities" is too strong. For example, while I suspect that most philosophers do not believe in God, some do, grounding their belief in a wide range of philosophical arguments not typically taken as beyond the philosophical pale.[14]

Of course, how *good* such arguments are is a matter of considerable controversy. But that's my point. I don't need to show that it is actually reasonable to believe in God; a considerably less controversial claim will suffice for my purposes. What counts as respectable, what counts as reasonable, is deeply controversial, and so long as there is no consensus among scholars about the intellectual respectability of religion it will be illiberal to keep religious voices out of the curricular conversation. In fact, what might appear to be a hostile consensus is, in part, the result of exiling religious scholars from universities to divinity schools, seminaries, and religiously affiliated liberal arts colleges. Or perhaps I should say the most vocal dissenters are exiled (or at least silenced), for many scholars keep their religion to themselves. As I have noted, faculty in colleges and universities are almost as likely to believe in God as are other folks.

Quite apart from this silent majority, however, there continues to be a lively religious counterculture that is intellectually respectable in the following sense. Various religious ways of making sense of the world are held by scholars, many with advanced degrees from our most prestigious research universities, who understand and work (largely) within the dominant categories of our intellectual life, but who also draw on religious traditions to rethink and reform the conventional wisdom of our time and place. To be sure, in order to be taken seriously religious scholars must have mastered the conventional scholarly wisdom of their disciplines, even if they reject the adequacy of it. But if some religion is mindless and disdains intellectual respectability, much isn't and doesn't. Most religious scholarship has not gone the way of astrology and alchemy or lapsed into purely private and irrational faith. Theologians and religious scholars continue to grapple in informed and sophisticated ways with secular modernity and postmodernity.

No doubt some scholars in the dominant intellectual culture find these efforts irrelevant, worthless, or perhaps even dangerous; indeed, I suspect that many assume that all religious thought is simply a variation on fundamentalist anti-intellectualism. But such naïveté does not justify excluding religious voices from the curricular conversation; to do so is both sadly uninformed and profoundly illiberal. As the neo-Marxist literary critic Terry Eagleton (no orthodox believer) puts it, "The truth is that a good many secular intellectuals with a reasonably sophisticated sense of what goes on in academic areas other than their own tout an abysmally crude, infantile version of what theology has traditionally maintained. . . . This straw-targeting of Christianity is now drearily commonplace among academics and intellectuals—that is to say, among those who would not allow a first-year student to get away with the vulgar caricatures in which they themselves indulge with such insouciance."[15]

But surely, a critic might respond, religion is a matter of faith and not open to critical thinking. In reviewing my first book on religion and education Alan Wolfe argued that "efforts to reintroduce faith into public universities" are a mistake. We have religious institutions for nurturing faith; the university should remain "committed to its core mission of *advancing and transmitting knowledge.*" It "is not the place for certainties."[16] D. G. Hart has argued on similar lines that the idea of initiating students into controversies that involve religion "would require the university to tolerate doctrines that are explicitly dogmatic and sectarian, and that appeal to sacred texts whose authority rests upon standards that modern scholarship is incapable of adjudicating."[17] Indeed, because the university simply can't deal with faith and dogma, the religion that it can tolerate tends to be thin and watered down. This being the case, the university may actually pay religion respect by excluding it from the conversation: "It may be time for faithful academics to stop trying to secure a religion-friendly university while paying deference to the academic standards of the modern university. If the old religions are right, in the new heavens and new earth there should be plenty of enduring rewards that will make promotion, tenure, and endowed chairs look like so much hay and stubble."[18]

Wolfe's ominous suggestion that I have proposed to reintroduce faith into the university (or public schools) should not need a response at this point—but let me be clear. I agree with him that the university's purpose is "advancing and transmitting knowledge," not nurturing uncritical faith. I am arguing not as a proponent of religion, much less as an advocate of uncritical faith. My primary concern is with liberal education, and a critical, reasoned search for truth is at the heart of a liberal education.

It is, of course, true that many religious believers are anti-intellectual and have no desire to participate in the rough-and-tumble of reasoned debate. (The same is true of some scientists.) But I would make three points in response. First, some (perhaps even many) believers can't be characterized in this way; they do believe that they are being reasonable and are game to discuss it (at least so long as the ground rules are fair). Second, whatever the beliefs of people in the pews, the major religions are grounded in rich intellectual traditions in which theologians and other intellectuals have developed—and continue to develop—ways of defending, rethinking, and reforming their traditions in response to intellectual developments. Third, even if religious faith were utterly and stupifyingly irrational, it is important for students to acquire some understanding of how such faith relates to the rest of their studies.

No doubt Hart is right that faith and the practice of religion have their home in religious contexts, not in the educational context of a university. Indeed, as Hart suggests, there is a danger that faith and religion will be misunderstood if wrenched out of context. This is why teaching about religion requires sophistication and time. But it is essential that students learn to recognize the tensions, conflicts, and complementarities between what they learn in their secular coursework and various religious faiths if they are to think critically about their secular studies and their religion—if they are to be liberally educated.

We need to break down the much too rigid distinction between religion and reason. As I suggested in chapter 4, faith has many meanings. In some contexts, faith need not be uncritical. Religion isn't simply a matter of blind uncritical faith—or maybe I should say that if some is, most isn't. Blanket condemnations, stark dichotomies, and rigid compartmentalization aren't helpful. All of this hopelessly oversimplifies our intellectual life and powerfully and uncritically reinforces the idea of religion as uncritical faith, as a kind of fanaticism. To be reasonable is not to follow (uncritically) science or any secular theory; it is to be open to a variety of ways of making sense of the world and then thinking critically about them. The university should be open and pluralistic, concerned with extending the reach of reason, building bridges between reason and religion, not burning them. In fact, religious beliefs (narratives, worldviews, or faiths) may turn out to be more reasonable than their secular competition, all things considered. This is surely still an open question.

In fact, one might wonder if the fault is in the eye of the beholder. The sociologist of religion Christian Smith finds among many of his university colleagues "a tenacious anti-religious sensibility." He suspects that they aren't aiming to be antireligious: "it just comes naturally to them, almost automatically, as if from a fundamental predisposition." They are, he speculates, "expressing a deeply interiorized mental scheme that is more prereflective than conscious, more conventional than intentional—yet one that has an immense power to reproduce a pervasive institutional culture."[19] They are so deeply immersed in a naturalistic (or at least secular) worldview they can't escape it. They can't be objective or self-critical. In effect, we might say, their secularism has become a faith for them.

In his *Autobiography* Darwin reflected on how, in his youth, he loved reading the romantic poets and Shakespeare, but in his old age he found them "intolerably dull." What accounted for this "curious and lamentable loss of the higher aesthetic tastes?" Darwin concluded that his "mind seems to have become a kind of machine for grinding general laws out of a large collection of facts."[20] He feared that the result may have been injurious to his moral character by enfeebling his emotional life.

Surely our philosophical commitments, our disciplinary blinders, can numb us—or blind us—to the richness of life and reality if we are not careful.

## Humility

Ninian Smart, the great scholar of comparative religions, once wrote that there is "neither a God-given nor a humanity-bestowed right to teach a debatable worldview as though it is not debatable, nor to neglect the deeply held beliefs and values of other people on the ground that you consider them foolish."[21] As we have seen, it is not at all obvious how to falsify or verify a worldview. It is not obvious where the truth lies. Indeed, scholars disagree deeply. This being the case, humility is a particularly valuable educational virtue.

My impression, however, is that textbooks (and most teachers) within a discipline present students with the truth, free of any doubts that their own discipline has gotten at least the fundamentals correct. The textbooks that I have read are not burdened by acknowledgments of humility or suggestions that students might profitably think about the subject matter at hand from the perspective of another discipline or worldview, much less a religious worldview.

Of course, there is no consensus, even among secular scholars, about many of the Big Questions to which religions have ventured answers—the origins of the universe, the origins of life, the origins and nature of consciousness and mind, what it means to be human, free will, morality, justice, and sexuality, to name but a few. Quite apart from religious alternatives, there is little agreement among scientific naturalists, traditional humanists (scholars using the categories of the humanities), and postmodernists about how to make sense of the world. So it is not as if secular thinkers have settled everything to everyone's satisfaction without religion. It might seem that a prudent humility would suggest that educators remain open-minded, constructing the curriculum in such a way as to encourage and enable students to take seriously religious as well as scientific and other secular ways of making sense of the world and their lives.

It is true that the track record of modern science is particularly spectacular, and one might be tempted to believe that science is cornering the market on truth to the disadvantage of its competitors. I have already suggested several reasons for being suspicious of the pretensions of modern science to explain everything. Here I might note that in 1894, the distinguished physicist Albert Michaelson (of the Michaelson-Morley experiments) argued that "the most important fundamental laws and facts of physical science have all been discovered, and these are now so firmly established that that possibility of their ever being supplemented in consequence of new discoveries is exceedingly remote. . . . Our future discoveries must be looked for in the sixth place of decimals."[22] He was wrong, of course, spectacularly wrong.[23] Julian Barnes has put the matter provocatively: "How can we be sure that we know enough to know? As twenty-first-century neo-Darwinian materialists, convinced that the meaning and mechanism of life have only been fully clear since the year 1859, we hold ourselves categorically wiser than those credulous knee-benders who, a speck of time away, believed in divine purposes, an ordered world, resurrection and a Last Judgement. But although we are more informed, we are no more evolved, and certainly no more intelligent than them. What convinces us that our knowledge is so final?"[24]

The philosopher of science, W. H. Newton-Smith has claimed that in science there is good inductive evidence for the claim that "any [scientific] theory will be discovered to be false within, say, 200 years of being propounded."[25] Of course, the great revolutions that shake science every now and then overturn not just theories but whole conceptual systems in ways that are likely to be inconceivable for adherents of the old views. Darwin, on at least some readings, overturned a worldview. Such a revolution might happen again—with somewhat different results. We might profitably heed Dean Inge's warning that whoever marries the spirit of the age will, in time, be a widower. In fact, virtually every academic discipline has passed through and beyond various orthodoxies over the course of the last century, revolutionizing its self-understanding.

We can trace the idea of critical reason far back beyond the Scientific Revolution and the Enlightenment to Greek philosophy, to Socrates, who was said to be the wisest of men. And why was he the wisest of men? Because, Socrates concluded, he was aware (unlike most people) of his own ignorance. And how do we find the truth? Not, Socrates thought, through blind faith or uncritical acceptance of tradition, but by open and reasoned discussion.

A measure of humility is in order. If there is as yet no consensus about how to make sense of the world and many of its enduring problems, and if religious ways of making sense of the world continue to be influential, then humility suggests that it may be reasonable that religious voices be included in the curricular conversation.

One further point. Robert Nash has wisely linked the educational virtues of humility and charity. Too often and too quickly we attribute foolishness and knavery to our intellectual and cultural opponents. We might better attribute "at least a modicum of wisdom and insight to others." Indeed, Nash concludes, the virtue of charity "is all about generosity and graciousness, and it is a virtue tragically missing in higher education today."[26] Amen.

## Conclusions

In chapter 4 I argued that public schools and universities perpetuate religious ignorance, fall far short of religious neutrality, and border on secular indoctrination. I said that these were potential problems. In this chapter it has become clear that given the nature of liberal education, religious ignorance and secular indoctrination are real problems. We will have to wait until chapter 7 to address neutrality.

In this chapter I have acknowledged the commonplace argument that students must learn something about religion if they are to understand history, literature, art, and politics. Much more important, schools and universities must take religion seriously if students are to be liberally educated. If students are to think critically about the world and about the other subjects they study— if they are to be reasonable—they must study religions in some depth, acquire an understanding of them from the inside, as live options, in critical and comparative perspective. I have argued that this need not open the floodgates to all kinds of views and I have addressed the concern, widespread among scholars, that religion need not be included in the conversation because it is not intellectually respectable. I've also noted that it is an act of hubris, given our current state of understanding, to assume that secular ways of thinking about life and the world are sufficient to make sense of the world and orient students in life. Humility requires that we take religion seriously.[27]

Finally, let me say explicitly what I trust is already clear: my arguments in this chapter are fully secular arguments.

# 6

# Moral, Existential, and Civic Arguments

As we saw in the last chapter, a good liberal education must take religion seriously. In this chapter I will consider three other kinds of arguments for requiring students to study religion. First, schools and universities have a responsibility to educate students morally, both by locating them in traditions and by enabling them to think critically about those traditions, and this can't be done without taking religion seriously. Second, a good liberal education will provide opportunities for students to explore those existential questions about the meaning of life that are inescapable for thoughtful human beings, and this can't be done without taking religion seriously either. Third, there are a set of related civic arguments for requiring some study of religion: students must understand religion to be thoughtful voters; justice requires that schools and universities take religion seriously; political liberty is incompatible with secular indoctrination; and both civility and respect for other people's rights require that students learn about their religions and religious liberty.

Finally, I will say something about a series of remarkable, widely endorsed, common-ground statements that address the importance of studying religion. Perhaps surprisingly, my position isn't all that far from that of a lot of people who think about such things.

## The Moral Argument

Persons are moral beings. To be a person is to have moral rights and responsibilities. I don't think this is particularly controversial.

There are three further, largely uncontroversial claims that I wish to make. First, even if there is a good deal of moral consensus, of agreement about fundamental values, it is also true that it is often not clear what morality requires of us. The world is a complicated place, and there are many options open to us. Second, moral problems are pervasive—they run through our private lives, our work lives, and our public lives. Third, our moral values and commitments have momentous implications for the suffering and well-being of human beings. In fact, every educational and social good can lead to great evil if not used morally. The pursuit of economic wealth can lead to exploitation and crass materialism. Science can create weapons of mass destruction and technologies that can destroy the environment. Liberty can be used for profane and mindless pleasures. Individualism can degenerate into self-interest and selfishness. Citizens can elect fascists in democratic elections or vote for politicians whose policies lead to imperialist wars. Reading and writing can be used for propaganda and pornography. Mathematics enabled engineers to build crematoria in the death camps and accountants to cook AIG's books. That is, students who are not firmly grounded morally may too easily become, in some part of their personal or professional lives, barbarians.

Now, if we are moral beings, if moral problems are pervasive, if morality has momentous implications for good and ill, and if the moral choices open to us are often controversial and complex, then it would seem that education must be responsive to these facts about the human condition.

I suggest that we think of three kinds, or levels, of moral education. First, there is the moral socialization that is necessary to develop and reinforce the idea that people are moral beings and that there are fundamental, widely shared, moral virtues and values. This is often called character education. Second, moral education should locate students in traditions that make sense of morality and provide moral guidance. Third, moral education should enable and require students to think critically about their lives and the traditions they have inherited in order to reform them, if necessary. The second and third tasks of moral education are integral to a liberal education and neither can be accomplished without taking religion seriously.

### Mores and Character Education

Children must learn to make sense of the world in moral categories, to understand the difference between right and wrong, and in time to think in terms of rights and responsibilities.

It is sometimes said that morality is caught more than taught, and there is something to this. Children aren't argued into morality. Rather, they learn to be honest, to work hard, to be compassionate, and to follow the rules by observing their parents and by internalizing the moral values of their communities. Much (though not all) of what is called character education in schools focuses on the importance of role models, exhortation, and stories (with morals) to begin this process of socialization. In fact, the term "character education" is something of a misnomer; "character socialization" might be more appropriate. This is not a criticism; children must be socialized before they can be liberally educated. Character is, to some considerable extent, formed early in our lives, and character education is particularly important in the early grades.

## Traditions and the Liberal Arts

Alasdair MacIntyre has famously argued that "I can only answer the question 'What am I to do?' if I can answer the prior question 'Of what story or stories do I find myself a part?' We enter human society, that is, with one or more imputed characters—roles into which we have been drafted—and we have to learn what they are in order to be able to understand how others respond to us and how our responses to them are to be construed.... Deprive children of stories and you leave them unscripted, anxious stutterers in their actions as in their words."[1] One problem with character education is that it often leaves character and moral values as relatively bloodless social conventions, mere mores, by failing to ground them in a tradition, a narrative, or a worldview that makes sense of them. Too often, as James Davison Hunter has put it, character education "reduces morality to the thinnest of platitudes, severed from the social, historical, and cultural contexts that make it concrete and ultimately compelling.... Without being anchored in any normative community, this morality retains little authority beyond its own aesthetic appeal."[2]

As I noted in discussing historical perspective in the last chapter, we live (granted, less now than in the past) in "communities of memory" that give shape and substance to our identities. We are not individuals, pure and simple, but members of communities (national, ethnic, linguistic, religious) shaped by traditions, by webs of influence and obligation that tie us to the past and the future. To be oblivious to the traditions we inherit, the stories in which we have roles, is a little like having amnesia: if we don't know where we've been, we don't know where we're going; indeed, we don't know who we are. (Maybe I should say that some character education programs are sensitive to giving children a past, to locating them in traditions; some aren't.)

In the last chapter I discussed Bruce Kimball's distinction between a liberal arts and a liberal-free education. A liberal arts education is largely a moral education; its purpose is to form character, to nurture virtue, to shape the identities of students by initiating them into a tradition that makes sense of, and gives direction to, their lives. (For advocates of the old liberal arts ideal, moral virtues were typically located in the classics of Greek and Roman literature and philosophy and, of course, the Bible.)

One purpose of a liberal (arts) education, then, is to ground our virtues and values in thick moral, civic, political, national, and religious traditions by way of teaching history and literature, and in universities, philosophy and religion. Of course, we often disagree about what literature to teach, and how to construct our historical narratives. Still, we don't disagree about everything. We agree (on a little reflection) that it is essential that students appreciate the importance of honesty and integrity, fairness and compassion, and great literature can do a great deal to nurture a nuanced understanding and appreciation of these virtues in students. We agree that students must be initiated into the American constitutional tradition. They must acquire the democratic virtues of citizenship and appreciate the obligations they have because of their location in a historical narrative defined, in part, by our constitutional commitments to liberty and human rights. And (though this may be a little more controversial) students must be located within the overlapping traditions—political, philosophical, literary, and religious—that constitute Western civilization and provide the context that makes sense of the moral and civic identities they inherit.

In the last chapter I noted the common argument that students cannot understand history and literature apart from religion. My point now is that the values and identities, the moral principles and commitments that students inherit by virtue of living in the United States are shaped in part by its religious history. I am not arguing that students should be taught that Christianity (or any religious tradition) is true, only that it, and other religious traditions, have played a constitutive role in shaping the institutions, culture, and moral traditions that go to make us the people we are.

We might say that this is the conservative agenda of a liberal education. It provides the cultural ballast needed to ground and balance the more liberal or liberating goal of critical thinking that is also essential to a liberal education. No doubt much education is a somewhat untidy mix of these two ideal types. Both are necessary. Alas, too much education is not motivated by either ideal.

## Critical Thinking and Liberal Education

Many conservatives, vividly aware of the sinfulness of people, believing in the Fall more than in moral progress, convinced that Truth is to be had within their own traditions, and wary of the Enlightenment and modernity, believe that Scripture and tradition are sufficient and properly constrain critical thinking about morality. There are several problems with this.

If students aren't given the resources and encouragement to think critically about the traditions into which they are initiated then moral education degenerates into training or indoctrination. Such a corruption of education is bad enough, but of course the practical results are often worse. Much of the world's evil is the result of business as usual; it is committed thoughtlessly. Too often people just follow orders or follow their traditions without thinking critically about them. But we cannot rely uncritically on our communities and traditions. All too many of us (of my age) learned sexism and racism from our communities and our traditions (including, sometimes, our religious traditions). The Germans (and many others) learned anti-Semitism from their traditions. Too many traditions have, in retrospect, turned out to be profoundly mistaken about very important things, sanctioning various kinds of evil. Everyone agrees that historically this has often happened, sometimes with devastating consequences (though we may not all agree on which traditions have fallen short). It is not enough to be a person of character; there are, after all, people of formidable character and considerable virtue who do the wrong thing for lack of critical judgment.

Clearly, we must attain a measure of critical distance on our traditions—on our character, our communities, and our culture—all of which require reforming from time to time. In fact, the possibility of progress in human affairs requires that we think critically about the fundamental ideas and ideals of our cultures and traditions.

Of course, whatever our commitment to critical thinking, we must each rely, in the beginning, on the virtues we acquired as children and the wisdom of the traditions within which we find ourselves. To some it will sound hopelessly old-fashioned to talk about the wisdom of our traditions, but if our traditions are continually rethought and reformed in the course of our ongoing cultural conversation then it makes sense to suppose that traditions are (often) progressive; and if there is moral progress (no matter how slow and halting) then it is reasonable to place some trust in those traditions; they aren't simply dead weights around our necks.

Nor do I want to deny that what morality requires of us is often simple and straightforward, in which case the problem is not that of determining what is right but of summoning the willpower to do what we know is right. In his great novel *Life and Fate,* Vassily Grossman writes movingly of the thoughtless kindness of "an old woman carrying a piece of bread to a prisoner, the kindness of a soldier allowing a wounded enemy to drink from his water-flask . . . the kindness of a peasant hiding an old Jew in his attic [and] the kindness of a prison guard who risks his own liberty to pass on a letter written by a prisoner."[3] Indeed, Grossman worries about what happens to such goodness when it gets caught up in the designs of ideologues. This is clearly a very real concern. And yet such goodness isn't sufficient. Too often we don't know what is right; sometimes our "instinctual" goodness leads us astray. In fact, not all letters should be smuggled out of prison, and not everyone should be hidden in one's attic.

Most obviously, we often disagree about what is right because the situation is so complex (as any election will make clear). We may disagree about what the facts are or which facts are relevant, what history shows, or what the likely implications of a course of action might be. We know that we should love our neighbor, but does this mean a more generous welfare state? How successful has the welfare state been (and what about European versions of the welfare state)? Might our neighbor live in the Third World? And what has been the effect of American foreign aid? We know that murder is wrong. But what about capital punishment? (And is it a deterrent or not? Does that make a difference?) Or euthanasia? Or abortion? Or killing in wartime? Or in self-defense? Of course, our assessment of which facts are relevant, or of the lessons of history, or of the likely outcomes of various actions given human nature, are often controversial matters of interpretation.

But the problem isn't simply the complexity of the facts, it's the moral traditions and theories we bring to our understanding of the facts. While some things, like honesty or simple kindness, turn out to be moral on almost any conception of morality, other moral issues—say, social justice, abortion, or capital punishment—may look quite different from the vantage point of different theories or traditions. Unlike past generations we must navigate a pluralistic sea of incompatible choices, defensible from the vantage point of different moral principles and traditions. Is morality a matter of maximizing happiness, human flourishing, enlightened self-interest, a social contract, obeying God's law (and whose God?), respect for other persons, compassion, love, evolutionary fitness, following local tradition—or something else? Is morality tied up with being an American—or a Russian or a Chinese? Of course, most people are members of several traditions (religious, civic, ethnic, political, cultural) that may impose conflicting obligations on them.

Even putatively nonmoral frameworks of interpretation are often morally controversial. As I've noted above, economics texts try very hard to avoid moral judgments, but if neoclassical economic theory is correct, if people are essentially self-interested utility maximizers, aren't there implications for morality? What is the relationship of cost-benefit analysis to moral judgment? And what are the implications of neo-Darwinian evolution for morality (not just for kin-group or reciprocal altruism)? If science can explain the brain in terms of deterministic causal laws, what happens to human responsibility? Can people be evil—or just mentally ill? Does cultural anthropology lead to moral relativism? Indeed, on some ways of making sense of the world it appears that the whole idea of morality becomes problematic.

As the last paragraph suggests, virtually everything students study has moral implications or is in some way caught up in webs of moral relevance. Indeed, I noted at the beginning of this section the dangers of virtually all educational goods when pursued apart from morality. The idea that one can specialize in ways that don't involve morality is naive and profoundly dangerous. (This is another angle on Hannah Arendt's argument about the banality of evil, of business as usual.) Arguably, being moral isn't just a matter of following rules or principles; it is a matter of acting thoughtfully and responsibly in the face of suffering and the possibilities for flourishing. Of course, much education, not least the study of history and literature, addresses human suffering (alienation, war, injustice, pain, illness, tragedy) and flourishing (social progress, justice, happiness, pleasure, art, joy, health). Morality requires that we use our insight, intelligence, and imagination to bring goodness, justice, and flourishing, out of a world of suffering.

We surely cannot expect families and religious communities to sort out all of this. Morality requires thoughtful, informed, educated judgments. Of course, how one sorts all this out is open to various interpretations, secular and religious. There are religious as well as secular ways of interpreting history, of assessing the significance of movements and institutions, of understanding human nature, and, of course, of making sense of morality. The whole point of the last chapter is that if students are to think critically, as a liberal education requires, they must understand the alternatives—religious alternatives included—from the inside, as live options, critically. No matter how convinced a scholar may be that secular ways of thinking about morality are the most reasonable, if students are to think critically about morality, if they are to be liberally educated, they must understand religious as well as secular way; of making sense of the moral dimension of our lives.

Once we acknowledge the importance of moral education (not just moral socialization) and recognize its relationship to critical thinking and liberal education, it follows that religion must be part of the conversation.

In chapter 5 I argued that to think critically students must be able to get inside other cultures and traditions. This is not easy. To the extent possible, I suggested, we should use primary sources, allowing people to speak for themselves. In particular we should use literature and art that nurture what Martha Nussbaum calls the "narrative imagination."[4] Much moral shortcoming results from a failure of imagination. One goal is to provide critical perspective on our own beliefs and values. Another is to get us beyond abstractions, to those personal expressions of suffering and flourishing that challenge any uncritical egotism or ethnocentrism. This makes it difficult to dehumanize people, a precursor to much of the great evil that has been done in human history. The English novelist Ian McEwan wrote of the 9/11 hijackers that if they "had been able to imagine themselves into the thoughts and feelings of the passengers, they would have been unable to proceed. It is hard to be cruel once you permit yourself to enter the mind of your victim. Imagining what it is like to be someone other than yourself is at the core of our humanity. It is the essence of compassion, and it is the beginning of morality. The hijackers used fanatical certainty, misplaced religious faith, and dehumanizing hatred to purge themselves of the human instinct for empathy."[5]

## Liberal Education as a Moral Enterprise

In the last chapter I argued that if schools and universities are to encourage truly critical thinking, then they must provide students with a liberal education. We might also argue for the importance of a liberal education on moral grounds. To be a person is to have responsibilities—as I have put it, the concept of a person is a moral concept—and surely one fundamental moral responsibility, perhaps our most fundamental moral responsibility, is to be thoughtful. One cannot be a morally responsible person if one practices business as usual, refusing to think critically about one's life. That is, morality requires a liberal education, which both situates students in traditions, and provides them the encouragement and resources to think critically about them.

In fact, a liberal education is inherently a moral enterprise. In taking alternative ways of thinking and living seriously a liberal education teaches humility. In encouraging and enabling students to think and feel oneself into the hearts and minds of others, education nurtures the critical moral virtue of empathy, which, in turn, may lead them to accord the people they study a measure of respect, and perhaps even lead to compassion as students become sensitive to the suffering of others. In learning to think historically, as a liberal education requires, students are caught up in communities of memory that nurture gratitude to those who suffered for us and create a sense of responsibility to those who come after us. In engaging other people, cultures, and traditions in conversation a liberal education nurtures civility, and in sustaining such conversations, it nurtures community.[6] The moral virtues and the intellectual virtues are entwined and it is impossible to disentangle them.[7]

## The Existential Argument

According to Huston Smith, the great scholar of world religions, "the ultimate questions human beings ask—What is the meaning of existence? Why are there pain and death? Why, in the end, is life worth living? What does reality consist of and what is its object?—are the *defining essence of our humanity*. They are not just speculative imponderables that certain people of inquisitive bent get around to asking after they have attended to the serious business of working out strategies for survival. They are the determining substance of what makes human beings human."[8]

This may sound a little grandiose to some, but Smith is surely right. Indeed, people need to be particularly thoughtless to avoid such questions or to believe them to be inconsequential. But if this search for meaning, this concern about the Big Questions, is an inescapable part of being human, then it should be an inescapable part of being an educated person. *What is truly important? How should I live my life?* In the last chapter I proposed that a liberal education must have existential depth. What could be more important?

There is, of course, considerable overlap between morality and these existential questions about meaning. Moral questions are among the Big Questions. Moreover, as we've seen, morality isn't intellectually free-floating; conceptions of morality are grounded in the ways in which we make sense of the world—in intellectual traditions, cultural narratives, and worldviews that provide answers to the Big Questions and shape our thinking about morality and meaning. But the existential domain of meaning is somewhat broader than that of morality. It has implications for how we live our lives that go beyond morality, to the meaning and significance of nature, friendship, love, sexuality, suffering, death, work, and beauty. To live one's life oblivious to the ways in which people and cultures have found meaning is to risk living superficially. The goal must be to live an examined life.

Now, if schools and universities are to address the Big Questions it is inconceivable that this can be done apart from considering religious answers to these questions. Or maybe I should say *almost* inconceivable, for some educators believe that questions of meaning can be disentangled from religion. In an often insightful book titled *The Soul of Education,* Rachael Kessler has argued that public schools should take on the largely spiritual task of responding to the need of students to find deep connections in their lives, search for meaning and purpose, and seek transcendence—all "gateways to the soul" as she puts it—but to do so apart from religious beliefs and dogmas that, she fears, would raise First Amendment problems.[9] My own view (about which I will say more in the next chapter) is that it should raise First Amendment concerns about neutrality to leave religion out of this discussion. In any case, surely it is deeply illiberal to pursue the search for meaning while excluding religious voices from the conversation. As with morality, once we locate the search for meaning within the context of a liberal education, religion cannot be shunted aside.

But if the search for meaning is part of the defining essence of our humanity, as Smith puts it, or even if it is just very important for most people, why don't schools and universities make more of an effort to address it? Needless to say, we can round up the usual suspects: our fixation on skills, testing, vocationalism, specialization, and the disciplinary blinders that force most teachers to at least explicitly ignore the Big (often transdisciplinary) Questions.

There can be little doubt that all of this is of considerable interest to students. A 2004 UCLA study of 100,000 incoming undergraduates found that 76 percent of them were searching for meaning and purpose in life.[10] At the same time, another UCLA study concluded that "over half of college students report that their professors never offered them any opportunities to discuss the meaning and purpose of life, and nearly half were dissatisfied because their college experience did not provide them with opportunities for religious/spiritual reflection."[11] (This study included students in religiously affiliated colleges—where professors were, I suspect, more likely to have been sympathetic to these goals than faculty in public colleges and universities.[12]) John Sommerville's rueful observation should not be surprising: "universities are not really where we look for answers to our life questions." In fact, he suggests, this makes them "seem marginal." And why is this? Well, size and specialization, but "they have also lost touch with important questions by their secularization."[13] Teachers simply don't see it as their task to address those questions of meaning that are at least potentially spiritual or religious.

Not surprisingly, the existential domain of education is entangled in pedagogy. Stephen Webb notes that too often "the message sent to the students is that they are productive members of the classroom only to the extent that they learn to bracket their personal lives and take control of complex intellectual issues." Students who are most likely to succeed are those who "learn to compartmentalize their intellectual and spiritual interests."[14] Barbara Walvoord discusses what she calls the great divide in religion courses between faculty goals, which typically focus on critical thinking, and students' goals, which are likely to be more directed at their own moral, spiritual, and religious development.[15] Bruce Grelle worries that "by striving for an objective and neutral approach to the study of religion that sets aside one's own presuppositions, experiences, and questions, there is a great risk of undermining students' sense of the relevance of the subject matter and its connection to their own personal lives."[16]

There are two somewhat different ways that teachers might respond. Some educators have distinguished between teacher-centered and student-centered pedagogies. The first is to structure courses that help students understand how other people (scholars, cultures, traditions, religions) have answered the Big Questions and found meaning in life. In the second approach teachers are not so much experts and instructors as facilitators who engage students in reflecting on their personal interests and concerns. Ronald Anderson argues that education must "address student questions, not just encourage student answers to teacher questions" and he quotes Paul Tillich who "said it well: 'The fatal pedagogical error is to throw answers, like stones, at the heads of those who have not yet asked the questions.' . . . The approach must be authentically student-centered with nonstandard assignments (i.e., student selected and defined) and great freedom in the manner of pursuing them, including student collaborations."[17]

It seems to me that these two approaches are entirely complementary. Clearly there is great value in the idea of teachers being responsive to their students' search for meaning and their desire to explore the Big Questions. There is also great value in learning about how other people, cultures, and scholars have addressed these questions so that students can make more informed and critical judgments about their own lives. In fact, the idea of a liberal education as a conversation captures some of the common ground between these positions. A good liberal education initiates students into an ongoing, critical conversation in which they have a voice along with all of those historical, cultural, and disciplinary voices that articulate ideas and values they must take seriously if they are to make educated judgments.

Clearly, the curriculum must be structured to raise and explore the Big Questions carefully and systematically, drawing out the implications for how students find meaning in their lives. Nel Noddings, formerly the dean of the School of Education at Stanford, has argued that existential questions "should form the organizing backbone of the curriculum, and they should be appropriate everywhere. We rob study of its richness when we insist on rigid boundaries between subject matters, and the traditional disciplinary organization makes learning fragmentary and—I dare say—boring and unnecessarily separated from the central issues of life."[18] (As a former mathematics teacher she has some interesting things to say about the relevance of existential questions to teaching mathematics.) She adds that "the unimaginableness of my scenario reveals the depravity in which we live and work."[19] Ah, yes.

Most important for our purposes, religious voices must be structured into this conversation. How could there be a discussion of the Big Questions, of life's meaning, that does not take religion seriously? It would be deeply illiberal.

Finally, two observations. First, I have discussed the importance of the existential dimension of education largely in terms of its critical value in putting our lives in perspective, in helping students orient themselves in life. But we might also think of its intrinsic value in giving students some sense of the richness of life, the joys of life, how people flourish. This is a gift education can give to students—an appreciation of the ways in which people find beauty, joy, and meaning in their lives.

Obviously literature and the arts have an important role to play in understanding people and cultures, in critical thinking about the moral and existential dimensions of life, but they are also immensely valuable as sources of beauty and joy. Of course, religious art, religious ritual, mystical experience, and religious ways of experiencing the world as suffused by the Sacred (the Divine, God's grace) are among the most profound ways in which people have found beauty, joy, and meaning in their lives and the world. In fact, to allow students to remain oblivious to all of this is an act of stinginess worthy of a pedagogical Scrooge. It is true that public schools and universities cannot require students to participate in religious rituals and mystical exercises, but they can require students to understand them, from the inside, imaginatively and vicariously.

Second, the idea that education should nurture wisdom would, I suspect, be viewed as embarrassingly naive by many. Of course, it is not easy to say what counts as wisdom. Indeed, it requires considerable wisdom. I don't claim any great wisdom, but it does seem to me that we often think of people as being wise when they have some ability to put life's problems in perspective, when they have a sense of what is truly important. And this is more likely if they have grappled with the Big Questions.

## Civic Arguments

I said in the last chapter that the most common argument for requiring students to study religion is that it is necessary if they are to understand history and literature. Perhaps the second most common kind of argument is a civic argument (of which there are many). Often advocates of such arguments start from the inevitability of conflict when religion is at issue, and the overriding question for them is about how we can live together in light of our deep differences.

A good example of this is the American Academy of Religion's *Guidelines for Teaching about Religion in K–12 Public Schools in the United States*.[20] Three premises shape the *Guidelines*: "illiteracy regarding religion 1) is widespread, 2) fuels prejudice and antagonism, and 3) can be diminished by teaching about religion in public schools using a non-devotional, academic perspective, called religious studies."[21] The primary goal of teaching about religion is the *civic* goal of encouraging understanding of different religious traditions "thereby hindering efforts aimed at promoting respect for diversity, peaceful coexistence, and cooperative endeavors in local, national, and global arenas."[22]

To achieve this goal, schools must promote a religious literacy that involves "a basic understanding of the history, central texts (where applicable), beliefs, practices and contemporary manifestations of several of the world's religious tradition and religious expressions as they arose out of and continue to shape and be shaped by particular social, historical and cultural contexts." This can be accomplished in a number of ways: by studying religion historically; through literature; through "traditions-based" approaches (often used in the study of comparative religion); and through a cultural studies approach (one often used by scholars in religious studies programs) with its emphasis on how a religion is "embedded in culture and cannot be understood in isolation from its particular social/historical expressions." This last approach "includes a consideration of social power and ways that race, class, and gender (among other factors) provide important categories of analysis" and is sensitive to the ways in which students, teachers, and texts are "interpreters of meaning."[23]

All of this is helpful, but it falls short of taking religion seriously. The *Guidelines* make nothing of the potential conflicts between secular and religious ways of making sense of the world or students' lives, the role of religion in moral (as opposed to civic) education, or the idea of liberal education as a systematic critical conversation.

This kind of position is not uncommon: some very good writers on religion and education stop short of the critical task of a liberal education, settling for civic arguments.[24] But, as we've seen, the most important purpose of education is to encourage and enable students to think critically about morality, meaning, and the secular disciplinary frameworks that are assumed throughout the curriculum.

That said, it is also true that we must learn to live with our differences—especially in a society of exploding religious diversity. The civic arguments are also important. I'll propose four of them.

## Informed Citizenship

Stephen Prothero has recently argued that the most important reason for religious literacy is the civic reason of creating informed citizens and voters.

"Today, when religion is implicated in virtually every issue of national and international import . . . US citizens need to know something about religion too. In an era in which the public square is, rightly or wrongly, awash in religious reasons, can one really participate fully in public life without knowing something about Christianity and the world's religions?" Prothero gives many examples of political issues with religious dimensions. When citizens lack religious literacy, he concludes, they "are too easily swayed by demagogues on the left or the right. Few Americans are able to challenge claims made by politicians or pundits about Islam's place in the war on terrorism or what the Bible says about homosexuality. This ignorance imperils our public life."[25]

This kind of argument is relatively uncontroversial. Insofar as schools should prepare students for their obligations as citizens, they must educate them about religion. No doubt having information about religion is often sufficient; but if one is to be a truly thoughtful citizen one must also have some sense of how reasonable religious ideas and values are. This requires a measure of religious understanding and some critical appreciation of the merits of contending religious and secular positions on important issues.

## Justice

Most Americans would be outraged at the idea of public schools or universities that ignored or privileged either Democrats or Republicans. Obviously there are good reasons for taking both political parties seriously if students are to think critically about politics and be informed voters, but this is also a matter of justice. When the public is deeply divided between political parties, public institutions (such as schools and universities) have an obligation to take each side seriously. The solution, happily, is simple: students should learn about the history, policies, and values of each of the major political parties, taking each seriously as live options.

A parallel argument can be made regarding religion. Americans are deeply divided over various secular and religious ways of making sense of politics—and morality, and human nature, and reality more generally. But whenever the public is divided about matters of importance, public schools and universities should ensure that all of the (live, major) voices in our cultural conversation are taken seriously.

Or take another example that I have used above. The traditional exclusion of women's and African American history and literature from the curriculum was unjust; it relegated many children to second-class status, and, as a result, massive efforts have been made over the last several decades to integrate public schools culturally, rebuilding them on common (rather than segregated) ground. If the voices of people of a particular gender, race, or ethnicity are excluded from the curricular conversation they are disenfranchised—much as if they couldn't vote or participate in the political process. There are good educational reasons for multicultural education; it contributes to critical thinking and the richness of students' understanding of the world. But it is also a matter of justice: in a democracy people have a right to participate in the discussion both politically by means of voting, and educationally by means of having their voices heard in the curriculum.

Unfortunately, the multicultural movement has been largely tone-deaf to religious cultures and subcultures. There are reasons for this. Multiculturalists have traditionally been concerned with those people who have been subject to cultural discrimination and oppression. As a result, they often defined themselves in opposition to the white, male, Eurocentric, Protestant establishment that had dominated American education for so long and was oppressive in matters of race, ethnicity, gender, and religion. Multiculturalism has been largely a movement of the Left. Moreover, beginning in the 1970s most of the vocal religious voices in battle over public schooling came from the Religious Right. Not surprisingly then, with a heritage of Protestant schools, and with the efforts of religious conservatives to restore prayer, creationism, and "traditional values" to public schools (if not dismantle them through voucher programs) multiculturalism has shown little sympathy for religion.

And yet, millions of Americans find the most profound sources of meaning in their lives in their religious traditions and define themselves less in terms of ethnicity, gender, or nationality than in terms of religion. Their primary identities are as Christians, Jews, Buddhists, or Muslims, rather than as blacks, women, or Americans. (No doubt all people have many identities.) Sometimes people's religious identities distinguish them from—and set them against—the dominant ideals and institutions of modernity; religious cultures are, to some considerable extent, "adversary cultures," sometimes more so than are subcultures grounded in race, ethnicity, and gender. Indeed, the tensions between religious subcultures and the dominant culture are often so marked, and the victory of the dominant culture over religion is so complete, that it may even make sense to talk now about the educational oppression of religious subcultures.

There were very good reasons of justice for multicultural education. Unfortunately, like most educators, multiculturalists have ignored religion. Given the alignment of combatants in our current culture wars this is, perhaps, unsurprising, but it is a betrayal of principles nonetheless. Religious voices too must be included in the conversation as a matter of justice.

## Liberty

A liberal political order, in its classical sense, is one that guarantees and respects liberty; it does not impose on citizens a particular conception of the good life but leaves them free to choose for themselves. Similarly, it has often been argued that education ought not to impose on students a particular conception of the good life. A liberal education, on this view, ought to promote the development of autonomous individuals.

This might mean a variety of things—not all of which are uncontroversial or defensible. I am not arguing that a liberal education should promote the idea of persons as morally unencumbered social atoms who can and should live apart from all tradition and obligations—one conception of autonomy. Indeed, as we have seen it is a purpose of a liberal education to situate students in traditions. But students must also be given the resources to think critically about those traditions and their past. What I believe is defensible—and relatively uncontroversial—is the idea that mature students (undergraduates certainly, but also high school students) must not be indoctrinated but should be free to make up their own minds so long as they are in a position to do so responsibly.

This right is inherent in the ideal of liberty in an open and free society. While indoctrination is permissible, even necessary, with children, as students mature the educational system should prepare them to think critically about the traditions (the culture, the values) they have inherited. Of course, there is no bright line (the age of sixteen, say) at which students acquire the right to be reasoned with, rather than indoctrinated. Rather, schools should gradually nurture the ability of students to make informed, reflective, responsible judgments.

This does not mean that students should be free to make up their beliefs and values, to define themselves as the existentialists would have it. Consider an analogy with science. A scientist should be free to follow the evidence where it goes, thinking critically about alternative theories. Still, there is a scientific truth to be found. Scientists cannot make it up. The analogy is not precise because scientists agree to accept scientific method, while there is no parallel agreed-upon moral or political method that everyone accepts. But just as scientists must not be indoctrinated into accepting theories, but must have the freedom to think critically about them, so mature persons (including students at some level) must not be indoctrinated into accepting particular conceptions of the good life but must be free to think critically about what is (truly) good. Teachers must reason with students, respecting their right to think critically about their lives and the world.

The philosopher E. M. Adams wrote, "The measure of one's provincialism and cultural slavery is the extent to which one is blindly in the grips of one's culture without critical understanding and mastery of it. The measure of one's education," by contrast, "is the extent to which one has a critical understanding and mastery of human culture."[26] To be a citizen rather than a slave one must be free to live one's own life, to make one's own judgments. To be free in the realm of the mind, rather than be a cultural slave, one must be liberally educated. If we are to respect students as individuals possessing the right to liberty, to not be indoctrinated, they must be free to judge for themselves where truth lies. And, as I argued in chapter 4, schools and universities now border on secular indoctrination. The cure is a liberal education that takes religion seriously.

## Rights, Respect, and Civility

The American experiment has been defined, in large part, by a commitment to liberty and human rights. This being the case, we should not be surprised by ensuing disagreements, culture wars, and social fragmentation. Charles Haynes has characterized our public square as "a hostile place where citizens shout past one another across seemingly unbridgeable distances. Incendiary rhetoric and personal attacks characterize many 'culture-war' debates [and] any notion of the common good frequently gets lost in the crossfire of charge and counter-charge."[27] But, as Haynes also argues, the ideas of civility and respect can bind us together. If we are to live together in spite of our deep differences, if the cultural politics of schooling are not to become dangerously polarized, if students are to take seriously different points of view as a good liberal education requires, then schools and universities must nurture the virtue of civility.

Such civility takes two somewhat different forms. First, all citizens must respect the *rights* of others—not least our constitutional right to religious liberty. They must understand the value of the civic and constitutional framework that defines America. But civility also requires that we understand one another's views. K. Anthony Appiah has argued that multicultural education is necessary to "reduce the misunderstandings across subcultures." It is "a way of making sure we care enough about people across ethnic divides to keep those ethnic divides from destroying us." Consequently, it must be "a central part of the function of our educational system to equip all of us to share the public space with people of multiple identities and distinct subcultures."[28] So it must be with regard to religion.

Historically, it has been a role of the public schools, the common schools, to nurture a sense of community—one that binds us together while respecting differences. The only way to find common ground when we disagree is to draw the circle widely enough so that we include everyone in the conversation, treating them with respect. If there is to be social peace, if the landscape of American education is not to be a battleground of warring ideologies and subcultures we must build schools and universities on common ground, and the only way to do this is to agree to treat one another with respect, talk civilly with one another, learn about one another, and establish the trust that is necessary to live together with our deepest differences—making room for everyone in the curricular conversation. Of course, respecting others doesn't mean that we must agree with them; it does, I think, commit us to understanding their ideas, values, concerns, and needs—as they understand them. Don't we want them to understand us in this way?

There is a case to be made that civility and respect are better served if we stop short of any kind of critical assessment of different cultures and traditions, settling for a tolerant and neutral respect for diversity. This has probably been the dominant position of the multicultural movement. Of course not all cultures deserve respect—and it is important to say this. We all agree about the evil of Nazi culture and antebellum slave culture. (Indeed, multiculturalists are themselves often committed to showing the injustice of the dominant culture in the United States.) Often, however, we disagree about how to assess other cultures, subcultures, and traditions. But we may disagree deeply all the while treating one another with respect as individuals, talking civilly with, and learning from, one another. We may disagree deeply about homosexuality, for example, while agreeing that gay bashing is reprehensible and not to be permitted.

My inclination is to argue for the importance of nurturing in students the capacity for reflective, informed, and critical judgment, leavened by a deep sense of humility in dealing with difficult and controversial matters in which they have something of a vested interest.[29] Of course, as we have seen, we can encourage a critical conversation about different theories, cultures, traditions, and worldviews, without passing judgment or taking an official position on their relative merits. This may often be the wisest position, not least with religious subcultures and traditions.

## Finding Common Ground

Perhaps surprisingly, in the midst of our culture wars over religion and public schools a good deal of common ground has been staked out—though far from everyone appreciates this fact. There is now a set of common-ground statements on religion and public education that have been endorsed by a broad spectrum of national educational, civil liberties, and religious organizations (conservative and liberal, Christian, Jewish, Islamic, and secular). The first of these statements, *Religion and the Public School Curriculum: Questions and Answers* (1988)[30] made several important claims: it is constitutional to teach about religion, teaching about religion must be done neutrally (as the First Amendment requires), textbooks are deficient in their treatment of religion, and it is important to teach about religion. Why is it important?

> Because religion plays a significant role in history and society, study about religion is essential to understanding both the nation and the world. Omission of facts about religion can give students the false impression that the religious life of humankind is insignificant or unimportant. Failure to understand even the basic symbols, practices and concepts of the various religions makes much of history, literature, art and contemporary life unintelligible. Study about religion is also important if students are to value religious liberty, the first freedom guaranteed in the Bill of Rights. Moreover, knowledge of the roles of religion in the past and present promotes cross-cultural understanding essential to democracy and world peace.[31]

Other common-ground statements followed, including *The Bible in Public Schools* and *A Teacher's Guide to Religion and Public Schools*. Hundreds of thousands, perhaps millions, of copies of these documents have been distributed, and in 1999, President Bill Clinton had several of them sent to every public school in the country. Cumulatively, the statements have established a new consensus in dealing with religion in public schools, providing a safe haven for teachers and administrators in schools that offer coursework in religion, often without controversy.

For Haynes, who has done more than anyone else to create and nurture this national consensus and help local school districts around the country find common ground, the starting point is the First Amendment, which provides a framework for living with our deepest differences. "In the spirit of the First Amendment," he argues, "all perspectives have a right to be heard, and each citizen has an obligation to protect the freedom of conscience of all others."[32] Finding common ground isn't simply a matter of political compromise, but of recognizing principles on which we can agree in negotiating our differences, principles that nurture an appreciation of rights, responsibilities, and respect.

As a result, Haynes suggests, we must reject the idea of a sacred public school (which promotes or privileges religion) and the naked public school (which is, in effect, a religion-free zone) for the civil public school, which respects everyone's rights and treats everyone with respect. It is his experience of many years that when we talk civilly and listen to one another, trust can be established, and with it a shared conception of public education that binds us together rather than separates us. But it is necessary that we take one another seriously, both in formulating school policies regarding religion (an exercise that every school district should go through) and in shaping the curriculum. We certainly need to recognize, Haynes argues, that "avoidance of religion and exclusion of religious perspectives is anything but neutral or fair. . . . All sides need to recognize that the current battles about 'world views' cannot be resolved either by excluding all religious perspectives or by establishing one religion (or world view) over all others."[33]

In 2007, the Office for Democratic Institutions and Human Rights of the Organization for Security and Co-operation in Europe coordinated the preparation of a seventy-page common-ground statement—the *Toledo Guiding Principles*—for addressing religion in European schools. While the constitutional contexts for dealing with religion vary across European nations, the *Principles* developed out of a "growing consensus among lawyers and educators" that is remarkably close to the American consensus.[34] The *Principles* are meant to "contribute to an improved understanding of the world's increasing religious diversity and the growing presence of religion in the public sphere. Their rationale is based on two core principles: first, that there is a positive value in teaching that emphasizes respect for *everyone's* right to freedom of religion and belief, and second, that teaching *about* religions and beliefs can reduce harmful misunderstandings and stereotypes."[35] Hence, "no educational system can afford to ignore the role of religions and beliefs in history and culture." Indeed, ignorance of religions "may fuel intolerance and discrimination."[36]

As with the American common-ground statements, the *Toledo Guiding Principles* adopt neutrality as the governing educational virtue in dealing with religion. In fact, the *Principles* overlap almost completely with the American common-ground statements (in spite of the absence of a European version of the First Amendment).[37] The bottom line is that there is now a broad consensus, in both Europe and the United States, that it is important for students to learn about religion, and that it should be done neutrally.[38]

These common-ground statements typically start from civic arguments for studying religion, complemented by the claim that students can't be well educated without understanding religions. They don't go so far as I do in arguing that education must take religion seriously (as a live option, in critical conversation with alternative ways of making sense of the world) though there is nothing in them that precludes my position. Indeed, the *Toledo Guiding Principles* discuss, among various pedagogies, a phenomenological approach (empathy and inside-understanding) as well as dialogical and multi-perspectival pedagogies that at least border on the critical approach I have proposed for taking religion seriously.[39]

## Conclusion

In spite of the common-ground statements and the new consensus it is dispiriting to see how far we still are from the ideal. Religion simply isn't taken seriously by the vast majority of public schools or schools of education. There are exceptions. Several states (California and Utah, most extensively) have developed "3Rs" projects—on rights, responsibilities, and respect—for dealing with religion and religious liberty in public schools, and individual school systems and teachers here and there are showing initiative.[40]

I am dispirited even more by the indifference of educators in both secondary and higher education to serious moral education. Our world is filled with suffering and injustice, so much so that it breaks one's heart, and yet we muddle on, preoccupied with so much that is less important. Maybe education is no worse in this respect than our culture generally—though one might hope for more from educated and, no doubt, caring people. There are, of course, many individual teachers who are exceptions to my crass generalization. Still, our organized, curricular efforts at moral education have been, at best, half-hearted and superficial—and, of course, they have proceeded all but oblivious to any role for religion.

Thus endeth the jeremiad. I will say something more about pessimism and optimism in chapter 8. I will say here that the new consensus does offer grounds for some hope, and a foundation on which to build that is very important.

Finally, I note an important shift in governing principles that comes with the common-ground statements: public schools *must be neutral* in dealing with religion. None of the arguments I have made in chapters 5 and 6 require neutrality. My arguments all require taking religion seriously (as a live option, in critical, comparative perspective) but they do not prohibit teachers or professors from, in the end, taking sides. Indeed, one might think that as our guides to what is reasonable, teachers should take sides. As we shall see in the next chapter, however, as the U.S. Supreme Court interprets it, the First Amendment to the U.S. Constitution requires religious neutrality. This is also part of the common ground we share in the United States.

# 7

# Constitutional Considerations

There is complete agreement among scholars that it is constitutionally permissible to teach about religion in public schools and universities. How to do this properly may be somewhat more controversial, though as I suggested at the end of the last chapter, there is also a good deal of consensus about this. The governing virtue—in both the common-ground statements and in court rulings—is neutrality. Public schools and universities are to be neutral in matters of religion. But, as I argued in chapter 4, schools and universities are not now neutral. To be neutral they must take religion seriously (in the strong sense in which I have defined it). I will argue in this chapter that, as the U.S. Supreme Court now interprets the First Amendment, schools and universities are required to take religion seriously. This is, I think, a claim of some importance.

While my primary concern is addressing the role of religion in the curriculum and classroom, I will say a little about a number of other educational issues relating to religion that are important and controversial: student rights, student speech, and school prayer.

In chapter 5, I argued that critical thinking and a good liberal education require historical perspective. I've organized two chapters of this book—chapter 3 and this chapter—historically. Given our culture wars, the claim that the United States is a Christian nation, confusion about the meaning of the phrase "separation of church and state," and the U.S. Supreme Court's changing (and always controversial) interpretation of the First Amendment, it is important to put our discussion in historical context.[1]

Religious Liberty in the American Colonies

Many Americans think of Puritan New England as the birthplace of the United States, forgetting that Catholic Spain was here long before the Puritan English, that a somewhat less godly lot had left England to populate Virginia a few years before the Puritans embarked for Massachusetts, and that Native Americans, with their own religious traditions, were here long before anyone else. The Puritans do have a special place in our history, however, precisely because they did come to North America for religious reasons. They came to North America for religious liberty—*their* religious liberty, I should say, not anyone else's (and they were not above ostracizing, branding, and occasionally hanging troublesome dissenters).

Puritan New England was not a theocracy; the responsibilities of minister and magistrate were separate. But Puritanism was the established religion, supported by the taxes people paid. Their laws were based on their understanding of the Bible, and there was no religious liberty. In all of this, the Puritans maintained the traditional European pattern of relating church and state. But that pattern would break down rather quickly for a number of reasons.

## Pluralism

As settlers came to the American colonies they brought their various religions with them. Different colonies had different establishments, and as every denomination was in a minority somewhere, there was reason, when a national government was created, to oppose any national establishment. This was, arguably, good for the cause of liberty. In *Federalist Number 10* James Madison argued that factions mutually ensure one another's relative powerlessness. "The influence of factious leaders may kindle a flame within their particular States," he wrote, "but will be unable to spread a general conflagration through the other States: a religious sect, may degenerate into a political faction in a part of the Confederacy; but the variety of sects dispersed over the entire face of it, must secure the national Councils against any danger from that source."[2] Religious pluralism makes religious liberty both necessary and possible.

## Evangelicals

In the 1720s and 1730s revivals spread across the colonies in what came to be called the Great Awakening. Salvation was possible outside the established churches with their theological orthodoxies. New churches and new denominations flourished. No longer was a person born into a church; one chose a particular church—or so many people came to believe. This made the idea of a unified relationship between a single church and community implausible. It was the evangelicals—and particularly the Baptists—who benefited the most, and they were particularly keen on religious liberty, both because they had been oppressed by establishments, and because of their theology. The logic of religious liberty was implicit in the Protestant Reformers' emphasis on conscience—what the sometime Baptist Roger Williams called soul liberty—and in its rejection of institutions (be they churches or states) that come between people and God. In the American colonies the conditions were right for this emphasis on liberty to come out of the shadows and flourish. Several colonies protected religious liberty from the beginning (e.g., Williams's Rhode Island and William Penn's Pennsylvania) and by the time of the American Revolution evangelical dissent was commonplace. In 1785, the Virginia Baptists resolved that it is "repugnant to the spirit of the gospel" to tax people for the support of religion; "the holy author of our religion needs no such compulsive measures for the promotion of his cause" and "the gospel wants not the feeble arm of man for its support."[3] Church and state should keep their distance. In fact, 150 years before Thomas Jefferson used the phrase, Roger Williams argued for a "wall of separation" between church and state.[4]

*Economics*

Already by the middle of the seventeenth century, the Puritans were fretting that Yankee merchants were undermining the purity of the Puritan City on a Hill. Purity requires isolation, while trade requires mobility, immigration, growth, material possessions, and the enjoyment of life. By the end of the century Cotton Mather wrote: "religion brought forth prosperity and the daughter destroyed the mother."[5] Often the English authorities adopted an explicit policy of religious toleration for economic reasons. So, for example, the Lords of Trade in London wrote to their colleagues in Virginia: "A free exercise of religion . . . is essential to enriching and improving a trading nation; it should be ever held sacred in His Majesty's colonies."[6] Religious freedom would motivate people to emigrate from England to the New World and do England's business. In spite of the Great Awakening, the late eighteenth century was a time of considerable religious indifference. Church membership may have been less than 10 percent of the population. In part this was the result of the inaccessibility of churches in a frontier society, but it was also partly the result of economics. Americans had mixed motives for religious toleration, some more pragmatic than others.

## The Enlightenment

Not a few Americans of the late eighteenth century fell under the influence of the Enlightenment. Unlike its more radical phase in France, the American Enlightenment was not hostile to all religion, but it was hostile to religious establishments. For Jefferson, truth is discovered through natural reason operating freely, and it needs no special favors from government: "It is error alone which needs the support of government." Difference of opinion, in religion, as in other pursuits, is advantageous in the search for truth. It is through reason that false religions are put to the test. "The effects of religious establishments," Jefferson argued, "have been the torture and imprisonment of millions of innocent people." Coercion only serves "to make one half the world fools, and the other half hypocrites."[7] Similarly, in his "Memorial and Remonstrance on the Religious Rights of Man" Madison argued that it is a fundamental truth that "religion, or the duty which we owe to our creator, and the manner of discharging it, can be directed only by reason and conviction, not by force and violence." Hence religion "must be left to the conviction and conscience of every man; and it is the right of every man to exercise it as these may dictate."[8] Religious liberty is a natural and inalienable right.

The commitment to religious liberty was not created by the Founding Fathers in one generation. Instead, there was considerable movement toward religious liberty over the course of the seventeenth and eighteenth centuries. Perhaps most interesting, much of that movement came from dissenting religious denominations, especially the Quakers and the Baptists, and from Enlightenment Deists who believed that natural reason, operating in a free culture, was the path to truth. This may have made for strange bedfellows, but it was the basis of an effective coalition in securing religious liberty in the new nation. Several times I have noted that deeply religious people may favor institutional secularism. By the end of the eighteenth century there was broad agreement among the American Founding Fathers that the new federal government should be secular.

## The U.S. Constitution

The only reference to religion in the Constitution (other than an incidental reference to the Sabbath, and dating it "in the year of our Lord") is in Article VI, Clause 3, which stipulates that "no religious test shall ever be required as a qualification to any office or public trust under the United States." Though short, this provision is significant: Muslims, Jews, Catholics, and atheists were to be treated the same as Protestant Christians with regard to holding office in the new federal government. The Constitution says nothing about religious liberty; indeed, there was no discussion of it at the Constitutional Convention, and little discussion of a Bill of Rights.

Why not? There are two answers. First, while the commitment to religious liberty was universal among the Founding Fathers, they believed that the Constitution gave the federal government no power to regulate religion or infringe on religious liberty. Neither an explicit protection of religion nor a bill of rights was necessary. Not everyone was convinced (Jefferson among them) and the ratification debates in the states showed considerable desire for a bill of rights. In response, the first Congress sent twelve amendments, constituting a bill of rights, to the states, ten of which were ratified. The first of those adopted began "Congress shall make no law respecting an establishment of religion or prohibiting the free exercise thereof."

The second answer is that the Founding Fathers—and the first Congress—chose to leave the power to regulate religion in the hands of the states (contrary to Madison's wishes). In fact, as it is written, the First Amendment is binding only on Congress. It is true that by the time the Constitution was drafted, freedom of conscience and a substantial measure of free exercise of religion were protected in all the new states, but this didn't mean that the new states had all abolished their religious establishments; six had not. (All six of these states had multiple establishments, meaning that voters in a community could choose which church to support with tax revenues that would typically fund ministers' salaries or new churches.) Keep in mind that a significant measure of religious liberty is compatible with religious establishments as many contemporary European countries still demonstrate. Even after the last state abolished its establishment (Massachusetts in 1833), many states retained religious tests for officeholders, religious oaths, Sunday closing laws, and laws prohibiting blasphemy.

So how did the First Amendment come to be applied to the states? Following the Civil War the Fourteenth Amendment was passed to restrict the power of the states. It said: "No State shall make or enforce any law which shall abridge the privileges or immunities of citizens of the United States; nor shall any State deprive any person of life, liberty, or property, without due process of law; nor deny to any person within its jurisdiction the equal protection of the laws." But what liberties could the states not deny their citizens? Beginning in the 1920s the Supreme Court answered: the liberties guaranteed in the First Amendment. In effect, they incorporated the First Amendment into the Fourteenth.

In 1940, in *Cantwell v. Connecticut,* the Supreme Court applied the Free Exercise Clause to the states for the first time when it overturned the conviction of a Jehovah's Witness who failed to comply with a Connecticut law requiring him to secure a license to engage in religious solicitation. This, the Court said, was an unconstitutional restriction of his religious liberty even though a state law, not a law enacted by Congress, was at issue. In 1947, the Court applied the Establishment Clause to the states for the first time in *Everson v. Board of Education* (which I will discuss below). The incorporation of the First Amendment into the Fourteenth was initially controversial, but it has become broadly accepted law. Only Justice Clarence Thomas, among current members of the Supreme Court, argues that the Establishment Clause of the First Amendment should not be binding on the states.

## Free Exercise

As in *Cantwell v. Connecticut,* the question in Free Exercise Clause cases is almost always whether or not members of a religious group are entitled to *exemptions from particular laws,* and for several decades after *Cantwell* the Supreme Court wrestled with developing a clear test for adjudicating such cases. In 1963, the Court first used what came to be called the compelling interest or Sherbert Test (so named for its first use in *Sherbert v. Verner*). At issue was whether a Seventh Day Adventist was entitled to unemployment compensation after refusing to take a job requiring her to work on Saturday, her Sabbath. The test requires courts to weigh the free exercise rights of individuals against the interests of the state: if the state's interests are not *compelling,* or if they might be realized in *some less burdensome way,* the Free Exercise Clause entitles the individual to an exemption from the law. While the test provides a procedure for settling the claim, it does not define what counts as burdensome or as a compelling interest; this must be decided by judges on a case by case basis. In this case, the Court found that an exemption from a constitutional law was required. As Justice William Brennan Jr. wrote for the Court: "To condition the availability of [unemployment] benefits upon this appellant's willingness to violate a cardinal principle of her religious faith effectively penalizes the free exercise of her constitutional liberties."[9]

We might look briefly at two important cases relating to education in which courts used the Sherbert Test. In *Wisconsin v. Yoder* (1972) the issue was whether the Amish should be exempted from obeying a Wisconsin law requiring children to attend school until the age of sixteen. (While they were willing to send their children to schools through the age of fourteen, they objected to the more worldly influence of a high school education.) Writing for the Court, Chief Justice Warren Burger acknowledged the state's interest in education, but argued that the "inherently simple and uncomplicated" way of life of the Amish is "difficult to preserve against the pressure to conform." The compulsory attendance law "carries with it a very real threat of undermining the Amish community and religious practice as they exist today; [the Amish] must either abandon belief and be assimilated into society at large, or be forced to migrate to some other and more tolerant region."[10] This, the Court held, would unduly burden their free exercise rights and the Amish were exempted from obeying the law.

In *Mozert v. Hawkins County Board of Education* (1987) the Sixth Circuit Court of Appeals denied fundamentalist children exemptions from a school district policy requiring the use of an elementary school reader that included stories with themes (feminism, one world government, witchcraft, and secular humanism) that, their parents claimed, burdened their Free Exercise rights. The Court held that as long as students were not required to affirm or act on the ideas and values in the books, they had no right to exemptions from the school policy; mere exposure does not burden religious liberty.

The *Mozert* ruling was controversial. For centuries the Catholic Church held that simply to read books included on its Index of Forbidden Books constituted a mortal sin. Arguably, what counts as burdening one's religious liberty must be a matter for each religious tradition to determine for itself, not for the courts. The federal district court had held that the policy did burden the families, and that while the state had a compelling interest in ensuring that students learn how to read, that interest could be satisfied in a less burdensome way—by allowing the children to use alternative textbooks they didn't find objectionable. This would be a reasonable accommodation. (When thinking about what kind of accommodations are reasonable, keep in mind the many ways in which schools bend over backward to accommodate the needs of athletes, gifted students, and handicapped students who have no constitutional claim to special treatment.) Some critics noted that the Amish were exempted from two years of schooling; the fundamentalists asked only for exemptions from reading a few stories. In any case, the Supreme Court declined to hear the case on appeal so the Sixth Circuit ruling was allowed to stand.

In 1990, the Supreme Court threw out the Sherbert Test. In *Employment Division, Department of Human Resources of Oregon v. Smith* (1990) the question was whether members of the Native American Church were entitled to exemptions from Oregon's drug laws so that they might use peyote in their religious ceremonies. (Peyote is not a recreational drug, and many states have exempted it from their drug laws when used in religious ceremonies.) Writing for the Court, Justice Antonin Scalia distinguished between laws whose direct object is to regulate religion—and are unconstitutional—and laws that have, as *an inci-dental effect,* the abridgment of free exercise. States cannot make laws prohibit-ing the use of wine in the mass—this would target Catholics—but they could prohibit the use of alcohol generally even if an incidental effect of such a law was to prohibit its use in the mass. The Oregon law was not directed at members of the Native American Church, but at drug users generally. If there is a *valid gen-eral law* (one that does not pick out a religious group for discrimination) then no free exercise claim can be made. Justice Scalia argued that the Sherbert Test opened the door to religious exemptions for every conceivable kind of law and that its rigorous application would be "courting anarchy." (One might respond that though the test had been used for more than twenty years, it had hardly led to anarchy.) If members of religious traditions don't like it, Justice Scalia wrote, they need to round up a democratic majority and change the law.

The *Smith* ruling was extremely controversial. Virtually all civil liberties and religious organizations (fundamentalist to liberal) saw *Smith* as eviscerat-ing the Free Exercise Clause. As a result, Congress passed the Religious Free-dom Restoration Act (RFRA) (1993), which required courts to use the Sherbert Test in adjudicating free exercise cases. The Supreme Court quickly ruled the RFRA unconstitutional as applied to state laws (because, the Court said, the act exceeded the constitutional powers of Congress) but let it stand regarding judi-cial review of federal laws. In the aftermath of the ruling, thirteen states (as of this writing) have enacted their own RFRAs.

So where do we stand? The Free Exercise Clause can no longer be used to appeal for exemptions from valid general laws—that is, laws that don't single out religions for discrimination—at the state level (where public schools and universities are governed). State laws can still be struck down as unconstitu-tional, however, if the law overtly discriminates against religion. For example, in 1993, only three years after *Smith*, the Court struck down a Hialeah, Florida, ordinance that transparently targeted members of the Santeria religion for engaging in ritual animal sacrifice (*Church of Lukumi Babalu Aye, Inc., v. City of Hialeah*). The Santerians weren't given an exemption from the law because the law itself was unconstitutional; it was not a valid general law but singled out their religion for discrimination.

There is a complication relating to education. (There is always a complica-tion in dealing with court rulings.) The Free Exercise Clause is most relevant when parents ask that their children be excused either from school activities or policies (e.g., Jehovah's Witnesses from holiday celebrations, Orthodox Jews from a no head covering policy, Muslims from class time to pray during the school day) or from reading texts they find offensive (as in the *Mozert* case). It would appear that after the *Smith* decision they have no free exercise right to request an exemption. The complication is that in his *Smith* decision Justice Scalia included a footnote indicating that hybrid rights—two or more rights, say, free exercise and parental rights to control their children's education—may still require the use of the Sherbert Test.

So what's a teacher or administrator to do? If your state has a RFRA requiring the use of the Sherbert Test you must accommodate students' free exercise claims unless there are compelling reasons for not doing so and there is no less burdensome way in which the school's purposes might be accomplished. If you don't live in such a state it is probably still a good idea to use such a test, though the question of hybrid rights remains unhappily murky. I will come back to the problem of excusal rights in later chapters.

There is one other complication I need to address. One result of the Court's weakening of the Free Exercise Clause is that the Free Speech Clause has been increasingly called into service to protect religious speech. (This is not an entirely satisfactory alternative in that much religious exercise is not speech, and may therefore go unprotected by the First Amendment.) In *Lamb's Chapel v. Center Moriches Union Free School District* (1993) and then again in *Good News Club v. Milford Central School* (2001) the Court held that if a public school allows some community groups to use its facilities it cannot discriminate against religious groups. Why? When a public school or university creates what the Court calls *a limited public forum* it must allow all groups equal access to that forum, not discriminating among them based on the content of their speech. A school or university could refuse access to all student groups, or to all community groups, but it cannot allow some and not others to use its facilities.

Perhaps the most important case of this kind was *Rosenberger v. Rector and Visitors of the University of Virginia* (1995) in which the Court held that the University of Virginia could not discriminate against a religious group that had applied for funding from student fees distributed by the student government to support the group's campus magazine. Writing for the Court Justice Anthony Kennedy warned against the viewpoint discrimination inherent in a university policy that "selects for disfavored treatment those student journalistic efforts with religious editorial viewpoints." A danger of such policies, he wrote, is "the chilling of individual thought and expression." This danger is "especially real in the University setting, where the State acts against a background and tradition of thought and experiment that is at the center of our intellectual and philosophic tradition. . . . For the University, by regulation, to cast disapproval on particular viewpoints of its students risks that suppression of free speech and creative inquiry in one of the vital centers for the nation's intellectual life, its college and university campuses."[11]

The majority ruling in *Rosenberger* provoked a vigorous response from the Court's minority, largely on two grounds. First, the religious magazine didn't simply comment on public issues (in which case viewpoint discrimination may have been relevant) but was a vehicle for promoting worship. Second, in using state money (albeit student fees rather than tax funds) to support a religious magazine it violated the Establishment Clause. The majority disagreed.

## Establishment

*Everson v. Board of Education* (1947) is the most important Establishment Clause case for two reasons: first, it was the first case in which the Supreme Court applied that clause to the states; and second, in his ruling Justice Hugo Black defined the clause in ways that have continued to shape the Court's interpretation of it. According to Justice Black, "The 'establishment of religion' clause of the First Amendment means at least this: Neither a state nor the Federal government can set up a church. Neither can pass laws which aid one religion, aid all religions, or prefer one religion over another. Neither can force nor influence a person to go or to remain away from church against his will or force him to profess a belief or disbelief in any religion. . . . No tax in any amount, large or small, can be levied to support any religious activities or institutions, whatever they may be called, or whatever form they may adopt to teach or practice religion. . . . In the words of Jefferson, the clause against establishment of religion by law was intended to erect 'a wall of separation between church and state.'"[12]

The metaphor of a wall of separation suggests that religion and the state should have nothing to do with each other.[13] This is obviously impossible. As Justice Black pointed out, the state rightly provides police and fire protection for religious organizations. Still, the Court has held to a fairly strict separation when it comes to matters of conscience, respecting the integrity of religious organizations and, until recently, the use of taxes for funding religion. (Hence the vigorous dissent regarding the use of state funds for a religious magazine in *Rosenberger*.)

But Justice Black also appealed to a second, quite different idea. The Establishment Clause requires the state *to be neutral* in matters of religion. In fact, two kinds of neutrality are required: the state must be neutral among religions, and cannot "prefer one religion over another"; and it must "be neutral in its relations with groups of religious believers and non-believers."[14] The state cannot promote religion but it cannot be hostile to religion either: "State power is no more to be used so as to handicap religions than it is to favor them."[15]

These two principles—separation and neutrality—have been the Court's touch-stones in addressing Establishment Clause cases, though, inevitably, the Court has developed variations on each.

The Court began to formulate a test for adjudicating Establishment Clause cases in *Abington School District v. Schempp* (1963). Justice Tom Clark, writing for the Court, asked, "What are the purpose and the primary effect of the enactment? If either is the advancement or inhibition of religion then the enactment exceeds the scope of legislative power as circumscribed by the Constitution. That is to say that to withstand the strictures of the Establishment Clause there must be a secular legislative purpose and a primary effect that neither advances nor inhibits religion." The underlying principle is neutrality: echoing Black in *Everson*, Justice Clark wrote that government "must maintain strict neutrality, neither aiding nor opposing religion." Justice Clark's two-prong test was given a third, more separationist prong by Chief Justice Burger in *Lemon v. Kurtzman* (1971): laws must also not foster "an excessive government entanglement with religion."[16] The purpose of the third prong is to prevent the intrusion of government and religion into each other's domains. (The word *excessive* indicates that the separation of the two can never be complete.) With the third prong we get the (in)famous Lemon Test that the Court has used often, but not always, in adjudicating Establishment Clause cases.

Justice Sandra Day O'Connor offered her own endorsement test, initially as an elaboration on the Lemon Test.[17] When government endorses religion it, in effect, distinguishes between insiders and outsiders, making some citizens less than full members of the political community. Like neutrality, endorsement can cut both ways: government may not disfavor religion either, making religious believers outsiders.

There have been a welter of Establishment Clause cases addressing education, and things get messy quickly. I will simplify the story considerably by saying just a little about school prayer and student speech before proceeding to the role of religion in the curriculum.

## School Prayer

No doubt the most controversial religion clause case in the history of the Court was *Engel v. Vitale* (1962), in which the Court ruled unconstitutional a prayer written by the State Board of Regents in New York: "Almighty God, we acknowledge our dependence upon Thee, and we beg Thy blessings upon us, our parents, our teachers and our Country." Schools had the option of opening the school day with this prayer, and the law required that they have an excusal policy allowing students to opt out of praying. Writing again for the Court, Justice Black held that there can be no doubt but that "the Regents' prayer is a religious activity. It is a solemn avowal of divine faith and supplication for the blessings of the Almighty. . . . We think that the constitutional prohibition against laws respecting an establishment of religion must at least mean that in this country it is no part of the business of government to compose official prayers for any group of the American people to recite as a part of a religious program carried on by government."[18]

That the prayer was nonsectarian made no difference for it still promoted religion; it was, in effect, not neutral between religion and nonreligion. The fact that schools had an excusal policy ensuring that students prayed voluntarily made no difference, for the Establishment Clause "is violated by the enactment of laws which establish an official religion whether those laws operate directly to coerce non-observing individuals or not."[19] The Court did not hold that students couldn't pray. It has never held this. It held that government (and agents of the government such as teachers) cannot pray in the course of official school activities.

Justice Black argued at some length that the ruling was not hostile to religion but rather respected religious liberty, and he cited a good deal of historical evidence to support his reading of the purposes behind the Establishment Clause. "It is a matter of history," he wrote, "that this very practice of establishing governmentally composed prayers for religious services was one of the reasons which caused many of our early colonists to leave England and seek religious freedom in America."[20] Indeed, "the history of governmentally established religion showed that whenever government had allied itself with one particular form of religion, the inevitable result had been that it had incurred the hatred, disrespect and even contempt of those who held contrary beliefs. . . . The Establishment Clause thus stands as an expression of principle on the part of the Founders of Our Constitution that religion is too personal, too sacred, too holy, to permit its 'unhallowed perversion' by a civil magistrate."[21] Not everyone was convinced.

The Court has heard two further prayer cases. In *Lee v. Weisman* (1992) the Court struck down a nonsectarian graduation prayer given by a clergyman (in this case, a rabbi). The ruling was something of a surprise, for in 1992 the Court had five conservatives, and many observers thought that it would approve graduation prayer and reject the Lemon Test with its emphasis on neutrality. Justice Kennedy (who has often been a swing vote) and the four conservatives on the Court argued that *coercion* rather than neutrality or endorsement should be the key consideration: it is permissible for the government to promote nonsectarian religion if no one is coerced into supporting it. (Hence, another Establishment Clause test.) But Kennedy broke with them over whether a graduation prayer is coercive. He argued that students were, in effect, coerced into participating in a religious ritual by virtue of attending their graduation ceremony. But, his conservatives colleagues argued, the students were not legally bound to participate in the graduation ceremony. Justice Kennedy responded that there was considerable social pressure on them to attend, and we can hardly expect them to stay away from their own graduations to avoid participating in a religious ceremony. Consequently, Justice Kennedy voted with the four moderates/liberals, though they disagreed about why the prayer was unconstitutional. While the liberal justices also objected to coercion, like Justice Black in *Engel* they argued that any official prayer would be unconstitutional simply because the government cannot conduct a religious exercise; this violates the neutrality required by the Establishment Clause whether anyone is coerced to participate or not.

In its final prayer case, *Santa Fe Independent School District v. Doe* (2000) the Court struck down nonsectarian prayers on the public address system before football games, even though they were given by students as a result of a student vote. The Court held that such prayers were coercive in that some students (the football team, the cheerleaders, and the band) were required to attend games and hence participate in the prayers. The prayers constituted a governmental endorsement of religion. The fact that the prayer was given by a student didn't make it private speech. Writing for the Court Justice John Paul Stevens held that "the delivery of such a message—over the school's public address system, by a speaker representing the study body, under the supervision of school faculty, and pursuant to a school policy that explicitly and implicitly encourages public prayer—is not properly characterized as 'private' speech."[22] The Court noted the school's long history of sectarian prayers at football games and suggested that the school district's mechanism of allowing students to vote on whether or not to pray was a disingenuous effort to get around the law.

So far, then, the Supreme Court has not allowed official school prayers, even if they are nonsectarian, even if there is an excusal policy, and even if they are voted on and given by students, so long as they are part of official school activities. I suspect that even the most conservative members of the Court would rule against explicitly sectarian (Christian) prayers, or prayers that students are legally required to participate in.[23]

Still, the Court has never prohibited *private* student prayers during the school day, if they are not disruptive, and, as I noted in discussing the Free Exercise Clause, the Court has upheld the right of student groups to use school facilities outside official school hours for religious meetings in which they might pray together so long as the school allows other noncurricular groups to use their facilities. The key consideration regarding prayer is whether it is fully private student speech (which is not bound by the Establishment Clause) or governmentally endorsed speech (which is bound, and must be religiously neutral). Of course, this problem arises in areas other than school prayer: should a student be free to express his or her religious views in a classroom discussion or in a written assignment or in a valedictory address? The First Amendment should protect their right to such expression, though at some point such speech may lose its protection if the student proselytizes or is disruptive, or if the setting conveys official school (hence governmental) endorsement. There is no easy way to address difficult cases, though the principle at issue is relatively clear. Teachers and administrators, as agents of the state, do not have a right to religious speech (in the role as teachers and administrators as opposed to in their private lives); their speech must be religiously neutral.

## First Amendment Politics

At the risk of oversimplifying a very complicated situation, I suggest that conservative justices tend to favor a weak reading of both the Free Exercise and Establishment clauses, while liberals tend to favor strong readings. That is, conservative justices have been less concerned about the dangers of establishment and less concerned to protect free exercise rights, particularly of religious minorities. Liberals, by contrast, have been opposed to any possibility of a religious establishment and they have been relatively more concerned to protect the free exercise rights of minorities.

There are several reasons for this. First, judicial liberals (like political liberals) have historically been concerned with liberties and rights, while conservatives have more often found virtue to lie in tradition, political order, and majorities. Hence Justice Scalia's advice to Native Americans who wished to use peyote in their religious ceremonies: find the votes to change the law. On Establishment Clause issues, conservatives have been much more willing than liberals to accommodate the interests of the majority—to allow government-sponsored prayers, for example.

There is a related reason. In a 1976 speech Chief Justice William Rehnquist argued that the Court does not have "a roving commission to second-guess Congress, state legislatures and state and federal administrative officers concerning what is best for the country"—as judicial liberals are sometimes wont to do. This is the traditional conservative complaint against activist judges and judge-made law. The problem with this argument is that over the last several decades, conservative justices have second-guessed Congress considerably more often than have liberals. The more important difference may be, as John Witte has pointed out, conservative support for federalism, for shielding state laws from federal regulation.[24]

Of course, most *religious* conservatives were not happy about the direction the Court's *judicial* conservatives took the Free Exercise Clause in *Smith* (the peyote case). As I mentioned, virtually all religious groups, right to left, were unhappy with *Smith*. Historically, religious conservatives have often favored a strong reading of the Free Exercise Clause (not least when they found themselves to be in the minority) and at least sometimes of the Establishment Clause as well. As I argued above, evangelicals (especially Baptists) were strongly opposed to religious establishments in the colonies, and maintained this opposition until the 1970s. Even then, most conservative Baptist leaders supported the Court's rulings on school prayer and funding for religious schools (and even, for a short time, abortion rights). The rise of the Religious Right at the end of the 1970s marked a sea change in Southern Baptist and evangelical positions on establishment.

Religious and judicial conservatives now typically agree that the Founders did not intend to build Jefferson's wall of separation between church and state (articulated in his letter to the grateful Danbury Baptists). They rightly point out that the First Congress—the one that wrote and passed the religion clauses of the First Amendment—authorized paid congressional chaplains and official days of prayer and thanksgiving. Surely, they argue, the Founders intended to accommodate religion. According to what has come to be called *accommodationism* the Establishment Clause was intended to prohibit the establishment of a state church or a particular religion but the state may legitimately promote religion nonpreferentially and noncoercively. So, for example, Chief Justice Rehnquist argued (in dissent) in *Wallace v. Jaffree* that the Establishment Clause "forbade establishment of a national religion, and forbade preference among religious sects or denominations . . . [but it] did not require government neutrality between religion and irreligion nor did it prohibit the federal government from providing non-discriminatory aid to religion."[25] In *McCreary County, Kentucky v. ACLU of Kentucky* (2005) Justice Scalia went further (in dissent) by arguing that the Establishment Clause allows government to support monotheism (Christianity, Judaism, and Islam) nonpreferentially. It is important to note that the argument of some religious conservatives that the United States is constitutionally a Christian nation finds no support among even the most conservative members of the Court.

My own view is that it is not at all clear what the Founding Fathers intended. In fact, it isn't obvious whose intentions count: members of the conference committee that wrote the religion clauses, members of the Congress that passed them, or members of the state ratifying conventions that adopted them? Of course, we don't know what the great majority of any of them intended. In any case, surely they didn't all agree. We know that Madison, the most influential of them (in chairing the conference committee) was not an accommodationist; nor was Jefferson (though he wasn't involved in these proceedings). Moreover, in the late eighteenth century a variety of somewhat different, if overlapping, notions were much in the air: religious liberty, freedom of conscience, free exercise, religious pluralism, religious equality, separation of church and state, and disestablishment.[26] No doubt people had somewhat different ideas of what these various terms meant, and the Founding Fathers most likely had different ideas of what they were writing into the First Amendment. Surely we shouldn't expect them to act consistently or see the implications of their principles clearly. Garry Wills has written that no "other government in history had launched itself without the help of officially recognized gods and their state-connected ministers. It is no wonder that, in so novel an undertaking, it should have taken a while to sift the dangers and the blessings of the new arrangement, to learn how best to live with it, to complete the logic of its working."[27] We also know that in 1797, the Senate (which included many members of the First Congress) ratified a treaty with the Muslim nation of Tripoli according to which "the government of the United States of America is not in any sense founded on the Christian religion."[28]

If we forget intentions and simply look at the text it is important to note that it doesn't read that Congress shall make no law respecting the establishment of a religion or a national church. The meaning would seem to be that religion generally is to be disestablished. In any case, many scholars (and Supreme Court justices) do not believe original intent is the proper criterion for determining what the Constitution means. In ruling "separate but equal" schools unconstitutional in 1954 the Supreme Court concluded that it could not turn the clock back to 1868 in deciding the meaning of the Fourteenth Amendment. In requiring equal protection of the laws, the authors of the Fourteenth Amendment clearly did not intend to eliminate segregated schools. Yet surely that is what equal protection of the law requires; we may recognize the moral implications of basic principles to which they were blind.[29] And so it may be with religious liberty. In our much more pluralistic culture it has become clear that disestablishment requires not just neutrality among religions or among monotheisms but neutrality between religion and nonreligion.

In any case, the Framers' original intent can hardly be binding when the Court has applied the First Amendment to the states by way of the Fourteenth. Certainly it was not the intent of the framers of either amendment that the First Amendment should be binding on the states. Our constitutional history is a living, developing tradition. In *Federalist Number 14* Madison wrote: "Is it not the glory of the people of America, that whilst they have paid a decent regard to the opinions of former times and other nations, they have not suffered a blind veneration for antiquity, for custom, or for names, to overrule the suggestions of their own good sense, the knowledge of their own situation, and the lesson of their own experience?"[30]

I don't claim to have settled anything. The arguments are much more complex than I've suggested, and the evidence is mixed. But however one sorts out the Framers' original intent, and however one interprets the text of the Constitution, we are bound by how the Supreme Court interprets the Constitution now. It is (finally) time to discuss the implications of the Court's current position for understanding the role of religion in the classroom and the curriculum.

## The Constitutional Argument for Teaching about Religion

The most important case by far in addressing the role of religion in the classroom and curriculum is *Abington School District v. Schempp* in which the Court distinguished between *devotional* Bible reading, which is unconstitutional, and the *academic study* of the Bible and religion—or, to use the Court's language, *teaching about religion*—which is constitutional. Writing for the Court, Justice Clark noted that "it might well be said that one's education is not complete without a study of comparative religion or the history of religion and its relationship to the advancement of civilization. It certainly may be said that the Bible is worthy of study for its literary and historic qualities. Nothing we have said here indicates that such study of the Bible or of religion, when presented objectively as part of a secular program of education, may not be effected consistently with the First Amendment."[31] In a concurring opinion Justice Brennan, the strictest separationist on the Court in recent times, wrote, "The holding of the Court today plainly does not foreclose teaching *about* the Holy Scriptures or about the differences between religious sects in classes in literature or history. Indeed, whether or not the Bible is involved, it would be impossible to teach meaningfully many subjects in the social sciences or the humanities without some mention of religion."[32] In another concurring opinion, Justice Arthur Goldberg added that it was clear that the Court recognizes "the propriety of . . . teaching *about* religion, as distinguished from the teaching *of* religion, in the public schools."[33] No member of the Court has ever dissented from this position.

The key consideration for each justice was neutrality. For Justice Clark, the Establishment Clause requires that "the Government maintain strict neutrality, neither aiding nor opposing religion."[34] For Justice Brennan the "State must be steadfastly neutral in all matters of faith, and neither favor nor inhibit religion."[35] For Justice Goldberg the "fullest realization of true religion liberty requires that government . . . effect no favoritism among sects or between religion and nonreligion." In essence, "the attitude of government toward religion must be one of neutrality."[36]

The Court did not draw out the implications for schools and universities (though it did go on to address the role of religion in regard to evolution in two later cases that I will discuss in chapter 11) and it offered us no further advice. Indeed, Justice Brennan wrote: "To what extent, and at what points in the curriculum religious materials should be cited, are matters which the courts ought to entrust very largely to the experienced officials who superintend our Nation's public schools. They are experts in such matters, and we are not."[37] (He might better have said that they *should* be the experts.)

Writing before *Schempp,* one member of the Court did suggest a fairly ambitious agenda for schools. In *McCollum v. Board of Education* (1948) Justice Robert Jackson wrote: "Music without sacred music, architecture minus the cathedral, or painting without the scriptural themes would be eccentric and incomplete, even from a secular point of view. . . . Even such a 'science' as biology raises the issue between evolution and creation as an explanation of our presence on this planet. Certainly a course in English literature that omitted the Bible and other powerful uses of our mother tongue for religious ends would be pretty barren. And I should suppose it is a proper, if not an indispensable, part of preparation for a worldly life to know the rules that religion and religions have played in the tragic story of mankind. The fact is that, for good or for ill, nearly everything in our culture worth transmitting, everything which gives meaning to life, is saturated with religious influences, derived from paganism, Judaism, Christianity—both Catholic and Protestant—and other faiths accepted by a large part of the world's peoples. One can hardly respect a system of education that would leave the student wholly ignorant of the currents of religious thought."[38] Education without religion would indeed be barren.

In fact, all commentators have taken *Schempp* to give public schools and universities permission to teach about religion—when done objectively or neutrally. (Perhaps I should say here that the Court has never explicitly addressed the role of religion in universities, the assumption being that the same rules apply.) There is nothing in *Schempp* (or any other Supreme Court ruling) that undercuts any of my arguments for taking religion seriously. All of my arguments for taking religion seriously in chapters 5 and 6 are entirely secular arguments. They all have a secular purpose. They neither endorse nor promote a particular religion or religion generally; they merely treat religion(s) neutrally along with secular ways of making sense of the world. This isn't to say that lines can't be crossed. Considerable sensitivity is surely required in assessing whether religious (or secular) beliefs or values are implicitly promoted or endorsed, and I will deal with a number of hard cases in chapters to come.

But constitutional neutrality doesn't just allow schools and universities to take religion seriously, it requires it. As I argued in chapter 4, public education is not religiously neutral (that is, neutral between religion and nonreligion) and, as Justice Black made clear in *Everson,* and as the Court has affirmed ever since, neutrality does not allow the state to oppose, denigrate, inhibit, or show hostility to religion. In *Schempp* Justice Clark wrote "that the State may not establish a 'religion of secularism' in the sense of affirmatively opposing or showing hostility to religion, thus 'preferring those who believe in no religion over those who do believe.'"[39] It is true that the state doesn't explicitly or avowedly prefer those who do not believe or those who do believe, but to require this would be to have an extraordinarily naive understanding of what's at issue. As Justice Goldberg warned in his concurring opinion, an "*untutored* devotion to the conception of neutrality" can lead to a "pervasive devotion to the secular and a passive, or even active, hostility to the religious."[40] There need be no smoking gun, no avowed hostility to religion, but if I am right in chapter 4, education *is implicitly* hostile to religion.

Justice Goldberg went on to argue, "Neither government nor this Court can or should ignore the significance of the fact that a vast portion of our people believe in and worship God and that many of our legal, political and personal values derive historically from religious teachings. Government must inevitably take cognizance of the existence of religion and, indeed, under certain circumstances the First Amendment may require that it do so. And it seems clear to me from the opinions in the present and past cases that the Court would recognize the propriety of providing military chaplains and of the teaching about religion, as distinguished from the teaching of religion, in the public schools."[41]

The distinguished legal scholar Douglas Laycock has argued that to protect religious liberty—the purpose of the religion clauses of the First Amendment—government should intrude as little as possible into people's religious beliefs and behavior. Government should leave things as they are. Sometimes this can be accomplished through laws and policies that are formally neutral—that is, that avoid religious classifications. Arguably, school and university curricula are formally neutral; they are neither designed nor defined in explicitly religious or antireligious categories. But, Laycock argues, the First Amendment also requires a *substantive neutrality* that hinges on judgments "about the relative significance of various encouragements and discouragements to religion."[42] If a law or policy discourages religious belief or practice, some compensatory acknowledgment of religion may be necessary, perhaps by exempting religious behavior from burdensome (if formally neutral) laws or by addressing religion, as in public school curricula. Hence, public schools (and, presumably, universities) "must teach about the role of religion in history and in contemporary society. It must teach about society's moral expectations, and it cannot do that honestly without noting that for many citizens, morality has a religious base. In such situations, government must be scrupulously even handed, treating the range of religious and nonreligious views as neutrally as possible."[43]

Currently, public schools and universities unrelentingly encourage students to think about the world and the subjects of the curriculum in exclusively secular ways, even though many of them are deeply controversial. This has the effect (religious people would say the primary effect) of advancing secular over religious ways of making sense of the world. Many religious parents believe that schools convey the message that they are outsiders by at least implicitly endorsing secular over religious alternatives. Arguably, this constitutes viewpoint discrimination. Most fundamentally, as the Court currently interprets it, the Establishment Clause requires neutrality between religion and nonreligion. Schools and universities are not free to take sides, even if unintentionally and only implicitly, in matters of religion. And if I am right in chapter 4, schools and universities are not neutral.

Let me be clear. Some critics argue that the idea of religious neutrality makes no sense. All education, all courses, all texts, they argue, assume a starting point within a historical, cultural, and philosophical context of beliefs and values—within a discipline or set of disciplines. It is true that if neutrality meant stepping outside all such contexts to a pristine neutral point of view it would be an incoherent notion. But this is not how I have defined neutrality. The core idea of neutrality is that of fairness to the major live alternatives when there are religious controversies—and then, not taking sides. I am willing to grant that fairness and neutrality can only be approximated. But greater rather than lesser fairness and neutrality remain important ideals in spite of this limitation.[44]

Perhaps ironically, if a conservative Supreme Court were to overturn the principle of neutrality between religion and nonreligion, it would abolish the constitutional case for taking religion seriously (while still *allowing* it, if only at the discretion of educators and voters).

## Conclusions

Whether or not one thinks that the Supreme Court has gone astray in interpreting the First Amendment, schools and universities are still bound by its rulings. Public schools and universities must be religiously neutral. They must be neutral among religions, and neutral between religion and nonreligion. They cannot privilege a particular religion (such as Christianity) or religion generally. Nor can they discriminate against religion. Here, of course, is the rub. As I argued in part 1, schools and universities do discriminate against religion; they are not neutral between religion and nonreligion. Hence, schools and universities are constitutionally obligated to set things right by including religion in the curricular conversation, by taking it seriously.

I might say that I do not believe that courts should attempt to manage (much less micromanage) the curriculum or classroom—though they may need to address egregious injustices. As Justice Brennan said, educators are the experts in these matters, not court justices. (Or, as I said, educators *should* be the experts.) Unfortunately, school and university administrators appear to be totally oblivious to any such responsibility.[45]

In part 3, I will spell out how schools and universities should take religion seriously, but first we must discuss a number of complications, clarifications, concerns about, and objections to the arguments I have made over the last three chapters.

# 8

# Complications, Concerns, and Clarifications

I have two tasks in this chapter. The first is to acknowledge a complication. I need to say something about academic freedom and resolve a potential tension between the positions I've taken in chapters 5 and 6 on the one hand, and chapter 7 on the other. The question is whether teachers have the right to take sides in matters of religion. The First Amendment would seem to forbid this, yet the logic of liberal education might seem to require it (at least sometimes), and academic freedom would seem to protect it (at least sometimes).

Second, I suspect that most readers will have at least a few concerns about the arguments of the last three chapters, and maybe many. I will consider what in my experience are some of the most common concerns loosely clumped together under a number of headings: the concerns of religious conservatives, the concerns of religious liberals, the concerns of atheists, and, finally, practical concerns (often coming from teachers and administrators).

## Academic Freedom

I have argued that a liberal education should take religion seriously by including religious voices in the curricular conversation, discussing them comparatively and critically as live options. In fact, all of my arguments in chapters 5 and 6 were arguments for some measure of fairness or inclusivity, not neutrality. And yet, the Establishment Clause, as I argued in chapter 7, requires neutrality.

It is true that religions can be discussed critically without taking sides, stopping short of conclusions. In this context critical and comparative study explores the relationships among various religious and secular ways of making sense of subjects and the world, considering tensions and conflicts from various points of view, but no judgment need be made about where the truth lies, or about what is most reasonable to believe.

And yet, a major purpose of a liberal education is to initiate students into a critical search for the truth, for what is most reasonable. No doubt most teachers believe that students (at least mature students) must learn to think for themselves, albeit thoughtfully and responsibly. Teachers aren't simply to dictate what students should believe. Yet teachers can't simply present even mature students with an array of options (about what to believe and how to live) and let them sort everything out for themselves. It would appear to be a general principle of education that teachers should guide their students, helping them to understand that some beliefs or theories, some intellectual or cultural traditions, are more likely to be true or more reasonable than others—and why. Because of their professional competence teachers are in a position to guide students who are less competent, less educated, less mature. (Mary Warnock once suggested that the image of teachers refusing to take sides in the battle of ideas is like "the nightmare of knitters at the guillotine."[1]) Teachers must sometimes, perhaps even often, take sides. In fact, this is a principle that teachers act on virtually every day. Of course, if it is the responsibility of teachers to guide their students, then surely they must have the freedom, the right, to do so.

The right to follow reason and the evidence wherever they lead has been institutionalized for university professors in the doctrine of academic freedom. (I will address public school teachers shortly.) Well into the nineteenth century the accepted ideal was that teachers, even in colleges, were simply to pass on the accumulated truths of tradition, not to challenge them or think for themselves, much less encourage students to think for themselves. With the rise of research universities, first in Germany, and then in the United States, in the second half of the nineteenth century, this changed dramatically. It became widely accepted that scholars must be free to research, to challenge old "truths," to discover new truths. For this they required academic freedom, not only in their scholarly research but in the classroom as well.

The American Association of University Professors (AAUP) first defined academic freedom in its 1915 *Declaration of Principles*. In all domains of knowledge, the *Declaration* asserts, "The first condition of progress is complete and unlimited freedom to pursue inquiry and publish its results."[2] Hence, the need for tenure and due process in hiring and firing, to protect scholars from the pressures and power of public opinion, trustees, legislators, donors, and administrators.

The *Declaration* goes on to say that "it is scarcely open to question that freedom of utterance is as important to the teacher as it is to the investigator." Indeed, the confidence of one's students "will be impaired if there is suspicion on the part of the student that the teacher is not expressing himself fully or frankly, or that college and university teachers in general are a repressed and intimidated class."[3] Teachers must also have freedom to pursue the truth in the classroom.

The *Declaration* singled out scholars who work in philosophy and religion—the domains of "ultimate realities and values"—as particularly in need of the protections of academic freedom, for in interpreting "the general meaning and ends of human existence and its relation to the universe, we are still far from a comprehension of the final truths, and from a universal agreement among all sincere and earnest men."[4] No doubt the authors of the *Declaration* were especially concerned, at the beginning of the twentieth century, to protect science and secular scholarship from religious dogmatism (and religious trustees). But if academic freedom protects the right of scholars to be critical of a particular religion or religion generally, shouldn't it also protect the right of scholars to be supportive of religion?

If university teachers are free to pursue the truth wherever it leads, does this mean that they are free to teach only their own point of view? The *Declaration* notes that in dealing with controversial matters the university teacher is "under no obligation to hide his own opinion under a mountain of equivocal verbiage." But he should also "set forth justly, without suppression or innuendo, the divergent opinions of other investigators; he should cause his students to become familiar with the best published expressions of the great historic types of doctrine upon the questions at issue." The goal is to enable students "to think for themselves, and to provide them access to those materials which they need if they are to think intelligently."[5] That is, academic freedom doesn't trump the responsibility to consider alternative points of view. Moreover, according to the AAUP's 1985 *Observations on Ideology,* where "ways of finding out and assessing the truth are precisely what is under debate, good teaching requires exposing students to all major alternatives. A department ought to try to insure that different currently debated and important approaches to its subject are presented to its students fairly and objectively, so that students are able to make informed choices among them."[6]

As we shall see shortly, this isn't without its problems. For now, however, the point is that academic freedom gives teachers the right to take sides, even in dealing with "ultimate realities and values," but this doesn't give them the right to exclude views other than their own. In fact, they have an obligation in their courses to present students with the major alternatives.

## The First Amendment

The U.S. Supreme Court only began to address academic freedom in the 1950s, largely as a consequence of legislative efforts to exclude communists from universities. (Of course, the First Amendment applies only to public universities.) Perhaps the most important case is *Keyishian v. Board of Regents* (1967), in which the Court anchored academic freedom in the First Amendment. Writing for the Court, Justice William Brennan held that "our nation is deeply committed to safeguarding academic freedom, which is of transcendent value to all of us and not merely to the teachers concerned. That freedom is therefore a special concern of the First Amendment, which does not tolerate laws that cast a pall of orthodoxy over the classroom."[7]

Unfortunately, the Court's occasional rhetoric on academic freedom has produced little in the way of results. Georgetown law professor J. Peter Byrne has expressed his distress over "the alarming tendency in the federal courts over the past decade to discount the significance of the academic enterprise. The distinctive needs and values of the intellectual life of a university have sunk from judicial view, as legal doctrines fashioned for the streets and the market are applied to the classroom."[8] Worse, some lower courts have not taken seriously the Supreme Court's few efforts to ground academic freedom in the First Amendment.

Perhaps even more troublesome for our purposes, the Supreme Court has never ruled on whether academic freedom carves out an exemption from Establishment Clause neutrality.[9] Though the situation is difficult, my own inclination is to argue that because college and university faculty have academic freedom they cannot be considered as agents of the state—they do not speak for the state—and therefore they are not bound by the Establishment Clause (which applies only to government and its agents). This means that the Establishment Clause should not apply to university faculty in aspects of their job involving academic freedom, such as the expression of their views in the classroom.

If this weren't the case the Establishment Clause would, in fact, cast a pall of orthodoxy over the university. It would be a striking limitation of academic freedom if teachers did not have the freedom to argue about and take positions on some of the most important questions in our intellectual life. This would mean that a Freudian psychologist could not argue that religion is a neurosis grounded in unconscious wish fulfillment, that a biologist could not claim that evolution disproves creationism, and that a philosopher couldn't agree with

Nietzsche in his critique of Christianity. (Or could they just defend aspects of Freud, Darwin, and Nietzsche, without discussing the religious implications, a kind of academic *don't ask, don't tell* policy?) Of course, if they can take positions hostile to some or all religion then surely they can argue for religious positions as well. We should keep in mind that no one questions the right of scholars to publish whatever they believe regarding religion. Why should academic freedom be more limited in the classroom? But, I have to add, the Court hasn't said this (or denied it).

## Limitations on Academic Freedom

Professors cannot gratuitously introduce discussion of religion (or politics) into their courses if they have no relevance to their subjects. According to the AAUP's "1940 Statement of Principles on Academic Freedom and Tenure," "Teachers are entitled to freedom in the classroom in discussing their subject, but they should be careful not to introduce into their teaching controversial matter which has no relation to their subject."[10]

Why? One reason is that academic freedom protects only competent speech. Academic freedom is not the same thing as free speech, which can, of course, be spectacularly stupid and incompetent. According to the *Declaration of Principles,* "The liberty of the scholar within the university to set forth his conclusions, be they what they may, is conditioned by their being conclusions gained by a scholar's method and held in a scholar's spirit."[11] So, for example, a historian who taught students that the Holocaust didn't happen would surely be incompetent—and could be fired for such incompetence.

And who determines competence? The AAUP's consistent answer: one's disciplinary colleagues. It is they (not trustees, not legislators) who understand "a scholar's methods." As Mark Edwards has recently put it, a scholar "enjoys academic freedom vis-à-vis outside interests only if one is a member of the disciplinary profession, and the price of that membership is reasonable fidelity to the goods and standards of the profession."[12]

This "price of membership" is not insignificant for our purposes. According to Edwards, this limitation means that disciplinary orthodoxies may prohibit taking religious positions or making religious arguments, for to do so would be to exceed one's competence as it is defined in most disciplines. He suggests, for example, that modern scientific method would not allow a biologist who argued for creationism to claim competence as a biologist and hence the protection of academic freedom (any more than the historian could deny the Holocaust and claim the protection of academic freedom). I suspect that Edwards is correct about this, though there are disciplinary exceptions. As I argued above, while many philosophers would disagree with a colleague who argued philosophically for the existence of God in his or her classes, they wouldn't (necessarily) call into question her competence as a philosopher.

Or consider the 2007 statement on academic freedom of the American Academy of Religion (AAR), the organization of professors of religious studies, which welcomes "all disciplined reflection on religion—both from *within* and outside of communities of belief and practice." The statement notes that "teaching about religion, in any educational context, essentially involves critical inquiry: questioning of assumptions, some of them long taken for granted; attending to multiple points of view, some of them disturbing; and engaging with the methods and findings of other scholars, some of whom are themselves religious, whereas others are not." Of course, the scholar's work can only be judged in terms of "shared scholarly norms, as understood by qualified peers. This is the core of academic freedom."[13]

In spite of these possible exceptions, there is a potential asymmetry that is worrisome. From within many disciplinary methodologies teachers cannot competently make religious claims, but they may, arguably, make claims that are hostile to, or that undercut, religious claims (as Freudian psychologists, Darwinian biologists, and analytic philosophers, often do). This is because many disciplines are committed to some form of methodological naturalism (which rules out any discussion of teleology or supernatural claims); as a result, they can only consider evidence and arguments that tends to cut against religion.

Should academic freedom give teachers, whatever their disciplines, the right to challenge such disciplinary orthodoxies in the classroom? Clearly, to be hired and given tenure scholars must fully understand and engage the orthodoxies of their respective disciplines. But that said, I am inclined to think that, having demonstrated their competence, teachers should be given rather wide latitude to challenge these orthodoxies. This is an implication of the commitment to critical reasoning—to being reasonable, not just rational within a discipline—that underlies liberal education and makes room for criticizing the foundational assumptions of the academic disciplines. The American Federation of Teachers' statement on academic freedom suggests something like this: tenure "not only protects faculty members from unwarranted interference in their professional work by 'outsiders,' it also ensures that faculty members cannot be sanctioned by their own colleagues for challenging conventional academic wisdom or utilizing unorthodox methods."[14] There is no clear place to draw lines, but this approach implies that the scholarly community as a whole, not one's disciplinary peers, should have the last word in determining competence.

There is another problem. As we've seen, teachers have the responsibility to expose students to divergent opinions and the major alternatives. But who defines the range of divergent opinions or major alternatives? The usual answer, unsurprisingly, is that each discipline does so for courses within its domain. But if each discipline limits discussion to the plausible alternatives within that discipline, then students are highly unlikely to hear religious voices or the voices of scholars who take religion seriously. Perhaps at this point we shouldn't be surprised that, once again, the greatest threat to taking religion seriously comes from the secular orthodoxies of the academic disciplines.[15]

It is this kind of worry with regard to politics that prompted a movement for a legally enforceable *academic bill of rights* that ensures that students be exposed to a diversity of political points of view. The problem with this (whether politics or religion is at issue) is that it makes the courts responsible for adjudicating very tricky questions of academic competence, diversity, and balance. While I'm not happy about the status quo, I suspect that courts have wisely deferred to universities in matter of internal governance—this is sometimes called institutional academic freedom[16]—regarding who gets to teach and what is taught. In this case the remedy might well prove worse than the illness.

I do believe that the Establishment Clause requires the *university* to be religiously neutral even if individual teachers need not be. Surely public universities cannot take official positions on religion; surely they cannot convert departments of religious studies into divinity schools. It is also surely the case that if they are to be neutral between religion and nonreligion universities have an obligation to take religion seriously. This requirement does not constrain the academic freedom of any faculty member (who is free to argue for, or against, any religious claims—or remain neutral). As I trust is clear, taking religion seriously is not a matter of advocating religion. But the faculty as a whole is not free—it is collectively not free—to ignore religion in the curriculum; the curriculum must be structured to take religion seriously (requiring, as I will argue in chapter 9, courses in religious studies).

Where does this leave us? Academic freedom is critical to the purposes of the university, and if teachers are to have genuine academic freedom they must be free to follow reason where it leads whether it be for or against religion. Neither the courts nor deans nor trustees can tell them what to say about religion or any relevant issue on which they are competent to teach. This means that they are under no obligation to be religiously neutral—though, as we shall see in the next chapter, there are often powerful pedagogical reasons for being neutral.

Perhaps I should also mention that academic freedom does not give teachers the right to require students to agree with them—though clearly they can require students to understand their positions. Nor does it void the obligation, grounded in liberal education and critical thinking, to expose students to a wide variety of points of view. Nor does it undercut the constitutional obligation, grounded in the Court's interpretation of the Establishment Clause, to take religion seriously as a matter of neutrality between religion and nonreligion.

## Public School Teachers

Because they aren't typically scholars by profession (possessing research degrees), public school teachers do not have the robust academic freedom that was created to protect university faculty members, although the Supreme Court has, on occasion, defended a limited freedom for schoolteachers. "It can hardly be argued," Justice Abe Fortas wrote for the Court in *Tinker v. Des Moines Independent Community School District* (1969) that "either students or teachers shed their constitutional rights to freedom of speech or expression at the schoolhouse gate."[17] In *Board of Education v. Pico* (1982) Justice Brennan held that the discretion of school boards "must be exercised in a manner that comports with the transcendent imperatives of the First Amendment," and he quoted from *Griswold v. Connecticut* (1965): "'the State may not, consistently with the spirit of the First Amendment, contract the spectrum of available knowledge.'"[18] Within this tradition, as Tyll Van Geel put it in his study of school law, the school board "retains its authority to control the basic curriculum, but at the same time the teacher is permitted, within limits, to bring to the students' attention alternative viewpoints and perspectives. This approach prohibits the board from simply requiring the teacher to read from a board-prepared script."[19]

For many scholars *Hazelwood School District v. Kuhlmeier* (1988) was a watershed case in which the Court began to tack sharply to the Right. In his majority opinion Justice Byron White explained, "School officials may impose reasonable restrictions on the speech of students, teachers, and other members of the school community" so long as their actions "are reasonably related to legitimate pedagogical concerns."[20] This ruling, Stephen Patrina has argued, "removed the legal framework for defending teachers' academic freedom in the United States." Indeed, from "this default position, the Supreme Court has since refused to hear K–12 academic freedom cases."[21] Hence, over the last two decades lower courts have often rejected claims to academic freedom, granting extensive rights for local school boards to limit the academic freedom of teachers.[22]

Even on a more expansive account of academic freedom, however, it cannot be doubted that unlike university teachers, K–12 teachers can make no claim grounded in academic freedom for taking sides in matters of religion. They are hired to teach an official, governmentally approved curriculum that must be religiously neutral; they are agents of the state and, as such, must remain religiously neutral.

Should teachers have the right to enlarge the conversation to include voices that are not part of the official curriculum? Should they be able to include (otherwise excluded) religious voices? Surely this can be done without violating neutrality. Such efforts cannot be gratuitous (but must be germane to the topic), the teacher must be competent to do so, and such occasions cannot be used to privilege a particular religion or proselytize. Of course, even if teachers can enlarge the curricular conversation, they do not have the right to disregard the official curriculum or to teach as true whatever they choose—and I must acknowledge that lower courts have not looked kindly on introducing religious ideas in science courses.[23] No doubt administrators might well argue that they have a "legitimate pedagogical concern" in forestalling controversy. Still, if my argument in chapter 7 is correct, neutrality between religion and nonreligion actually requires that religious voices be included in the conversation where they are relevant.

Can a teacher ever say what he or she believes regarding religion? The *Teacher's Guide to Religion in Public Schools* (a common-ground document) says that if asked what he or she believes, a teacher "may choose to answer the question straightforwardly and succinctly in the interest of an open and honest classroom environment."[24] There is a difference between *official* and *personal* speech. As a teacher one must remain officially neutral, but it may be possible to step outside that role and speak personally, as least with more mature students. (Courts have placed a great emphasis on maturity, fearing that immature students are more likely to confuse a teacher's personal views with the official position of the school and the state.) Indeed, there may be good pedagogical reasons for speaking personally from time to time. It may well be that in doing so teachers convey the valuable lesson, as Charles Haynes points out, "that people with deep convictions are able to teach and learn about the convictions of others in ways that are fair and balanced."[25] But teachers must be officially neutral.

I suspect that the traditional distinction between public school and university teachers is typically drawn too starkly. Arguably, some spectrum of possibilities should be marked out distinguishing elementary school, middle school, high school, and college teachers (not all of whom are scholars). Surely high school teachers, for example, are not just pedagogical technicians, hired to teach the state's curriculum. The demands of a liberal education require them to be at home in the world of ideas, and as they acquire graduate degrees (in their teaching fields, not in education) they also acquire greater competence to make informed judgments about the importance and relevance of ideas and perspectives that might reasonably be included in the official curriculum. Until that Day of Enlightenment dawns, however, teachers cannot rely on academic freedom to justify their efforts to take religion seriously.

In chapter 5 I considered two objections, often made by scholars, to my proposal for taking religion seriously: first, the claim that if we take religion seriously then we also have to take seriously astrology, fascism, and other discredited ways of making sense of the world; and second, that because religion has itself been intellectually discredited it need not be taken seriously. Neither objection, I argued, holds water. Now I want to discuss a number of potential objections to my position from religious conservatives, religious liberals, atheists, members of minority religious traditions, and school administrators.

## The Concerns of Religious Conservatives

Religious conservatives resisted the liberalizing and secularizing tendencies of public education from the beginning. Much of their criticism has addressed noncurricular issues—particularly school prayer. Conservative religious criticism of the curriculum has often been scattershot, directed at a variety of targets of the moment—evolution, values clarification, sex education, stories in literature anthologies, and the role of religion in history textbooks—though evolution has had remarkable staying power. There is a more systematic critique of public education, however, that has often been framed in terms of secular humanism—a pervasive ideology religious conservatives find underlying public schooling. Whatever we think of secular humanism (I'm not going to get into it here), religious conservatives are largely right that there is a deep conflict between their religious traditions and what their children are taught in public schools and universities, and I expect that many of them will be sympathetic to my analysis of the problem.

Some religious conservatives will not, however. They will reject the idea of liberal education, critical thinking, and constitutional neutrality if this requires, as it does, that a variety of religious as well as secular ways of making sense of the world be taken seriously. But religious conservatives don't always agree. Some—perhaps many, perhaps even most—will find my solution to the problem acceptable so long as *their* religion is taken seriously, so long as *they* have a place at the table.

## Parental Rights

Many religious conservatives argue that parents have the right and the responsibility to teach their children religion—and that public schools and universities must respect this right, leaving religion to them.

It is true that parents have the constitutional right to bring up their children within a religion or, so far as that goes, no religion. Moreover, it is clear that schools and universities do not have the right (as a matter of constitutional law or of the principles of liberal education) to teach religion in the sense of proselytizing or indoctrinating children. Rather, it is the right and responsibility of schools and universities *to educate* students about various religions. This is a quite different right and responsibility. Of course, some parents believe that their task is made more difficult by such education. Be that as it may, we must be clear that the rights and responsibilities of parents on the one hand, and of schools and universities on the other, are quite different—and are (for most people, at least) complementary rather than antagonistic.

It is important that schools be sensitive to maturity in dealing with religion, however. Elementary schools can certainly begin to develop a relatively uncontroversial religious literacy (regarding history, symbols, and holidays, for example) among students. A deeper religious understanding—one that get students to think themselves inside various religious traditions—requires greater maturity, and engaging religion in a critical, comparative conversation requires yet greater maturity and is perhaps best deferred until high school and college. Parents would rightly object to schools that pushed children into attempts to understand and critically address religion at too young an age.

## Neutrality

Many religious conservatives believe that religious neutrality is the wrong educational ideal in addressing religion. Some believe that we should vote on how to handle religion in schools. We are a democracy, after all. (Of course, the results of any such election would be somewhat different depending on whether they were tabulated by local community, by the state, or by the nation.) We are not a pure democracy, however, but a constitutional democracy that grants rights to its citizens—those rights enumerated in the Bill of Rights that, as the Supreme Court has interpreted them, require religious neutrality of public education. Needless to say, many of the Court's critics believe that the Court has misinterpreted the Establishment Clause. Some believe that the United States is a Christian nation. While this may be true demographically, it is not true constitutionally: no member of the Supreme Court, not even the most conservative, accepts this view. It is possible that some day a conservative Court may overturn the long-standing requirement that government be neutral between religion and nonreligion, but it is less likely that it will drop the requirement that government and schools be neutral among religions, allowing Christianity to be privileged. In any case, until the Court changes its collective mind, schools and universities are legally obligated to be religiously neutral.

## Implicit Relativism

There is a danger to which religious conservatives are particularly sensitive, that students are likely to confuse neutrality with relativism. They may find it all too easy to slide thoughtlessly from a neutral survey of different points of view to the claim that none are any better (more true, more reasonable) than the others. No doubt efforts to be neutral sometimes go awry for lack of sophistication. About complicated and controversial matters teachers may often say "There is no right answer." If this means that for the purpose of the course there is no right answer, fine; if it means there *is* no right answer, then we have relativism—and students must understand the difference. Or, to take another example, Charles Haynes has pointed out that "in an attempt to sound 'tolerant' or 'neutral,' people speak of all religions as 'all the same' underneath their differences." As Haynes notes, however, "For many religious people . . . such 'toleration' from others distorts their faith and is anything but neutral. . . . The view that all faiths are ultimately the same may be compatible with some world views, but this is itself a philosophical position."[26] Indeed, this is a typically liberal position—which does not make it wrong but does keep it from being religiously neutral.

Clearly, neutrality—fairness and not taking sides—must be carefully distinguished from relativism, from the view that there is no (objective, reasonable) right or wrong. Disagreements among various religious and secular scholars are typically disagreements about what the truth is. If students come to believe that choosing a religious (or a political or scientific) position is like choosing what to eat from a buffet line they will have badly misunderstood what's at issue. From within each tradition, some foods are poisonous, others are healthy; and students certainly should not choose them simply as a matter of taste. Teachers need to explain very carefully why they must be religiously neutral in dealing with religion in the classroom, distinguishing neutrality from relativism. Alas, many teachers may not be entirely clear about the distinction themselves.

A related problem is that educators often place considerable emphasis on tolerance, a virtue in some ways akin to neutrality. Many religious conservatives understand tolerance as a matter of finding all beliefs and values equally good (a kind of relativism) and, consequently, don't want their children taught to be tolerant. Some liberals may accept some such relativistic understanding of tolerance, though I suspect most don't. The ideal of tolerance surely extends to beliefs and values that we find misguided, untrue, perhaps even offensive, but neither tolerance nor neutrality commits us to the claim that all beliefs or values are equally true or good.

## Is Neutrality Neutral?

Even if teachers are able to convey the difference between neutrality and relativism there may be problems. Neutrality is sometimes thought of as a liberal virtue and one might argue that religious neutrality is not itself neutral between religious conservatives, who often would have their children learn only about their own religious traditions, and religious (or secular) liberals, who often want their children to learn about various religious traditions and think critically about them. No doubt many religious conservatives find little to be said for treating the truth of their tradition (as they understand it) neutrally with various religious and secular beliefs and values they believe to be false. Of course, this is only one instance of a more general concern; after all, schools teach students about cultures, political parties, and moral values different from those of their parents. Religion raises no new problem in this regard.

For some religious conservatives the only truly neutral position is that of educational choice and vouchers, where the government neutrally funds private religious schools (which need not themselves be religiously neutral) as well as secular private and public schools. Still, if there are to be public schools and universities they must be religiously neutral.

There is no solution to this problem that will satisfy some religious parents. Clearly they can't be given a veto over the curriculum because they object to neutrality; that wouldn't be neutral but would privilege their religion. Yet that is exactly what would seem to be required by those who are opposed to neutrality. In fact, this would make neutrality impossible in principle.

My own sense of the situation is that most conservative religious parents (not all by any means) would accept a neutrality in which their own views are taken seriously along with the views of others.[27] After all, fairness is at the heart of neutrality as I have defined it, and fairness is a common value. Most people are willing to listen to the views of others if their own views are taken seriously; that is only fair. What most people want is a seat at the table; they don't insist on dictating the curriculum. The problem is that many religious parents feel deeply alienated from public education because they believe (often rightly) that their

views aren't taken seriously. No doubt it will take a considerable effort to establish trust. Of course it is also true that many parents and children—Catholic,
Jewish, Muslim, Hindu, agnostic, and atheist—also feel excluded, often for
good reasons. Clearly the goal of neutrality is to take the beliefs and values of *all*
students seriously insofar as this is practically possible.

## The Concerns of Religious Liberals

Over the last few decades religious liberals have expressed little concern over
the role of religion in public universities or public schools (other than criticizing the Religious Right for its designs on public education). In fact, my
greatest disappointment in twenty years of trying to make the case for taking
religion seriously has been the utter indifference of religious liberals to any
serious study of religion in public schools (with a very few exceptions).[28] Unlike
conservatives, liberals fail to see that there is even a problem. Why?

First, religious liberals have accepted, sometimes rather uncritically, the
ideas and ideals of secular modernity, not least those of modern science. As a
result, they have had little to say about the dangers of secularism and secular
education. Not surprisingly, conservative critics have often responded that in
their search for respectability in a secular world, liberals have negotiated an
ill-advised peace with modernity, granting secular scholars and scientists a
trump card to play against any religious claims.

Second, perhaps the dominant concern of religious liberals over the last
century has been justice, which they take to be central to the work of God in the
world. It follows for them that the great problem of modernity is injustice, not
secularism. The liberal religious crusades regarding education have been for
integration, equality of access, gender equality, and multiculturalism. In his
history of divinity schools, Conrad Cherry argues, "The preponderant cultural
and social reality with which university divinity schools have had to contend in
the late twentieth century is American pluralism, not American secularism.
The assertive diversity of religious and cultural worldviews, not the marginali-
zation or elimination of sacred worldviews, constitutes the heart of the challenge."[29] Liberation theology, so powerful in the seminaries, has driven much
liberal and mainline thought in this direction.[30]

Third, like secular liberals, religious liberals are sensitive to maintaining
the constitutional "wall of separation" between church and state. Liberals see
religious conservatives strenuously attempting to break down the wall, not least
in matters of schooling, and this has generated a powerful response, leading
them to align themselves with secular liberals in defense of a strict separationist

interpretation of the First Amendment. In fact, our culture wars have led, as James Davison Hunter has argued, to a series of tactical alliances between religious and secular liberals, presenting a united front against those on the Religious Right who would make the United States into a Christian country and our schools into Christian schools.

Fourth, as we saw in chapter 3, liberals have insisted that religion be voluntary and have rejected as a matter of principle coercive religious practices (such as prayer or chapel) traditionally found in schools and colleges. Arguably, this concern has carried over to any required study of religion. They know that public schools were once Protestant schools and believe that many conservatives would like nothing better than to return to the good old days. Perhaps it is not surprising that liberals are wary of all talk of religion in the schools; as they see it, it is the proverbial camel's nose under the tent. Some religious liberals find it hard to believe that there can be any reasons for taking religion seriously in public schools or universities that aren't conservative religious reasons. (I remember once being cornered at a conference by a participant whose response to my entirely secular arguments for taking religion seriously was to try to browbeat me into admitting that I was really a fundamentalist.) As a result, liberals have too often uncritically accepted "religion-free" schools as the only alternative to religious schools.

If such views are not surprising, they are disappointing and shallow. No doubt the cognitive dissonance between the curriculum and religion is greater for religious conservatives than for liberals, but unless they have compromised everything they believe (some have, of course) liberals too should be deeply troubled by modern education.

Because the problem is (largely?) nonexistent as they see it, my solution to the problem is likely to lack both urgency and cogency for many liberals. Yet liberals should find my emphasis on liberal education, critical thinking, fairness, sensitivity to all religious traditions, and constitutional neutrality acceptable, even important. Moreover, I reject the solution to the problem proposed by the Religious Right (privileging conservative Christianity). One might say that to a considerable extent conservatives are right about the problem, but that liberals come closer to accepting the principles that shape the solution. I hope that most liberals and conservatives might, on reflection, actually find common ground in reflecting on the problem and its solution.

## The Concerns of Atheists

The primary concern of many atheists is that religion not be given credibility, that it not be taken seriously as a live option. Many atheists (not all) appear to assume that all religion must be mindless, anti-intellectual fundamentalism. In fact, the militant *New Atheists*—Richard Dawkins, Daniel Dennett, Christopher Hitchens, and Sam Harris—show little familiarity with theology and are completely uninterested in nurturing a critical dialogue among scholars and theologians. I have already addressed this concern in chapter 5. While atheists may prove right in the end, their position is still extremely controversial and certainly cannot be used to exclude religious voices from the curricular conversation.

That said, Richard Dawkins and Daniel Dennett (the brightest of the brights) have argued for teaching students about the Bible and world religions—though certainly not for taking religion seriously. Dawkins confesses that he has been "taken aback" by students' ignorance of the Bible—and, he asks, how can they understand culture without understanding the Bible?[31] Dennett writes: "Let's get *more* education about religion into our schools, not less." Of course, Dennett argues that students should be taught the negative as well as the positive influences of religion—for example, "the Inquisition, anti-Semitism over the ages, [and] the role of the Catholic Church in spreading AIDS in Africa through its opposition to condoms."[32]

I agree with Dennett, and none of my arguments for studying religion require that religion be presented in an unduly favorable light. In fact, we all agree that religions have often been the source of great evil; it's just that most of us think that such evils are the consequence of other people's religions. Of course, sorting out the influence of religions for good and evil is a matter of some controversy, but this only means that students should be introduced to different interpretations of the influence of religions for good and evil; controversy doesn't mean that the question should be ignored. (Still, this is not any easy thing to do fairly.)

Should students learn about atheism?

There are reasons for not requiring the study of atheism. I have argued that the major (the most influential) ways of making sense of the world need to be included in the conversation. Ninety percent of Americans believe in God, while most surveys show that atheists and agnostics together total less than 5 percent of the population. True, scholars and intellectuals are somewhat more likely to be atheists, agnostics, or skeptics of some kind.

We also need to remember that we already teach secular ways of making sense of everything in the curriculum. It is true that "secular" means nonreligious, not antireligious; still, in effect, students are already learning how atheists think about history, science, and economics.[33] Atheists don't typically argue for teaching history, economics, or science differently from how we now teach them. What's important in this context is to make room for religious voices in the curricular conversation.

But what if we teach a course in religion—say, in world religions? Shouldn't there be some discussion of atheism as part of any critical conversation? But consider an analogy. We don't require that critics of women's studies or African American studies be included in courses on those subjects. A part of the point of such courses is that women's voices and minority voices haven't been taken seriously, so let's make sure that *those* voices have a place in the curriculum. My point is that religious voices have been excluded from the curricular conversation. Why now insist on including the voices of atheists in a religion course?

All of this said, in the end it does seem to me important to discuss atheism and various critiques of religion in teaching history (in addressing Marxism, for example) or literature (in teaching about existentialist literature, for example) and if there is to be an introductory course on religion or world religions (as I will argue there should be) it is important to devote some time to atheism. One of the most fascinating, and in our culture increasingly important, questions is why people believe or don't believe in God. Again, the point of a liberal education is to initiate students into an ongoing cultural conversation, helping them to make sense of it.[34]

There is another factor that must be considered. As I've noted above, scholars in the social sciences and in religious studies have devoted considerable effort into developing theories of religion that attempt to explain it in terms of the secular disciplinary categories of the humanities, social sciences, and (increasingly) the natural sciences (such as evolutionary biology). Dennett argues, for example, that "as we discover more and more about the biological and psychological bases of religious practices and attitudes, these discoveries should be added to the curriculum, the same way we update our education about science, health, and current events."[35] This is an increasingly important (if often controversial) domain of scholarship and students might well be introduced to it in an introductory course. But let's keep our priorities straight: discussions of atheism or secular theories of religion must constitute a relatively small part of any introductory course the primary purpose of which is to take religion seriously, to include religious voices in the curricular conversation.

## Practical Objections

There are some people who will say that my proposals are fine in theory, but in practice they won't work and may even prove disastrous—for a number of reasons.

*Religion Is Too Controversial*

This is the first refuge of school administrators who fear criticism and potential lawsuits from either the Religious Right or the Secular Left.[36] Who can deny it? Religion *is* controversial, and schools (not usually universities, which are much better insulated from public opinion) might well get swept up into bloody battles in our culture wars. And yet, this is not a good argument for a number of reasons.

Schools already live with many controversial issues—politics, gender, race, and sex education, among them; controversy can't be a deal breaker only for religion. Moreover, courses in religion (good courses in religion) have been taught in some schools for years without problem.[37] (I know some of the teachers.) Of course, both good and bad courses are taught in schools without political or legal battles largely because they are elective courses; students don't have to take them (defusing the objections of skeptical parents). If religion courses become required (as I will argue in chapter 9 should be the case) controversy might be a more important problem (though I will argue there that this needn't be the case).

Perhaps most important, all schools should have religion policies that address the role of religion in the curriculum. Such policies should be developed by school districts at a time of peace—as my friend Oliver Thomas likes to say, the time to buy a fire truck is before the fire—not in the midst of a heated local battle over the curriculum. All of the stakeholders, secular and religious, public and professional, should be involved in crafting a common-ground policy so that all are vested in its success. My sense of the matter is that most (not all) controversies can be avoided if a community thinks through the issues and everyone is given a place at the table so that they are vested in the policy.

I might also point out that leaving religion out of the curriculum is also controversial. It is precisely because so many public schools don't take religion seriously that parents raise a ruckus or desert them for private schools or home schooling. In fact, I think that my position is, all things considered, in the long run, the least controversial position.

*It Can't Be Done Well*

Many teachers feel insecure in addressing religions other than their own (and sometimes their own as well). Many parents from minority religious traditions fear that teachers will misunderstand their traditions or privilege the teacher's own religion, if only unintentionally. In this context Randall Styers has warned that "when state power and resources are mobilized on behalf of religion, the majority perspective almost always wins out."[38] Liberals typically fear that the line between proselytizing and academic teaching about religion is difficult to draw, and teachers will not be able to observe it in practice. No doubt most teachers try to be fair and neutral, but, alas, it is also true that most teachers do not have the educational background to teach about religion competently.

The problem of competence is a nagging concern and a recurring theme in Kent Greenawalt's very helpful book on religion and public education *Does God Belong in Public Schools?* Greenawalt argues that religion has an important place in the curriculum (he doesn't go quite so far as I do) but over and over again he backs away from the practical implications of his argument: "Although from the standpoint of a fully liberal education, much may be said in favor of a searching examination of religious perspectives, that ambition presents serious risks that educators may reasonably decide not to undertake. . . . Schools may teach less religion less deeply than would be ideal, were all the teachers of that subject to be well trained and appropriately sensitive, and were parents to be fully accepting of diverse religions being taught from an academic perspective."[39] In other words, he concludes, "If religion is *too* sticky or controversial, selective ignoring of religion is defensible."[40]

I acknowledge that most teachers are not adequately prepared to take on the task I'm giving them. That being the case, it is completely understandable that many parents worry about my arguments—especially parents in minority religious traditions that are less likely to be understood or taken seriously than the majority Christian tradition in the United States. Clearly, schools must proceed with caution in phasing in serious study of religion. Teachers must be given the training to do the job well. I will say more about this in chapter 9. I note, however, that though Greenawalt is deeply concerned about this problem he doesn't propose a solution. Consider an analogy. Several decades ago, most teachers were woefully unprepared to deal with women's and minority history and literature (also areas of some sensitivity and controversy). Educators did not say "Well, we better not teach that stuff." (OK, some did say that.) Rather we started preparing teachers to deal with multiculturalism. So we should prepare them to deal with religion.

Greenawalt also makes a somewhat stronger argument: "the counsel of circumspection is not *just* a matter of teachers being inadequately trained. The issues can be so complex and controversial that almost anyone should be skeptical of his ability to present the religious perspectives in a detached and fair way."[41] Again, he is right, but again his caution shouldn't settle the matter. Teachers aren't responsible for everything that goes on in the classroom. They have textbooks *that, if well written,* will address complex and controversial issues in an informed and responsible way. Alas, textbooks are no better written (as we saw in chapter 2) than teachers are prepared. But just as teachers could be better prepared, so textbooks could be better written, and I will have more to say about how this might be done in chapter 9.

Still, shouldn't we leave well enough alone and stop addressing religion until we can do it properly? If only it were so simple. The thrust of my argument is that there is no "well enough" to leave alone. Education is now scandalous (at least with regard to religion). Education is now deeply biased against religion. Indeed, it is unconstitutional. The status quo is simply not acceptable. What I grant is that we can't simply immediately implement the reforms I am proposing; we must do what is reasonable now (which is rather more than we are doing) and take seriously the task of preparing teachers and textbooks.

## There's Not Enough Time for Everything Now

Let me start with public schools. It is true that textbooks now weigh seven or eight pounds and the curriculum is bulging at the seams with pressures to add more on every side, all the while legislators are pressuring schools to devote more and more time to preparing students for tests in a narrow range of subjects. My proposal is that we take a deep breath and step back from the details and minutia and ask, All things considered, what's really important?

I've read more than a hundred high school textbooks. They are crammed full of stuff, some important, much not. The history books are filled with endless facts and details and very little perspective on what's important. The science textbooks are filled with facts and formulas and very little perspective on what it all means. The economics textbooks are . . . well, a lost cause. So what *is* important?

We teach students a lot about things that *all things considered* aren't particularly important when compared to those deep and inescapable existential questions about morality and meaning that are so obviously important, and that we either shy away from or totally ignore. We fail to give students critical perspective on any of the secular ways of making sense of their lives that pervade the curriculum. Unfortunately, most educators have little appreciation of the relevance of religion to the curriculum (at least outside of history) because most of them have been illiberally educated. They have learned to compartmentalize religion and education. And, of course, most legislators (and many parents and educators) are unreasonably fixated on the economic purposes of education.

What about actually requiring a course in religious studies (as I will propose in the next chapter)? Surely this would be extravagant. Let me pose a question. Which is the better education: twelve years of arithmetic/mathematics and no religious studies, or eleven years of arithmetic/mathematics and one year of religious studies? If you said the former, you flunk. As important as mathematics is (yes, it is very important) there is no good reason to require four years of high school math. (Two years should be sufficient, though, of course, math courses should be available as electives to students going into math, engineering, and the sciences.) The fact that we can't see this proves that our priorities are messed up.

As for universities, there is no good reason not to tack on a required course or two in religious studies and, if need be, eliminate an elective or two.


## Conclusions

Some of the concerns and objections that I have considered are serious and are not easily addressed in practice. I believe that teachers' lack of preparation, and their ignorance of the proper governing framework for taking religions seriously, are problems that are sufficiently great to warrant considerable caution, but they also highlight the urgency of beginning to think about religion seriously.

Unfortunately, there is little respectable constituency for change. I have mentioned that several decades ago textbooks and curricula said little about women and minority cultures. Educators then were naive about the need to include multicultural voices in the curriculum, were largely incompetent to do it, and considered the whole business deeply controversial. Still, multicultural education is now commonplace. Things change with a little enlightenment and a strong enough lobby for change, and one might find some hope in this.

Unlike the multicultural movement, a movement of the Left, there is no lobby for taking religion seriously (in some sense) apart from the Religious Right—and for most educators the embrace of the Right is a prelude to the kiss of death. Too easily, discussion of religion in the curriculum gets caught up in the polarizing rhetoric of our culture wars. And yet, there is also, as I noted in chapter 6, common ground on which educators can stand in taking religion seriously in ways that are constitutionally acceptable and pedagogically sound. This is tremendously important, and provides perhaps the major reason for hope.

We might also remember that fifty years ago few public universities had departments of religious studies. Now a significant minority do. The field of religious studies is not without its problems, and can't be uncritically transplanted in public schools. Still, it is also a part of the solution and perhaps provides a measure of hope. I will say more about religious studies and the implications of my position in the next chapter.

It may be helpful to review where we are as I draw the curtain on section 2. I concluded section 1 by arguing that public schools and universities perpetuate religious illiteracy, fall far short of religious neutrality, and at least border on secular indoctrination. All of these potential problems turn out to be real problems given what a good education should be. In section 2, I provide eleven arguments for requiring some study of religion, in most cases for taking religion seriously (in my sense) in schools and universities.

In chapter 5 I argued (1) that a modicum of religious literacy is necessary if students are to understand history, literature, and other subjects in the curriculum. (2) A liberal education should nurture critical thinking—the ability to be reasonable—by providing students a broad understanding of the major ways in which humankind has made sense of the world, religious ways included. (3) Given the fact that worldviews are contestable, and there is no agreement among secular scholars about the solution to any of the Big Questions, humility requires openness to religious as well as secular worldviews.

In chapter 6, I proposed a series of moral, existential, and civic arguments for taking religion seriously. (4) Education must locate students historically within traditions that give them some sense of moral values and cultural identity; religious traditions have shaped much of contemporary culture. (5) Education inevitably addresses important moral controversies, and it would be illiberal to leave religious approaches to these controversies out of the conversation. (6) A liberal education has an obligation to address those Big Questions of meaning that any thoughtful person asks; again, it is illiberal to leave religion out of that conversation. (7) In a democratic society we have a civic obligation to be informed citizens and thoughtful voters; this is impossible apart from a substantive understanding of religion. (8) Justice requires that traditions (at least the major ones) and subcultures of the United States be given voice in the curricular conversation. (9) Within a liberal state, one that protects and nurtures liberty, indoctrination is forbidden; but unless schools and universities take religion seriously they will be engaged in secular indoctrination. (10) A democratic society requires civility and a measure of respect for other people and their rights; if we are to take one another seriously we must understand one another. I noted at the end of chapter 6 that there are now many widely endorsed common-ground statements, both in the United States and Europe, that require serious study of religion (even if they stop a little short of what I mean by taking religion seriously).

In chapter 7, I considered the constitutional context for dealing with religion in public schools and universities, arguing that not only is it constitutionally permissible to teach about religion, to take religion seriously (a completely uncontroversial claim) but that (11) constitutional neutrality actually requires it.

Finally, let me say once more that all of my arguments for taking religion seriously are entirely secular arguments. They might be advanced by atheists as well as by religious believers (though each may well have legitimate concerns about how schools and universities act on these arguments). No doubt there are also religious arguments for studying religion, but I have not made them.

Now that the basic principles are in place, we can draw out the implications for the classroom and curriculum, putting a little meat on the bones of these somewhat abstract arguments and principles.

# PART III

# Implications

# 9

# The Basics

In section 2, I proposed a set of respectably secular reasons for taking religion seriously in schools and universities. In section 3 my task will be to draw out the implications for teaching, coursework, and the curriculum of schools and universities. What would they look like if we were to take religion seriously?

In this chapter I will propose that if schools and universities are to take religion seriously they must require students to take at least one course in religious studies. This doesn't mean that religion can be ignored in all other courses, however; far from it. There must be courses in religion and there must be religion in (other) courses. I'll say something about textbooks and teacher education, both of which must be reformed if religion is to be taken seriously, and we'll wade at least knee-deep into pedagogical waters as I propose a few broadly pedagogical considerations for teachers to keep in mind in teaching about religion.

Finally, if there are to be required courses in religion it is essential that religious studies be a field of study in all public universities and in all public schools. I will characterize the field as it now exists, say something about the relationship of religious studies to theology and philosophy, and sketch how religious studies should be defined with regard to public schools.

Having settled on the basics, we can move on, in the final three chapters, to what it would look like to take religion seriously in specific courses.

### Religion in Courses? Courses in Religion?

No doubt it is easier to incorporate some study of religion into existing courses, especially history and literature courses, than to create new courses in religion. Indeed, as we have seen, some discussion of religion is relatively common in such courses. This is sometimes called *natural inclusion*—including some study of religion wherever it naturally comes up.

There are three reasons why natural inclusion won't do the job, however. First, given the amount of material that must be crammed into most courses (often required by state standards), few pages and little time will be given to religion. Second, teaching about religion requires sophistication, and most teachers, whatever their level, are poorly prepared by their educations to take religion seriously (no matter how religious they might be in their personal lives). Third, the disciplinary structure of the curriculum all but ensures that religion won't be taken seriously. Indeed, including any discussion of religion in some courses—in economics and biology courses, for example—would be viewed by many as quite *unnatural*.[1]

We must keep in mind the distinction between subjects—which are open to a variety of interpretations, secular and religious—and disciplines, particularly interpretive and methodological approaches to subjects. While it is true that students might encounter religious subject matter in some courses, they will inevitably learn how to think about it in the categories of the host disciplines, which are always secular. So, for example, a course in psychology might address religious experience, but the point of studying religious experiences in psychology courses is to understand them as psychologists do, not as theologians do or as they are understood within a particular religious tradition. Even in history courses, students typically learn to think about religion in secular historical categories; they don't learn to think about history religiously. But if religion is to be taken seriously, religion must not just be interpreted in the secular categories of the host discipline; students must come to understand religious ways of making sense of the world.

As I have argued, taking religion seriously requires that religion is understood from the inside, studied in sufficient depth to make sense of it, treated as a live option in its most compelling forms, and allowed to contend with secular traditions, narratives, worldviews. This will be possible only if students take a course in religious studies, taught by a teacher competent to teach it, and this will be possible only when religious studies is accepted as a field of study. All public (and private) universities must have such departments, and a parallel field must be created in public secondary education. Of course, not all courses in religious studies take religion seriously. I will say a good deal below about the field of religious studies in higher education, and the need to develop a version of it in public schools.

So if schools and universities must take religion seriously they must require that students take at least one yearlong course in religious studies.[2] Why not two? An even better idea to be sure, but even more controversial, so, being practical, I will stick with one. I'll say something about what such a required course should look like in the next chapter.

Does this mean that all discussion of religion can be shunted into the one required course? No. Any course that addresses religion or subjects that are religiously important and controversial must at least acknowledge the relevance of religion to what is being discussed. This follows from the nature of critical thinking and liberal education. A liberal education must be a conversation, not a series of monologues. Critical thinking requires more than just a sequential understanding of contending ways of making sense of the world; it requires that students be initiated into a conversation about contending ways of interpreting the world—and the subjects of the curriculum. When any course deals with religion or matters that are religiously controversial students should be given some sense of what is at issue religiously, and they must have some sense of the contending interpretations and be involved in the broader curricular conversation.

I might put this in terms of two kinds of fairness. First, the curriculum must be *robustly* fair by requiring that students take at least one course that takes religion seriously. Second, all courses must be at least *minimally* fair by acknowledging religious interpretations of the subject matter, even if they aren't taken seriously. That is, students must appreciate the fact that the approach taken in a text or a course is only one of several and that it's controversial—perhaps not within the host discipline, but within culture and in other disciplines. In this case, there will not be time, and there is no obligation, to take religion seriously, especially if students have the opportunity to do so in a course in religious studies. But if students are to be educated rather than indoctrinated they can't be left to assume that they have been given the only way of making sense of their respective subjects. They must learn something about religious ways of thinking about any subject—economics, biology, history, or sexuality, for example—that is religiously contested when the conflict or tension is of some importance. I'll give examples of how this should work in the chapters to come.

So I make a two-pronged proposal: first, robust fairness by way of a required course in religion that takes religion seriously; and second, minimal fairness to religion in other courses that deal with religiously important and controversial material.

A further word about neutrality is in order here. No doubt most courses are officially or formally neutral in that they aren't explicitly hostile to religion. But, as we've seen, they often encourage, by way of the categories of the host discipline, ways of making sense of their subject matters that are at least implicitly in tension with, and may even conflict with, religious alternatives. I have argued that coursework often has the (unintended) effect of nurturing a secular mentality that marginalizes and discredits religion, and that borders on secular indoctrination. So even if such courses are officially or formally neutral, they are not substantively neutral. Only by shifting our attention to the curriculum as a whole and requiring a course that takes religion seriously is any kind of substantive neutrality—and robust fairness—possible.

## Legal Considerations

The U.S. Supreme Court hasn't ruled on the constitutionality of a required course in religion. The question is whether an elective course that is clearly constitutional would become unconstitutional if it is required. One might argue that requiring a course in religious studies might appear to promote or endorse religion. Yet given the many secular reasons for taking religion seriously, this argument isn't plausible. Requiring one or even two courses in religion would fall well short of promoting religion (if taught properly) given the overwhelmingly secular thrust of the curriculum.

I suspect that a required Bible course would be unconstitutional (where an elective course on the Bible need not be) for such a course would most likely privilege a particular religion, Christianity (or perhaps Christianity and Judaism)—at least in the absence of a companion required course on the scriptures of other religious traditions. It is true that there are powerful secular reasons for requiring students to learn about the Bible, but this should be done in some context that doesn't so explicitly privilege a particular religion. I will say more about Bible courses in the next chapter.

Even if it is constitutional to require a religion course one might ask whether there should be an excusal policy. In chapter 7 I discussed the rather murky situation we are in regarding excusal policies and the Free Exercise Clause, and I am not going to retrace that torturous ground. I will only say that while I think limited excusal policies are wise and should be defensible on Free Exercise grounds for young students, I'm much less sympathetic with regard to older and more mature students. Exposing them to views they find objectionable is essential to a liberal education.[3]

That said, it may still be good politics for schools to have an excusal policy for students who object to taking a religion course as a matter of conscience.

Some religious students (or their parents) may believe that their religious or moral values will be unduly burdened by such a course. Such a view would likely be shortsighted—not least because such a course would give students critical perspective on their secular courses—though the parents might not see it that way. Liberal or secular parents may fear that their children will be religiously indoctrinated. In any case, an excusal policy would diffuse most political controversy surrounding the course. It might turn out in some communities that many children would ask to be excused, but I suspect that if the course is educationally and constitutionally sound the number of dissenters would be small and would decrease over time. (In fact, one public school system has required a world religions course for some years now with little controversy.[4]) What is important is that school districts and states make the case for requiring serious study of religion (even with an excusal policy) rather than simply making it an elective possibility, a regrettably feeble alternative.

I suspect that requiring a religion course of undergraduates at public universities would be much less controversial among students and parents than it would be in high schools; alas, it would be much more controversial among the faculty.

Textbooks

In the preceding chapter I took seriously Kent Greenawalt's concern about the ability of teachers to deal with religion in all of its complexity and controversy. One response I proposed is better teacher education. I will say something about this shortly. Another is better textbooks. Teachers aren't alone in the classroom; good textbooks help structure courses, provide background, and contribute a wealth of detail, context, and nuance for dealing with difficult and controversial subjects.

As we saw in chapter 2, there are major problems with textbook treatments of religion. Such problems aren't limited to religion, of course, but are systemic. Textbooks are big business. As such, they tend to be bland and safe, minimizing controversy to maximize profits. While scholars may write the first editions of a text, their texts are often edited and rewritten in later editions by in-house editors who don't have the scholarly credentials the original authors had. In responding to state standards, textbooks squeeze in as much detail as possible (thus demonstrating their responsiveness to the standards) all but ensuring that it will be impossible for students to discern large patterns in the profusion of detail. Textbooks are often written in leaden prose. They often border on incoherence as students are challenged to keep track of the narrative amid a confusing profusion of pictures, boxes, charts, and various entertaining diversions. And yet, in spite of this jumble, textbooks tend to speak in a single interpretive voice; they are not anthologies that expose students to a variety of interpretive voices. They are written from a disciplinary perspective that inevitably ignores other disciplinary perspectives.

Obviously, textbooks could be better, *much* better. Indeed, for many purposes (especially in the humanities) the ideal must be eliminating textbooks, replacing them with primary sources or anthologies of primary sources. It is also true, however, that for younger students the coherence of a textbook may be as important as the encounter with contending points of view for older students. It takes considerable intellectual maturity to work though the often-confusing mix of voices found in primary sources. Of course, it need not be one or the other; primary sources can be used to supplement textbooks.

I can't address all of the problems I've just mentioned, but I do want to make a proposal for how to think about the role of religion in textbooks.

### The 5 Percent Rule

Textbooks often have an opening chapter on methodology that more or less defines the disciplinary approach that will be taken. These chapters (in high school textbooks at least) are desultory and superficial, and they rarely say anything substantive about alternative approaches to the subject matter. But, I have argued, all textbooks must locate the host discipline within the context of a liberal education—in our ongoing conversation about how to make sense of the world. What other points of view (disciplines, intellectual traditions, conceptual nets, worldviews) address the subjects that are to be considered? What are their relationships to one another? Do they conflict, are they in tension, or are they complementary? Historically, how has the discipline developed, and what are its basic philosophical commitments? What in the text is deeply controversial? How does the discipline (and the course) relate to fundamental questions of morality and meaning? If students are to be educated and not just trained or socialized within the disciplinary framework, they must have some sense of the answers to these questions. In fact, a good deal in addition to religion—philosophy, morality, and politics—must be woven into this discussion; I need not engage in any special pleading for religion.

My own view is that ideally about 10 percent of a textbook should be devoted to these contextual, historical, philosophical, normative (moral, existential, and religious) matters. Given the fact that most textbooks devote 0 percent of their pages to these matters, I will be cautious and in the spirit of compromise propose what I will call the 5 percent rule. Textbooks must devote at least 5 percent of their pages to locating the host discipline in the interdisciplinary conversation that is central to a liberal education. While this context would certainly be helpful in an opening chapter, it might also be necessary at points in the text that deal with particularly controversial material. In any case, anything less than 5 percent is simply unacceptable (and more is better). The 5 percent rule should also apply to class time.

Given the limitations of space, such discussions cannot take religion seriously, but they should be sufficiently substantive to give students some sense of what is at issue, and some range of ways of thinking about the subject matter and the host discipline. (That is, while they cannot be robustly fair, while they cannot take religion seriously, they must be minimally fair.) Of course, if these discussions of religion are to serve their purpose in a liberal education they cannot simply reflect the conventional understanding of religion held by scholars in the textbook's host discipline. They must be sophisticated, not simplistic or one-dimensional. They must be written in collaboration with scholars in religious studies (and politics, ethics, and philosophy).

It is true that religion is often controversial, but this is not a reason for ignoring it; this is a reason for including it. (All right, here I'm talking about educational reasons, not the economic considerations of publishers, or the political reasons of administrators.) The treatment of religion in textbooks will often be controversial, but what's important is that students have some sense of the controversy and some context for understanding it. No doubt some interpretations of the subject will often be better than others given the disciplinary framework of the textbook. This can be made clear too.

As we shall see in the next several chapters, what this means is that it may be necessary to address religious conceptions of justice in economics textbooks, religious ways of thinking about evolution in science textbooks, and religious ways of thinking about sexuality in health or sex education textbooks.

## Teacher Education

Textbooks don't teach themselves. Teachers have to be competent to teach the text and, when textbooks fall short of adequacy, they need to interpret, supplement, or even correct them.

Only a small minority of undergraduates in public universities take courses in religious studies, and they aren't likely to encounter religion anywhere else. I suspect that students who wish to become teachers are even less likely to take a course in religious studies given the demands of a disciplinary major together with education courses. I don't know of any recent statistics, surveys, or studies of religion and teacher education programs—perhaps evidence in itself of how unimportant the subject is taken to be—but my sense of the matter is that teacher education programs and schools of education are largely tone-deaf to religion. I suspect that what little attention is paid to religion is directed to constitutional considerations (prayer, the practice of religion, maybe vouchers) rather than the role of religion in the curriculum.

Only a few scholars take seriously the idea of taking religion seriously in the curriculum, and most of them are in fields other than education. In fact, the number of books published on religion and public education over the last decade can be counted on one's fingers and toes. There is one quite good but modest (in terms of subscribers) journal that addresses such things (*Religion and Education*). A few years ago I found that only two of more than five hundred presentations at the annual meeting of the American Educational Studies Association (whose members teach those social foundations courses where religion might be considered) addressed religion. I know of only one college or university that offers an interdisciplinary degree program in religion and education—Harvard's MTS Program in Religion and Secondary Education.[5]

The American Academy of Religion (AAR) has done a little better—but not much. It has for some time had an active but small section on religion and education that sponsors sessions at the annual meeting. Unfortunately, it has had little impact on the field as a whole (though professors of religious studies are known to bemoan the religious ignorance of the students they inherit from public schools). Only a very few professors of religious studies have chosen to write about religion and K–12 education, and there are few courses in departments of religious studies on religion and education—though again the evidence is anecdotal because I know of no studies.

I will make six proposals.

(1) First, and most important, teachers must be liberally educated. They need to be more than specialists, they should be intellectuals, at home in the world of ideas. This is clearly important quite apart from religion. Teachers should have some sense of how what they teach relates to other subjects and disciplines, and to broad moral, political, religious, and existential issues, concerns, and controversies. Alas, few teachers—indeed, few undergraduates—receive a good liberal education.

(2) Some substantial discussion of the role of religion in education should be included in every prospective teacher's education by way of a required course in social foundations or the philosophy of education. In particular, students must be introduced to the idea of taking religion seriously in the curriculum and in the courses they will teach.

(3) Schools of education (or departments of religious studies) should offer at least one course in religion and education (perhaps team-taught by someone in education and someone in religious studies) that allows future administrators and teachers in particularly sensitive areas of the curriculum (such as Bible courses) to acquire a sophisticated understanding of the relationship of religion and education.

(4) Teachers should be given the opportunity, be encouraged, and ideally be required to take a course in religion and their particular subject matter (religion and literature, religion and science, religion and economics, etc.). Such courses are no doubt best taught in departments of religious studies but they might also be taught in other disciplines (such as history or literature). Such courses should count toward certification in their subject area, something that state departments of education often don't do.

(5) States and individual school systems should offer, and teachers should be encouraged or even be required to participate in, various in-service programs addressing religion and education. One model is the statewide 3Rs projects I mentioned in chapter 6 (in California and Utah), developed by the First Amendment Center. Diane Moore suggests several other possibilities (for preservice as well as for in-service courses) in her helpful book.[6]

(6) If they are to be competent to teach Bible or religion courses, teachers must have at least a minor in religious studies. That is, if there are to be courses that take religion seriously, then religious studies must become a certifiable field of study in public schools.

## Pedagogy

We know a good deal about successful pedagogy. We know that good teachers are enthusiastic, they care about their students, they engage them in discussion, and they are well organized and clear about their goals and in conveying course content.[7] I am not going to rehearse these familiar points, but say something about pedagogy regarding religion in particular.

### Interpretation and Worldviews

I begin with a general claim that is particularly important for our purposes. All subjects of the curriculum are open to different interpretations, religious interpretations included, which, in turn, are embedded in broader cultural and intellectual traditions, narratives, and worldviews. Teachers must be aware of these contexts of interpretation and, given the goals of a liberal education, begin to make students aware of them. In most courses this kind of inquiry cannot be a major theme, but it should be a minor theme, subject to the 5 percent rule and minimal fairness.

## Empathy and Primary Sources

Education requires the ability to get inside of other cultures, subcultures, intellectual traditions, historical periods, and religions, understanding them as advocates of those cultures and traditions, employing their categories, not our own, for making sense of the world. If we can't do this, we can't acquire critical perspective on our own beliefs and values and we can't think critically. This makes primary sources—including theological texts, biographies and autobiographies, imaginative literature, art, guest speakers, filmed interviews, dramatic films, and visiting religious sites—particularly important. If textbooks are often necessary, they should, as much as possible, be supplemented by primary sources. Of course, this requires substantial time, more time than most teachers can give to religious texts (hence, the need for courses in religious studies).

## Contemporary Religions as Live Options

A liberal education must locate students in traditions, in historical ongoing conversations about how to make sense of the world, but it is essential to bring the conversation up to the present. What are the live options for making sense of the world now? Clearly, to understand religious traditions students must understand something about their scriptures and classic formulations, but they should also understand something about how religions have responded to modernity. How have their beliefs, values, and practices developed? What do people in different traditions believe and value now? Often courses in world religions focus on scriptures and classical texts, but if students are to be liberally educated and take religion seriously they must have some understanding of those religions now.

## Complexity

All cultures, traditions, and worldviews are complex. As I've just noted, religions change over time. Any religion will have various branches or denominations. Catholics and Pentecostals have quite different understandings of

Christianity; Shi'i and Sunni Muslims have quite different understandings of Islam. There are geographical and cultural differences in how religious traditions are practiced, and there are typically liberal and conservative inter- pretations of religious traditions. We often assume that intellectuals—usually theologians—get to define religious traditions, but their understanding of their traditions is often different from that of priests or preachers who, in turn, may understand them differently from people in the pews or temples. Clearly, we can't expect teachers to be scholars of every religious tradition, sensitive to all complexities, but they must have some sophistication regarding the com- plexity of different traditions and be wary of generalizations and stereotypes.

There is, of course, a particular danger in assuming that other religions are fundamentally like one's own. In the introduction I mentioned Ninian Smart's seven dimensions of religion (doctrine, ethical and legal teachings, social insti- tutions, myth or sacred narratives, rituals, religious experiences, and art). All religious traditions may have these various dimensions, but they aren't equally important. Christians are apt to think of doctrine and belief as basic to religion because Christianity was, almost from the beginning, defined in terms of creeds, and Christians have often held that salvation hinges on what one believes. But most religions are different from Christianity in this respect; they may value morality, mystical experience, ritual, or tradition more than correct beliefs about God or the gods.

## Critical Conversation

What are the implications of these varying interpretations of life, religious traditions, and academic subjects for each other? Are they compatible? Are they in tension? Or do they conflict? As I've said (over and over) education should be a conversation, not a series of monologues; a liberal education must be interdisciplinary, even transdisciplinary. It isn't enough that education exposes students to a variety of views or interpretations. The point is that some are more reasonable than others. The fundamental purpose of a liberal educa- tion is to make students informed, thoughtful, reasonable—competent to make responsible judgments about what to believe and how they should live their lives.

I am not saying that teachers need to single-mindedly focus all discussion on where the truth lies or which interpretations are most reasonable. In fact, such questions will not typically be up front; they are more often background questions and concerns. In many contexts it is sufficient to understand what a particular culture or tradition believes or values, or how it relates to an alterna- tive, but leave aside the bottom-line question of which is more reasonable, and who might have the truth. Yet the question of truth and reasonableness must inevitably be the background consideration of students and teachers in that a goal of a liberal education is to enable students to think responsibly about what to believe and how to live their lives.

## Neutrality

Public school teachers must be religiously neutral for constitutional reasons. I have argued that neutrality requires fairness to contending points of view when there are deep and important disagreements, and then not taking sides. As I argued in chapter 5, teachers can convey inside understandings of religions and conduct critical conversations in which various ways of sorting out the compatibility, tensions, and conflicts among different points of view— secular and religious—are discussed, fairly, without themselves taking sides, maintaining neutrality. I have also suggested that at least with mature students, teachers might carefully express their personal views, at least if asked, so long as they are careful to distinguish them from the official views of the course (which must be religiously neutral). We should also remember that students can take sides; they are not agents of the state bound by the Establishment Clause.

I have argued that faculty members in universities have the academic freedom to take sides, so long as they don't do so gratuitously and so long as they are within their areas of competence. That said, I think it is often pedagogically prudent to remain neutral in dealing with matters of great controversy that are of intense personal importance to students, especially if the goal is to encourage students to think for themselves. Moreover, in the end, truth is often elusive, not least when religious interpretations are at issue for, as I've argued above, it is not at all easy to assess contending worldviews (which typically have contending conceptions of evidence and argument). In chapter 5, I argued that in such situations, a measure of humility is required—in which case neutrality might well be the best policy.

Of course, withholding all judgment may implicitly suggest that all positions are equally good—a kind of relativism. In fact, I think there is some merit in university teachers acknowledging their own positions and the reasons for them, so long as this is done in the context of a fair discussion of alternatives, and so long as they stop short of a concerted effort to convince students of the reasonableness of their position. Teachers should always respect the right of students to disagree with them in the classroom and on tests (though students can surely be held responsible for understanding positions with which they may disagree).

## Models of Teaching

There are times, particularly with younger students where the goal is basic religious literacy, when the teacher (who is, after all, the expert) must simply instruct students regarding important facts about religion and its role in history and culture. And there are times, particularly with mature, bright, and motivated students when the ideal is for the teachers and students to engage in a critical conversation of ideas and texts together by way of a seminar. In this case the teacher serves more as a facilitator than an instructor, and students may even help set an agenda that is responsive to their interests and concerns. Insofar as a liberal education must address those existential questions of meaning that are often of great personal concern to students it is particularly important that students participate in and help shape the discussion. Unfortunately, seminars must be small classes, a luxury in most schools and universities. As I proposed in chapter 6, most of the time a third, middle position is most appropriate, one in which the teacher structures a conversation among contending authors and texts, assumes the role of instructor in providing context for understanding the texts and the issues the texts address, but also encourages a good deal of questioning and discussion, initiating students into a larger, ongoing conversation.[8]

If students are to speak candidly about sensitive, controversial, perhaps even personal matters, as they would be asked to do in the second and third models, it is essential that teachers establish trust, openness, and mutual respect among students, whatever their views.[9]

## The Principle of Cultural Location and Weight

Clearly, teachers and texts must not convey the idea there is only one interpretation of a religion, a sacred text, or an academic subject, when there are many. Nor is there usually a simple dichotomy of views; there are typically many, some of which may be more influential than others. An important (but sadly unappreciated) principle of education is relevant here—what I call the *Principle of Cultural Location and Weight*. Teachers and textbooks have an obligation to locate different interpretations of their subjects on a conceptual map of alternatives, indicating the weight different views have within different intellectual and cultural contexts. In particular, students must be given some sense of whether the teacher or text is idiosyncratic or is taking a consensus position (within a discipline, or a culture). Do all historians or biologists agree? Do all Muslims or Christians agree? Which, if any, positions are consensus positions? And for what groups? And which are minority views? If students are to make responsible judgments they must have some sense of who holds which views, and how influential those views and their advocates are.

## Relativism and Pluralism

Some scholars are relativists—that is, they believe that it makes no sense to say that any point of view (or tradition or cultural narrative, or worldview) is more reasonable or true than another. Relativism is certainly not a foolish position, but it is deeply controversial, not least in matters of morality, politics, and religion. Indeed, most scholars—like most people—are concerned to find the truth of the matter, not just have a position. Consequently, it is important to remind students that the disagreements among different religious and secular traditions are typically about what the truth is (or what is most reasonable). I noted in the last chapter that too often I've heard teachers say, in discussing a matter of controversy, "there is no right answer" and sometimes in an effort to be tolerant teachers say that (deep down) all religions are fundamentally the same or equally true. Not surprisingly, many religious folks see this as (at least implicit) relativism. At the least, such claims are controversial.

Mature students should have some idea what relativism is and why some scholars are relativists. But teachers must understand, and in their teaching convey to students, the difference between relativism and pluralism (the idea that societies should be open to and tolerant of a variety of beliefs and values). There are many good (nonrelativist) reasons why societies should be pluralistic. One is that a pluralistic society is more apt to progressively discern the truth than one in which only a single conception of Truth is allowed. Another is that people have rights to their beliefs and values.

## Religious Studies

If we are to take religion seriously there must be courses in religion. If there are to be courses in religion, universities must have departments of religious studies and the field of religious studies must become a certifiable field for high school teachers. But we must take some care to define the field to ensure that it serves our purposes.

As we saw in chapter 3, as a result of the increasing secularization and specialization of scholarship over the course of the nineteenth century, theology was exiled from the undergraduate curriculum to seminaries and divinity schools and by the end of that century it had largely disappeared from public colleges and universities. There continued to be Bible courses here and there, but it was only after World War II that a significant movement developed for departments of religion, and it was only in the 1960s that they became relatively common, with a substantial minority of public universities creating departments or interdisciplinary curricula in religious studies. This growth was facilitated by the assurance provided by the Supreme Court's 1963 ruling in *Abington Township v. Schempp* that the secular study of religion is constitutional. Of course, 9/11 played an important role in exposing our ignorance of world religions (of Islam in particular), providing evidence of the need for greater opportunities to study religions.

At first, faculty in the new departments of religious studies were drawn, of necessity, from other disciplines—from history, sociology, philosophy, literary criticism, the ancient languages, Near Eastern and Asian studies, and theology. With this kind of interdisciplinary background scholars in religious studies have fretted about whether it is actually a discipline (with a common methodology) and many would say that it is not.[10] Like women's studies or environmental studies, scholarship in religious studies is united more by its subject rather than by any disciplinary methodology. Still, for all of its diversity, I will risk a few generalizations.

First, while there continues to be some controversy about the relationship of theology to religious studies (more on this shortly), the conventional wisdom is that religious studies is a secular rather than a religious field. According to the AAR's 1991 self-study, religious studies is the name of the "scholarly *neutral* and *nonadvocative* study of multiple religious traditions."[11] As William Scott Green once put it, "Religion is the subject we study, not the way we study it."[12] Religious studies continues to be a multidisciplinary field, but its epistemological and methodological commitments are clearly those of secular scholarship, rooted in the social sciences and humanities. No doubt there continues to be some suspicion of religious studies on the part of university faculty and administrators who worry that they may be divinity schools in disguise.[13] Such suspicion is usually misplaced.

Second, the old focus on the Bible and Christianity has been broadened to take in all of the world's religions and the various ways people and cultures are religious. (This transition was formally marked when, in 1963, the National Association of Bible Instructors changed its name to the American Academy of Religion.) Scholars in religious studies are typically wary of essentialist definitions of religion and the traditional focus on sacred texts such as the Bible. They are more likely to explore the strikingly different ways in which religions are practiced and understood. The field is comparative and intercultural. Scholars have shown particular interest in non-Western religions, as well as the religions of neglected and oppressed peoples—Third World and minority religions, oral traditions, and women's religion. This transition from a focus on Christianity to world religions was accelerated by 9/11 and a growing awareness of our ignorance of Islam and world religions.

Third, students who take courses in religious studies are inevitably confronted by the profound moral and existential concerns and commitments that are at the heart of the religious traditions they study. As the AAR's 2008 white paper on the religion major puts it, in studying religion students will "examine and engage religious phenomena, including issues of ethical and social responsibility, from a perspective of critical inquiry," addressing complex problems relating to "issues of life, death, love, violence, suffering, and meaning."[14]

Fourth, as in the humanities generally, courses in religious studies typically introduce students to primary sources, to texts written from within many religious traditions—not just sacred and theological texts, but literary and autobiographical texts and artistic works—that give students an inside, empathetic, and imaginative understanding of those traditions (scholars often call this a phenomenological approach). As a 1990 AAR task force report said, the study of religion should be both empathetic and critical, but if "criticism is uninformed by an empathetic understanding of the criticized, it chiefly serves to confirm the moral or cultural superiority of the critic. For that a liberal education is scarcely needed."[15]

Fifth, if courses often give students an inside understanding of particular religions, such study is almost always framed by broader (outside, secular) considerations. As I noted above, much study of religion is comparative, and many teachers and scholars in religious studies take it as their task to explain religion. In his study of the field, Walter Capps concluded that the "overall intent" of religious studies has been to make "the subject of religion intelligible by utilizing analytical and interpretive methods that were sponsored and, thus, legitimated, by the Enlightenment."[16] Of course postmodernism has also had a major influence in religious studies—as it has elsewhere in the humanities—undermining much of the old Enlightenment conviction about objectivity, and the interpretive turn (away from objectivity) characterizes much scholarship in religious studies. Still, the governing idea often is that in attempting to render religion intelligible it is approached from the outside using categories and methods drawn from the secular scholarship rather than from within religious traditions.

I have argued that a good liberal education requires that religious voices be included in the curricular conversation, that they be studied in sufficient depth for students to make sense of them, and that they be allowed to contend, as live options, with secular voices. Clearly, much coursework in religious studies allows students to hear religious voices—to encounter primary source texts drawn from various religious traditions—that address fundamental moral and existential concerns and issues, and to study those texts critically, in depth. It is also true, however, that much coursework is historical, and it is not at all clear that religious ways of thinking and living are (typically) presented as live options (in their most compelling forms) for understanding the world here and now. Moreover, it is not clear how often religious ways of thinking and living are allowed to contend with secular alternatives. Does coursework allow discussion of the reasonableness of alternative religious and secular epistemological and methodological commitments—both in the study of religion itself, and in the study of other domains of life? I suspect the answer is sometimes yes, but often no. The potential shortcoming of the field from my point of view is that because of its secular epistemological and methodological commitments, coursework in religious studies may not be allowed to challenge (at least in any direct way) the secular commitments and methodologies of the disciplines in the academy that, cumulatively, marginalize religion from our intellectual life and that result in illiberal education.

John Dixon once put it this way: because "religious studies" makes studies rather than religion its primary focus, students learn that "truth is in the systems of study" rather than in the religion that is studied—though he acknowledged that the "actual effect is far more muddled than that, simply because so much of the material we study is more powerful than the prejudices of the methods we apply to them, and many teachers are exceedingly respectful of the integrity of their subject."[17] Still, because there is a tendency for everything sacred to become grist for the mill of secular scholarship, students often don't learn how to think religiously so much as they learn to think in secular ways about religion.

Consider an analogy. Political scientists often assume that the truth is to be found in the scientific method they employ rather than in the (normative) ideological, philosophical, and political beliefs and values of the politicians, voters, and writers they study—and, as a result, they don't teach students to think politically so much as to think scientifically about politics. But surely what is most important in studying politics, at least from the perspective of a liberal education (and from the perspectives of many students) is sorting out whether Democrats or Republicans, capitalists or socialists, have the more reasonable position. What is justice? How should I live?

Similarly, the primary value of religious studies as part of a liberal education lies in its ability to enable students to think in an informed and critical way about the moral, existential, spiritual, and religious dimensions of life. The secular methodological commitments of the field may discourage teachers from grappling with these questions; indeed, such questions may be thought to be less than respectable.

Of course, it is important to keep in mind that the mission of the field of religious studies goes well beyond that of providing a liberal education for undergraduates. Research and advanced study may well focus on efforts to understand and explain religion using the methodologies of the humanities and social sciences. (No doubt I am drawing this distinction much too starkly and more nuance is needed.) Moreover, the "second-order" secular study of religion can often enlighten our thinking about first-order religious claims.

## Philosophy

Philosophers have often been more open than scholars in religious studies to considering whether God exists, and what the implications might be if God does exist—that is, to questions about whether religious claims *are true or reasonable*. After all, the existence of God is a traditional philosophical problem, debated by many of the great philosophers of history. It is true that over the last century philosophers have not been particularly sympathetic to religious ways of making sense of the world; still, the philosophy of religion continues to be a respectable philosophical specialty, and if philosophers argue for the existence of God they will not automatically be tarred and feathered (or even lose tenure). In fact, over the past few decades there has been something of a renaissance of interest in the philosophy of religion and in arguments about God's existence and nature. Of course, the point of philosophical study is not simply to understand what the great philosophers of history thought about God, but rather to discuss whether it is in fact reasonable to believe in God, and what the implications are.

The philosophy of religion is also a specialty within religious studies, though it has often been noted that philosophers think somewhat differently depending on their disciplinary homes.[18] Perhaps most important, philosophers within religious studies tend to be considerably more wary (than philosophers in departments of philosophy) of questions about whether God exists. I have noted that there is an academic suspicion of departments of religious studies, and it is no doubt safer for scholars in long-established philosophy departments to take on questions of religious truth. Merold Westphal has pointed out that philosophy "does not make people nervous in the same way that the study of religion does."[19] And then there is the fact that, as the philosopher Stephen Evans puts it, "philosophers are thought to be eccentrics who tolerate all kinds of weird ideas."[20]

## Theology

As I suggested above, there has been a long-standing debate among scholars of religious studies regarding theology. I suspect that few scholars in religious studies would deny that the history of theology is an appropriate specialty and subject of study, at least when approached using the categories of a secular historian. What is problematic for many of them is *doing theology* (especially with students, in class) for this requires scholars to use religious categories for making sense of the world and it would appear to undercut the secular foundations of the field. In the introduction to their very helpful collection of essays on the relationship of theology and religious studies, Linell Cady and Delwin Brown write that most scholars of religious studies are threatened by any "rapprochement of the fields, recognizing that the intellectual legitimacy of the modern academic study of religion has been secured through its oppositional contrast to theology. Diminishing the opposition is experienced as endangering the academic status of the field within the context of the liberal arts and sciences."[21] And yet, theology continues to have its advocates—as well as its critics—within religious studies.

Among its critics, Russell McCutcheon frets that "for a number of us working in the field today, there is a weariness in tackling this question [of the relationship of theology and religious studies] yet again because we happen to think that it was settled to our satisfaction quite some time ago—possibly as early as David Hume's theory of religion in the eighteenth century."[22] Settled, that is, so as to exclude theology from serious academic study of religion. Similarly, Donald Wiebe has argued, "If the academic study of religion wishes to be taken seriously as a contributor to knowledge about our world, it will have to concede the boundaries set by the idea of scientific knowledge that characterizes the university. . . . A study of religion directed toward spiritual liberation of the individual or of the human race as a whole, toward the moral welfare of the human race, or toward any ulterior end than that of knowledge itself, should not find a home in the university; for if allowed in, its sectarian concerns will only contaminate the quest for a scientific knowledge of religions and eventually undermine the very institution from which it originally sought legitimation."[23]

Not surprisingly, the idea of sectarian (or confessional) theology—that is, theology done from within a particular religious denomination or tradition—has few advocates within religious studies. The more common argument is for academic, critical, or philosophical theology that allows academic theologians in religious studies to critique religious and secular traditions independently of particular denominations or traditions but still using religious categories for making sense of the world.

But, critics argue, theology has often been taken to be grounded in revelation or a faith tradition and, as such, is not open to falsification or assessment by critical reason. It is not a fit approach, particularly within a public university. Many theologians respond, however, that they are willing to run the gauntlet of critical assessment. For example, Robert Neville has argued for including theology as a specialty within religious studies so long as it is "publicly objective," for theologians "need to make themselves vulnerable to criticism from all sides and to sustain themselves through the process of correction."[24] For David Ray Griffin, theological claims "are not assumed to be products of infallible revelation, but are treated as hypotheses to be tested" by "seeing whether they can lead to an interpretation of reality that is . . . more self-consistent, more adequate to all the relevant data of experience, and more illuminating of those data."[25] As Griffin has noted, given other "professions of belief that are regularly made as a natural part of university teaching, it would be arbitrary to exclude in principle professions of belief in the existence and causal efficacy of a being who would in our tradition most naturally be called 'God.'"[26] After all, no other discipline—not physics, philosophy, or psychology—is required to bracket questions about the nature of ultimate reality: why must religious studies do so? And as we have seen, philosophers continue to wrestle with the existence of God. Why then shouldn't scholars in religious studies argue about the existence of God and a host of other religious claims drawn from a variety of religious traditions?

Of course, a part of what is at issue here is what is to count as evidence, as reasonable. Some advocates of academic theology point to the postmodernist contention that all theories and disciplines are grounded in "faith communities" so that, epistemologically, science, social science, and theology are in the same boat. So, for example, Stephen Webb claims that postmodernism vitiates the old distinction between theology and religious studies: everyone models ways in which "the particularity of faith hangs together (or does not hang together) with various critical discourses." Indeed, "it can be said that every teacher of religion (and the provocation is intentional) is a theologian now."[27] George Marsden has argued that if scholars are going to operate on the postmodern assumption that all judgments are "relative to communities" then we should "follow the implications of that premise as consistently as we can and not absolutize one or perhaps a few sets of opinions and exclude all others." Universities should foster a broad pluralism that allows "all sorts of Christian and other religiously based intellectual traditions back into the discussion."[28]

I would put it this way. All scholars are embedded in intellectual and cultural traditions—the most rigorously skeptical scientists and philosophers as well as the most dogmatic theologians. The question is whether they are going to teach those traditions uncritically or open the discussion to alternative interpretations, risking falsification (or at least some measure of cognitive dissonance) in the process. Scientific, philosophical, and theological claims can each be taught dogmatically, or they can be critically assessed. As I argued above, the key to reasonableness (and critical thinking) is not some particular method—scientific method, for example—but the willingness to think critically about one's most basic assumptions, engaging in conversation.[29] Of course if one assumes that the only respectable knowledge is scientific (as does Wiebe) this will make no sense. But we certainly can't assume that Wiebe is right. Surely there is considerable merit in a pluralism of approaches to religion that allows more than one kind of flower to bloom.

Arguably, the intellectual and cultural task of theology is simply too important to the purposes of a liberal education to ignore. For Delwin Brown, "academic theology is *important*, because the power of religions for good and ill is too great to be ignored by the academy, and because *the scrutiny of academic analysis is too valuable to be denied to religious beliefs.*"[30] Griffin argues that "given a broad view of the history of modernity, there is surely no question more central to the cultural realm than that of the *validity of religion*."[31] And, as Linell Cady argues, eliminating theology from religious studies would make it "unresponsive to the clearly existential motivations and concerns that drive most of its students."[32]

I agree, but I suggest two cautionary notes. First, some scholars have trouble with the term "theology," finding it historically tainted by its association with authority and faith. Moreover, it appears to privilege theism over nontheistic religions and, some would argue, it privileges Christianity, where the term is most comfortably used. In fact, Cady finds the term "inflammatory and misleading" though she endorses the critical task of what others call academic theology.[33] Fearing misunderstanding, Griffin, who had previously argued for keeping the term "theology," now prefers the term "philosophy of religion" for those activities that might also be called theology.[34] The term itself is something of a problem.

Second, the task of academic theology (or the philosophy of religion) carries considerable political risks in a secular university both with regard to the public and to other faculty members. Many scholars (not least in religious studies) would say that the secular character of religious studies is critical to its legitimacy. Hence, I need to acknowledge the risks of departing from neutrality even if academic freedom permits it, and the purposes of a liberal education justify, even require, such theological departures.

## Religious Studies and Public Education

If there are to be high school courses in religion then religious studies must become a certifiable field of teaching, but we need to take some care in defining it. We can't assume that the university model can be uncritically transposed to public schools. Whatever one might think of the merits of doing theology in universities where professors have academic freedom, it would clearly be unconstitutional to do theology, or to take positions on theological issues, in public schools (although teaching about theology historically should be constitutional). I also worry that much undergraduate coursework in religious studies doesn't take religion seriously (in my use of that phrase), either because it is narrowly historical or because it focuses on explaining religion in ways that may be reductionistic. That is, theological and reductionist approaches to religion, both of which are legitimate approaches in universities, are inappropriate approaches in public schools where the primary purpose of high school courses in religious studies is to take religion seriously in ways that are constitutionally neutral.

The two religion courses most commonly taught in high schools are Bible courses and world religions courses. There are four ways to prepare prospective teachers to take religion seriously in their teaching. First, if there are going to be Bible courses, prospective teachers should take courses in the Bible that give them both contemporary secular and religious ways of understanding the Bible for reasons that I will discuss in the next chapter. As we shall see, a Bible course must introduce students to the major different ways of understanding the text, maintaining neutrality among secular and religious interpretations.

Second, whatever the religion course, the teacher must have some understanding of world religions, at least of several major traditions, in both their classical and contemporary guises. Even Bible teachers must understand something of Judaism and Jewish as well as Christian interpretations of the Bible.

Third, any religion teacher must have some understanding of the moral, social, and existential dimensions and implications of religions and religious texts. Obviously, teachers would acquire some of this in undergraduate coursework in world religions, but other courses (in religious ethics or the philosophy of religion) would be helpful.

Finally, religion teachers should have some sense of how religious ways of making sense of the world relate to secular alternatives—to modern science, to history, to literature and the arts, to economics and politics and morality—if they are to help initiate students into the kind of interdisciplinary conversation that is central to a liberal education. There is no easy way to pursue this kind of competency apart from specific courses in religion and literature, religion and science, and so on.

Anyone who teaches a religion course should have at least an undergraduate minor in religious studies comprising the kinds of courses I have just suggested. Of course, there is no way one can just study religion and then teach it. As we've seen, a whole raft of constitutional, political, moral, and pedagogical considerations are relevant to teaching about religion, and prospective teachers must take an education course that addresses them. Needless to say, few if any of these courses are offered at most public universities. All public universities must have departments of religious studies (for their own students, even if they don't prepare teachers) and all departments of religious studies at teacher-training institutions must offer courses designed to prepare prospective teachers to take religion seriously in their classes.

## Conclusions

All courses that address subjects that are religiously controversial (which is to say most courses) must be minimally fair to religious ways of interpreting those subjects. If teachers are to address religion in their classes, they need the help of a new generation of textbooks (that respect the 5 percent rule) as well as of teacher-education programs that prepare them for the task. While some courses in history and literature may do a great deal to help students understand religion, if religion is to be taken seriously high schools and universities must each require a yearlong course in religious studies. Hence, all universities should have departments of religious studies, and religious studies (in a somewhat modified form) must become a certifiable field of teaching in public schools.

With the basics now in place, I will draw out the implications for particular courses in the three chapters that follow.

# 10

# Taking Religion Seriously across the Curriculum

Finally to the nitty-gritty. What are the implications of my position for specific courses?

In the last chapter I argued that there must be at least one required yearlong high school and university course in religious studies. In this chapter I'll sketch what such an introductory course might look like. I'll also say something about Bible courses. As we've seen, however, it isn't enough to require a course in religion. Many other courses should address religion. We need to take some care about how they do this, and how they fit into the curricular conversation that constitutes a liberal education. I will focus my comments here on high school history, literature, and economics courses. I begin with them.

## History

The first problem is that history texts (and, I suspect, most history courses) simply don't say enough about religion. (Call me old-fashioned, but I think that texts should say more about religion than railroads.) The texts' accounts of the origins, "basic teachings," and early development of the great religions are too brief to actually make sense of those religions, and in the absence of a required course in religion it falls largely on history texts and courses to do this. The texts say little about the theological development of religions, freezing them in their classical shapes, and less about religious responses to modernity.

Indeed, religion largely disappears from the texts as we page past the seventeenth century (and, as we've seen, when religion does resurface in the twentieth century it is usually as a cause of war, violence, and social conflict). Finally, in the occasional closing chapters on long-term trends, religion is conspicuous by its absence.

The usual response to any such concerns has been to mention religion a little more often. Unfortunately, given the massive amount of material that history texts must cover there is little hope that much more can be said about religion—that is, short of requiring an additional course in history, a truly excellent idea. (My own view is that high school students should be required to take three years of history.[1])

A part of the problem is the preoccupation of the texts with political, social, and military history, at least in addressing the last several centuries. It is not just religion that is marginalized, so is cultural and intellectual history more generally. And yet, perhaps the most important thing for students to understand in using history to think critically about their own lives is how people in other times have made sense of their lives—often, of course, religiously. Needless to say, religion has not gone away; people continue to grapple with religious ways of making sense of the world and their lives, and religious institutions have continued to influence the larger world for good and ill. So why don't the texts say more about religion?

I'll mention just a few twentieth-century religious themes that are either underplayed or ignored in the texts: the ways in which various modern social, political, and intellectual movements are hostile to religion; the growth of religion (especially Islam and evangelical and Pentecostal Protestantism) in the developing world; increasing religious pluralism in the United States; ecumenical religious dialogue; the role of religion, both pro and con, in the great rights movements (civil rights, women's rights, gay rights) in the second half of the twentieth century; scholarly and theological understandings of the Bible; theological responses to modernity and the transforming events and movements of the twentieth century (modern science, capitalism and industrialization, colonialism, the Holocaust, and globalization); liberal theology among Jews, Protestants, and Catholics; the development of spirituality in the West; conservative reactions to religious and political liberalism; religion and the arts (existentialism, religion in popular art, conflicts over the arts in our culture wars); the new science/religion dialogue; and the religious and spiritual dimensions of the environmental movement. If the texts (rightly) discuss religious contributions to conflict, war, and terrorism (though punches are sometimes pulled) they might find more to say about the many ways in which organized religion nurtures humanitarian responses to war and suffering (in addition to the standard box on Mother Teresa).

There are good reasons to favor an approach that integrates the study of religion into the political, social, cultural, and intellectual narratives of history. Historically, religions have been part of the warp and woof of culture. Yet something can also be said for an occasional chapter that focuses on theology and religious responses to, and influences on, politics, society, culture, and our intellectual life. If there can be occasional chapters on railroads or popular culture why can't there be an occasional chapter on religion? This is probably the easiest way to take religion a little more seriously. The danger is that all discussion of religion might be shunted into such a chapter.

The second major problem is that texts and teachers must be more sensitive to religious interpretations of history. As I have said several times, students should learn something about religious interpretations of history, not just secular historical interpretations of religion. And how do various religious and secular interpretations relate? Are they complementary or might they conflict? I am not saying that religious interpretations of history must be given equal time or that a religious interpretation of history must be used by scholars to shape the dominant narratives in texts or teaching. Of course not. Academic history is thoroughly secular. My point is that the philosophical assumptions (the worldviews) that shape the text's historical narrative must be made clear to students and located on a conceptual map of alternatives if they are to think critically about history. This might be done in several ways.

History texts typically have a preface or introductory chapter that discusses history as an interpretive discipline that sorts out the causes and meaning of historical change. Such a chapter should also discuss various religious interpretations of history. A great deal could be made, for example, of the religious reasons for our systems of dating (e.g., B.C./A.D., B.C.E., C.E.) and periodizing history. Here I might distinguish between what I will call strong and soft religious interpretations of history. A strong religious interpretation holds that God (by whatever name) is actively shaping history by divine intervention, as religious conservatives often believe. Religious liberals are more likely to hold a soft religious interpretation, according to which God acts more indirectly, through individuals and religious institutions, ideas and ideals. But interpretation resists reductionist accounts that explain history in terms of more narrowly economic or materialist factors that typically undercut any substantive explanatory role for God or for religious ideas and ideals.

In addition to a general introduction to these interpretive frameworks, students should be made aware of conflicting interpretations of particular events, movements, and periods of history. When a text discusses ancient Israel, students should learn something about how that history is understood in biblical texts (with their strong religious interpretations) and not just how contemporary secular historians interpret it. But even more recent events and movements—such as the origins of modern science, the origins of capitalism, the religion clauses of the First Amendment, the abolition of slavery, or the civil rights movement—are open to different interpretations, some of which give much more of a soft explanatory role to religious influences than do others.

One high school history text that I reviewed devoted a page or two at the end of each major section to reviewing major disagreements among historians about how to interpret that historical period.[2] If teachers and students took these sections seriously they would see that the subject of history is anything but cut-and-dried (as most history textbooks implicitly suggest). Historians often disagree deeply about how to make sense of history, and their frameworks of interpretation change significantly over time. Moreover, these differences often have implications regarding human nature, the causes of change, the heroes and villains of history, the question of progress, grounds for hope, implications for politics, the broad lessons of history, and, at least sometimes, the role of religion in history. No doubt this is not easy material for students (who often simply want to know the facts about which they will be tested). I suspect, however, that if taken seriously and well taught, multiple interpretations make history exciting.

There is one other way in which texts (and the standards) address the meaning and significance of history, by addressing in their closing chapters long-term historical trends (which as I've noted, typically ignore religion). Such an effort is important, for it is all too easy for students to get lost in the welter of historical facts that are squeezed into the texts. History courses should end not in a rush to get past World War II to the present day, but in reflection on the long sweep of history, and the implications for where we find ourselves. What is the meaning (if any) of the story? Is there moral or social progress in history and, if so, why? Are we closing in on the end of history (of ideological conflict), or are we caught up a clash of civilizations (caused by deep cultural and religious differences)? What have been the moral and religious implications of modern science and capitalism? And there are a dozen other questions, most of which have some religious significance.

I am wary of leaving all discussion of alternative interpretations of history to an opening chapter, to special sections at the end of major sections, or to a closing chapter on long-term trends, because the controversies over interpretation are often important enough to be included in the main narrative of the text. In any case, the general principle should be clear: students must learn that history has been and continues to be subject to multiple interpretations, some of which are religious. Altogether, I expect that this exploration of varying ways of interpreting history and its lessons should require at least 5 percent of the text as I proposed in the last chapter.

The third problem is inherent in textbooks no matter how sensitive they are to religion. Written as they are in (often leaden) prose from within a particular disciplinary perspective, they simply cannot provide the imaginative inside understanding of different cultures and traditions that primary sources provide. In a sense the solution is easy. Supplement texts with a collection of primary sources drawn from traditions—including religious traditions—other than the textbook author's. Supplemental readings from the Bible or Buddhist Sutras or the Qur'an, or from theological and imaginative literary texts written from within religious traditions would be very helpful, though, of course, their use would require sophistication, time, and money (none of which may be available). This problem could best be addressed if history and literature courses (using anthologies that include religious scriptures and literature) were taught in parallel (or, better yet, were team-taught, a luxury, I realize). This would allow typically dull history textbooks dominated by a single narrative voice to be supplemented by a variety of authorial perspectives embodied in texts that may be imaginatively rich and compelling. Why can't this be done more?

Finally, neutrality again. No doubt history texts are formally neutral; they are not overtly hostile to religion. But because students will inevitably learn to interpret history in secular categories that are likely to ignore or marginalize religious interpretations of history, a substantive neutrality between religion and nonreligion is impossible. I have argued that substantive neutrality and robust fairness should be understood as a requirement on the total curriculum, not individual courses. Still, individual courses must be at least minimally fair by acknowledging controversies involving religion, and giving students some sense of what is at issue.

We also need to consider neutrality among religions. Diane Moore has recently argued that the study of American and Western history (along with the Western literary canon) "valorizes" the Christian tradition so that "the 'default assumption about religion in our culture in general and our schools in particular is that of Christianity." Hence, "Christianity is still deeply embedded in 'secular' schools in ways that subtly promote unintentional Christian sectarianism."[3] There is something to this, though the point can be overstated. Of the world's religions, Christianity has been far and away the dominant influence on Western, European, and American history; students simply can't understand Western history apart from Christianity. It would be ludicrous to require that courses in American, European, or Western history pay equal attention to (all?) other religious traditions. A good historical education must devote more time and space to Christianity than to other religions on entirely secular grounds.

So is there a neutrality problem here? Do texts and courses (at least implicitly) valorize Christianity? This might be the case if we taught only Western history. But, of course, a good liberal education also requires the study of non-Western countries and cultures with their religions. I suppose one might ask why we don't teach just world history. Why tilt the scales in the direction of Western or American history (and Christianity) at all? I don't think this is a serious question, though there are many answers that might be given. As I have argued, it is one task of a liberal education to root students in traditions that make sense of the moral and political values that they have inherited (as Americans, for example). We can't turn students loose on the world rootless, somehow equally shaped by all traditions (or no traditions). In the end, neutrality—and what we take seriously—must be determined on the basis of the entire curriculum, not individual courses.

## Literature

Much more than the typically dry prose of history textbooks, the stories, poems, plays, films, and novels that students encounter in studying literature have the potential to excite and enrich the imagination, nurture empathy, and provide an inside understanding of religious traditions. Moreover, literary texts often address Big Questions and those inescapable existential concerns about the meaning of life that too seldom surface in history texts. So let me repeat my lament from the last section: if only we taught history and literature in parallel courses!

And yet, literature texts and courses also fall short of taking religion seriously for a number of reasons. As I noted in chapter 2, literature anthologies that are organized historically (far from all are) typically include religious literature, sometimes even excerpts from scriptures, but these selections are always short and lack context. (This is a general failing of the texts: even at 1,200 or 1,400 pages, they almost always anthologize relatively brief excerpts from longer works, presumably necessitated by the need to be inclusive and squeeze a great deal into a limited space.) Hence, the texts don't provide a broad or systematic understanding of religions so much as occasional insights. Moreover, the texts rarely include recent literature that conveys to students the sense that religion is a live option here and now. So what should be done?

### 1. *The Big Questions*

Most literature wasn't written for narrowly aesthetic reasons—art for art's sake as it were. The great Greek tragedies were integral to civic festivals and had deep moral and religious meaning for their audiences. *Paradise Lost* is a theological as well as a poetic work. *Crime and Punishment* is about sin and redemption. In the past, religious ways of making sense of life and the world suffused literature and the arts just as they did morality, politics, and science.

Clearly, great literature must be studied not simply for aesthetic reasons but for its success in addressing and grappling with the Big Questions, with morality and the sources of meaning in life. In fact, this is why the study of literature should be required in schools and universities. No doubt it is good that students learn about plot and characterization, symbolism and meter, but it is essential that they acquire the imaginative understanding of good and evil, justice and injustice, sin and salvation, to be found in great literature. One important reason for choosing which texts to read in a literature class (or to anthologize in a textbook) is the ability of those texts to illuminate important moral and religious concerns and traditions. Teachers should not avoid the moral, political, and religious meaning and significance of texts, but embrace the opportunity they provide for discussing the Big Questions. More particularly, they should explore with their students the sacred and religious literature that addresses the Big Questions and the religious dimensions of people's lives.[4]

## 2. *The Sacred*

Some of the deepest and most influential answers to the Big Questions are found in the sacred literature of religious traditions. As we have seen, literature anthologies typically include brief excerpts from sacred texts. These excerpts should be longer, and students should learn what it means for a text to be sacred or canonical within different religious traditions.

Even more important, literature classes are the only place in the curriculum (other than courses in religion) in which students might acquire some inside understanding of the sacred more generally. People have often experienced the world—or particular times and places in the world—as sacred or as holy. Traditionally, religion has not just been a matter of believing propositions; religions involve distinctive ways of experiencing reality and, arguably, being oblivious to the sacred or the holy is a little like being tone-deaf to music. Surely acquiring some sense of the sacred is part of being well educated. The sensitivity to symbolism, to metaphor and myth and mystery, to beauty and wonder, to those aspects of nature and life that move us deeply, in literature and the arts, can imaginatively convey to students ways of experiencing the world that transcend the mundane, the literal, the merely secular.

## 3. Disciplines and Interpretation

Teachers have an obligation to take authors seriously, just as we take cultures or intellectual traditions seriously, by trying to understand them in their own categories, rather than automatically imposing our own favored interpretive framework on them. At least this is where we must begin. Of course, writers work within traditions (including religious traditions) and their works in time become part of traditions, so, to make sense of their meaning and influence, students need to understand those traditions. In fact, to get at the meaning and significance of many texts teachers need to draw on religious traditions and the categories they provide. (I'll say more about this in discussing the Bible below.)

Unfortunately, neither the New Critics who dominated literary criticism for much of the last century, nor the professors of cultural studies who have been so influential for the last several decades, have typically been much interested in or sensitive to religious traditions. Hence, given their training, teachers are not likely to be sophisticated about them either, and will typically approach texts in narrowly secular aesthetic or political and critical categories. Too often close readings of texts decontextualize them, allowing them to float free of the traditions (religious traditions included) that make sense of them. Sometimes an overly narrow aesthetic focus dictates a preoccupation less with *what* is said—its potential truth and its claim on us—than on *how* it is said. For other critics, religious themes will be "deconstructed" from the vantage point of a hermeneutic of suspicion that exposes the hidden (class, gender, and racial) prejudices and purposes of writers and dismisses out of hand any religious claims they might make.

The danger, once again, is that academic disciplines will constrain the vision of teachers and students. Like all academic disciplines, literary criticism is largely secular. As a result, teachers have some obligation to expand their own sensitivity to, and understanding of, the religious traditions (and experiences of the sacred) that shape literature. No doubt an undergraduate course on religion and literature would prove helpful for prospective teachers.

## 4. Literature and Our Culture Wars

As I mentioned in chapter 1, literature and the arts are caught up in various battles in our culture wars over religion (battles between conservatives and liberals, the sacred and the secular, Islam and the West). Often these battles play out in local school districts, sometimes in the U.S. Congress, occasionally on the international stage. This shouldn't be surprising, for literature often conveys profoundly controversial conceptions of good and evil. Literature courses must nurture the ability of students to understand the implications and significance of literature and the arts for religion in our public life.

## 5. Popular Literature

T. S. Eliot once confessed to the "alarming" realization that it was not great literature but literature read "purely for pleasure" that had the most powerful and potentially insidious influence on us because we read it so uncritically.[5] This is even more the case regarding popular media such as television, film, video games, music, and the Internet, which are all profoundly influential within youth culture. These media are often as deeply controversial on moral and religious grounds as they are influential, and students must learn to think critically about them.

## 6. Secularization

Just as in studying history, so also in studying literature, it is easy to lose sight of the forest for the trees, of long-term trends for immersion in the particulars (in this case literary texts rather than historical facts). Students should understand the significance of the secularization of literature and arts, the loss of transcendence and meaning that writers may mourn or celebrate, its causes and its implications for culture. Of course, even as literature has become more secular, some writers have continued to grapple with the problem of God, transcendence, and the loss of meaning. As I noted in chapter 1, there continue to be poets and novelists who write within religious traditions, who can only be adequately understood in the context of those traditions, while others have attempted to re-symbolize God and the spiritual dimension of life, rejecting traditional religious symbols and myths in the process. Students need to understand something about how literature and the arts play into our larger cultural conversation about God, religion, spirituality, and the ways in which we find meaning in life.

## 7. The Humanities

Finally, it is important that both literature and history teachers think of their teaching in terms of the humanities. The critical point here is that historically the disciplines of the humanities make sense of persons, history, and society within a broadly humanistic rather than naturalistic framework of thought.

(Maybe I should say that sometimes the term "humanism" is used as a synonym for "atheism." I *don't* mean this. Scholars often refer to the disciplines of the humanities as humanistic disciplines.) While the humanities are secular disciplines, their basic categories overlap in important ways with those of religion. I'll give three examples. First, the great Western religions—Judaism, Christianity, and Islam—all understand reality as a narrative; history has a plot line, with a central character, God, who also happens to be (in some way) the author of the story. Similarly, most scholars within the humanities contend that we best understand persons in terms of their place within a narrative or set of overlapping narratives. Second, literature, like religion and the humanities more generally, insists on thick descriptions of people—accounts that locate the intelligibility of our beliefs and actions in a rich meshing of reasons, purposes, intentions, and cultural contexts and meanings, rather than in an abstract matrix of scientific laws. Third, the study of literature, like the study of art and religious studies, is particularly sensitive to symbols, metaphors, and myths that express or point to dimensions of reality that can't be caught in the literal, factual categories and languages of the sciences and the hard social sciences. Hence, even though their categories of interpretation are secular, the disciplines of the humanities often overlap religious categories. (Again, secular means nonreligious, not antireligious.) Unfortunately, the concept of the humanities is largely absent from K–12 education. This merits much more discussion than I can give here.

## Economics

As we saw in chapter 2, economics is typically taught as a hard social science in which neoclassical economic theory provides the governing framework of interpretation. Because this framework is assumed in textbooks and the standards, students are taught uncritically to accept certain controversial views of human nature (that people are essentially self-interested), rationality (that it is rational to act on the basis of self-interest), values (which are understood as personal preferences), and, at least implicitly, morality (which is typically replaced by some form of cost-benefit analysis).

Now there may well be good reasons for adopting a neoclassical framework for understanding the economic domain of life. The problem is that it is deeply controversial (less so, no doubt, among economists than in other academic disciplines and in the larger culture) and as such, a good liberal education should initiate students into a critical conversation about economics and neoclassical theory—one that claims at least 5 percent of an economics text. A substantive opening chapter should locate neoclassical theory on a conceptual map of contending ways of thinking about economics historically and in contemporary culture, religious ways included. Put in terms of my Principle of Cultural Location and Weight, students must be given some sense of how controversial neoclassical theory is, and for whom. (Students might also learn that not all economists accept neoclassical theory; there is, for example, growing interest in behavioral and neuroeconomics, neither of which, alas, is any more sensitive to religion.)

So far I'm asking for very little. As we have seen, most economics textbooks include a chapter on Marxism and socialism. There could easily be another chapter (or two) on various religious (and philosophical) interpretations of human nature, rationality, and morality.

No doubt economists will argue that they should be free to define the content of economics texts and courses, leaving all discussion of religious or philosophical issues to other courses. If we were to accept this proposal, then there must be some other course in which economics is discussed from religious and philosophical perspectives, and in the absence of a required course on religion or ethics, what course might that be? In any case, this wouldn't suffice. No doubt economists should be free to choose the primary theory that students are required to learn, but this doesn't absolve them of their responsibility to initiate students into the critical conversation that constitutes a liberal education. The study of economics—or any subject—cannot be a disciplinary monologue if it is to serve the purposes of a liberal education.

Of course, the study of economics by almost anyone's definition (other than an economist's) is shot through with moral and spiritual issues and concerns. I've already mentioned what I take to be the most important of them in chapters 1 and 2. What follows here is largely a reminder.

One of the biggest of the Big Questions is that of justice (as it applies to taxes, welfare programs, race, gender, the rich and poor, and the Third World). How can economics textbooks ignore the problem of justice and contending theories of justice? Students must learn something about justice and intellectual and cultural traditions (secular and religious) within which interpretations of justice are embedded. Perhaps this is even more important than understanding the Federal Reserve system, the subject of lengthy chapters in all economics textbooks. Of course, our current economic crisis has made clear the importance of the Federal Reserve (the Fed); it also makes clear the importance of understanding the implications of the Fed's actions for justice. This might even help students vote more intelligently.

In chapter 2 I noted that the economics texts all discuss poverty, presenting considerable information documenting the extent and causes of poverty and inequality, but they provide no moral, political, or religious context for thinking about poverty as a moral or spiritual problem about which something ought to be done. In 2008, the World Bank concluded that 1.4 billion people live in poverty—that is, on goods and services equivalent to what $1.25 a day would buy in America. As Peter Singer has put it, "This kind of poverty kills."[6] Poverty is an evil of immense proportions. Singer rightly argues that a problem as great as world poverty must be addressed in various courses. But surely there is a special responsibility to address it in economics courses that do not shy away from putting it in various moral, political, and religious perspectives.

Textbooks should raise questions about personal ethics as well as social justice. Granted, this is something of a challenge when the texts are committed to ignoring morality, but as an unending series of scandals (some of immense proportions) makes evident, too many executives fail to understand and act on their moral responsibilities. No doubt such behavior is made much easier by the conventional wisdom of neoclassical theory that business is one thing, morality another (or the dubious proposition that ethical behavior is always in one's long-term self-interest, which suggests that morality requires an economic justification). Moreover, texts should discuss compassion and altruism and not uncritically assume that human nature is essentially self-interested. (All religions are based on the idea of overcoming our self-interest in order to act compassionately.) And they should discuss why, in various philosophical and religious traditions, charitable giving is so important.

Texts and courses should discuss the meaningfulness of work, the dignity of labor, human rights relating to labor, and work as a calling (as fulfilling fundamental moral or spiritual obligations). They must discuss consumerism or materialism as a moral and spiritual problem (as is the case within every religious tradition). And they must discuss the relationship between economics and the environment as a moral and spiritual problem regarding obligations to future generations, the moral dangers inherent in technology, the stewardship of nature (including the idea of the sacredness of nature), and, of course, the implications of social justice.

In spite of this robust agenda, I am not arguing that economics texts and courses should be made over into courses in moral theology or philosophy. So long as most economists accept neoclassical theory, the texts can employ it as the primary framework for interpreting the economic domain of life. But clearly, there is a major problem with teaching economics entirely as a hard social science. It is profoundly illiberal insofar as it screens out immensely important moral and spiritual Big Questions and contending philosophical and religious ways of answering them. Indeed, the idea that we can separate economics from morality and religion contributes powerfully to the secularization of our culture. A large part of the problem, once again, is disciplines. Economics should be taught more as a subject open to various interpretations and concerns, religious as well as secular.[7]

Finally, we should keep in mind the importance of primary sources, particularly in addressing moral and religious concerns. Textbooks should always (at least for older students) be taught in conjunction with primary sources including, I suggest, literature, both secular and religious, that brings alive moral and spiritual problems relating to justice and the economic dimension of people's lives.

## Bible Courses

There can be little doubt that the Bible is the most influential book in the history of humankind, and if any book warrants serious study, it is the Bible. As I noted in chapter 8, even Richard Dawkins, the world's most prominent atheist, has claimed that students must learn about the Bible if they are to understand culture. And it continues to be immensely influential. So all students should study the Bible. But where? And how?

In public schools and universities the answers to both questions must be constitutionally acceptable. As we've seen, in *Abington v. Schempp* (1963) the U.S. Supreme Court approved of academic (but not devotional) study of the Bible when it is taught objectively as part of a secular program of education. In chapter 7 I argued that we need to parse objectivity in terms of neutrality, the Court's touchstone since its *Everson* ruling in 1947. Any study of the Bible must be religiously neutral—it must be both neutral among religions and neutral between religion and nonreligion.

Courts have found no problem with elective courses in the Bible so long as they are properly taught. I suggested in the last chapter that a required Bible course may implicitly endorse Christianity and, as such, raises a neutrality problem. One might respond that a required Bible course could be justified simply on the basis of the Bible's influence.[8] (Similarly, we can justify paying more attention to Christianity than to other religions in courses in American or Western history and literature, as a matter of its influence.) But if there is going to be only one required course in religious studies, there are many reasons relating to both neutrality and liberal education for casting our net to catch much more than the Bible. My own proposal is to incorporate significant study of the Bible into a world religions course or the introductory course I will sketch below. Of course, some discussion of the Bible is also important in world history courses, and excerpts from the Bible should be included in world literature anthologies.

There is now an effort in the legislatures of a few states to enable and encourage (but not require) Bible courses in the public schools, and several states have passed "Bible bills." Unhappily, too many legislators have gotten caught up in battles over the curricula of these Bible courses and ended up arguing theology in ways that are neither constitutional, enlightened, nor edifying.[9] At issue are two nationally distributed curricula.

The first, distributed by the National Council on Bible Curriculum in Public Schools, while professing to be nonsectarian, is a distinctively conservative Protestant curriculum that encourages students to use the King James Bible (the Bible of choice for many conservative Protestants). The curriculum is a teacher's guide, and there is no textbook other than the Bible itself, which is to be read free of interpretive commentary: "Study about the Bible should center on the biblical text itself rather than the extraneous material and theories which might express a particular theological position rather than the historical presentation found in the Bible."[10] This is, of course, a peculiarly conservative Protestant approach to the Bible—an approach that would be rejected by Catholics, Jews, liberal Protestants, and secular scholars of the Bible.[11] One of the problems with just reading the Bible is that this throws students on their own, typically meager, resources for making sense of ancient texts written in different languages and cultures. In their review of this curriculum, Brennan Breed and Kent Harold Richards conclude that it assumes that the Bible is "infallible and thus historically accurate," that "critical inquiry into the Bible and its backgrounds is not to be trusted," and that a "'literal method' of reading the Bible without reference to alternative views" is to be adopted.[12] Yes the curriculum also ventures into the politics of church and state and advocates a conservative Christian Americanism according to which the Founding Fathers created the United States to be a distinctively Christian nation. (In fact, the cover of the 2005 edition pictures the Declaration of Independence and a flag, not the Bible.) In one of his several reviews of the curriculum, Mark Chancey concludes that the curriculum promotes "the idea that the Protestant Bible is the cultural standard, that conservative Protestant beliefs about the Bible are the scholarly norm, and that the Old and New Testaments consist primarily of easily harmonized historical accounts. In short," he concludes, "students will leave this course with the understanding of the Bible apparently held by most members of the [council's conservative board] with little awareness of views held by other religious groups or within the academic community."[13]

The second curriculum, distributed by the Bible Literacy Project, takes the form of a lavishly illustrated textbook that is to be used in conjunction with a Bible of the student's choice. The textbook works through the Bible, sometimes noting different interpretations of important passages (it is sensitive to Jewish interpretations) and discussing the influence of various passages on art, literature, and, occasionally, politics. The text has shortcomings: it says little about scholarly textual and historical criticism, avoids any discussion of the relationship of science and the Bible, says little about the relationship of biblical texts to controversial moral issues, and is not very helpful in enabling students to understand the differences between the ways conservatives and liberals read the Bible. Still, it is a significant improvement on the curriculum used by the National Council on Bible Curriculum in Public Schools, and has been favorably reviewed by many religious journals and both secular and religious scholars from diverse traditions. Not surprisingly, it has been denounced by advocates of the National Council on Bible Curriculum in Public Schools curriculum, often for discussing multiple interpretations of the Bible, as well as by (the liberal) Americans United for the Separation of Church and State, which finds it too uncritically sympathetic to religion.

The two basic questions to ask in assessing these (or any) curricula are whether they are religiously neutral, and whether they promote the ideals of a liberal education. Constitutional neutrality requires fairness to alternative religious and secular interpretations. A liberal education requires that students be initiated into a discussion of the major ways in which cultures and scholars have made sense of the Bible. Happily, we can draw on a common-ground statement, *The Bible and Public Schools: A First Amendment Guide* (1999), that has been endorsed by sixteen national educational and religious organizations (Jewish, Christian, Islamic; conservative and liberal), as well as People for the American Way. While the statement is framed primarily in terms of neutrality, it tracks the requirements of a liberal education closely. (The Society of Biblical Literature, the primary national organization of academic biblical scholars, has also issued guidelines, "Bible Electives in Public Schools: A Guide from the Society of Biblical Literature" (2009), which takes largely the same position as the common-ground document.)[14]

The common-ground statement emphasizes neutrality in two contexts. First, whose Bible? I have so far written as if there is a single Bible when, as the *Guidelines* note, Jews, Catholics, Protestants, and Orthodox Christians have different Bibles—their own set of canonical texts arranged in different orders. The most fundamental difference, of course, is that Christians have a New Testament, while Jews don't (and, because Jews don't have a New Testament they don't have an *Old* Testament either: Jews have the Hebrew Bible, or Hebrew Scriptures, or *Tanakh*). Students should learn about the different Bibles. Of course, particular translations will also be more or less acceptable within different religious traditions. Students should understand why translations matter, and explore how important passages are translated and what difference this makes.

Second, whose interpretation? According to the *Guidelines*, "Because there are many ways to interpret the Bible—religious and secular—public school teachers should expose students to a variety of interpretations. Teachers should allow students to encounter the text directly (like any primary source), and then draw on the resources of different religious and secular interpretative traditions for understanding its meaning and importance. To do this effectively requires the use of secondary sources that provide a discussion of various religious and secular approaches to the Bible."[15] There are, for example, fundamental differences between Jewish and Christian readings of Scripture. Does the "Suffering Servant" passage in Isaiah 53 refer to Jesus or to Israel? Is the narrative of Adam and Eve the story of the Fall? Jews and Christians have historically disagreed about both.

Just as in reading Homer or Plato, or any ancient secular text, biblical scholars employ modern historical and literary scholarship. Beginning in the nineteenth century the resources of such scholarship (in history, philology, and archaeology) were brought to bear on the Bible. For example, most scholars agree that the Torah or Pentateuch wasn't the work of Moses but the "redaction" of at least four different sources, and biblical texts (such as the Noah narrative) were variations on nonbiblical stories common in the Ancient Near East.[16] In our century, liberal and mainline Jewish and Christian theologians have drawn on such scholarship to interpret the Bible and rethink their traditions, while conservative Christians and Orthodox Jews have typically reaffirmed that the Bible is inerrant.[17]

I might add a related question, whose emphases? It has often been argued that the Bible can be quoted in support of any cause. This is an exaggeration, but there is a point to it. Some biblical texts were quoted by slaveholders, others by abolitionists. Different religious traditions have valued (and sometimes denigrated) different portions of the Bible. Jews will not read the Hebrew Bible as a precursor to the Christian New Testament—and will pay much more attention to the ritual and legalistic themes of the Torah that Christians ignore. Liberals are likely to emphasize the moral/political theme of liberating the oppressed found in the great Hebrew Prophets and the synoptic Gospels, while conservatives will likely place greater emphasis on passages addressing personal salvation and the afterlife. Students should read enough of the Bible to acquire some sense of its recurring themes and internal emphases, but if they can't read all of the Bible (an unlikely possibility) teachers must be careful in selecting (and interpreting) the parts they do assign.

Needless to say, all of this requires considerable sophistication on the part of teachers. No doubt a modest level of factual biblical literacy (learning the stories) is possible without venturing far into the deep waters of controversy, but any substantive discussion of the meaning of biblical texts will become controversial quickly.

Schools occasionally offer Bible history courses that are likely to compound the controversy. The danger here is that the veracity of biblical accounts of history and miracles are deeply controversial. Religious conservatives often argue that historical and archaeological research corroborates the Bible's account of history, while most mainline and secular scholars find little evidence for such claims, and a good deal of evidence that casts doubt on significant stretches of biblical history. (Here is another place where my Principle of Cultural Location and Weight is critical: how much support do different positions have, and among which scholars?) The common-ground guidelines prudently suggest that Bible-as-history courses are likely to be too controversial, and propose that if there are to be Bible courses they should adopt a literary approach.

It is true that courses on the Bible in Literature (that is, the influence of the Bible on later literature) can be taught without too much controversy, but they aren't likely to give students much understanding of the Bible itself. Study of the Bible as literature (that is, study of biblical texts themselves) is likely to be more difficult and controversial. Literary study often raises questions of authorship and dating that are controversial, and literary study cannot avoid questions of *meaning and interpretation* that are inherently controversial.[18]

No doubt there is some value in simply reading the creation narratives in Genesis 1–3, in just knowing the story. But it is hard to understand how there could be thoughtful discussion of those narratives apart from a whole host of theologically controversial questions. How do the first and second creation narratives relate to each other? Indeed, are there two narratives or one? And who wrote it/them? Some curious students will ask about Genesis 1 and evolution. And what is the relationship of the account of the creation of women in Genesis 1 with the creation of Eve in Genesis 2? Is the serpent Satan (and since the text doesn't say that, where does that idea come from)? Is this the story of the Fall? What is the best translation of the Hebrew in Genesis 1:1 (that is, does God create from nothing or from a preexisting chaos)? When God says in 1:26 "let us make man in our image" who is the "us"? Well, enough. These are neither unimportant nor uninteresting questions. Can they be ignored? Or would this be to suggest the text should be read literally?

My own view is that English teachers must be prepared (by their coursework and by competent teacher's editions of their texts) to know something about the basic scholarship, secular and theological, of those biblical texts included in their anthologies. They must be able to give students some sense of the major interpretations (while maintaining their neutrality). Teachers who teach a Bible course that adopts a literary approach must themselves have studied the Bible in some depth. All things considered, however, I think it best that any substantive study of the Bible be incorporated into a world religions course or the introductory course in religious studies that I will propose below.

There is a final point of some importance regarding approaches to the Bible. It is no more permissible to privilege a secular interpretation of the Bible (one that draws exclusively on secular historical and textual criticism) than it is to privilege a particular theological interpretation (such as that of conservative Protestantism). An introductory Bible course should be neutral among religious interpretations and neutral between religious and secular interpretations, a daunting task. No doubt an exclusive emphasis on secular historical and textual criticism and social science is much more likely in universities than in high schools, and there, academic freedom grants professors considerable leeway in shaping their courses. Still, there is, I suggest, considerable wisdom in adopting rough neutrality as the relevant pedagogical principle. The purposes of a liberal education require that students be introduced to a variety of ways of interpreting Scripture, theological and secular.

## Introductory Courses in Religion

In his book *Religious Literacy* Stephen Prothero argues for requiring two religion courses in public schools—one on the Bible, the other on world religions.[19] He doesn't say whether these are to be semester-long or yearlong courses. If he is proposing two yearlong courses I reluctantly dissent simply because the idea of one required religion course will be sufficiently outrageous for most educators (though I admire his spunk). So we must figure out a way to incorporate some serious study of the Bible and world religions into a single, yearlong course.

If there is to be only one required course—I'll simply call it an introduction to religion—it must, of course, take religion seriously. I've summarized the major guidelines for teaching about religion in my discussion of pedagogy in the preceding chapter. Here I will just say that an introductory course in religion must give students an inside understanding of several religions, as live options, as part of the critical conversation that constitutes a liberal education. It should prepare students to think in informed and reflective ways about religious ways of making sense of the moral and existential dimensions of their lives. It is important that students acquire some sense of the internal diversity of religions, especially conservative and liberal versions of them. Care needs to be taken regarding who gets to define or speak for a religion, and teachers must be sensitive to the different dimensions of religions (doctrine, myths or sacred narratives, ethical teachings, rituals, religious experiences, social institutions, and art). Of course, public school teachers need to remain religiously neutral in teaching the course.

Given the potentially controversial nature of the study of religion it is wise to discuss with students the constitutional status of religion in public schools (or public universities), establishing the civic, constitutional, and pedagogical ground rules, including the importance of respecting (not agreeing with) students from other religious traditions or no religious tradition.

I need to be clear that in an introductory course it is impossible to take religion seriously without taking several religions seriously. This is a requirement both of neutrality (among religions) and of the breadth that is essential to critical thinking and a liberal education. In each case we are pushed toward breadth, diversity, inclusiveness, and fairness. It is, of course, impossible to take all religions seriously, treating each one fairly and neutrally. There are too many. The only feasible way of proceeding is by limiting the field to major world religions. (Typically, world religions courses deal with five, six, or seven of the major world religions, defined largely in terms of their influence and the number of their adherents.) Of course, the more religions discussed, the more superficial the discussion will be. Inevitably, there must be trade-offs in terms of breadth and depth of treatment.

We need to be sensitive, however, to the fact that influence may vary in different cultural contexts. In the context of American and Western education, and in the lives of most students, Christianity will be much more influential and relevant to a wider range of educational purposes than other religions. If a greater emphasis on Christianity can be justified in terms of influence and relevance, however, Christianity cannot be privileged by any suggestion, explicit or implicit, that it is the true religion. On the other hand, given that students are likely to learn more about Christianity than other religions in studying history and literature there is some reason to ensure that other religions are not slighted in a world religions course. Moreover, some minor religions may be particularly influential in a local community or state, and there is merit in including study of either African or Native American religions along with the more influential religious traditions. I should add that the First Amendment doesn't require equal time for all religions, an impossible requirement, but there must be valid, educational (nonreligious) reasons—such as influence—for giving some more time than others.

I propose that in a yearlong introductory course one semester might be devoted to the Bible, Christianity, and Judaism, and the other to Islam and Eastern religions. (Teachers need to make clear that Judaism is largely a postbiblical religion growing out of rabbinic traditions, and they also need to be careful about lumping Eastern religions together as if they are interchangeable.) A case can also be made for discussing spirituality as an alternative to institutionalized religion in modern cultures.

There is also an argument to be made for the comparative study of secular religions or worldviews. Ninian Smart, the great scholar of world religions, argued forcefully for treating such religions or worldviews (e.g., liberal humanism, Marxism, scientism, or nationalism) side by side with traditional religions, in order to enable students to think critically about their similarities and help them decipher their deepest values.[20] There is considerable merit in exploring the ways in which secular frameworks of interpretation and worldviews function religiously, often as matters of faith. I agree, but I would argue a little differently, that an essential goal of the introductory course is to think critically about the differences between religious and secular disciplinary frameworks of interpretation. This is essential to the critical conversation that a liberal education must nurture. Religion must not be marginalized or privatized, exiled to the periphery of the curricular conversation as if it had nothing to do with how to interpret the subjects studied in the rest of the curriculum. So, for example, the introductory course should make students informed about and sensitive to the tensions between various live religious and secular ways of understanding morality, sexuality, economics, and nature. Clearly, the course must explore what counts as religious.

It might appear that requiring a course in religion that promotes an empathetic, inside understanding of religion could imply that religion is being endorsed or promoted. There is, of course, a difference between empathy and sympathy. It is not the task of such a course to nurture sympathy for (or agreement with) a particular tradition or religion generally; it is a task of such a course to nurture empathy—an inside understanding of various religious traditions. In any case, the whole point of taking religion seriously enough to require a course in religion is to balance the scales, to restore neutrality to a curriculum that implicitly favors secular over religious ways of making sense of the world.

What about the 5 percent rule? In this case the goal might be to make students aware of secular interpretations or theories of religion (rather than, as in other courses, of religious interpretations of secular subjects) or arguments about atheism, agnosticism, and various forms of skepticism. But most of the time must be devoted to understanding religious ways of making sense of the world and the subjects of the curriculum. The fundamental task, after all, is to take religion seriously, providing a robust neutrality to the curriculum.

All of this adds up to what may be an impossibly rich and complex agenda, and I suspect that it can be accomplished only in limited ways. (Hence the need for at least a yearlong course.) There is, of course, a good deal of overlap between what I am proposing and a typical course in world religions. It is essential for my purposes, however, to frame the purposes of an introductory course in terms of religions as live options and a critical conversation among religious and secular ways of making sense of the world, more than is often done in most world religions courses.

The course that I have proposed must be a high school or undergraduate course, for it will require maturity on the part of students. While I don't believe that an opt-out provision is constitutionally necessary for high school students, it may be politically wise. As I noted in the last chapter, parents on both the religious right and the secular left may be suspicious of any such course. It is absolutely essential that school districts have done their homework, establishing constitutional ground rules for high school courses with the cooperation of the community.

## Conclusion

Although I have argued that there must be required courses in religion if schools and universities are to take religion seriously, educators might make a serious dent in the problem by addressing religion more thoroughly, along the lines I have proposed, in history and literature courses.

I expect most educators will view my proposal for a required yearlong course in religion as extravagant and unrealistic: there simply isn't room in the curriculum. As I indicated in chapter 8, I would make room for a high school course in religion by dropping a required math course (making that math course an elective for students who wish to pursue careers in math or the sciences). This is to me *an easy call*, though I recognize that our national fixation on mathematics and the entrance requirements of most colleges and universities make this a problematic proposal for the moment. No doubt there are other possibilities for carving time out of electives or less important courses. In any case, the course I have proposed is necessary if there is to be constitutional neutrality, and it is absolutely necessary if students are to become liberally educated human beings.

Most undergraduates have many more electives than high school students, and it should be easier to make room in the undergraduate curriculum for a required course in religious studies, though I don't want to minimize the problems of disciplinary turf wars over curricular requirements and the academic balance of power, and there would be immense suspicion of any required course in religion at most public universities.

Finally, I fear that this chapter feels like a rather breathless forced march though a thicket of technicalities. I can't say that our pace will become more leisurely in the final two chapters, but at least these chapters will be devoted to a single subject each.

# II

# Religion and Science Courses

Too often the media version of our culture wars over science and religion is that of an endless series of battles over evolution between fundamentalist creationists on the one side, and all the rest of us reasonable folk who accept evolution on the other. As we shall see, there are more than two positions on evolution (fundamentalists aren't the only religious folk with a horse in this race) and, as important as evolution is, there are other important controversies regarding science and religion. Because there is some value in working through a particular issue more thoroughly than I have done so far, I will spend much of this chapter on evolution, but I will also say something about several other controversies—over cosmology and over consciousness—at the end of the chapter.

I will argue that schools and universities are obligated to educate students in introductory science courses about alternative ways of making sense of nature, religious alternatives included, rather than simply train them in good science, even if scientists are confident that they have the truth firmly in their grasp. As I hope is clear by now, my position involves no special pleading for religion (much less, in this case, for some form of creationism); rather, I will simply apply to science education the same principles that govern the role of religion in all parts of the curriculum given the requirements of a liberal education.

## Science and Liberal Education

There is considerable controversy among scholars about how much of reality science can explain. Many secular philosophers reject in principle the claim that science can explain either mind or morality, both of which require that we draw on a quite different set of categories (from the humanities). Indeed, scientists acknowledge that they are not yet able to explain everything, though scientific method (or methodological naturalism—the commitment to materialistic explanations that makes no appeal to purpose, design, or causes that have a supernatural source) has proved extraordinarily successful in expanding the range of scientific understanding.[1]

So what are the requirements of a liberal education when it comes to science? From our previous discussions of history, literature, and economics the answer should be obvious. If students are to think critically about matters about which there is considerable controversy, matters with profound existential implications, they must learn about the disagreements and listen to the contending voices. True, students don't need to learn about every cultural or scholarly controversy, only the important ones. But those revolving around the relationship of science and religion are important—indeed, we might say they are of cosmic importance.

The curriculum must initiate students into our ongoing conversation about religion and science. But where in the curriculum should this take place? The usual answer of the science and education establishment is that students should learn about science in science classes, and religion somewhere else— probably in a history or social studies class. Of course, students *don't* learn anything about religion and science in history or social studies classes now. But even if they did, this wouldn't absolve science texts and courses of the responsibility to be part of the conversation. Like history and economics courses, science courses must be at least minimally fair to religion. They must acknowledge controversies and provide some context for making sense of them, helping to initiate students into an interdisciplinary conversation.

No doubt the primary purpose of science courses is to teach students good science as scientists understand it, but it can't simply be to train scientists. Science education must serve the purposes of a liberal education. High school and introductory undergraduate science courses must situate students in our ongoing scholarly and cultural conversation about how to make sense of nature and the world.[2] Nel Noddings has put it well: science teachers "have a special obligation to pass on to students the most widely accepted contemporary beliefs in science together with the evidence used to support them. But *as educators,* they have an even greater responsibility to acknowledge and present with great sensitivity the full range of solutions explored by their fellow human beings."[3]

Science texts and courses do not now convey to students anything like the "full range of solutions." We typically teach science as one more disciplinary monologue that students must listen to uncritically. In fact, because science texts don't take seriously contending interpretations of nature, students typically come to accept the claims of science as a matter of faith in the scientific tradition rather than of critical reason.

## Faith and Reason Again

No doubt the practice of science requires a highly sophisticated use of reason, and no one can doubt that scientific method enables scientists to know many very important things about the world, but it is also true that scientists often make claims that are deeply controversial and conflict with claims made in other disciplines (in the humanities as well as in religion). The scientists who make these claims may well prove right. The problem is that no matter how scrupulously rational scientists are within the methodological framework of science, if the philosophical assumptions that define that framework are not themselves held up to critical scrutiny they will be held as a matter of faith.

As I said in chapter 4, I don't mean by "faith" irrational belief. Rather, I mean trust—and trust may be reasonable, all things considered. But to judge whether it is reasonable we must step outside the governing framework—methodological naturalism—and consider its relationship to alternative frameworks of intelligibility, drawn from other disciplines. As we've seen, this is necessary in teaching history, literature, and economics. It is not enough to teach students to be rational within a discipline; students must have some understanding of how that discipline relates to others if they are to make reasonable judgments.

The great historian and philosopher of science Thomas Kuhn once claimed that the education of scientists "is a narrow and rigid education, probably more so than any other except perhaps in orthodox theology."[4] Scientists are not typically educated to understand the historical or philosophical issues that underlie modern science, Kuhn argued; nor are they taught about the mistakes and blind alleys of science. They are taught largely through textbooks that present them with "the truth" rather than (as in the humanities) a variety of conflicting historical and philosophical texts that force them to think through alternative ways of understanding the world. One might argue that Kuhn understates the case. Students of religion are not able to avoid extensive exposure to science at all levels of their education—science that may be deeply critical of their religion.

But I know of no public university that requires students who are pursuing a degree in science to take coursework in theology or religion. The education of scientists is much narrower when it comes to religion, than that of clergy or theologians when it comes to science.

In effect, students—indeed, most people in our culture—are taught (implicitly) to accept the conclusions of science as a matter of faith; they accept science because they trust their teachers (just as in premodern cultures people accepted their religious views on the authority of the church and the educational establishment of the day). Of course, one might respond that their teachers and the scientific tradition have proved trustworthy; in fact, science has been enormously successful and this provides strong evidence for trusting that science will explain more and more of the world. But this is not conclusive by any means. There continue to be gaps in the scientific understanding of reality and controversies over the adequacy of science to bridge them. There continue to be whole domains of culture (such as morality and the mind) where even the relevance of scientific interpretations is deeply controversial. Yet students are typically provided no critical distance on science and these controversies in their science courses.

In practicing science, scientists develop a trust both in the methods of science and in the ultimate scientific intelligibility of the world just as theologians often develop a trust in their theological tradition and discern patterns of religious intelligibility in the world. Albert Einstein once wrote: "I have never found a better expression than 'religious' for this *trust* in the rational nature of reality and of its peculiar accessibility to the human mind."[5] According to the distinguished chemist Michael Polanyi, "No one can become a scientist unless he presumes that the scientific doctrine and method are fundamentally sound and that their ultimate premises can be unquestioningly accepted. We have here an instance of the process described epigrammatically by the Christian Church Fathers in the words: *fides quarens intellectum,* faith in search of understanding."[6]

As a result of such faith, the sociologist Edward Shils wrote, "Confidence in the powers of reason and science became a tradition accepted with the same unquestioning confidence as the belief in the Judeo-Christian accounts of the origins and meaning of human existence had been earlier."[7] Most scientists cling to this faith, even though it may close them off to other patterns of intelligibility in the world. This is not to say that modern science is, in the end, unreasonable. It is to say that scientists, like almost everyone else, live and think within a tradition, a worldview, that makes sense of the world for them, and by virtue of their educations they are not well equipped to make judgments about the adequacy of their tradition—their faith—compared with others.

Modern science has justly prided itself on its openness to new evidence and to the potential falsification of its theories. There is, nonetheless, a kind of scientific fundamentalism, in which methodological naturalism functions much as does Scripture for religious fundamentalists: just as fundamentalists are not open *in principle* to scientific evidence that falsifies Scripture, so many scientists are not open *in principle* to nonnaturalistic evidence, claims, or theories that might be taken to falsify, qualify, or define the limits of science. The mathematician and philosopher Alfred North Whitehead wrote some hundred years ago (but it is perhaps still true) that "nothing is more curious than the self-satisfied dogmatism with which mankind at each period of its history cherishes the delusion of the finality of its existing modes of knowledge. Skeptics and believers are all alike. *At this moment* scientists and skeptics are the leading dogmatists. Advance in detail is admitted: fundamental novelty is barred."[8]

As I've said, there are powerful, if not quite conclusive, reasons why scientists should adhere to methodological naturalism. But unless the nature and possible limitations of methodological naturalism are themselves the subject of discussion, unless methodological naturalism is itself open to potential falsification, this commitment will be, in effect, an uncritical trust or faith—and surely there is some risk in uncritically trusting that all of reality can be explained in naturalistic categories.

Now it may be that a measure of faith is essential to the practice of any intellectual tradition. (I suspect that it is; we must all acknowledge, with some humility, the potential limitations of our various conceptual nets.) But public schools and universities should not be in the business of nurturing uncritical faith, whether it is in religion, politics, economics, *or science*. A liberal education should encourage critical thinking, and this can only be done when we are willing to lay bare and question our fundamental assumptions. Certainly one of the most important of these assumptions is the adequacy of scientific method. What are its limitations? When might it need revision? In what intellectual contexts might the use of scientific method be a mistake?

Of course, how to sort this all out is controversial. No doubt being reasonable requires appeals to evidence, arguments, and critical thinking; it cannot tolerate appeals to uncritical faith. But there are many ways of understanding evidence, arguments, and critical thought. Some are found in the sciences, others in philosophy and the humanities, yet others in religion.

## The Relationship of Science and Religion

There are four positions that are often taken regarding the relationship of science and religion.[9] (There are more; I'm simplifying.)

## 1. Biblical Creationism

Scripture trumps science when they conflict, and Scripture, especially Genesis 1, should be read literally. No doubt good science would agree with Scripture, but, unhappily, not all science is good science. Scientific creationists (as that term is often used) begin from the assumption that the truth about nature is to be found in Scripture, and then search for scientific evidence that confirms what they already know to be true. This is a position taken by fundamentalists and many religious conservatives.

## 2. Scientific Naturalism

Science trumps religion when they conflict. Indeed, science provides us with our only true knowledge of nature. If the scientific conceptual net doesn't catch something, it's because it doesn't exist. Because science is naturalistic (because it does not allow appeals to design, supernatural causes, or teleological explanations) scientific naturalism implies atheism. Sometimes this position is called scientism or scientific materialism (to distinguish it from a merely methodological naturalism). This is a position taken by many (but far from all) scientists and philosophers.

## 3. The Independence or the "Two Worlds View"

Properly understood, science and religion can't conflict because they are incommensurable; each has its own methods, each has its own domain. There are many variations on this theme: science asks objective "how" questions while religion asks personal "why" questions; science is concerned with what is, religion with what ought to be; science is concerned with facts, religions with meaning; religion is about our existential situation, not physical reality; religion is about the meaning of life, not its chemical composition. In each case the conceptual nets of religion and science capture aspects of reality so different that they have no logical implications regarding the other; hence, each can be true (or false) in its own terms. Religion and science can be compartmentalized.

Over the last two centuries many theologians have taken this position, some taking their cue from Immanuel Kant, others from Romanticism, yet others from Karl Barth and neoorthodox theology. In each case, they have ceded nature to scientists. Scripture is not a science textbook, and ought not to be read literally. God relates to us personally and in history, not in nature. Many scientists, too, have taken this position. In fact, this has been for some time the orthodox view of the science establishment.

## 4. Integration and Dialogue

Science and religion can conflict, for they each make claims about the same world. Because they are each competent to illuminate aspects of the same reality, a fully adequate picture of reality must draw on—and integrate—both. Hence, the need for dialogue. On this view, scriptural passages about nature should not be taken literally, but they must still be taken seriously; they still tell us something important about nature.

Over the last several decades there has been something of a shift from independence to dialogue and integration among theologians and scientists. Why? It is often argued that developments in twentieth-century science made nature a somewhat more complicated—perhaps even mysterious—place more open to religious interpretation than the old deterministic billiard ball world of atoms and classical science. At the same time, liberal theologians have worked to reconcile their religious traditions with modern science, modifying their understanding of how God works in the world (less by way of supernatural intervention than through the processes of nature). For them, theology is a critical discipline and theological claims are testable—though not in quite the same way as scientific claims. That is, theology and science are not nearly so different as has often been believed, and integration has become a possibility— or so it is often argued.

There is, of course, a theological risk in this position, for it leaves religious claims open to the possibility of revision, even falsification, by modern science. Perhaps the greatest problem is that of reconciling the idea of purpose or design in theology—the idea that nature fulfills God's purposes—with the methodological naturalism of modern science that allows no references to design, purpose, or supernatural influences. Still, some theologians and scientists would agree with Arthur Peacocke, the distinguished biochemist and theologian, who claimed that religion and science are "ultimately converging" in that "the scientific and theological enterprises" are "interacting and mutually illuminating approaches to reality."[10]

## Textbooks and the 5 Percent Rule

Science textbooks typically include a perfunctory opening chapter on scientific method, but these chapters never include any substantive discussion of the relationship of religion (or philosophy) to scientific method; indeed, rarely do they say anything about religion at all. When they do, it is usually to affirm a two-worlds view, according to which science and religion are conceptual apples and oranges. Because they are assumed to be incommensurable, the authors of science texts feel themselves absolved of the responsibility to say anything about religion. Of course, the two-worlds view of the relationship is deeply controversial and itself needs critical discussion. In fact, the nature of the relationship is a theological or philosophical problem of a kind that can't be settled scientifically.

I've argued that in teaching any introductory course that addresses important matters of religious and philosophical controversy, at least 5 percent of the textbook should be devoted to locating the discipline at hand in our ongoing conversation about how to make sense of the world—or in this case, nature. I'll make four quick points about how a textbook chapter might take on this task. First, the textbook should put the conversation in historical perspective, perhaps going back as far back as Greek philosophy and the Bible. Second, it should address a variety of philosophical and cultural perspectives including, of course, religion. Third, it should be sensitive to the existential (moral, political, spiritual) significance of conceptions of nature. Fourth, it should outline the major live, contemporary ways of relating science (and the particular science at hand, biology, say, or physics) and religion.

Moreover, when the texts deal with particular religiously controversial themes (such as evolution) they need to provide some context for making sense of what is at issue. This need not be an in-depth discussion, one that takes religion seriously in the full-blown sense for which I've argued. But it must be minimally fair, acknowledging the controversy, situating students in (yet another) ongoing interdisciplinary discussion. Texts must alert students to the fact that they are about to study something religiously controversial. The point isn't to convert science courses into theology courses; it is to locate scientific interpretations of nature in the context of our larger cultural conversation, transforming a monologue into an interdisciplinary discussion.

I might note that according to the *National Science Education Standards,* science curricula often integrate topics from different school subjects "such as science and mathematics, science and language arts, or science and history." Not surprisingly, then, teachers need to be able to make "conceptual connections" to "other school subjects." The *Standards* claim that scientific inquiry requires the ability "to distinguish between what is, and what is not a scientific idea"—a matter of some controversy. The seventh of eight proposed content standards requires that science education "give students a means to understand and act on personal and social issues" such as health, sexuality, and the environment—all areas of our social life where, the *Standards* acknowledge, religious beliefs and values are relevant. The eighth content standard requires that students learn that "science reflects its history and is an ongoing, changing enterprise." Indeed, the *Standards* acknowledge, "scientists are influenced by societal, cultural, and personal beliefs and ways of viewing the world. Science is not separate from society but rather science is a part of society." Consequently, students should learn the role "that science has played in the development of various cultures."[11] That is, while the *Standards* certainly don't require that religion be discussed (indeed, religion is hardly mentioned) they do require considerably more than simply teaching good science.


## Evolution

Fundamentalists and many religious conservatives reject evolution, holding that it is incompatible with Genesis read literally. To teach that evolution is true is, in effect, to teach that the Bible is false.

Many scientists (and other scholars) agree that evolution and the Bible are incompatible; hence, evolution gives us good reason to reject belief in God. Many of the greatest evolutionary biologists of the twentieth century—Ernst Mayr, George Gaylord Simpson, Jacques Monod, E. O. Wilson, James Watson, Francis Crick, Stephen Jay Gould—have been atheists. Richard Dawkins, an ardent Darwinian and the world's most prominent atheist, has claimed that "Darwin made it possible to be an intellectually fulfilled atheist" and the *New Atheism* (of which Dawkins is the leading bright) is grounded very much in evolutionary biology. Only 7 percent of the members of the prestigious National Academy of Sciences (NAS) believe in a personal God, and only 42 percent of biologists believe in a God of any kind.[12] Perhaps not surprisingly, some of this skepticism takes on an evangelical tinge. The Darwinian philosopher Michael Ruse has written: "I have spent the past 30 years fighting creationism in its various guises. One thing that has become apparent to me is that in some ways the creationists and intelligent-design theorists have a very good point. Science, or at least its leading spokespeople, tends to be strongly antireligious. No subgroup of scientists is more vocal than the biologists."[13]

Darwin himself was an agnostic, or so he claimed in his *Autobiography*, written shortly before his death. In fact, Darwin sat on his theory, refusing to publish it for several decades, fearing the public's response to its religious implications. When he finally had to publish in 1859 (lest Alfred Russel Wallace, who had also come up with the idea of natural selection, get credit) it turned out there was surprisingly little religious reaction. He went on to publish *The Descent of Man* (that important species unmentioned in *On the Origin of Species*) and was at his death interred with the saints in Westminster Abbey. And why was there so little reaction? Most theologians and religious thinkers simply took evolution to be God's way of creating people. That was the purpose of evolution. God was still at work in nature, we just needed to take a longer view. Of course, these theologians didn't insist on reading Genesis 1 literally.

So what about evolution led so many biologists to atheism? Darwin didn't just make the case for evolution in general, he argued for a particular mechanism of evolution: natural selection acting on chance variations (shaped as scientists now believe by random genetic mutations. Hence, according to neo-Darwinism (the synthesis of natural selection and genetics) evolution is a purposeless process. There is no design in evolution; it is not the fulfillment of what ought to be, of God's purposes. I quoted Stephen Jay Gould in chapter 1 as saying that on this account, human beings are not the crowning glory of the evolutionary epic, but rather a minor species in the Age of Bacteria (which will long survive us). This is how Darwin made it possible to be an intellectually satisfied atheist: he provided a compelling explanation for the appearance of design in nature while explaining evolution in fully naturalistic categories. True, scientists don't yet know how life came to be in the first place, but neo-Darwinism has explained so much that biologists have great confidence (faith as trust) that it will eventually explain everything.

Of course, not all biologists agree that neo-Darwinism provides an adequate account of evolution; there are a number of naturalistic competitors in the scientific marketplace.[14] Nor do all scientists believe that atheism follows in the wake of neo-Darwinism; there are those surveys that show that 40 percent of biologists still believe in God. So we can't say that everything is settled.

If fundamentalists and some conservative theologians reject evolution, most Jewish, Catholic, and mainline Protestant theologians accept evolution while rejecting the claim of atheists that evolution is incompatible with belief in God. Some continue to hold the old two-worlds view, while others take a more integrationist view on which there are many variations. Some believe that God started the ball rolling (perhaps with the big bang) and then let the world roll on, governed by laws and chance that, in time, led to human beings, more or less as neo-Darwinism proposes. Others find God working through quantum indeterminacy or through top-down forms of causality that hinge on non-reductionistic, evolutionarily emergent forms of meaning (much as our minds act on our brains without violating the laws of nature). Some believe that the basic laws of nature—the physical context for evolution—are fine-tuned to produce life. (I'll say a little more about this claim in discussing cosmology below.) Catholic theology accepts evolution (of some kind) but claims that science cannot account for the development of persons with souls (which requires divine intervention). Process theologians argue for a God of limited power who works within the processes of nature, slowly bringing order and goodness out of chaos. Much recent controversy has centered on those scientists who accept some form of intelligent design in nature (some of whom accept evolution, while others don't). And there are other views.

Of course, whatever one's view, evolution isn't simply a matter of technical scientific interest. Questions about the origins of life and human beings are among the biggest of the Big Questions; for many scholars and ordinary folk they have had and continue to have important implications regarding religion, morality, and our humanity. Surely students must learn something about the existential significance of evolution for morality, politics, and religion.

As I mentioned above, if biology textbooks mention religion at all, it is to affirm the independence or two-worlds view of the relationship of science and religion: evolution has no implications for religion so religion need not be discussed in biology texts. According to a 1981 resolution of the NAS, "Religion and science are separate and mutually exclusive realms of human thought whose presentation in the same context leads to a misunderstanding of both scientific theory and religious belief."[15] The NAS essentially reaffirmed this view in 1998 and again in 2008.[16] I must say that I find an official resolution about the relationship of science and religion rather curious—as if the matter could be settled by a vote of scientists. What gives scientists the authority or expertise to settle this when theologians disagree? And how is it that only 7 percent of NAS members believe in God if science has no implications for religion? Dawkins has suggested that the authors of the NAS statement belong to the Neville Chamberlain school of evolutionists—that is, they are appeasers—and the atheist Sam Harris has charged that the NAS statement "is stunning for its lack of candor."[17] In fact, Dawkins and Harris notwithstanding, this is an old and respectable view, held by many theologians and scientists, and it may be the right view. But it is not the only view; indeed, it is controversial on both sides of the aisle.

The science establishment argues that if religion is to be brought up at all in relationship to science or evolution this should be done elsewhere, perhaps in history or social studies texts, but surely the customary four paragraphs in history texts (two on Darwin and religion, two on the Scopes Trial) don't do the job. Nor is any discussion of the contemporary controversy likely in the next generation of history texts. Nor would it be given more than two paragraphs if it were to be discussed in history textbooks. Nor would most history teachers be prepared to address either the relevant theology or science. Nor are there courses in philosophy or religion in public schools where such discussions might take place. In any case, questions about religion and evolution will inevitably come up in biology courses if students are thoughtful, and this is as it should be, for introductory courses in biology are part of a liberal education (not some specialty in which future professionals are to be trained) and, as such, they must situate students in the scholarly and cultural conversation, providing some context for understanding what is at issue.

So how should they do it? Though references to evolution appear throughout biology texts, they typically have several chapters (or a section) that focus on evolution, sometimes put in historical context with some discussion of Darwin. Given the importance of what is at issue and the requirements of a liberal education, the texts should devote five or ten pages to religion and evolution, setting out the major points of view. In doing so, there are several things to keep in mind.

First, it is often claimed that *both* points of view should be taught. But as I've noted, there aren't just two alternatives. There are at least three major alternatives (no evolution, evolution directed in some sense by God, and evolution without God). Moreover, there are many variations on the theme of evolution with God, and students should learn something of several of the most important of them. And then there are nontheistic religions, some of which have a spiritual understanding of nature.

Second, I am not arguing for any kind of balanced treatment. Biology texts should teach biology as the vast majority of biologists understand it (just as economics texts should teach neoclassical economics, and history texts secular history). If most biologists believe that neo-Darwinism is true (which I take to be the case), students should learn this. But texts and courses cannot leave out connections to other disciplines and major controversies that are important to a liberal education.

Third, it is tremendously important that the alternatives are presented not simply as abstract possibilities, but in historical and cultural context (as required by the Principle of Cultural Location and Weight). Neo-Darwinism, biblical creationism, the two-worlds view, theistic evolution, and Intelligent Design aren't simply alternatives from which students should be free to choose depending on their tastes. If students are to make informed and reasoned judgments, they must have some sense of where alternative theories acquire their authority, of what traditions they are a part, and how controversial they are within those traditions and within our culture more generally. Students must understand that the vast majority of scientists accept neo-Darwinism (though they may disagree about the religious implications). Which are consensus views? Which are controversial views? And for whom? And what can advocates of each view say in defense of that view or in criticism of its competitors?

Fourth, this section must be written fairly (with the help of historians, philosophers, and theologians) and not simply used as an opportunity to bludgeon critics of establishment science. It should give students some sense of what the major arguments are. Having done this, the texts should then be free to teach what their authors take to be good science.

Fifth, because what is at issue is complex as well as controversial, teachers cannot be left to fashion their own resources for undertaking this task. The vast majority of them are not prepared to undertake this task. The issues must be addressed in textbooks or (carefully vetted) short resource books or textbook supplements.

Many scientists are concerned that too often students aren't taught about evolution because it is controversial. Some teachers avoid it. Others discuss it along with their personal religious views. According to a recent study of nearly one thousand biology teachers, one in eight of them teaches some form of creationism as a "valid scientific alternative to Darwinian explanations of the origin of species."[18] Some states, either through their legislatures or state boards of education, have threatened what many scientists see as the integrity of the science curriculum. At the same time, many religious people are concerned that nowhere in the public school curriculum do students learn about religious ways of understanding nature, or about critiques of evolutionary theory.

I am arguing with regard to the concerns of scientists that biology and science textbooks should teach only the prevailing evolutionary theory as good science. With regard to the concerns of religious critics, textbooks should also (briefly but fairly) teach about critiques of evolution and alternative ways of understanding nature in context-setting chapters that address historical, cultural, and philosophical issues. I put this forward not as a political compromise, however, but as a principled and logical implication of what a good liberal education requires—one that I hope the advocates of various positions can accept as providing common ground even when we disagree deeply about evolution and the relationship of science and religion.

Is this a radical proposal? I've mentioned that although the *National Science Education Standards* don't discuss religion they do require that science be taught in historical context and address personal and social issues. The Web site of the National Center for Science Education suggests that teachers might assuage students' religious concerns about evolution by reviewing with them a spectrum of views regarding the relationship of religion and evolution, adding that it would make for an "engaging lecture." (I would say a lecture *or two*.) I might also note that even the economics textbooks (which are so objectionable) all include chapters on Marxism and socialism; that is, their clear commitment to neoclassical economic theory—to economics as a science—does not preclude some discussion of alternative political and philosophical ways of thinking about economics.

## Intelligent Design

The vast majority of scientists believe that Intelligent Design theory (ID) is not science, and that it has no place in science courses. So what is ID? Advocates of ID argue that when biologists are unable to explain the evolutionary development of "irreducibly" complex aspects of nature (such as DNA or the structure of cells) in terms of the incremental steps required by neo-Darwinism, it is legitimate to give a design explanation. This isn't a theological move, they argue, but good science, at least when science is freed of its philosophical commitment to naturalism. (Maybe I should add that ID needn't be hostile to evolution, which might be designed, but it is clearly hostile to neo-Darwinism, which denies the idea of purpose or design in evolution.)

Critics of ID argue that if we don't yet have good (naturalistic) neo-Darwinian explanations of something, they are forthcoming, that good science is naturalistic and hence rules out appeals to supernatural causes (a designer-God), and that ID makes scientifically unfalsifiable claims. Intelligent Design is, in effect, thinly veiled religion; it is fundamentalist creation-science hidden in a Trojan horse. I am skeptical of these last two charges.[19] Still, in giving design explanations ID clearly does violate the rules of methodological naturalism; it simply isn't science as most scientists understand it.

That said, the first point I want to make is that even if ID is a religious theory, this does not mean that it should not be discussed in science textbooks and courses as an alternative to neo-Darwinism. It should be included for at least two reasons.

First, debates over ID have become a staple in our culture wars, and students should learn about major public controversies involving science. Second, ID acquires some importance as yet another in a long history of philosophical, religious, and scientific efforts to show there is design in nature, going back to the Bible and Greek philosophy. That is, it is part of a tradition that should be taken seriously. The Darwinian Michael Ruse ends an article on design theories by leaving his reader "with the reflection that the argument from design has had a long and (I would say) honorable history, and that this history seems to be unfinished."[20]

Of course, advocates of ID argue that it should be taken seriously as science. As I have said, the vast majority of scientists reject this claim. Advocates of ID respond that scientists do so because of a philosophical commitment to naturalism (or materialism) that prevents a truly open-minded consideration of possible explanations. For example, the distinguished geneticist Richard Lewontin once wrote, "We take the side of science *in spite* of the patent absurdity of some of its constructs, *in spite* of its failure to fulfill many of its extravagant promises of health and life, *in spite* of the tolerance of the scientific community for unsubstantiated just-so stories, because we have a prior commitment, a commitment to materialism. It is not that the methods and institutions of science somehow compel us to accept a material explanation of the phenomenal world, but, on the contrary, that we are forced by our a priori adherence to material causes to create an apparatus of investigation and a set of concepts that produce material explanations, no matter how counterintuitive, no matter how mystifying to the uninitiated. Moreover, that materialism is absolute, for we cannot allow a Divine Foot in the door."[21] That is, it is atheism that dictates methodological naturalism.

I suspect that many, perhaps even most, scientists would reject Lewontin's claim and argue that there are good reasons for sticking with methodological naturalism, the most important of which is that naturalistic science has been remarkably successful. In any case, I'm inclined to think that scientists should get to decide what science is. I do not favor efforts of governments or state boards of education to redefine the nature of science. Of course scientists may change their minds; they may prove to be mistaken. Scientific revolutions have occasionally redefined what science. This happened when Darwinists excluded design explanations from science. Conceivably, scientists could reverse themselves once more.

And yet, as I have argued above with regard to every discipline, it is always important for students to think critically about the basic assumptions of their disciplines.[22] So it is with science and methodological naturalism. Why not accept design explanations? What are the arguments on all sides? Students should understand something about this. Indeed, scientists should encourage study of the idea of design in nature, not necessarily as good science, but because questions of design are important and they don't go away. Why, for example, isn't there a journal of design studies in which advocates *and* critics of design argue about the empirical and philosophical issues?

Of course, if science is committed to methodological naturalism and design explanations are ruled out a priori, this leaves us with a major educational problem, for what a reasonable person will want to know is not just what the best scientific explanation of nature is (though that is very important) but what the best explanation is *all things considered*. Is there evidence for design in nature whether scientific, philosophical, or religious? If science refuses to take this question seriously then it must be addressed elsewhere in the curriculum. Of course, it isn't.

So where does this leave us? Science texts and courses have no obligation to take ID seriously as a scientific alternative to neo-Darwinism (and certainly not as part of some balanced-treatment scheme). But they do have an obligation to discuss ID in two contexts. In the opening chapter on the history, philosophy, and methodology of science it is important to discuss the relationship between design explanations (historically, philosophically, religiously) and methodological naturalism. Second, in a contextual chapter on evolution, ID should be discussed along with various other religious and philosophical alternatives to neo-Darwinism. These discussions should be fair; ID (and other theories) should be discussed fully enough to give students some sense of the basic arguments. The historian of science Will Provine, an atheist and ardent Darwinian, argues that biology teachers should encourage students to discuss evolution and ID because it makes the study of evolution exciting as well as fair.[23] But apart from these introductory and contextual chapters, the textbooks should be free to teach students the dominant understanding of evolution among biologists. Indeed, students should learn that the great majority of scientists accept neo-Darwinian evolution, and that the ID movement is a small minority movement among scientists, but they should also learn that ID is another effort to understand nature in terms of design, and that the idea of purpose or design has a long and respectable history in philosophy, theology, and (pre-Darwinian) science.

Virtually everyone who writes about ID—other than advocates of ID—deny it any place in the science curriculum. This stems, I suggest, from not appreciating the role of science courses within the context of a liberal education and from failing to make the simple distinction between teaching about ID (within a broad, historical, and philosophical context) and taking it seriously as good science. I trust it is clear that I propose teaching about ID, not endorsing it as true or as good science, and I certainly don't advocate balanced treatment. Still, it should have a place in the conversation.

## Further Constitutional Considerations

The U.S. Supreme Court has twice addressed evolution. In *Epperson v. Arkansas* (1968) the Court struck down an Arkansas law that prohibited teaching evolution. The First Amendment, Justice Abe Fortas wrote, "mandates governmental neutrality between religion and religion, and between religion and nonreligion."[24] The purpose of the Arkansas law, however, was "to blot out a particular theory because of its supposed conflict with the Biblical account, literally read."[25] Because its purpose was to protect Christian fundamentalism it was not religiously neutral.

If the teaching of evolution could not be prohibited, then perhaps teaching creation-science could be required, but in *Edwards v. Aguillard* (1987) the Court struck down Louisiana's "balanced-treatment" act. The problem again was that the purpose of the act was to shore up fundamentalist Christianity (in that creation-science is part of a conservative religious movement), and this isn't neutral either. Justice William Brennan cited a paper trail of comments from Louisiana legislators that made it clear their purpose was to promote conservative Christianity.[26]

Because the purpose of both the Arkansas and Louisiana laws was religious they ran afoul of the neutrality required by the Establishment Clause. But the Court has also held that a religious purpose need not invalidate a law or policy if there is also a secular purpose for it. Justice Fortas could find none for the Arkansas law; nor could Justice Brennan find any for the Louisiana act. But surely there is at least one powerful secular reason for requiring students to learn about religious accounts of nature: a good liberal education requires it. If students are to think in an informed and critical way about matters of controversy and importance (like the origins of the universe, life, and human beings) they must understand religious as well as secular points of view.

It shouldn't be controversial to claim that the First Amendment allows students to be taught about religious interpretations of nature. What is controversial are my claims that neutrality requires this, and that it should be done (in part, at least) in science courses.

Interestingly, almost everyone acknowledges that evolution conflicts with fundamentalism, but the scientific and educational establishments typically argue that there is no conflict between science and religion properly understood, true religion. But this is a theological judgment, and a controversial one at that. Should it be permissible for schools to undermine conservative religion so long as they can reconcile science and some varieties of liberal theology? Is this neutral among religions—as the Establishment Clause requires? Of course, some liberal theologians also have difficulty with neo-Darwinism and its purposeless conception of nature (and some scientists believe that evolution does undermine all religion).

No doubt many, perhaps even most, claims made by scientists and secular scholars can be reconciled with much religion. It is at the level of conceptual nets or worldviews that there is often tension or conflict. The problem is that we teach students to interpret, or make sense of, experiences and evidence in exclusively secular, naturalistic ways, and then we convey the adequacy of those secular interpretations uncritically. Arguably, by keeping students ignorant not just of creationism and conservative religion, but of liberal ways of integrating science and religion, science education nurtures a secular mentality and profoundly biases the thinking of students.

Clearly, the solution can't be to censor science education by giving religious folks a curricular veto—this is hardly a neutral scheme. As I have argued, the only way to be neutral when we disagree is to be fair to the alternatives. Neutrality requires that students understand modern science (including, of course, neo-Darwinism) and various religious ways of conceiving nature. No doubt there is a practical problem here that stems from the number of alternatives, but there are not so many *types* of view. In any case, when neutrality is hard to come by it would seem incumbent on us to approximate rather than ignore it.

It has sometimes been argued that Justice Brennan's ruling in *Edwards* prohibits teaching about religious accounts of origins in science classes, but, as I've said, Brennan ruled the Louisiana act unconstitutional because it had a religious purpose, leaving open the possibility that a properly secular purpose could justify discussion of religion in science courses. I can't see any principled reason why it should be permissible to teach about religion in a social studies class but not in a science class when religion is relevant to the subject under discussion and is not introduced gratuitously but serves the purposes of a genuinely liberal education. In fact, I do not find anything in Justice Brennan's ruling in *Edwards,* or in any other Supreme Court ruling, that would prohibit this. Hence, I take it that with the proper secular purpose, where we teach about religion is an educational rather than a constitutional question. Of course, no religious view can be advocated or promoted (or denigrated); my argument is that students must learn something about religious understandings of nature in studying the historical and cultural context of modern science.

It is sometimes argued that singling out evolution for special treatment betrays a religious agenda. For some, no doubt, it does. But my proposal is not a Trojan horse for creationists or theologians. To the extent I single out evolution it is because it has historically been a Big Question with important implications for how we understand the human condition. But, in fact, I am not singling it out at all, because there are other controversies relating to religion that warrant parallel discussions in biology and physics courses as we shall see. I might add that this does not mean that advocates of astrology or a flat earth need to be included in the discussion; as with any subject, it is the most influential ideas and important controversies that must be included.

Finally, a word is in order about *Kitzmiller v. Dover Area School District* (2005) in which a federal district court judge ruled the Dover, Pennsylvania, schools unconstitutionally promoted religion in requiring teachers to read a short disclaimer to biology students to the effect that Darwinism is only a theory and that Intelligent Design provides an alternative. The court rightly found that the purpose of the school board's purpose was to promote conservative Christianity and this is unconstitutional. Judge John Jones didn't stop there, however, but went on to address a number of philosophical and educational issues arguing, among other things, that ID is religion, not science, in a long opinion that is often misguided and disturbingly naive.[27] Still, I don't think there are any major implications of the ruling for the position I have taken. The ideal of liberal education provides a fully secular purpose for discussing ID in science courses (along with other philosophical and religious positions) and I don't claim that ID is science, only that students should learn something about the controversy over science and the various ways in which philosophers, theologians, and scientists have used design explanations historically and now.

I might add that the National Center for Science Education acknowledges that it is constitutional to teach about religious views in a science classroom.


## Other Issues

There are at least five other issues regarding science and religion that are as important as evolution. I will say a little in the next chapter about three of them: morality, the environment, and technology. Here I will say something first about cosmology and then about consciousness, minds and souls.


### Cosmology

Surely one of the Big Questions is about the origins of our universe. What are we to make of the big bang and its relationship to religious ideas of creation? For several decades after it was first proposed in 1927, some scientists rejected the big bang theory in part, at least, because they believed that it seemed to provide evidence for creation. While some theologians have made a good deal of the big bang, more have argued that it is irrelevant to religious ideas of creation, which is a continuing process, not a once-and-for-all event. Still, there are several fascinating questions here: What, if anything, caused the big bang? Is it simply a brute fact? Can it be explained naturalistically? Or might some kind of religious explanation be necessary or at least reasonable?

Just as interesting is the lively discussion of the last few decades about cosmological fine-tuning (anthropic arguments) to the effect that the basic laws and physical constants of nature are precisely what they must be for life to be possible, leading to a new design argument for the existence of God (or at least some kind of cosmic designer). This evidence and these arguments have engaged many distinguished scholars. Some scholars have also argued that the fact that the laws of the universe are intelligible mathematically in ways we can understand gives reason to think that the human mind and the universe have a common origin in the mind of God. (Why would natural selection select for minds that can eventually do calculus? Of what survival value is this?)

These are Big Questions, and physics texts cannot ignore them if they are to serve the purposes of a liberal education. The 5 percent rule requires that a substantive part of any physics text should be devoted to historical and philosophical discussions of scientific method, the development of modern physics, the relationship of physics to philosophy and religion, and those Big Questions that have existential significance in thinking about the nature of life, the universe, and God. (The philosophical problem of determinism and free will is also relevant to physics.) I might add that it strikes me that astronomy and cosmology should get much greater play than they do in physics texts given their historical relevance to the Big Questions.

## Consciousness, Minds, and Souls

Science doesn't rest content with explaining physical nature, but attempts also to explain the mind and consciousness. We know from medical histories, brain surgery, animal studies, and brain-imaging technologies that it is possible to correlate with some (but hardly complete) precision brain states and mental states; as a result, there is considerable confidence among neuroscientists that science will ultimately be able to explain consciousness, the mind, and human action using only naturalistic categories appropriate for talking about the brain as a physical system. Consciousness and mind are (in some sense) *nothing more* than the brain—or so it is often argued.[28] Many scholars have taken this to challenge traditional claims about free will, morality, rationality (the idea that we think and act as we do for reasons rather than because of the causal processes in our brains), and, of course, the existence and immortality of the soul. In fact, the agenda of modern neuroscience may prove to be more threatening to religion than that of neo-Darwinian evolution.

And yet, this scientific agenda has critics—not only theologians but many philosophers and some scientists. Certainly nothing is yet settled. How the mind and brain are related (the so-called hard problem of consciousness) is still a mystery. Even Sam Harris, a neuroscientist and one of the most vocal of the New Atheists, acknowledges that "while there is much to be said against a naive conception of a soul that is independent of the brain, the place of consciousness in the natural world is very much an open question. The idea that brains *produce* consciousness is little more than an article of faith among scientists at present and there are many reasons to believe that the methods of science will be insufficient to either prove or disprove it. . . . [The problem is] that nothing about a brain, when surveyed as a physical system, declares it to be a bearer of that peculiar, interior dimension that each of us experiences as consciousness. . . . The fact that the universe is illuminated where you stand, the fact that your thoughts and moods and sensations have a qualitative character, is an absolute mystery."[29] Of course, the problem of consciousness and mind is also an evolutionary problem: how and when did consciousness come into existence out of nonconscious matter? How do primitive nervous systems give rise to perceptions and thoughts? This is part of the mystery. Or might mind go all the way back?

Even if science can't explain the origins of consciousness, or precisely how minds and brains relate to each other, there is no shortage of scientific theories, many of which are reductionistic, explaining thought and action in naturalistic, causal categories. Biological theories of morality, neuroeconomics, and genopolitics attempt to explain naturalistically our predispositions to various kinds of moral, economic, and political behavior. Of course, many philosophers and secular scholars resist these movements, arguing that mind and human action can only be understood and explained in the categories of the humanities (that is, in terms of meaning, intentions, values, and reasoning). In fact, some scholars argue on scientific grounds that there is considerable evidence for top-down causality in which the mind can not only influence the body (consider placebos, for example) but even reprogram the brain.

Of course, all of this leaves us well short of the soul and the possibility of an afterlife. My point is twofold: first, the scientific agenda doesn't stop with physical nature, but seeks to explain everything naturalistically (at considerable cost to traditional religious ways of thinking); and yet, second, all of this is very controversial.

Although biology textbooks deal with the development of the nervous system and the brain, they never bring up such matters. Arguably, they leave students with the impression that the mind is nothing more than the brain and nervous system. This is yet another lost opportunity to promote critical thinking about Big Questions and matters of existential importance. Biology (and psychology) textbooks should devote several pages to mapping the major points of view (secular and religious) on these questions.

## Conclusions

Science textbooks (and, I suspect, most science teachers) are not overtly hostile to religion. As I suggested in chapter 2, if anything, the texts typically pull their punches to avoid controversy (and many teachers may do so as well). And yet, my impression from reading the texts is that students are likely to be lulled by the inexorable flow of innumerable details, the elegance and power of the theories, the confidence of the authors, and the absence of any non-naturalistic alternatives, into uncritically assuming that science can explain everything—at least in the long run.[30] The texts give students no sense that anything in them is controversial (except insofar as scientists occasionally disagree among themselves). They uncritically nurture (without explicitly endorsing) a secular, scientific mentality and worldview. In their preoccupation with teaching good science the texts and most teachers are oblivious to the task of putting science into any kind of historical, philosophical, or cultural perspective. No matter how well they teach the consensus view of good science, they fail to address the role of the sciences in a liberal education.

I do worry that even if science texts made their 5 percent donation to the cause of liberal education those pages would be biased toward the conventional interpretations of the science establishment. But perhaps I worry unnecessarily, for I'm not optimistic about there being any takers on my proposals. Scientists fear (with some reason) that any argument for broadening the purpose of science education (and the content of science textbooks) will open the door to the Religious Right to spread their prejudices. This being the case, I would argue for a twenty- or thirty-page textbook supplement (perhaps online) that would enable educators to avoid the nasty politics of textbook approval, especially if it could be a common-ground document endorsed by a wide-ranging group of religious, educational, and scientific organizations.

Of course, any such supplement is not likely to give students any deep understanding of religious ways of understanding nature. Hence the need, once again, for a course in religious studies where nature can be explored in the context of religious worldviews rather than within the context of the naturalistic worldview of science texts and courses.

# 12

# Religion and Moral Education

In addressing the secularization of education in chapter 3, I said something about the demoralization of education. In fact, the two have gone together to some considerable extent. Through much of the nineteenth century it was an important task of public schools and colleges to ground students morally in the Bible and Protestant Christianity. As religious pluralism, modern science, disciplinary specialization, and the economic purposes of education eventually eliminated religion from the curriculum, these movements also marginalized—though never quite eliminated—moral education. Certainly moral education had to be rethought in secular categories, and by the end of the nineteenth century, or at least by the end of the first few decades of the twentieth century, moral education had become almost entirely secular, grounded a little uneasily in Americanism and our civic traditions, in the study of literature and Western civilization, and the social sciences (particularly in the guise of progressivism).

In fact, the idea of moral education continues to be controversial and intellectually problematic. Character education programs are too often superficial add-ons in the elementary school curriculum, undergraduate ethics courses are almost always electives, and there is little in the way of moral education that falls betwixt and between. Either educators don't think morality to be very important, or they simply don't know how to go about doing it.

I have suggested that it is the primary task of schools and universities to make students good people. This is not widely accepted for a number of reasons (perhaps the most important of which is that it isn't even considered a possibility). Why? First, morality is of momentous importance; without it, people become barbarians. Second, the requirements of morality are complex (not always, but often enough) and require sophisticated—that is to say, educated—judgment. And third, moral responsibilities are pervasive; there is no escaping them in our private lives, our work lives, or our public lives; morality is relevant to virtually everything students study and do with their lives.

I'm not going to insist that you agree with me that the primary purpose of education is moral, but I will assume (based on the arguments I made in chapter 6) that moral education is very important and must be taken seriously. I begin this chapter by rehearsing the three-level scheme for thinking about moral education that I proposed in chapter 6, drawing out the implications for the role of religion. I go on to consider whether moral education can be adequately pursued by way of natural inclusion in existing courses, or whether there should be required courses in ethics. As with religion, I will argue that a double-prong strategy is required: virtually all courses must be sensitive to moral concerns, but there must also be required courses in ethics or what I will call morality and meaning, at both the high school and undergraduate levels.

To put a little flesh on the bare bones of my argument I will take as a case study how schools should address sexuality. I will also say a little (too little) about what may be the major moral problem of our time, the environmental crisis. Finally, given our concerns in the preceding chapter, I will also say a little about the implications of science and technology for morality.

## Religion and the Types of Moral Education

In chapter 6 I discussed three types or levels of moral education. First, schools should initiate students into the conventional moral consensus (such as it is); this is often called character education. Second, schools and universities should situate students within the traditions that ground and make sense of morality. Third, a liberal education should nurture critical thinking about our moral traditions; it should nurture the thoughtfulness that is essential if students are to responsibly orient their lives, if they are to live examined lives.

### 1. Character Education Should Have Three Goals

The first is the absolutely fundamental task of ensuring that students make sense of their lives in moral categories. The second is to think in terms of a particular understanding of right and wrong. The third is to motivate students to act in terms of what is right. No doubt character education is first of all the responsibility of parents, but morality is sufficiently important that schools must reinforce their efforts.

How is this done? Not so much didactically as by ensuring that schooling is a pervasively moral enterprise in which moral categories of right and wrong, rights and responsibilities, are routinely used to assess behavior. Students must understand that they are expected to be moral. Teachers and administrators should serve as role models. Everyone should be treated with respect. Teachers must draw out the morals of stories, especially in teaching history and literature.[1] The point is to create a moral ethos within which morality comes naturally. This is absolutely critical for children. If they do not come to understand their actions and relationships in moral categories, education has failed.

But which virtues and values in our pluralistic culture are schools to encourage? As a practical matter, character education programs typically proceed by way of local efforts to identify those virtues and values on which people agree, removing the prohibitive threat of controversy. In spite of our moral pluralism there happily continues to be a significant (if perhaps shrinking) moral consensus about some very important moral virtues—responsibility, integrity, hard work, honesty, and kindness—at least in principle if not always in practice. If all goes well, children are socialized by their parents, their religious and civic communities, and their schools to be honest, hard-working, and compassionate people who, when confronted with moral challenges, will act honestly, diligently, and compassionately.

Moreover, children need moral stability, a starting point from which they can begin to think critically about the world. Elmer John Theissen has asked whether "the anomie and rootlessness so pervasive in our societies is in part related to our liberating children too soon from the present and the particular in which they are raised? Are they exposed too soon to a 'Babel of values' in our public schools?"[2] If so, he suggests, students may need a greater degree of coherence and stability in their lives—even if our eventual goal for them, in the end, is moral autonomy. Of course, as they mature, "they begin to ask questions, and these need to be encouraged and taken seriously. But what children want are answers, not doubts, and it is as absurd as it is cruel to treat children at this stage with a heavy dose of 'critical thinking.'"[3]

All of this said, there are significant limitations to character education. First, it usually deals almost exclusively with personal morality, rather than with social and political issues relating to the public good—which are, after all, often controversial. Second, character education typically ignores the deep justifications of moral virtues and values in political, philosophical, and religious traditions because, again, such justifications are controversial. As a result, third, character education is less a matter of critical thinking about morality than about efforts at socialization. (This isn't a criticism so much as a limitation; children must be socialized before they can be educated.) Fourth, because character education is typically a curricular add-on that teachers must integrate into existing classes (usually with little help or preparation) it is often superficial. All of this makes character education, in the eyes of many of its critics, a notably conservative program, one that reinforces conventional morality without challenging it.

For our purposes it is also important to note that with few exceptions leaders of the character education movement have bent over backward to avoid religion—not because they are hostile to it, but because religion is controversial and doesn't fit the character education model of socialization. Religion can't be practiced in public schools; the ethos of public schools must be secular rather than religious. Character education cannot use religious exercises or role models to nurture the development of character. That said, surely some of the stories and some of the history that students read should make clear that people's moral convictions are often grounded in religious traditions. This can be done in fairly uncontroversial ways. In fact, to suggest (implicitly) that religion is irrelevant to morality is, arguably, hostile to religion.

In spite of these criticisms, I believe that character education is important when taken seriously and done well. It is essential that students learn to think in moral categories and develop a commitment to those virtues and values that we share and agree are important.

## 2. Traditions

In chapter 6 I quoted Alasdair MacIntyre, who claimed that we know how to act only when we know what stories (or narratives) we have roles in. I also quoted James Davison Hunter who argued that by severing morality from its roots in traditional communities character education fails to be either concrete or compelling to students, in which case morality becomes a matter of mere convention. For Hunter and MacIntyre moral education should situate students in narratives, in cultural contexts, in traditions, that make sense of their moral roles, providing deep justifications for them.[4]

For advocates of the old liberal arts ideal, the moral virtues were typically found in the classics of Greek and Roman literature and philosophy and, of course, the Bible, and there are still advocates of the classics—the Great Books— some of which continue to be taught in high school literature and undergraduate humanities courses. We might be tempted to dismiss the classics as products of their time and place with no obvious relevance to us, yet the classics, not least the Bible, continue to be rewoven into the fabric of the living traditions we inherit.

There is, of course, a good deal of suspicion of the Great Books. Some would enlarge the canon to include overlooked great books by women, members of minority groups, and non-Western writers. Other critics find fault in the very idea of "great" books. As we become more multicultural (and come to recognize the multicultural strains that have always been here) we find, not surprisingly, that we often disagree about which literature and which interpretations of history to teach.

But we don't disagree about everything. There is, for example, a good deal of agreement that students must understand their roles (and responsibilities) as American citizens. The question is, how do we make sense of the U.S. Constitution so that it isn't a lifeless document, a bare catalog of laws? What are the deep justifications underlying it? To understand the Constitution it must be situated within a historical narrative about the ideas and ideals (and limitations) of the Founding Fathers and their generation, the ways in which it has been amended over time, particularly in the Bill of Rights and in the Thirteenth and Nineteenth amendments, each of which can only be understood in terms of developing ideas of rights and justice. That is, one can't just study the Constitution; students must understand its location within a welter of developing ideas and ideals regarding liberty, slavery, democracy, and human rights.

Of course, this is the case not just with regard to the Constitution. Our private virtues and our social policies are all embedded in the cultural, political, philosophical, and religious narratives that go to make up Western civilization.

There are several implications of this that are essential for our purposes. History and literature teachers aren't just teaching value-free history (the facts) or literary texts devoid of moral meaning and influence. They are situating students in normative traditions in which they come to understand and make sense of their personal and public lives in moral categories. I am not saying that the lessons of history or literature should be taught didactically. Rather it is a matter of nurturing the ability of students to make sense of the historical development of culture and civilization from the inside (ideally by way of primary sources) so that they come to understand and imaginatively feel the force of the moral ideas and ideals internal to these narratives. I trust this will not come as a surprise to most teachers.

Of course, scientific and economic theories are also rooted in traditions that have been shaped by various cultural, political, philosophical, and religious ideas and ideals. The history of modern science has its heroes of conscience (Galileo and Darwin, not least), its contributions to human welfare, and its occasional

evils (weapons of mass destruction, for example, or the widespread commitment of scientists to eugenics in the first part of the twentieth century). Similarly, the history of economic theory is saturated with passionately held moral
ideals (in, for example, debates over socialism, Marxism, and capitalism), in the
aspirations of the working classes, and in competing conceptions of human
welfare and social justice. Clearly, both science and economics should be taught,
in part, historically. Their narratives are entwined with some of our deepest
moral concerns, and both have had, in turn, a powerful influence on the moral
dimension of culture.

I am not arguing that students must accept as morally binding any particular tradition (or any particular interpretation of a tradition). What is essential
is that they understand (and feel) the deep justifications of contemporary moral
ideas and ideals, controversial though they may be. In making sense of our
values students may well find them reasonable—though the deep disagreements that students will also encounter in studying history and historical literature often don't lend themselves to such conservative domestication. Still, this
is, so far, a (relatively) conservative approach to moral education.

Of course, these narratives inevitably have religious subplots and overlap
with religious narratives. As we saw in chapter 7, the Constitution says virtually
nothing about religion, still religion had a great deal to do with the historical
origins of the Constitution, as well as the all important First, Thirteenth, and
Nineteenth amendments. I am not arguing that the Constitution should be
understood as a Christian document. But the Founders and the reformers who
amended it were deeply influenced by Christian ideas and ideals, and it developed in a historical and cultural context that was, in large part, religious. The
ideals of liberty and freedom of conscience are rooted in Protestant theology as
much as in the Enlightenment, and ideals of justice and equality are rooted in
part, at least, in the Bible. (Of course, the Bible and Christian theology were
used both to justify and to condemn slavery and the oppression of women.)
Religion also played a role both in giving rise to, and in censoring, modern
science, and religious ideas and ideals flow though the historical debates over
social justice and the economy. I trust that I don't need to argue once again that
we can't understand history (including the history of science and economics)
apart from religion.

The great virtue of a liberal arts education is that it situates students in
thick moral, civic, and religious traditions—traditions that make sense of our
moral values and provide deep justifications for them (and give students ground
on which to stand in confronting the materialism and often mindless individualism of popular culture and the relativism of so much of our intellectual life).
It provides the roots of morality. That said, I must note again that such efforts

will inevitably be shallow in the absence of a course in religious studies that actually takes religious traditions seriously. If students are to understand the deep justifications of much of our moral life, they must take a course in religious studies.

## 3. Critical Thinking and Liberal Education

Of course, students inevitably discover that they are the inheritors of many traditions—indeed, of conflicting traditions. They find themselves situated in the American constitutional tradition and Western civilization, to be sure, but not everyone interprets the American constitutional tradition in the same way, and Western civilization comprises conflicting cultural, ethnic, racial, gender, political, philosophical, moral, scientific, literary, artistic, and religious strands. Even the venerated Great Books, so often criticized for their narrowness, convey no single tradition, but a welter of conflicting views. There is no way to reconcile Homer, Plato, Dante, Milton, Newton, Hegel, Smith, Marx, Freud, and Dostoyevsky. Indeed, we might think of Western civilization more as a developing conversation with recurring themes rather than as a single tradition or narrative. And now with globalization and the increasing cultural and religious pluralism of our own society, we are caught up in conversations (and conflicts) among even more traditions.

In chapter 6 I argued that if our culture wars are not to divide and polarize us, if we are going to be able to live together in spite of our deep moral differences, we must respect one another. This doesn't mean that we must agree with one another; it does mean that we need to listen to and understand one another. That is, there is a civic argument, one that is sometimes incorporated into character education programs, for teaching students how to talk with, and listen to, others about our differences, openly, honestly, and fairly.

The point of moral education, however, is not just to enable citizens to live together, as important as this is. If students are to be educated they must understand and think critically about different traditions. History demonstrates beyond any doubt that all too often our traditions have been oppressive and unjust, requiring reformation. The possibility of moral and social progress requires that we think critically about our traditions. In fact, the complexity of our lives and our world, together with the momentous consequences of our actions, make uneducated moral judgments dangerous. If one is to be a moral person, responsible for one's actions, one must be thoughtful; one must live an examined life.

All along my argument has been that schooling *uncritically* initiates students into secular ways of making sense of their lives. We teach students to think of themselves and their lives in the pervasively secular categories of the academic disciplines—of history, economics, psychology, and science. But if students are to be liberally educated about the moral dimensions of their lives, rather than simply socialized or indoctrinated, they must learn to take seriously religious alternatives as well.

Some courses—in economics, civics, or sex education, for example—may be explicitly normative; even if they resist explicitly moral language they are concerned with how students should live their lives. Other courses—in history, or psychology, or the sciences—while less explicitly normative, provide conceptual frameworks for making sense of the world and human nature within which morality (or specific conceptions of morality) may or may not make sense; as a result, those frameworks may be controversial on religious or moral grounds. Morality, as I've argued, isn't intellectually and culturally free-floating; it is grounded in ways of making sense of the world, some of which are supportive while others aren't.

So, for example, we saw in chapters 2 and 10 how neoclassical economic theory—the disciplinary conceptual framework of most introductory economics courses—stands in tension with traditional moral and religious categories for making sense of human nature, rationality, morality, and decision making. As a result, critically important moral and spiritual concerns relating to poverty, justice, work, consumerism, charitable giving, the sacred, and obligations to future generations can't even be raised. In chapter 10 I applied the 5 percent rule to economics texts and courses, arguing that they must address contending moral, religious, and philosophical concerns and ways of making sense of the economic dimension of life, initiating students into a conversation about the discipline of economics, not simply socializing them uncritically into the dominant approach of economists. Indeed, it is a requirement of a liberal education that any text or course situate students within a conversation about those moral concerns and controversies, ideas and ideals, theories and traditions, that bear on its subject matter, even if they don't fit the disciplinary framework of interpretation.

It is true that secular and religious folks agree on a great deal. For example, many economists and theologians agree that the United States should extend its welfare state, while other economists and theologians agree about a more libertarian conception of the political economy. Religious folks often disagree among *themselves*, as members of different religions, or as conservatives and liberals within the same religions do.[5] Still, there are fundamental differences between secular and religious ways of making sense of morality that students must learn to appreciate: morality isn't simply a matter of actions or policies but is grounded in what I have called deep justifications that make sense of it.

For religious folks, the world is (in some sense) the creation of God. Nature is (in some sense) sacred. People have souls (or there is a spiritual dimension of reality that can't be reduced to biology). There is wisdom in scriptural and religious traditions. People have obligations to God as well as to all of God's creation. Morality is in some sense grounded in religious narratives and ways of making sense of the world.

There are particular moral values or virtues that are typically taken to be of greater importance within religious rather than secular traditions: charity, mercy, forgiveness, love (as a public rather than just a private virtue), humility, reverence, and a sense of the sacred. No doubt many secular folks share some of these values in part, at least, because religious traditions have, through the centuries, shaped secular thinking. Arguably, secular conceptions of justice and equality have, in part at least, religious origins, and it is important to recognize the powerful interplay between religious and secular moralities and traditions. Of course, for many religious thinkers, the basic moral problem isn't so much with particular moral or social issues; rather it is that modern culture has generally lost its moral bearings.

Three conclusions seem inescapable. First, moral education cannot simply be a matter of how students (or people more generally) should act. It is also about why they should act in some ways rather than others; it must be grounded in deep justifications that must be subjected to critical thought if students are to live examined, responsible lives. Second, religions provide critiques of secular society that are absolutely necessary if students are to think critically—if they are to be liberally educated—about the dominant, secular culture. Third, because of the complexity of these matters and their importance, we can't expect them to be adequately treated by way of natural inclusion in existing courses.

## Courses in Ethics, Morality, and Meaning

No doubt it would be easier to incorporate some study of morality into existing courses, especially history and literature courses, than to create new courses, and, in fact, some discussion of moral issues is not uncommon in such courses. As with religion, however, natural inclusion isn't likely to do the job for at least three reasons. First, there simply isn't time for substantive discussion of complex and controversial moral issues (and relevant deep justifications) given the amount of material that is crammed into most courses. Second, because morality is complex and controversial, moral education requires sophistication, and most teachers, whatever their level, are poorly prepared by their educations to take morality and its deep cultural, religious, and philosophical justifications seriously. Third, the disciplinary structure of education all but ensures that morality often won't be taken seriously for, as with religion, it will not seem natural in many courses—in economics or biology, for example. And, while it is true that students might encounter moral and religious subject matter in a variety of courses, they will inevitably learn how to think about them—to interpret them—in the categories of the host disciplines, which are always secular and are typically nonmoral.

There is no small irony in the fact that for all the importance commonly attributed to morality, ethics courses are nonexistent in secondary schools and are typically electives in higher education (though courses in professional or applied ethics have often become required in professional schools). Indeed, it can only be astonishing, on reflection, that we require students to learn about the most abstract, complicated, and obscure scientific theories but leave them completely ignorant of all moral theories and traditions. How many students have any understanding of utilitarianism, Kantian ethics, social contract theory, or liberation theology? How many have even heard of John Rawls or Reinhold Niebuhr, arguably the greatest American moral philosopher and moral theologian of the last century? The de facto position of the educational establishment is that students need not be educated about morality.

In higher education, specialization ensures that ethics is typically compartmentalized (or departmentalized) within philosophy departments. There are two problems with this. First, other disciplines have been so demoralized that there are few (if any) resources in the categories of those disciplines for addressing morality in any substantive or systematic way. Second, the fact that ethics has become a philosophical specialty means that theological voices are typically left out of the discussion. (Why include Reinhold Niebuhr along with John Rawls?) As I noted in chapter 2, while philosophy courses in the history of ethics may include religious thinkers (but virtually never later than Kierkegaard), recent and contemporary religious voices are almost always left out.

One might also fret about the abstractness of philosophical ethics. As in any discipline, abstraction simplifies the messiness of reality, and this has real advantages (particularly in terms of clarity and logical rigor) but it also has disadvantages. Most important, it decontextualizes ethics from historical and cultural settings. Yet moral judgments and theories are inevitably entangled in complex webs of social, cultural, scientific, and religious beliefs, assumptions, and traditions. Moral judgments are tested, in part, by their implications for human suffering and flourishing—and this requires some sense of how, historically, moral ideas and ideals have played out in the past. Moreover, appreciating the moral demands on us requires empathy and sensitivity to people's suffering that is better gained through literature and the arts than philosophy. This isn't to say that philosophical ethics isn't essential to our critical thinking about morality; it is to say that it isn't sufficient. Moral education must be embedded in a historically and culturally textured liberal education.

In fact, instead of thinking of ethics, which has a somewhat narrow and academic feel to it, I suggest that all high school and undergraduate students should be required to take at least one yearlong course in morality and meaning. Such a course should have several characteristics. First, it should address several major moral concerns or problems—the environmental crisis, poverty, war, abortion, or homosexuality—introducing students to various ways of interpreting what is at issue, initiating them into a cultural conversation about these issues. Second, it should help them explore those related existential concerns about justice, love, suffering, happiness, flourishing, beauty, death, and the meaning of life that are inescapable for thoughtful human beings. Third, such a course must put these moral and existential concerns and problems in the context of traditions, theories, and worldviews—including, of course, religious traditions, theories, and worldviews—that enable students to make sense of various positions and think critically and systematically about their lives and our culture. That is, it must explore deep justifications—and basic concepts such as free will, responsibility, obligation, virtue, and human nature—in terms of which we make sense of morality.

Fourth, a course in morality and meaning should be broadly interdisciplinary, drawing on texts, ideas, and traditions from across the curriculum—from literature and the arts, from history and the sciences, from philosophy and religion. Indeed, it should explore interdisciplinary tensions—between, say, understandings of human nature in economics, biology, and the humanities. Needless to say, fifth, students should read a great deal of primary source material, particularly imaginative literature that makes moral and existential concerns, suffering and flourishing, imaginatively vivid to students (written, of course, from different points of view). Finally, I noted in chapter 6 that some emphasis on student-centered pedagogies is important in dealing with moral and existential concerns. Ideally, such courses should be seminars or small classes in which students are encouraged and enabled to express their own views and concerns.

In high schools, a senior course in morality and meaning would logically follow and build on the course in religious studies I have proposed (which might best be taken during students' junior year). Indeed, what could be more important to students than bringing together the disparate strands of their education in a capstone course, focusing their attention on the implications of their educations and our cultural conversation for the kind of society we should have, the kind of persons they should be, and how, in their life's work, they might make the world a better place? No doubt many educators will again point out that there is not time for such courses. I've responded to a similar argument regarding religion courses that it is astonishing that we find time for twelve years of mathematics, but no time for any serious study of religion. I now point out that we might, with similar justification, eliminate two required mathematics courses to make room for a course in morality and meaning. What is most important after all?

Such courses would need teachers. Happily, the same teacher might teach both the religious studies and morality courses (producing an economy of scale). The ideal teacher preparation would include coursework in both philosophical ethics and religious studies—or perhaps even better, an interdisciplinary degree with work in both of these disciplines as well as in history and literature (if I might be allowed to be wildly utopian).

In large universities such a capstone course would be virtually impossible if required of all students. Who would teach all those courses? Given the tyranny of specialization there probably is no solution to this problem—though such a course might be possible in small, liberal arts colleges where specialization is less a tyrant. Perhaps the best that can be done in universities is to require *an* ethics course (which might be taught in religious studies as well as in philosophy departments).

## Pluralism and Relativism Again

I have mentioned the danger of relativism as a side effect of critical thinking; this is particularly important when morality is at issue. One of the most difficult tasks for teachers is to convey to students the difference between pluralism and relativism. The civic and constitutional ground rules of our democracy and the ideal of liberal education require that we respect the pluralistic nature of our society and take seriously the different views of participants in our cultural conversation about morality. But teachers must not uncritically convey to students the deeply controversial idea that all positions are equally good, reasonable, or true—that is, relativism—not least when morality is at issue. After all, almost all moral disagreements are about what is truly right and good, or what justice actually requires.

Not surprisingly, in discussions of moral education the question is invariably asked, whose morality is going to be taught? In a sense, the answer is everyone's. Where there is broad agreement public schools should initiate students into the moral consensus—as character education programs do. When there is deep disagreement students should be taught about the alternatives (including the religious alternatives) fairly, taking the contending points of view seriously.

Because there is broad consensus about honesty, slavery, and democracy we should teach students to be honest, that slavery is evil, and to take seriously their obligations as citizens in a democracy. Because we disagree about abortion and politics and the deep justifications of morality we should teach students about the alternatives, initiating them into an interdisciplinary conversation about where the truth lies. Of course, neutrality is constitutionally required when religion is at issue, but it is often wise as a matter of sustaining broad public support for schools, in order to create the conditions for openness and trust in classes composed of students with various moral, political, and religious values. While teachers may acknowledge their personal convictions with mature students, courses and curricula shouldn't take official positions on controversial political, moral, or religious issues.

In universities, academic freedom protects the right of scholars to take moral positions on controversial matters or to argue for moral relativism (when either is within their area of competence) though here too there may be good pedagogical reasons for withholding judgment. I have argued that whether or not a scholar takes a moral position in the classroom, the idea of critical thinking requires that students be exposed to various points of view. Academic freedom does not protect indoctrination.

Perhaps I should note here that it is sometimes claimed that because religious accounts of morality are absolutist, religion, by its nature, cannot tolerate dissent and is, as a result, ill-suited for the give-and-take of an educational setting. While this has been a common religious position it has also been a common secular position over the last century (among Nazis and communists, for example). But some religious traditions have placed considerable emphasis on a free conscience, and if some religions have claimed to know God's law with considerable certainty, others have emphasized humility. Just as scientists can believe in objective truth and yet favor an open society in which we debate what that truth is, so religious folk can believe in moral truth and yet favor an open society in which we pursue it individually, openly, with humility. If some traditions have favored religious establishments and are intolerant of dissent, others value freedom of conscience and the separation of church and state.

## Sex Education, Abortion, and Homosexuality

I want to shift now from discussing the structure of moral education to its content by way of a case study.

We might distinguish four common purposes of sex education: promoting abstinence, teaching the biology of sexuality, giving students the technological know-how about condoms and birth control that enables them to avoid pregnancy and STDs, and locating sexuality within a broadly cultural context (relating to psychology, dating, love, the family, law, morality, and perhaps religion). Each of the first three goals is typically a matter of instruction rather than the critical thinking that engages students in a conversation about contending ways of making sense of sexuality and sexual morality.

Most people agree that it is legitimate and important to teach *children* sexual abstinence and not engage them in critical thinking about sexuality. Most would agree that it is important for students at some age to understand the biology of sexuality. Condoms are more controversial. Not surprisingly, many parents (including many religious conservatives) view the technological know-how approach as legitimizing sexual promiscuity and favor abstinence only. Many educators respond that it is naive to teach only abstinence because most adolescents will inevitably engage in sexual behavior and they must learn how to protect themselves and others. The pragmatic middle ground has become "abstinence *but*": teach students abstinence but include something about condoms and birth control as well.

Whichever position we take, however, requires that we give students reasons for abstinence or for using condoms. It can be argued that this is in students' long-term self-interest, and much sex education focuses on the unhappy consequences of unplanned pregnancies and STDs. Some students will recognize the risks and alter their behavior accordingly—though adolescents are not always strong on long-term self-interest and deferred gratification. It is also essential, however, that sex education makes students aware of the fact that sexual behavior is universally held to be subject to moral as well as prudential reasoning. Indeed, to be ignorant of this is to be uneducated.

So how do we introduce moral reasons into sex education? Some health textbooks I have reviewed adopt a *values clarification* approach.[6] On this approach, it is the task of texts and teachers to help students clarify their values, not guide them morally (which would be indoctrination). Students should consider the consequences of their actions on themselves and on others, and then act in a way that maximizes whatever it is that they value most. These texts often conclude that as a result of such considerations, students will practice abstinence. Unfortunately, this conclusion requires a considerable act of faith, for what students value most is up to them—and students are given no reasons for thinking of their actions as morally right or wrong. For these texts, values are ultimately personal and subjective. And yet, virtually everyone still believes that some actions are morally right and other actions are morally wrong.

Pedophilia is morally wrong. Not telling one's sexual partner that one has an STD is morally wrong. Honesty in relationships isn't just a matter of personal, subjective values; it is morally binding. If students don't understand this they are woefully ignorant and morally irresponsible.

Character education offers a quite different approach to sex education. Sexual relationships, like all relationships, should be characterized by honesty, loyalty, and respect for the feelings, privacy, and well-being of others—and, happily, there is broad consensus about this (though perhaps more in principle than in practice). Prudence, self-control, and a willingness to defer gratification are virtues of great importance in all aspects of life, but particularly in matters of sexuality. And we all agree that it is wrong for children to have sexual relationships. No doubt the moral consensus on sexuality is limited and fragile (many would say that the rules are different for adults, and we disagree about when children become adults) but because there is still considerable agreement, schools can and should teach these consensus moral values in health and sex education courses. Sex education must also be moral education.

But this takes us only so far. Earlier in this chapter I argued that character education would better be called character socialization, for it (usually) avoids controversial issues and the deep justifications of morality in political, cultural, and religious traditions. If sex education is to be truly educational (and not simply a matter of socialization into a moral consensus) it needs to situate students in moral, cultural, and religious traditions that make sense of sexuality— traditions that are often controversial—and they need to think critically about those traditions. Here we need to move to the fourth goal of sex education, locating sexuality within a broad cultural context—one in which not everyone agrees.

What is most important for our purposes is that students learn about religious as well as secular positions regarding abstinence, birth control, and sexuality more generally. They should understand why, within religions, marriage is a holy or sacramental (and not just a legal) institution. They should understand the policy positions on controversial sexual issues taken by religious organizations and theologians. They should learn about religious conceptions of the sanctity of life. Once again, students are illiberally "educated" if they learn to think about sexuality only in the secular categories.

Consider abortion. For many religious people, abortion is the most important moral issue of our time—and it is also the most important consequence of unwanted pregnancies and sexual promiscuity. Yet much sex education ignores abortion. I once reviewed a health textbook that devoted a single paragraph to abortion, explaining only that it is a medically safe alternative to adoption. That paragraph concludes: "this procedure has sparked a great deal of controversy."[7]

Well, yes—though some might consider this an understatement. That's why to be an educated person in the United States at the beginning of the twenty-first century it is so important to understand abortion; its relevance to sex education is immediate and tremendously important.

So what does it mean to be educated about abortion? Certainly, students should understand the point of view of the Roman Catholic Church and those religious conservatives who believe that abortion is murder. They should also understand the point of view of those religious liberals who are pro-choice. They should understand feminist positions on abortion. They should learn about the key U.S. Supreme Court rulings and different ways of interpreting the implications of political liberty for the abortion debate. Students should read primary source documents written from within these traditions.

Or consider homosexuality, like abortion a matter of great controversy, and also, like abortion, a matter of sufficient importance to make education about it mandatory. Many would say that after civil rights and women's rights, gay rights is the great human rights movement of our time. Because we disagree deeply about homosexuality students must learn about the major points of view, liberal and conservative, secular and religious, again using primary sources and imaginative literature. Students should learn something about how genetics, psychology, and politics relate to homosexuality and gay rights. They must learn that in some states gay marriage is legal (but they should also understand that morality and legality are not the same thing). They must learn something about different religious understandings of homosexuality. Of course, all of this is controversial, and the conversation must respect the different positions (drawing on the principle of cultural location and weight). Amid all of this controversy, however, it is proper and important to teach children to respect the rights of everyone and that name-calling and gay bashing are not permissible; happily, there is a fairly broad consensus about this so that it is a proper matter for character education.

What then would an adequate sex education curriculum look like? It must, of course, be age appropriate. Lessons and courses for young children should adopt the character education model, and great care must be taken to ensure that we don't prematurely encourage sexual behavior. Students must learn that everyone agrees that sexuality must be understood in moral categories, though there is considerable disagreement about how morality applies to some aspects of sexuality. Mature students need to be educated about some matters of great importance about which we disagree deeply, such as abortion and homosexuality. When we do this, however, we must initiate them into a conversation that includes all of the (major) voices, religious as well as secular. This will not be uncontroversial, and it may well be that there should be opt-out provisions—though I suspect that if parents were convinced that their moral and religious views were taken seriously, fewer would have their children opt out.

I recognize that adequate materials are lacking, and few sex education teachers are prepared to include religious perspectives on sexuality in their classes. It is no easy task to make sense of the soul (when discussing abortion), sacramental understandings of marriage or love, or guilt and alienation as they are explored in imaginative literature that grapples with the moral and spiritual complexity of sexuality.[8] Sex education teachers are usually from health education, psychology, or coaching rather than the humanities, and they may have no background in religious studies to help them make sense of religious perspectives on sexuality. In fact, sex education might best be taught by literature teachers (though they would also require considerable retooling to take on this task) or it might be team-taught. Once again, the difficulties of addressing religious perspectives on sexuality provide further reason for a required course in either religion or morality and meaning that takes religious perspectives on sexuality seriously.

## The Environmental Crisis

If many religious conservatives believe that abortion is the major moral issue of our time, many other folks believe that it is the environmental crisis (and many religious conservatives have come to believe that it is an issue of great importance) for the fate of the earth and its peoples literally hangs in the balance. It is for our time what the possibility of nuclear war was for the second half of the twentieth century. Students cannot leave high school (much less college) without a sophisticated understanding of what is at issue. Of course we don't agree entirely about the nature and extent of the crisis, so students must be initiated into a conversation about its causes, its seriousness, and ways of addressing it. Needless to say, the environmental crisis requires an interdisciplinary interpretation and response. It is necessary to understand something about (various perspectives on) the scientific understanding of the crisis and possible technological responses to it, the relevant political issues and responses (not the least of which relate to justice and the relationship of the First and developing worlds), economic issues (particularly as they relate to consumerism, lifestyles, sustainability, and justice), and of course religious ways of making sense of nature and responding to the crisis.

Arguably, capitalism, modern science, and technology have in various ways legitimated a utilitarian ethos that has been taken to justify the exploitation of nature. While organized religion came slowly to the environmental movement, religions provide a great deal of spiritual capital for addressing the problem. Religions understand nature as sacred (as God's creation, or as spiritual or divine). Religions take the long view much better than can economics or politics, and it is essential that students understand the importance of thinking in terms of obligations to future generations rather than cost-benefit analyses that typically discount the future and avoid the category of obligations. Religions have typically advocated simpler lifestyles, and warred against the consumerism and materialism that fuels unsustainable growth. Moreover, there has been a wealth of theological work on ecology (or ecotheology) as well as on poverty and justice regarding the Third World.

Given its importance, some discussion of the environmental crisis must be included in biology, economics, and civics courses, in each case with some acknowledgment of interdisciplinary connections to ethics and religion. It also merits a prominent place in a course on morality and meaning. Finally, an introductory religion course should consider the ways in which theology and our religious traditions provide resources for addressing it.

## Science, Technology, and Morality

Through most of history, morality has depended on religion, though there are quite different accounts of just what this relationship is. During the nineteenth century some scholars argued that by discrediting belief in God, science had also discredited morality. (One of Dostoyevsky's characters famously asserted that if God is dead, everything is permitted.) More scholars have argued that it is possible to make sense of morality apart from God—though how to do so is controversial. Indeed, the whole relationship of science, religion, and morality continues to be deeply controversial.

It has long been the conventional wisdom that science cannot justify moral values: it is conceptually impossible to move from the "is" statements of science (whether factual or theoretical) to the "ought" statements of morality; science can tell us what *is* the case, but it cannot tell us what *ought to be* the case—what is morally required. This need not be a problem so long as we don't believe that science provides us with a complete account of reality. But, of course, some scholars do believe that science provides a complete account of reality. Science appears to be constructing, slowly but surely, a cumulative case for scientific naturalism as research in evolutionary biology, genetics, neuroscience, and the hard social sciences provides fully naturalistic accounts of human nature and behavior, undercutting, in the process, traditional folk beliefs (as they are often called) about free will, morality, and God. So, for example, the idea of moral responsibility for our actions appears increasingly problematic as scientists provide deterministic (genetic, chemical, neurological, environmental) explanations for behavior. Nowadays, Darwinian explanations for the origins and development of morality are much in vogue. To the extent that students come to understand nature from the value-free sciences, and human nature from the value-free social sciences, morality may well seem irrational, without any grounding in reality.

Science textbooks don't say that science makes morality problematic, even if some scholars have come to this conclusion. Indeed, it is safe to say that there is no agreement among scholars (including scientists) about these things. My own view is that a full-blown scientific naturalism is an incoherent position in that the practice of science presupposes the much broader categories of the humanities (including those that ground free will and morality). Of course, some scholars continue to argue that morality presupposes the existence of God (in some way); morality makes sense only within a religious conception of reality. Because the relationship of science, religion, and morality is controversial and important, it surely warrants discussion in courses in ethics (or morality and meaning). Indeed, some discussion of their relationship may well be warranted by the 5 percent rule in other contexts—in courses on evolutionary biology, psychology, and economics, for example.

And then there is technology. No doubt technology has been a great boon to humankind, and dramatic technological advances will be necessary for addressing problems such as poverty and the environmental crisis. And yet, technology carries within it the potential for disaster. As Terry Eagleton has noted, "The Apocalypse, if it ever happens, is far more likely to be the upshot of technology than the work of the Almighty. . . . Who needs an angry God to burn up the planet when as mature, self-sufficient human beings we are perfectly capable of doing the job ourselves."[9] In fact, we almost did it with nuclear bombs.

The new GNR technologies—germline genetic engineering, nanotechnology, and robotics—may create even greater, if somewhat more subtle, dangers to humankind if misused. Some of these technologies are particularly dangerous because they don't require the massive resources of the state that nuclear weapons do, but are possible given small teams of scientists and modest amounts of venture capital. In fact, all too often, technology gets ahead of our ability morally or theologically to assess its meaning and consequences, leading at least a few scientists and scholars to propose moratoriums on research in the case of particularly troubling kinds of technology.[10]

A large part of the problem is that just as science is value-free, there is no moral compass built into the development of technologies that, consequently, can be used for great evil as well as for great good. So, for example, many scientists, in both the United States and Nazi Germany, succumbed to the lure of the eugenics movement. While some scientists resisted the development, testing, and use of nuclear weapons, more served on the government payroll. As Hannah Arendt argued in the aftermath of the Holocaust, altogether too much evil has been committed by good (or at least by normal) people, including, of course, scientists, who were oblivious, or at least insensitive, to the moral and spiritual significance of what they were doing. In fact, the technological acceleration of our time can be profoundly disorienting politically, morally, and spiritually (not least in the developing world, especially when yoked to the massive engine for change of capitalism).

Arguably, our reliance on (our addiction to?) technology encourages a technological ethos that encourages people to think technologically, bypassing moral and social approaches to problems for the quick technological fix. Educators have hardly been immune to the charms of technology, and public clamor for scientists and engineers who sustain our competitive advantage in the world and the pleasures of a consumer economy leave less and less room in the curriculum for the humanities.

Both theoretical and applied science must be taught together with ethics and moral theology. Textbooks must make science students aware of the moral and spiritual significance of the science they are studying and the technology they are creating. More generally, all students should be more thoughtful of the immense potential of science *for good and for evil*, a critical topic for any course in religion or morality and meaning.

## Conclusions

So what would be the effect of the reforms I have proposed? Would a good education make students moral? It has often been pointed out that many highly educated Germans—including doctors, scientists, and college professors—were Nazis. But I asked whether a *good* education makes students moral. German education in the early twentieth century was not, I suggest, a good education (for a variety of important reasons).

Clearly, whether students become good people is the result of much besides their formal educations. They benefit immensely from good parents, caring communities, and a humane culture. And, no doubt, personal psychological problems and powerful cultural or subcultural influences can counter the influence of the best teachers and courses. Character education programs are often touted for reducing incidents of violence, or improving manners, in schools. If this is in fact the case, this is important. But the deeper goal of moral education is to give students ways of thinking that make sense of their lives morally and enable them to live examined lives. The goal of moral education is to make students informed, empathetic, motivated, and thoughtful. The changes a good moral education brings about are deep, and not easily measured in crude, easily quantifiable ways.

In the end, a great deal depends on the ability of education to shape the culture (or better, the cultural conversation) within which individuals are enmeshed. Too much education is relentlessly fixated on economic and techno-logical development—both of which are important, of course. But students must learn that the greatest sources of goodness, joy, and meaning in life come not from wealth and technological wizardry but from altogether different realms of experience. In fact, if students are to be adequately oriented in life they should be educated somewhat less about its material dimensions and somewhat more about morality and those forms of community that bind us together in webs of meaning (and conversation) with our fellow human beings, with the past, with our posterity, and perhaps also with ultimate reality. In any case, it is hard to believe that students will be more likely to live good lives if they are thoughtless about the moral and spiritual dimensions of life, if they fail to live examined lives.

# Conclusions

## A Review of the Argument

I have argued that education in public schools and universities leaves students ignorant of religion. More problematic for constitutional reasons, such education is not neutral with regard to religion. Indeed, it borders on secular indoctrination. Given what education should be, this is scandalous.

A truly liberal education would devote sufficient time and effort to religions to enable students to understand them, from the inside, as live options for making sense of the world, and would be allowed to contend with secular positions. That is, it would *take religion seriously*. I have also argued religion must be taken seriously given the moral, existential, and civic purposes of education, and to achieve the neutrality that is required by the Establishment Clause of the First Amendment.

I have acknowledged that there are immense problems in correcting the situation. The public is deeply confused and divided about the proper role of religion in the curriculum. Few educational administrators have much sense of the relevance and importance of religion in the curriculum. Most teachers are not prepared by their educations to take religion seriously in their courses. Schools of education are tone-deaf to the problem. Textbooks utterly fail to take religion seriously.

While departments of religious studies make the situation less bleak in higher education, they hardly solve the problem. After all, the majority of public universities do not yet have departments of religious studies, courses in religious studies are invariably electives where departments do exist, and not all courses in religious studies take religion seriously.

So what, then, is to be done?

I have argued first for requiring a yearlong course in religious studies of high school students and undergraduates (taking religion seriously, robust fairness); and second for the 5 percent rule, which requires that all courses that deal with morally, philosophically, politically, and religiously controversial material devote 5 percent of textbook space and class time to making students aware of these controversies, situating them within the conversation that constitutes a liberal education (minimal fairness).

Many educators will view my solution to the problem as naively idealistic (if not simply wrongheaded). I have often fretted about what strategy to adopt in response to the problems I have discussed. I realize that it can be counterproductive to point out how far short of the ideal we fall, for there is a not entirely unreasonable temptation, in response, to throw up one's hands in despair and move on to problems with feasible solutions. I would be disappointed if I have discouraged teachers and administrators from taking on the task of taking religion seriously by making that task appear too daunting. Recognizing that danger, I have chosen, nonetheless, to emphasize the great distance we have to go, hoping that some sense of scandal might motivate some action.

## Realism and Idealism

But it is not a matter of all or nothing. It is possible to approximate the ideal incrementally through a series of stages.

(1) Individual teachers can make themselves better informed regarding religion and how to integrate more substantive study of it into their courses. This is likely to require a good deal of continuing education (whether formal or informal) on their part. I am aware of the danger of the rogue teacher who thinks that he or she knows much more than in fact is the case about either religion or the pedagogical and constitutional constraints regarding teaching about it. I do not recommend that teachers undertake radical changes in their courses in ways that depart from the established curriculum in order to incorporate serious study of religion into their classes, only that they know enough about various religions (and ways of teaching religion that are constitutionally and pedagogically sound) so that they can be more thoughtful on those occasions when religion does come up or should come up in textbooks and

class discussions. In higher education, academic freedom gives professors much more leeway in designing their courses, though even here there are important (sometimes controversial) questions about exceeding one's disciplinary competence. Teachers might also be lobbyists for further steps, such as the next one.

(2) Every school system should have a religion policy that addresses the role of religion in the classroom and the curriculum (as well as concerns about the practice of religion and religious liberty rights). As I've already said, developing such a policy can be controversial if undertaken in the midst of a crisis, but it need not be controversial if done right—which is to say that the task is taken on at a time of calm, involves all the various stakeholders (so that no major group is marginalized and everyone buys into it), and draws on the common-ground statements I discussed in chapter 6.[1] I don't expect such policies to issue clarion calls for taking religion seriously in my sense of the term, but they will, if they are developed thoughtfully, make clear that some study of religion is important and can be undertaken in ways that are pedagogically and constitutionally sound and not particularly controversial.

(3) Faculty members in schools of education can propose and teach elective courses on religion and education designed for prospective teachers and administrators, or at least give somewhat greater attention to religion in existing courses on teaching methods and in courses in the philosophy and social foundations of education. Faculty members in departments of religious studies can develop and teach courses that would be helpful to teachers (on religion and education, religion and literature, religion and science, or religion and economics). Needless to say, the fact that such courses are offered does not mean the prospective teachers will take them. Some groundwork must be laid to ensure that prospective teachers are aware of such courses and that they satisfy credentialing requirements.

(4) Parents and teachers can lobby for elective religion courses in public schools. World religions courses are taught in many schools with no controversy. Bible courses will usually be more controversial and, as I've suggested, will be more difficult to teach well. New religion courses might be modeled on the introductory courses I have described. Of course, teachers need to be competent to teach such courses. I've suggested that this means at least an undergraduate minor in religious studies. But when taught by competent teachers, in a school district that has a good religion policy, elective religion courses need not be controversial. In fact, such courses might even take religion seriously in my sense.

The following two steps will be somewhat more difficult and controversial, though they may still be feasible in some places.

(5) The reform of textbooks is a difficult and controversial business. In the meantime, there is some good supplementary material that might be used in conjunction with textbooks and more could easily be developed.[2] I particularly encourage the development of supplementary resource material designed to address my 5 percent rule that could be made available, either as published booklets or online. Such material might take the form of common-ground documents endorsed by educational, religious, and civil liberties groups.

(6) States might develop common-ground statements that largely replicate the national common-ground statements that I discussed in chapter 6, but in this case they would be endorsed by the state organizations whose parent, national organizations endorsed the national common-ground statements. Such statements might demonstrate a broad measure of local support for courses that take religion seriously.

Finally, six more challenging goals.

(7) State boards of education should require that schools of education take religion seriously by offering courses that address the role of religion in the curriculum and in public education more broadly.

(8) State boards of education should revise official curricula in history, social studies, and literature—and, ideally, in economics and the sciences—to include some study of religion (as well as of philosophy, ethics, and politics, in response to the 5 percent rule).

(9) State boards of education should encourage (or require) textbook publishers to incorporate serious study of religion in textbooks (again in response to the 5 percent rule).

(10) State boards of education (or local school districts) should require that all high school students take a course in morality and meaning that also takes religion seriously.

(11) State boards of education (or local school districts) should require that all high school students take a yearlong course in religious studies that takes religion seriously.

(12) Universities should require that all undergraduates take a yearlong course (or sequence of courses) in religious studies and in ethics or morality and meaning.

## Perspective

I fear that some readers will still think that the issues that I have dealt with in this book are marginal issues, both to education and to culture generally. It is probably too late, now, to change their minds, but I want to make a last effort to put my argument in broad historical and philosophical perspective, to explain why it's so important.

## Religious Perspective

For virtually all of human history—until at least the last century or two in the West—culture was pervasively religious (though religions could be wildly different). Some evolutionary biologists have argued that the ubiquity of religion suggests that evolution has somehow hardwired us to be religious. Some theologians argue that the presence of God makes belief understandable and reasonable. Whatever the explanation, the virtually universal presence and influence of religion are remarkable. On the human timeline it is only quite recently, and only in our part of the world, that belief in God has been called into question and sometimes rejected. The staying power of religion is remarkable not least because, as I noted at the end of chapter 1, many of the most influential political, social, and intellectual movements of the last century tried very hard to wipe religion out—with little success. Belief in God (by some name) appears to be a massive and perhaps unalterable fact of human existence.

True, we cannot deny various kinds of secularization, but we can overstate the extent of secularization—as intellectuals often do. Religion isn't disappearing from the world, even if it has lost much of its influence in a few places—in Western Europe and among Western intellectuals. The United States continues to be deeply religious and much of the rest of the world is becoming more religious. Moreover, religions refuse to be safely shunted into the private corners of people's lives. Because of its wide-ranging implications for how we make sense of the world and our lives, religions continue to be profoundly influential for both good and evil.

Of course, many scientists and secular scholars argue that whatever the numbers, religion is no longer intellectually respectable. I've argued not that this is wrong, but that it is deeply controversial. No doubt modern science and secular scholarship pose a challenge to religion—although, as we've seen, there are various ways of reconciling them. I do think we need to be wary of the claim that methodological naturalism—the ideal of scientific method in the natural and the hard social sciences, especially economics—is adequate to provide us with a complete account of reality. Scientific method requires scholars to abstract away from the messy richness of lived reality, screening out the personal, normative, and spiritual dimensions of reality, leaving us with a thin and abstract account. Moreover, in spite of the extraordinary successes of modern science and secular scholarship there is little agreement among secular scholars about how to answer the great existential questions—the Big Questions—that have long perplexed people.

## Civic Perspective

For most of human history, people lived within societies that were largely homogenous both culturally and religiously. Modernity has altered this situation dramatically. American culture is increasingly pluralistic. Moreover, we live in a much smaller world, one in which we simply can't avoid contact—and often conflict—with other cultures. In fact, we Americans are caught up in many clashes of cultures, values, traditions, and religions. I suppose that 9/11 and its aftermath made this most clear, but the United States' own culture wars, many of them shaped by religion, have raised many of the same concerns and fears even if on a smaller scale.

Religious pluralism is a massive fact of modernity. This being the case it seems even more obvious now than a decade or two ago that we must learn how to live with out deepest differences—which are often religious. The religion clauses of the First Amendment provide a remarkably helpful way of doing so within the United States. Of course, it is important to recognize, as the U.S. Supreme Court has often, but not always, done that the religion clauses were not designed to protect us from religion, but to protect the right of Americans to be religious (or not religious so far as that goes). The clauses provide a framework, a set of ground rules, for living together, peacefully, amid our religious differences.

But, as I argued in chapter 6, a purely legal framework for addressing our differences and resolving conflicts isn't sufficient, not least because it can't take in the rest of the world. There is also a civic imperative to understand one another, to take one another seriously, if we are to counter the constantly polarizing rhetoric of our various culture wars and live in peace rather than in fear, suspicion, conflict, and war. I don't suggest that such understanding is a panacea, but it can remove misunderstandings, puncture stereotypes, and reveal our similarities (as well, of course, as our differences). I am not saying that we must agree with one another or that we should give in to some kind of cultural relativism. The challenge is to keep our cultural and religious differences from destroying us, and for this conversation, understanding, and an enlarged sense of community, is essential.

## Moral Perspective

History gives us good reason to think that without powerful civilizing traditions and institutions people become barbarians. It is striking to me, as I've said several times along the way, how casual, even dismissive, educators are regarding moral education—as if we're doing just fine so that schools and universities needn't worry about it.

Here, too, modernity creates problems as traditional communities give way to rootless individuals, especially under the pressures of technology and capitalism. Modern cultures often suffer from the sin of presentism, in which people live their lives largely oblivious to the sacrifices of their ancestors and their responsibilities to posterity. Science, social science, and technology encourage us to adopt nonmoral intellectual frameworks for rethinking what it means to be a person and what our place is in the larger scheme of things. Specialization enables people to avoid considering the moral consequences of their professional actions, enabling those often banal evils that have devastating consequence for humankind writ large. Modernity carries with it some rather nasty baggage.

It is certainly true that traditional cultures and religions could be profoundly oppressive and promote great evils. (No doubt we are more inclined to recognize this regarding other cultures and religions than our own; humility is a helpful antidote here.) And I don't want to deny that a healthy measure of individualism, science, technology, capitalism, and specialization has helped people escape from many of the evils of traditional, often oppressive cultures.

It isn't obvious whether we need religion to underwrite (to provide deep justifications for) morality. No doubt atheists can be good people and the secular societies of Western Europe often appear more morally advanced than our own. But it may be that societies live for centuries off of the interest earned from the religious capital of their civilizations. In any case, the continuing moral shortcomings of most people's lives and of all societies suggest that we ought not to be sanguine about moral progress—or even about sustaining the fragile moral consensus about basic rights and responsibilities that we have. It may turn out that secular morality will prove sufficient to the occasion—though there is virtually no agreement among them when it comes to deep justifications for morality. But it may also be the case that religious ideas and ideals provide a balancing corrective to many of the limitations of modernity. I am thinking of the sacredness of nature, the sanctity of life; equality in the eyes of God; love, mercy, forgiveness, humility, and compassion for those who suffer, including, of course, the least of God's creatures.

No doubt institutional religions have often botched their moral responses to the human condition; so have secular societies and ideologies.

## Educational Perspective

I am struck by how little public discussion and scholarly study is devoted to the ultimate purposes of education. Mostly we argue about means, not ends. But what should students study? What kinds of understanding are essential to being a good or a wise person? The conventional assumption, internal to modernity, is that we must promote those skills and that knowledge necessary for economic success, whether for individuals or for the United States. Let me be clear once more: the study of math and science, technology and economics, is tremendously important. Indeed, we are in such desperately deep trouble with regard to natural resources, the environment, poverty, and health care that short of divine intervention we must count on massive doses of technological and economic aid to survive. That said, our educational priorities reflect all too much, and all too thoughtlessly, the priorities of modernity that have created and exacerbated many of the problems that beset us. The solution to our problems cannot simply be more science, technology, and economic development. The humanities are absolutely critical if we are not to succumb to the enthusiasms of our time.

I have proposed dropping two required high school math courses to make room for a required religion course and a required course in morality and meaning. I am not optimistic that my counsel will be heeded but surely it is foolish to require so much math if that means no study of religion and morality! This should be as obvious as anything can be educationally, and yet we are utterly blind to it. (I think of this as a kind of Rorschach test for educational and cultural sanity.)

We need to rethink the curriculum of both secondary schools and colleges and universities. Religion isn't going away. If anything, it is becoming more influential (for good and for evil) on the world stage. We have to learn to live with our (often deep) religious differences. We need to nurture in students a deeper understanding of, and commitment to, the moral dimensions of our lives. Schools can't continue to home in on professional and economic goals; the end result will be barbarism. Socrates was right: the unexamined life is not worth living. An educational system that ignores the great existential questions—political, moral, spiritual, religious—is not worthy of respect, indeed, it shouldn't count as educational at all.

But we rarely think about these things. We are fixated on the mundane world of business as usual. As a result, public schools and universities uncritically take sides in a matter of momentous historical, cultural, and philosophical importance, guiding students thoughtlessly toward exclusively secular ways of making sense of the world and living their lives. I am not saying that atheism is false. I am not saying that any religion is true. We disagree about these things. But precisely because we disagree any education that is to be called liberal education cannot avoid the question of God's existence. Does God make a difference to how we should think about education? Of course. Public schools and universities must take religion seriously.

# Notes

INTRODUCTION

1. John Micklethwait and Adrian Woodridge, *God Is Back: How the Global Revival of Faith Is Changing the World* (New York: Penguin, 2009).

2. This new national consensus, embodied in a series of common-ground statements that I will discuss in chapter 6, has contributed significantly to developing respect for First Amendment religious liberty rights. It has had much less influence on the role of religion in the curriculum (though its potential is considerable).

3. No doubt most educators do not intend to be hostile (or even indifferent) to religion and they often respond to critics by testifying to their own religious convictions. On average, schoolteachers and administrators are about as religious as most Americans—though university professors, as we shall see, are somewhat less religious. But all of this is beside the point. The hostility at issue is not only unintended, it is unrecognized. It is the result, for the most part, of a deep naïveté, a result of educators' own limited, illiberal educations.

4. Perhaps I should note that all of this is a nonproblem for most scholars. Given the violence of our culture wars and our deep disagreements about the role of religion in public life, one might expect a vast scholarly literature on the role of religion in American education. Not so. Only a handful of scholarly books address these issues in any significant way. This fact is itself eloquent testimony to the irrelevance of religion in the academy. For most educators the problem of religion and education is the purely political problem of how to keep religious conservatives from taking over school boards, censoring textbooks, and passing voucher legislation. The truth of

the matter is a good deal more complicated—and much more interesting and much more important—than most folks suspect.

5. John Hick, *A Philosophy of Religion*, 4th ed. (Englewood Cliffs, N.J.: Prentice Hall, 1990), 18.

6. Wilfred Cantwell Smith, *The Meaning and End of Religion* (New York: Mentor, 1964), 22. For example, we typically take religions to be discrete traditions, institutions, or systems of belief that stand alongside others (science, politics, and economics, for example). But in traditional cultures what we call religion pervaded all of life—history, nature, morality, politics, economics, and psychology; religion was part of the warp and woof of lived culture.

7. John Hick, *An Interpretation of Religion* (New Haven: Yale University Press, 1989), 22.

8. J. Milton Yinger, *Scientific Study of Religion* (New York: Macmillan, 1970), 7, 11–12.

9. Will Herberg, "Religion and American Education," in *Religious Perspectives in American Culture,* ed. James Ward Smith and A. Leland Jamison, 28 (Princeton: Princeton University Press, 1961).

10. *Torcaso v. Watkins,* 367 U.S. 488, 495n. (1961), my emphasis.

11. *United States v. Seeger,* 380 U.S. 163, 174, 176 (1965).

12. According to a 2007 survey conducted by the Institute for Studies of Religion at Baylor University, 10 percent of Americans say that they are spiritual but not religious; 57 percent claim to be spiritual and religious; 17 percent religious but not spiritual; and 16 percent claim to be neither. See Rodney Stark, *What Americans Really Believe* (Waco: Baylor University Press, 2008), 88–89.

13. Ninian Smart, *Worldviews: Crosscultural Explorations of Human Beliefs* (New York: Scribner's, 1983).

14. E. J. Dionne Jr., *Souled Out: Reclaiming Faith and Politics after the Religious Right* (Princeton: Princeton University Press, 2008), 44.

15. Robert Nash has provided an intriguing, alternative typology in his book *Faith, Hype, and Clarity* (New York: Teachers College Press, 1999) where he distinguishes between the fundamentalist narrative, the prophetic narrative, the alternative spiritualities narrative, and the post-theist narrative. (The first three map very roughly onto my categories of fundamentalism, liberalism, and spirituality.) A part of the joy of Nash's book is his account of how he engages students in discussions of these alternatives.

16. Alan Wolfe argues, contrary to Hunter, that religious movement in the United States is toward the middle rather than to the conservative and liberal ends of the spectrum. So, for example, "talk of hell, damnation, and even sin has been replaced by a nonjudgmental language of understanding and empathy. Gone are the arguments over doctrine and theology. . . . Religions can be astonishingly different, while human beings can be surprisingly the same. Study theology, and one comes away impressed by differences. Study real people, and one is more likely to notice the similarities." He concludes: "We are all mainstream now" (*The Transformation of American Religion: How We Actually Live Our Faith* [Chicago: University of Chicago Press, 2003], 3–5).

17. In the third volume of his monumental three-volume history of American liberal theology Gary Dorrien argues that the "fundamental divide in Christian theology is between various forms of conservative orthodoxy and progressivism" (*The Making of American Liberal Theology: Crisis, Irony and Postmodernity, 1950–2005* [Louisville: Westminster John Knox, 2006], 6). For Dorrien, "progressivism" is the umbrella term under which he locates liberal theology, neoorthodoxy, liberation theology, and postmodern theology. I am using "liberal theology" rather than "progressive theology" as my umbrella term (and I'm running roughshod over a number of distinctions that Dorrien very helpfully makes).

18. Some scholars have argued that fundamentalism isn't conservative at all, but reactionary, in that it rejects tradition (which is to be conserved) in favor of going back to original texts. Others have argued that in its insensitivity to historical scholarship fundamentalism often misses the "intended" or original meanings of scriptural texts (which are likely to be broadly metaphorical and not at all literal) for their own interpretations—interpretations that are often, unwittingly, influenced by the literalism of modern science.

19. See Robert Wuthnow, *After Heaven: Spirituality in America Since the 1950s* (Berkeley and Los Angeles: University of California Press, 1998).

## CHAPTER I

1. According to a 2006 Gallup poll, 73 percent of Americans are convinced God exists; 14 percent believe God probably exists but may have a little doubt; 5 percent say that God probably exists but they have a lot of doubt. According to a recent survey of the Institute for Studies of Religon at Baylor, 63 percent of Americans agree that "I have no doubt that God exists." According to the 2008 American Religious Identification survey, 69.5 percent say that a personal God "definitely exists."

2. A 2008 survey of 35,000 Americans by the Pew Center on Religion and Public Life found that 1.6 percent call themselves atheists, 2.4 percent agnostics, and 12.1 percent claim to be "nothing in particular," meaning that 16.1 percent of Americans are religious unaffiliated. The 2007 Baylor Survey puts the percentage of atheists at 4 percent, which Rodney Stark notes is identical to the percentage of atheists in America in 1944. See Stark, *What Americans Really Believe* (Waco: Baylor University Press, 2008), 117.

3. According to the 2007 Baylor Survey (63 percent of Americans are "absolutely sure" that heaven exists, while another 19 percent are "pretty sure"; 73 percent of Americans believe that hell absolutely or probably exists). According to a 2007 Gallup poll 57 percent of Americans say that religion is "very important in their own lives," 26% say that it is "fairly important," and 16% say it is "not very important."

4. "Donating Our Dollars and Hours," *Newsweek* (July 3/July 10, 2006), 65.

5. 2005 Eurobarometer Survey http://ec.europa.eu/public_opinion/archives/ ebs/ebs_225_report_en.pdf, 12. If these three options were given to Americans, the percentage who believe in God would surely go down. According to the 2008 Religious Identification Survey, 69.5 percent of Americans believe in a personal God, while 12.1

percent believe there is "a higher power but no personal God." A 2004 Bliss Institute (University of Akron) survey found that 40 percent of Americans believe in a personal God, while 41 percent believe that God is a spirit or force, and 19 percent acknowledged that they don't know what they believe. Of course, what these terms mean to people is not at all clear.

6.  Peter Berger, *The Desecularization of the World* (Grand Rapids: Eerdmans, 1999), 2, 10. Noting the very secular convictions of many of the intellectuals who have advocated the secularization thesis, some scholars (e.g., Jeffrey Hadden and Christian Smith) have agued that it is more an ideology than an empirical theory.

7.  This very careful survey of a representative sample of faculty yielded a sample of 1,471 responses of which: 10.0 percent were atheists, 13.4 percent were agnostics, 19.6 percent believe not in a personal God but in a higher power of some kind, 4.4 percent believed sometimes but not always, 16.9 percent acknowledged doubts but claimed to believe in God nonetheless, and 35.7 percent believed in God and had no doubts. While 23.4 percent of the total sample were atheist or agnostic, 36.6 percent of faculty members at research universities were atheist or agnostic (though even here they are a minority). See Neil Gross and Solon Simmons, "The Religious Convictions of College and University Professors," in *The American University in a Postsecular Age,* ed. Douglas Jacobsen and Rhonda Hustedt Jacobsen, 22–23 (New York: Oxford University Press, 2008).

8.  *Spirituality and the Professoriate: A National Study of Faculty Beliefs, Attitudes, and Behaviors* (a report of the Higher Education Research Institute at UCLA), available at http://www.spirituality.ucla.edu/docs/results/faculty/spirit_professoriate.pdf.

9.  *Gallup Poll Briefing* (May 2006).

10.  *The Church of the Holy Trinity v. United States,* 143 U.S. 226, 232 (1892).

11.  Appleby, *The Ambivalence of the Sacred* (Rowman and Littlefield, 1999), 122.

12.  Joseph Schumpeter, *Capitalism, Socialism, and Democracy,* 3rd ed. (New York: Harper, 1972), 83.

13.  National Conference on Catholic Bishops, *Economic Justice for All* (Washington, D.C.: United States Catholic Conference, 1986), vi–vii, 12.

14.  Maybe I should say that the vast majority of scientists and theologians are not part of the science/religion dialogue, but many are. The important point is that there is a substantive conversation among theologians, scientists, and philosophers. The conventional picture of warfare between scientists and fundamentalist creationists is badly out of date.

15.  Anthony Flew, the most prominent atheist among philosophers of the last fifty years, recently acknowledged that he now finds the evidence for a cosmic fine-tuner convincing. See his *There Is a God* (New York: HarperOne, 2007).

16.  William Barrett, *Irrational Man* (Garden City, N.Y.: Anchor, 1962), 56, 24.

17.  Andrew Delbanco, *The Death of Satan* (New York: Farrar, Straus, and Giroux, 1995), 220, 212.

18.  According to Baylor University's Institute for Studies of Religion, an astonishing 30 percent of Americans have read *The Da Vinci Code,* and another 20 percent have read the *Left Behind* series; 44 percent of American adults have seen

Mel Gibson's *Passion of the Christ*, and 58 percent have watched the television series *Touched by an Angel*. See Stark, *What Americans Really Believe*, 172, 174.

## CHAPTER 2

1. *Education Week* (April 12, 1995): Special Report, 5.

2. I have conducted three reviews of high school textbooks, the first of texts published in the late 1980s, the second of texts published in the mid-1990s, and most recently of texts published between 2003 and 2006. In all, I've reviewed more than one hundred high school textbooks in history, literature, biology, physics, economics, and health.

3. Frances FitzGerald, *America Revised* (New York: Vintage, 1980), 18, 27.

4. Susan L. Douglass, *Teaching about Religion in National and State Social Studies Standards* (Fountain Valley, Calif.: Council on Islamic Education; Nashville: First Amendment Center, 2000), 88.

5. See Diane Ravitch, *The Language Police* (New York: Vintage, 2003). For Seawell's reviews see the Web site of the American Textbook Council at http://www .historytextbooks.org/islam.htm. For the response of the Council for Islamic Education see www.cie.org/news/SewallResponse.asp.

6. *National Standards for World History* (Los Angeles: National Center for History in the Schools, UCLA, 1994), 245. The *Standards* suggest that students "debate the proposition that the late 20th century is a time of religious ferment and vitality in the world" (283). There is no correlative standard for American history.

7. *National Standards for World History*, 17.

8. *Prentice Hall Economics* (Upper Saddle River, N.J.: Prentic Hall, 2003), 68. My emphasis.

9. *Glencoe Economics: Today and Tomorrow* (New York: Glencoe/McGraw-Hill, 2003), 23.

10. National Council on Economics Education, *National Content Standards in Economics* (New York, 1997), 8.

11. Robert H. Frank, Thomas Gilovich, and Dennis T. Regan, "Does Studying Economics Inhibit Cooperation?" *Journal of Economic Perspectives* 7 (Spring 1993): 159–71.

12. National Council on Economics Education, *National Content Standards in Economics*, viii. For a more thorough discussion of religion, economics, and education (and bibliographical references), see my book *Taking Religion Seriously across the Curriculum* (Washington, D.C.: ASCD, 1998), 105–16.

13. In a *Parade* magazine story Duvall is quoted as saying that "teachers, parents and others are often afraid that economics can't be separated from ideology and politics." The author then writes: "That's not true, Duvall adds. Indeed, the National Council's standards for an economics curriculum are basic principles with no ideological content. . . . These principles are just common sense." Lynn Brenner, "What We Need to Know about Economics," *Parade* (April 16, 1999).

14. *Economics: Principles and Tools*, 3rd ed. (Upper Saddle River, N.J.: Pearson Prentice Hall, 2003), 432.

15. Robert Wuthnow, *Christianity in the Twenty-First Century* (New York: Oxford University Press, 1993), 200.

16. National Research Council, *National Science Education Standards* (Washington, D.C.: National Academy Press, 1995), 201.

17. Ibid., 138.

18. *Conceptual Physics* (Upper Saddle River, N.J.: Prentice Hall, 2002), 6–7.

19. *Glencoe Biology* (New York: Glencoe/McGraw-Hill, 2005), 21.

20. *Physics: A Worldview,* 5th ed. (Pacific Grove, Calif.: Thomson-Brooks/Cole, 2004), 10.

21. Ibid., 344.

22. Edward Larson, *Trial and Error* (New York: Oxford University Press, 2003), 200.

23. Lawrence S. Lerner, *Good Science, Bad Science: Teaching Evolution in the States* (Washington, D.C.: Thomas B. Fordham Foundation, 2000), 12, 26.

24. *Glencoe Biology,* 388.

25. *Physics: A Worldview,* 616.

26. According to the *Standards for the English Language Arts* (Urbana, Ill.: International Reading Association and the National Council of Teachers of English, 1996) texts chosen for study should "reflect the diversity of the United States' population in terms of gender, age, social class, religion, and ethnicity" (28). In discussing cultural diversity the standards suggest that students might explore "the history of oral cultures and their many philosophical and religious traditions" (41–42). At another point, the standards note that African folk narratives and Greek myths "can be read as delightful, entertaining stories, as representations of mythic archetypes or as cultural, religious, or philosophical histories of particular regions or people" (27).

27. I looked at three world literature, three British literature, and three American literature anthologies, all with copyright dates of 2006 or 2007. I thank Martha Dill for her help in reviewing these texts.

28. The one Advanced Placement text I reviewed gave a little more than 1 percent of its pages to religion (primarily by cataloging the religion clauses in U.S. Supreme Court rulings in a seven-page section); the other three texts each gave somewhat less than 1 percent of its pages to religion.

29. The sole exception is a nine-week course required in the Modesto, California, schools that has been offered since 2001 without incident.

30. If the fact that God comes up so rarely is unsurprising, there is, nonetheless, an irony in it. As I noted in chapter 1, most professors believe in God and, as George Marsden has noted, "Keeping within our intellectual horizons a being who is great enough to create us and the universe . . . ought to change our perspectives on quite a number of things. One might expect it to have a bearing on some of the most sharply debated issues in academia today. . . . Why, in a culture in which many academics profess to believe in God, do so few reflect on the academic implications of that belief?" (*The Outrageous Idea of Christian Scholarship* [New York: Oxford University Press, 1997], 4).

31. For discussion of the AAR study see Linell Cady, "What Does the Census Data Say about the Study of Religion?" *Religion Studies News* 17, no. 2 (March 2002): 7, 21; and Hans Hillerbrand, "The 2000 Survey of Departments of Religion," *Religious Studies News* 19, no. 2 (March 2004): 6, 19.

32. According to the 2009 *Chronicle Almanac* 78 percent of American undergraduates attend public institutions and 22 percent attend private colleges (August 28, 2009), 6. The numbers would be even more lopsided if we consider two-year schools.

33. According to the AAR study, about 4 percent of public universities that offer coursework in religion require that students study religion (in some way).

34. Conrad Cherry, Beter A. DeBerg, and Amanda Porterfield end their helpful book *Religion on Campus* (Chapel Hill: University of North Carolina Press, 2001) with the following assessment (which is somewhat different from mine): "We found both the practice and the study of religion to be vital aspects of the slices of American higher education that we observed. . . . It is possible that young people in American culture have never been more enthusiastically engaged in religious practice or with religious ideas" (294–95). But, I would respond, we cannot extrapolate from their in-depth study of four universities to public universities generally. Only one of the four universities they studied was a public university, and unlike the majority of public universities it had a department of religious studies. Nor do they pay adequate attention, in this concluding generalization, to the elective nature of religion courses, or the extent to which courses may be highly specialized or narrowly historical.

35. Alan Wolfe, "Higher Learning," in *Lingua Franca* (March/April 1996): 70.

# CHAPTER 3

1. *The Annotated McGuffey*, ed. Stanley W. Lindberg (New York: Van Nostrand Reinhold, 1976. The second greatest number of references is to death.

2. Ruth Miller Elson, *Guardians of Tradition: American Schoolbooks of the Nineteenth Century* (Lincoln: University of Nebraska Press, 1964), 338.

3. Julie Reuben, *The Making of the Modern University* (Chicago: University of Chicago Press, 1996), 17.

4. Laurence Veysey, *The Emergence of the American University* (Chicago: University of Chicago Press, 1970), 48.

5. Jon Roberts and James Turner, *The Sacred and the Secular University* (Princeton: Princeton University Press, 2000), 21.

6. Horace Mann, "Twelfth Annual Report of the Secretary of the Board of Education of Massachusetts (1848), reprinted in *Religion and Constitutional Government in the United States*, ed. John Semonche, 123 (Carrboro, N.C.: Signal, 1986).

7. Quoted in Robert Michaelsen, *Piety in the Public School* (London: Macmillan, 1970), 67.

8. Charles Glenn has argued that the common schools were "profoundly subversive of the beliefs of most Protestants"—at least most conservative Protestants—and much of the early opposition came from them. See Glenn, *Myth of the Common School* (Amherst: University of Massachusetts Press, 1987), 150.

9. Douglas Laycock, "Summary and Synthesis: The Crisis in Religious Liberty," *George Washington Law Review* 60 (March 1992): 845.

10. Elson, *Guardians of Tradition*, 282.

11. Ibid., 314.

12. Michaelsen, *Piety in the Public School*, 150.

13. Sidney Hook, *Education for Modern Man* (New York: Humanities, 1973), 115–16.

14. C. Kenneth Shannon, "The Religious Content of Secondary School American History Textbooks, 1860–1938," unpublished manuscript, 1996, 7.

15. Frances FitzGerald, *America Revised* (New York: Vintage, 1980), 75–76.

16. Ronald Reagan, "Farewell Address to the Nation," www.ronaldreagan.com /sp_21.html.

17. Quoted in Andrew Cremin, *American Education: The Colonial Experience* (New York: Harper Torchbooks, 1970), 238.

18. Elson, *Guardians of Tradition*, 222.

19. FitzGerald, *America Revised*, 171.

20. David Tyack and Margaret Hansot, *Managers of Virtue: Public School Leadership in America* (New York: Basic, 1982), 106–7.

21. George M. Thomas, Lisa R. Peck, and Channin G. de Haan, "Reforming Education, Transforming Religion, 1876–1931," in *The Secular Revolution*, ed. Christian Smith, 379 (Berkeley and Los Angeles: University of California Press, 2003).

22. Kraig Beyerlein, "Educational Elites and the Movement to Secularize Public Education: The Case of the National Education Association," in *The Secular Revolution*, 191.

23. National Education Association, *Proceedings* (1903), quoted in Beyerlein, "Educational Elites," 192.

24. B. Edward McClellan, *Moral Education in America* (New York: Teachers College Press, 1999), 55–56.

25. What was required, according to Thomas, Peck, and de Haan, "was a science-based curriculum that fostered a moral code that was functional for industrial society. . . . Children should be taught to reason from experience about morality, not simply accept traditional values" ("Reforming Education," 380).

26. Elson, *Guardians of Tradition*, 17.

27. Ibid.

28. Ibid., 19.

29. Edward Larson, *Trial and Error: The American Controversy over Creation and Evolution* (New York: Oxford University Press, 2003), 20.

30. Ibid., 18.

31. Ibid., 22.

32. Ibid., 81–92.

33. Ibid., 91.

34. George Marsden, *The Soul of the American University: From Protestant Establishment to Established Nonbelief* (New York: Oxford University Press, 1994), 99.

35. Roberts and Turner, *The Sacred and the Secular University*, 28.

36. Ibid., 29.

37. Quoted in Reuben, *The Making of the Modern University*, 63. Also see 61–71.

38. By the end of the nineteenth century even scholars of religion were committed to studying religion and the Bible scientifically. Reuben argues, "Between 1890 and 1920 the scientific study of religion flourished. Most scholars in the new

field were sympathetic to religion and wanted to show that it had an important role in modern scientific culture. To demonstrate its value, intellectuals focused on its psychological and social functions. This approach, however, did not produce modern religious beliefs, as predicted. Instead, the scientific study of religion only affirmed religion's intellectual marginality" (*The Making of the Modern University*, 101). Also see 107.

39. James Turner, *Without God, Without Creed* (Baltimore: Johns Hopkins University Press, 1985), 240.

40. Sigmund Freud, *The Future of an Illusion* (Garden City, N.Y.: Anchor, 1964), 63.

41. Robert Bellah, "Between Religion and Social Science," in *Beyond Belief: Essays on Religion in a Post-Traditional World* (New York: Harper & Row, 1970), 250.

42. Douglas Sloan, *Faith and Knowledge: Mainline Protestantism and American Higher Education* (Louisville: Westminster John Knox, 1994), 20.

43. Turner, *Without God, Without Creed*, 240.

44. Marsden, *The Soul of the American University*, 187.

45. Roberts and Turner, *The Sacred and the Secular University*, 92.

46. Frederick Rudolph, *Curriculum: A History of the American Undergraduate Course of Study Since 1636* (San Francisco: Jossey-Bass, 1977), 103.

47. Quoted in Veysey, *The Emergence of the American University*, 84.

48. Smith, *The Secular*, 76.

49. Rudolph, *Curriculum*, 156–57. Reuben puts it this way: Because of specialization, "by the early twentieth century, the ideal of the unity of truth did not seem plausible to younger intellectuals trained in the new universities. Twentieth-century academics embraced the separation of facts and values because it fit the scholarly and educational practices that had developed over the previous fifty years. The separation of knowledge and morality was an unintended result of the university reforms of the late nineteenth century" (*The Making of the Modern University*), 4.

50. Reuben, ibid., 135–36.

51. Ibid., 211–29.

52. See Kronman, *Education's End* (New Haven: Yale, 2007), 37–90. Roberts and Turner argue, "There was in fact nothing specifically Christian, nothing essentially theistic, in the humanities." Indeed, because of their turn-of-the-century commitment to historicism, "the humanities emerged in the long run as more than passive abettors in the deconstruction of the religious framework of knowledge; ironically, they proved to be active undercover agents; a fox welcomed into the henhouse. For historicism eventually had the effect of sapping Christianity, indeed undermining any conviction of objective truth transcending human beings" (*The Sacred and the Secular University*, 118–19).

53. Marsden, *The Soul of the American University*, 158.

54. Marsden, *The Secularization of the Academy*, 28–29. As James Burtchaell tells the story, liberals "unwittingly deprived their institutions of any capacity to retain their Christian identity when exposed to a secularist faculty" in succeeding generations ("Decline and Fall of the Christian College, I," in *First Things* [April 1991]: 29).

55. Bradley Longfield, "From Evangelicalism to Liberalism," in Marsden, *The Secularization of the Academy* (New York: Oxford University Press, 1992), 46.

56. James Prothero, *Religious Literacy* (San Francisco: HarperSanFrancisco, 2007), 106.

57. Sloan, *Faith and Knowledge*, 23.

58. Quoted in Sloan, *Faith and Knowledge*, 23.

59. See my *Religion and American Education* (Chapel Hill: University of North Carolina Press, 1995), 168–79; or my essay "Humanism and the Humanist Manifestos" in the *Praeger Handbook on Religion and Public Education*, ed. James C. Carper and Thomas C. Hunt, 2: 245–48 (Westport, Conn.: Praeger, 2009).

60. Smith, *The Secular Revolution*, 1.

61. Ibid., 1. Smith argues, "Many modern Western intellectuals exhibit a propensity for hostility toward religion. This is because historically they are themselves the direct products of emancipation from church control, and because religion is often implicated in established social orders which frequently they more generally condemn. It is also because intellectuals aspire to an autonomy and engage in discursive practices that are both in many ways at odds with religious sensibilities and practices" (46).

62. Joan DelFattore claims that on the eve of the Supreme Court's rulings twelve states required some kind of religious observances in its public schools, while nine states (with Blaine Amendments) forbade them. She also notes, "Long before the U.S. Supreme Court began ruling on school prayer, state courts throughout the country had soundly rejected the once-prevalent notion that public schools have the right to impose majoritarian religious practices on all students. Beyond that, several courts had declared that school officials may not sponsor such observances even if dissenters are excused. To be sure, attitudes toward state-sponsored school prayer were not changing at the same rate or in the same way in all states, and there were serious disagreements about the extent to which opt-out policies protect minority rights. Nevertheless, the Supreme Court's rulings were nowhere near so unprecedented as its critics sometimes claim" (*The Fourth R: Conflicts over Religion in America's Public Schools* [New Haven: Yale University Press, 2004], 53, 60). According to Jonathan Zimmerman, a 1962 survey indicated that 42 percent of school systems had Bible reading without comment and about a third of public schools conducted some kind of daily devotional services (*Whose America? Culture Wars in the Public Schools* [Cambridge, Mass.: Harvard University Press, 2005], 138, 163).

63. As late as 1890, President James Angell of the University of Michigan reported that twenty-two of twenty-four state universities he surveyed conducted chapel services; at twelve, chapel was required.

## CHAPTER 4

1. Prothero, *Religious Literacy: What Every American Needs to Know—and Doesn't* (San Francisco: HarperSanFrancisco, 2007), 21–38.

2. Prothero argues that a true religious literacy would be more than just "the accumulation of facts." It would require the ability to understand and use religious facts, symbols, stories, and practices. See ibid., 14.

3. I take the term "live option" from William James's famous essay "The Will to Believe." For James, whether an option was live depended on whether or not it was a significant option for an individual. As I am using the term, an option may be live for a culture. A teacher or a course can present live options to students even if the students or teachers don't accept them as such in their own lives.

4. Stephen Toulmin, *Return to Reason* (Cambridge, Mass.: Harvard University Press, 2001), 140.

5. Ibid., 41.

6. Eric Weislogel, "The Transdisciplinary Imperative," *The Global Spire,* December 12, 2008, http://www.metanexus.net/magazine/tabid/68/id/10669/Default.aspx.

7. John Hick, *Death and Eternal Life* (San Francisco: Harper & Row, 1980), 297–98.

8. It has become commonplace, since Kant, to claim that we do not experience reality as it is in itself. Rather, we interpret it in terms of sensory and conceptual frameworks or grids that we bring to our encounter with it. Clearly, the world will appear quite different depending on whether one is a bee or a bat, or a pig or a person. Our sense organs carve the world up differently, enabling animals to see different colors, for example, or perhaps navigate the world without color and sight at all. It is true that there may be categories (or basic concepts) in terms of which all persons experience the world (space, time, and causality, for example) but there may also be significant differences given the fact that languages and cultures provide us with different ways of making sense of the world. Of course, as we grow into a language and culture, the interpretations they provide seem natural and inevitable. If we are brought up, as most children still are, knowing only one linguistic and cultural tradition, we come to believe that we experience the world as it really is. Knowing what we now know about other languages and cultures, our natural tendency to believe we know reality for what it is has become problematic.

9. One might argue that we should have different terms to distinguish between indoctrination that is intentional and that which isn't. Arguably, many Christian academies intend to indoctrinate their students, while most public schools don't (and their teachers and administrators would be aghast at the idea that they do). We might distinguish between hard indoctrination (which is intended) and soft indoctrination (which is not). Still, the end result is the same.

10. Allan Bloom, *The Closing of the American Mind* (New York: Simon and Schuster, 1987), 249.

11. Karl Popper, *Conjectures and Refutations: The Growth of Scientific Knowledge* (New York: Harper Torchbooks, 1963), 356.

12. For a number of variations on this theme see Hillary Putnam, "Two Conceptions of Rationality," in *Reason, Truth and History* (Cambridge: Cambridge University Press, 1981), 103–27; Stephen Toulmin, *Cosmopolis* (New York: Free, 1990), 198–201; *Human Understanding* (Princeton: Princeton University Press, 1972), esp. 478–503; and *Return to Reason* (Cambridge, Mass.: Harvard University Press, 2001), passim. My distinction is similar to that drawn between soft and hard rationality by William

Abraham in his *Introduction to the Philosophy of Religion* (Englewood Cliffs, N.J.: Prentice Hall, 1985), 98–129.

13. See Marsden, *The Outrageous Idea of Christian Scholarship* (New York: Oxford University Press, 1997).

14. I find Ian Barbour's discussion of how to assess rival paradigms in science and in religion particularly helpful. See his *Myths, Models, and Paradigms* (New York: Harper & Row, 1974), esp., 92–146. I also find helpful Basil Mitchell's idea of cumulative case arguments, which appeal to all the evidence. See Mitchell, *The Justification of Religious Belief* (New York: Oxford University Press, 1981); and *Faith and Criticism* (Oxford: Clarendon, 1994).

15. According to Ian Barbour, "If *faith* were simply the acceptance of revealed propositions or assent to propositions, it would be incompatible with *doubt*. But if faith means trust and commitment, it is compatible with considerable doubt about particular interpretations. Faith does not automatically turn uncertainties into certainties. What it does is take us beyond the detached speculative outlook which prevents the most significant sorts of experiences; it enables us to live and act amid the uncertainties of life without pretensions of intellectual or moral infallibility. But it does not give us wisdom or virtue transcending the limitations of human existence" (*Myths, Models, and Paradigms*, 137).

## CHAPTER 5

1. *Time* magazine (April 2, 2007), 43.

2. Bruce A. Kimball, *Orators and Philosophers: A History of the Idea of Liberal Education* (New York: Teachers College Press, 1986).

3. Fareed Zakaria notes that "while America marvels at Asia's test-taking skills, Asian countries come to America to figure out how to get their kids to think. . . . American culture celebrates and reinforces problem solving, questioning authority, and thinking heretically. . . . It rewards self-starters and oddballs" (*The Post-American World* [New York: Norton, 2008], 194–95). That is, at our best schools and universities we teach students to think outside the usual boxes; we encourage them to explore alternative perspectives on the conventional wisdom.

4. John Stuart Mill, *On Liberty, The Essential Works of John Stuart Mill*, ed. Max Lerner, 287 (New York: Bantam, 1965).

5. Gerald Graff, *Beyond the Culture Wars* (New York: Norton, 1992), 13.

6. Brand Blanshard, *The Uses of a Liberal Education and Other Talks to Students* (La Salle, Ill.: Open Court, 1973), 283.

7. Graff, *Beyond the Culture Wars*, 12.

8. Alasdair MacIntyre, *Three Rival Versions of Moral Enquiry: Encyclopaedia, Genealogy, and Tradition* (Notre Dame: University of Notre Dame Press, 1990) 231.

9. There is, of course, a danger that scholars in the university will take their own views to exhaust the realm of possibilities when there are serious (live, influential, important) moral and intellectual traditions in our culture that they don't take seriously. We must also be wary of using intellectual seriousness to

define out-of-bounds the views of oppressed people who have not had the opportunity to sustain their traditions.

10. Pinker, "Less Faith, More Reason," *The Harvard Crimson*, October 27, 2006, http://www.thecrimson.com/article.aspx?ref=515314.

11. Edington, "God: Amen. Discuss," *The Chronicle Review*, December 1, 2006, http://chronicle.com/weekly/v53/i15/15b01601.htm.

12. Pinker, "Less Faith, More Reason."

13. Hollinger, "Enough Already: Universities Do Not Need More Christianity," in *Religion, Scholarship, and Higher Education*, ed. Andrea Sterk, 47–49 (Notre Dame: University of Notre Dame Press, 2002). In another article, Hollinger argues that in my book *Religion and American Education* I gave priority to the ballot box over the laboratory because I insisted on including religious as well as scientific voices in the curricular conversation. But this is a crude misreading of my argument. In that book, as here, my primary argument for taking religion seriously was grounded in liberal education, not politics. See Hollinger, "The Secularization Question and the United States in the Twentieth Century," *Church History* 70, no. 1 (March 2001): 142.

14. Some understand religious experiences (visions, voices, mysticism, numinousness, conversion) to provide evidence for the existence of God. There are philosophical arguments for the existence of God (ontological, cosmological, and teleological). Design arguments have recently been given new life by the discovery of cosmological evidence that the universe appears to be fine-tuned for life. Some philosophers argue that morality (or at least an objective morality) presupposes a God. Some philosophers have argued that orderliness of nature or consciousness or rationality presupposes the existence of an underlying intelligence or a teleological dimension to reality. Some philosophers argue that while none of this evidence provides, by itself, a knock-down or convincing case for God, it is still reasonable to believe in God in light of a cumulative case built out of a wide range of complementary and mutually reinforcing evidence; such cumulative case arguments hinge on what I have called being reasonable, all things considered. Some philosophers and theologians, working within the tradition of Reformed epistemology, argue that we can have a basic belief in God, analogous in some ways to our perception of the physical world, in which our sense of God's existence is immediate, not simply inferred from evidence or as the conclusion of an argument.

15. Terry Eagleton, *Reason, Faith, and Revolution: Reflections on the God Debate* (New Haven: Yale University Press, 2009), 49, 52.

16. Alan Wolfe, "Higher Learning," *Lingua Franca* (March/April 1996): 77, my emphasis.

17. D. G. Hart, *The University Gets Religion* (Baltimore: Johns Hopkins University Press, 1999), 250.

18. Ibid., 250–51.

19. Christian Smith, "Force of Habit," *Books and Culture* (September/October 2002): 20.

20. *The Autobiography of Charles Darwin and Selected Letters*, ed. Francis Darwin, 53–54 (New York: Dover, 1969).

21. Ninian Smart, *Religion and the Modern Mind* (New York: McMillan, 1987), 20.

22. Quoted in Simon Singh, *Big Bang* (New York: Harper Perennial, 2005), 267.

23. For a provocative (if occasionally frustrating) meditation on humility and the overreach of science see David Berliner, *The Devil's Delusion: Atheism and Its Scientific Pretensions* (New York: Crown Forum, 2008).

24. Julian Barnes, *Nothing to Be Frightened Of* (New York: Knopf, 2008), 24.

25. W. H. Newton-Smith, *The Rationality of Science* (Boston: Routledge & Kegan Paul, 1981), 14.

26. Robert Nash, "A Clash of Opposing Worldviews," *Religion and Education* (Fall 2006): 110.

27. Some scholars have argued that rather than focusing so directly on religion we should focus on worldviews: after all, the issue isn't religion in particular, it is worldviews in general. See, for example, Perry Glanzer, "Taking the Tournament of Worldviews Seriously in Education: Why Teaching about Religion Is Not Enough," *Religion and Education* (Spring 2004): 1–19. This may indeed be a wise strategy; something will be gained by deflecting attention away from controversies connected with religion in particular. It is certainly true that there need be no special pleading for religion. In fact, my argument in this chapter regarding religion is simply one example of a larger case for taking various worldviews seriously as part of a liberal education.

## CHAPTER 6

1. Alasdair MacIntyre, *After Virtue* (Notre Dame: University of Notre Dame Press, 1981), 201.

2. James Davison Hunter, "Leading Children beyond Good and Evil," *First Things* (May 2000): 39. Also see Hunter's important book-length critique of character education, *The Death of Character* (New York: Basic, 2000).

3. Vassily Grossman, *Life and Fate*, trans. Robert Chandler (New York: Harper & Row, 1980), 407–10.

4. See Martha Nussbaum, *Cultivating Humanity* (Cambridge, Mass.: Harvard University Press, 1997), 85–112.

5. Ian McEwan, "Only Love and Then Oblivion," *The Guardian* (September 15, 2001).

6. Karl Popper called this the rational unity of mankind. When we take other people seriously enough to talk and argue with them, even learn from them, we are united with them in webs of meaning, in community.

7. See Mark Schwehn, *Exiles from Eden* (New York: Oxford University Press, 1993), 44–65.

8. Huston Smith, *Why Religion Matters* (San Francisco: HarperSanFrancisco, 2001), 274, my emphasis.

9. See Rachael Kessler, *The Soul of Education: Helping Students Find Connection, Compassion, and Character at School* (Alexandria, Va.: Association for Supervision and Curriculum Development, 2000). Also see Ronald Anderson's helpful

contrast of Kessler's and my positions in *Religion and Spirituality in the Public School Curriculum* (New York: Peter Lang, 2004), 64–78.

10. The authors of the study concluded that undergraduates "are searching for deeper meaning in their lives, looking for ways to cultivate their inner selves, seeking to be compassionate and charitable, and determining what they think and feel about the many issues confronting the society and the global community" (Larry A. Braskamp, "The Religious and Spiritual Journeys of College Students," in *The American University in a Postsecular Age*, ed. Douglas Jacobsen and Rhonda Hustedt Jacobsen, 125–26 [New York: Oxford University Press, 2008]).

11. Braskamp, ibid., 130–31.

12. Only 16 percent of faculty in public universities believed that they should be concerned with facilitating students' spiritual development. (Perhaps one should be impressed with how high this percentage is; of course, a lot hinges on what is meant by "spiritual.")

13. C. John Sommerville, *The Decline of the Secular University* (New York: Oxford University Press, 2006), 8–9.

14. Stephen H. Webb, *Taking Religion to School* (Grand Rapids: Brazos, 2000), 66.

15. Barbara E. Walvoord, *Teaching and Learning in College Introductory Religion Courses* (Malden, Mass.: Blackwell, 2008), 13–55. Walvoord acknowledges that this "divide" is one of tendencies and is not at all sharp.

16. Bruce Grelle, "Defining and Promoting the Study of Religion in British and American Schools," *Religion and Education* (Spring 2005): 32.

17. Anderson, *Religion and Spirituality*, 75. Diane Moore concludes on the basis of her thirteen years of teaching secondary school students that "adolescents hunger to ponder fundamental questions of meaning in an atmosphere where their views will be engaged and respected" and argues for a "learner-centered and inquiry-based" pedagogy in response to which students "recognize that 1) they are taken seriously as individuals, with thoughtful and meaningful ideas to share and 2) they can raise and address issues and questions that really matter to them" (*Overcoming Religious Illiteracy* [New York: Palgrave Macmillan, 2007], 163–64).

18. Nel Noddings, *Educating for Intelligent Belief and Unbelief* (New York: Teachers College Press, 1993), 8.

19. Ibid., 17.

20. American Academy of Religion, *Guidelines for Teaching about Religion in K–12 Public Schools in the United States* (2010), http://www.aarweb.org/Publications /OnlinePublications/CurriculumGuidelines/AARK-12CurriculumGuidelines.pdf

21. Ibid., ii.

22. Ibid., 5

23. Ibid., 12. The *Guidelines* emphasize three other important claims: first, students must recognize that religions are *internally diverse*; second, religions are *dynamic*; and third, religions are *embedded in cultures* (so that we can't understand culture without understanding something about religion, and we can't understand religions without understand their cultural context). A long series of case studies provide teachers helpful examples of how to address these important aspects of religion.

24. I am thinking here of Moore, *Overcoming Religious Illiteracy*; James W. Fraser, *Between Church and State: Religion and Public Education in a Multicultural America* (New York: St. Martin's, 1999); and Robert Kunzman, *Grappling with the Good: Talking about Religion and Morality in Public Schools* (Albany: State University of New York Press, 2006).

25. Prothero, *Religious Literacy: What Every American Needs to Know—and Doesn't* (San Francisco: HarperSanFrancisco, 2007), 10.

26. E. M. Adams, "Philosophical Education as Cultural Criticism," in *Teaching Philosophy* 3, no. 1 (Spring 1980): 1–2.

27. Charles C. Haynes, "From Battleground to Common Ground: Religion in the Public Square of 21st Century America," in *Religion and American Public Life: Living with Our Deepest Differences*, by Azizah Y. al-Hibri, Jean Bethke Elshtain, and Charles C. Haynes, 97 (New York: Norton, 2001).

28. K. Anthony Appiah, "Culture, Subculture, Multiculturalism: Educational Options," in *Public Education in a Multicultural Society*, ed. Robert K. Fullinwider, 84 (Cambridge: Cambridge University Press, 1996).

29. Fullinwider puts it this way: "Students should learn to respect what is respectable and learn to appreciate what is *worthy* of appreciation." The real question, he suggests, is "What standards of discrimination should we use to identify the respectable and the worthy in matters of culture?" In promoting "a broad-mindedness and generosity of judgment, multiculturalism must avoid a vacuous relativism" (ibid., 14, my emphasis).

30. Reprinted in Charles Haynes and Oliver Thomas, *Finding Common Ground: A Guide to Religious Liberty in Public Schools* (Nashville: First Amendment Center, 2001), 95–100 (or http://www.freedomforum.org/publications/first/findingcommonground/FCG-complete.pdf). The statement was endorsed by The American Academy of Religion, the American Association of School Administrators, the American Federation of Teachers, the American Jewish Congress, the Americans United Research Foundation, the Association for Supervision and Curriculum Development, the Baptist Joint Committee for Religious Liberty, the Christian Legal Society, the Church of Jesus Christ of Latter-day Saints, the First Amendment Center, the Islamic Society of North America, the National Association of Evangelicals, the National Conference of Community and Justice, the National Council of Churches of Christ in the USA, the National Council for the Social Studies, the National Education Association, and the National School Boards Association.

31. Haynes and Thomas, ibid., 98.

32. Ibid., 6.

33. Haynes, *Finding Common Ground* (Nashville: First Amendment Center, 1994), 1:3.

34. *The Toledo Guiding Principles on Teaching about Religions and Beliefs in Public Schools* (Warsaw: OSCE Office for Democratic Institutions and Human Rights, 2007), 13.

35. Ibid., 11–12.

36. Ibid., 18.

37. A number of Americans were consultants on the *Toledo Guiding Principles*, including Charles Haynes, the primary author of the American common-ground statements.

38. While endorsing neutrality in dealing with religion, the *Toledo Guiding Principles* leave open the possibility that some European nations, given their constitutions, may fund religious schools, but students must have the freedom to be exempted from religious teaching that violates their liberty.

39. *Toledo Guiding Principles*, 46–49. Though the *Principles* don't say much about dialogical approaches or their importance, they do suggest that among various learning outcomes students might understand "that there are various legitimate ways to view history and historical developments (multi-perspectivity)" and they might be aware "of similarities and differences between different religions and beliefs" (49).

40. For several decades now only one person in the entire country—Charles Haynes of the Freedom Forum First Amendment Center—has worked full-time on issues relating to religion and religious liberty in public schools. He has, of course, had help—beginning with Nick Piediscalzi and his colleagues at Wright State University who initiated the task of defining common ground in the wake of *Abington v. Schempp*. Over recent years, Oliver Thomas, Charles Kniker, Bruce Grelle, Marcia Beauchamp, Martha Ball, Michael Waggoner, and others have contributed in important ways to the effort.

## CHAPTER 7

1. According to a 2007 Freedom Forum "State of the First Amendment" survey of Americans: 58 percent want teacher-led prayers in schools; 50 percent would allow public school teachers to teach the Bible as a "factual text" in history classes; 65 percent agree that our nation's Founders intended the United States to be a Christian nation; 55 percent believe that the U.S. Constitution establishes a Christian nation; 28 percent believe that "freedom to worship as one chooses" was never meant to apply to religious groups that the majority of the people consider "extreme or on the fringe." See Charles Haynes, "What Part of 'Secular Nation' Do We Not Understand?" September 16, 2007, http://www.firstamendmentcenter.org/commentary.aspx?id=19049.

2. James Madison, *Federalist Papers* (New York: Bantam, 1982), 48.

3. Quoted in William Estep, *Revolution within a Revolution* (Grand Rapids: Eerdmans, 1990), 145.

4. Williams viewed the Puritan ideal of a New Israel fusing church and state as an Old Testament ideal that is incompatible with the New Testament requirement that God's kingdom be a spiritual kingdom. If Jefferson was primarily concerned that mixing religion and politics would corrupt politics, Williams believed that the wall of separation is necessary to protect religion from the spiritual wilderness of politics.

5. Quoted in Lawrence Cremin, *American Education: The Colonial Experience, 1607–1783* (New York: Harper & Row, 1970), 238.

6. Quoted in Winthrop Hudson, *Religion in America*, 3rd ed. (New York: Scribner's, 1981), 11.

7. Thomas Jefferson, "Notes on the State of Virginia," in *The Life and Selected Writings of Thomas Jefferson*, ed. Adrienne Koch and William Peden Querry 17, 272–77 (New York: Modern Library, 1944).

8. James Madison, *A Memorial and Remonstrance on the Rights of Man*, reprinted in *Religion and Constitutional Government in the United States*, ed. John Semonche (Carrboro, N.C.: Signal, 1986).

9. *Sherbert v. Verner*, 374 U.S. 401, 406 (1963).

10. *Wisconsin v. Yoder*, 406 U.S. 205, 211, 217–18 (1972).

11. *Rosenberger v. Rector and Visitors of the University of Virginia*, 515 U.S. 819, II (1995). Justice Kennedy also argued that the funding policy was religiously neutral so that it did not violate the Establishment Clause.

12. *Everson v. Board of Education*, 330 U.S. 1, 15–16 (1947).

13. In *Everson* the Court allowed the state of New Jersey to reimburse parents for bus fares for children attending parochial schools. In spite of the "wall of separation," the Court noted that the benefit went to children and their parents, not the parochial schools, and it was distributed neutrally (to parents of children attending both public and private schools). While the other eight justices agreed with Black's interpretation of the Establishment Clause, four split with the majority on its implications for the New Jersey law.

14. *Everson v. Board of Education*, 300 U.S. 1, 18 (1947).

15. Ibid.

16. *Lemon v. Kurtzman*, 403 U.S. 602, 614. Burger is here quoting from *Walz v. Tax Commission of the City of New York* (1970).

17. See her concurring opinion in *Wallace v. Jaffree*, 472 U.S. 38 (1985).

18. *Engel v. Vitale*, 370 U.S. 421, 424–25 (1962).

19. *Engel v. Vitale*, 370 U.S. 421, 430 (1962).

20. *Engel v. Vitale*, 370 U.S. 421, 425 (1962).

21. *Engel v. Vitale*, 370 U.S. 421, 431–32 (1962).

22. *Santa Fe Independent School District v. Doe*, 530 U.S. 290 (2000).

23. Perhaps a fourth ruling should be mentioned. In *Wallace v. Jaffre* (1985) the Court held unconstitutional an Alabama law authorizing a one-minute period of silence "for meditation or voluntary prayer." Justice Stevens concluded from the history of the statute that the legislators had no secular purpose; in fact, the clear purpose of the law was to promote prayer and religion. Most commentators believe that a truly neutral minute of silence policy or law (one that allows but doesn't privilege prayer) would be constitutional.

24. See John Witte, *Religion and the American Constitutional Experiment* (Boulder: Westview, 2005), 151.

25. *Wallace v. Jaffree*, 472 U.S. 38 (1985).

26. See Witte, *Religion and the American Constitutional Experiment*, 41–70.

27. Garry Wills, *Under God: Religion and American Politics* (New York: Simon and Schuster, 1990), 383. Thomas Curry argues, "Customs like days of prayer and thanksgiving appeared not so much matters of religion as part of the common coin of civilized living. Sabbath laws enjoyed widespread support and were so little the subject of dissent that citizens never even felt challenged to think how those laws might impose a particular religious viewpoint. . . . The contradiction between their theory and their practice became evident to Americans only later, with the advent of

a more religiously pluralistic society" (*The First Freedoms: Church and State in America to the Passage of the First Amendment* [New York: Oxford University Press, 1986], 218–19).

28. "Treaty of Peace and Friendship between the United States and the Bey and Subjects of Tripoli of Barbary," Article 11, http://www.stephenjaygould.org/ctrl/treaty_tripoli.html. In their study *The Search for Christian America,* the historians Mark Noll, Nathan Hatch, and George Marsden, all evangelicals, conclude: "The key to understanding the American Revolution is balance. The Revolution was not Christian, but it stood for many things compatible with the Christian faith. It was not biblical, though many of its leaders respected Scripture. It did not establish the United States on a Christian foundation, even if it created many commendable precedents. . . . America is not a Christian country, nor has it ever been one" (*The Search for Christian America* [Westchester, Ill.: Crossway, 1983], 100, 102).

29. I owe this analogy to Christopher Mooney. See Mooney, *Boundaries Dimly Perceived: Law, Religion, Education, and the Common Good* (Notre Dame: University of Notre Dame Press, 1990), 110.

30. Madison, *Federalist Papers,* 66–67.

31. *Abington School District v. Schempp,* 374 U.S. 203, 225 (1963).

32. Ibid., 300.

33. Ibid., 306.

34. Ibid., 225.

35. Ibid., 299.

36. Ibid., 305–6.

37. Ibid., 300.

38. *McCollum v. Board of Education,* 333 U.S. 202, 236 (1948).

39. *Abington School District,* 374 U.S. at 225.

40. Ibid., 306.

41. Ibid.

42. Douglas Laycock, "Formal, Substantive, and Disaggregated Neutrality toward Religion," *DePaul Law Review* 39 (1990): 1004.

43. Douglas Laycock, "Religious Liberty as Liberty," *Journal of Contemporary Legal Issues* 7 (Fall 1996): 348.

44. There is an alternative approach taken by some scholars and, notoriously, by Judge Brevard Hand in his unjustly ridiculed ruling in *Smith v. Board of School Commissioners of Mobile County,* 827 F.2d 684 (11th Cir. 1987). On this analysis, schools should be recognized as teaching the *religion* of secular humanism or scientific materialism. In my introduction I mentioned that it has often been claimed that Marxism, nationalism, Americanism, and secular humanism may function as religions do in people's lives, are analogous to traditional religions, or have overlapping characteristics with traditional religions. We might call them secular religions. The claim here is that since schools teach a secular religion (uncritically, as a matter of faith) and since the Establishment Clause requires neutrality among religions (as well as neutrality between religion and nonreligion), schools must also teach about traditional religions. This is not an implausible position—though I believe my analysis

more plausible and less controversial. I don't require that we think of any secular ideology or worldview as a religion—an implausible claim to many. While I do argue that schools and universities teach secular ways of thinking and living uncritically, as a matter of faith, I don't believe that schools teach secular ways of thinking and living as religions. I don't propose that the Supreme Court should accept secular religions for Establishment Clause purposes (an unlikely development). My position is that the clearest conflict is between (traditional) religions and nonreligion, not among religions (including secular humanism).

45. Perhaps I should add that over the last several decades teachers and administrators have become much more sensitive to the free exercise rights of students, largely in response to growing religious pluralism, the multicultural movement, court rulings, and the widespread distribution of common-ground statements. This is all to the good, but it hasn't resulted in any parallel sensitivity to the implications of the Establishment Clause for taking religion seriously in the curriculum.

## CHAPTER 8

1. Mary Warnock, "Neutral Teacher," *Progress and Problems in Moral Education,* ed. Monica Taylor, 110 (Windsor: NFER, 1975). Warnock argues that "unless the teacher comes out into the open, and says in what direction he believes that the evidence points he will have failed in his duty as a teacher" (107).

2. AAUP, *Declaration of Principles* (1915), http://www.aaup-tnconf.org /Documents_PDF/1915_Declaration_of_Principles.pdf, 5.

3. Ibid.

4. Ibid.

5. Ibid., 7.

6. AAUP, "Some Observations on Ideology, Competence, and Faculty Selection," *Academe* 72 (January–February 1986): 2a.

7. *Keyishian v. Board of Regents,* 385 U.S. 589, 603 (1967).

8. "Constitutional Academic Freedom in Scholarship and in Court," *The Chronicle of Higher Education* (January 5, 2001): B14.

9. While the Supreme Court has never weighed academic freedom against the Establishment Clause, an appallingly bad ruling by the 11th Circuit Court does cut against the grain of my position: see *Bishop v. Aronov,* 926 F.2d 1066 (11th Cir. 1991). I discuss the details of this decision in *Religion and American Education: Rethinking a National Dilemma* (Chapel Hill: University of North Carolina Press, 1995), 269–74.

10. AAUP, "1940 Statement of Principles on Academic Freedom and Tenure," in *Two Policy Documents and Reports,* 9th ed. (Washington, D.C.: AAUP, 2001).

11. AAUP, *Declaration of Principles,* 7.

12. Mark U. Edwards Jr., *Religion on Our Campuses* (New York: Palgrave Macmillan, 2006), 118. Edwards notes, "To be a full *professional* member of a disciplinary community demands strong self-identification with the discipline; an

intuitive grasp of the goods, practices, standards, and interpretive schemes of the discipline; and heavy emotional and intellectual investment. . . . In fact, the formation of today's academic is hardly less rigorous than the traditional formation of a nun or monk, requiring as it does extensive training, a long probationary period, years of submission to the judgment of superiors and (willing or not) to the continued judgment of peers, and, arguably, considerably intellectual asceticism and self-denial" (165).

13. "AAR Statement on Academic Freedom and the Teaching of Religion," *Religious Studies News* (March 2007): 3, my emphasis.

14. American Federation of Teachers, "Academic Freedom in the 21st-Century College and University: Academic Freedom for All Faculty and Instructional Staff" (2007), http://www.aft.org/pdfs/highered/academicfreedomstatement0907.pdf, 9.

15. Louis Menand has argued that "the structure of disciplinarity" in research universities "is philosophically weak" and "it encourages intellectual predictability, professional insularity, and social irrelevance. It deserves to be replaced." But with what? And who would determine professional competence? Administrators? See "The Limits of Academic Freedom," in *The Future of Academic Freedom*, ed. Louis Menand, 19 (Chicago: University of Chicago Press, 1996).

16. The idea of institutional academic freedom stems from a comment from Justice Felix Frankfurter who noted the "'four essential freedoms' of a university—to determine for itself on academic grounds who may teach, what may be taught, how it shall be taught, and who may be admitted to study" (*Sweezy v. New Hampshire*, 354 U.S. 234, 263 [1957]). There is a problem with institutional academic freedom that I've not discussed. It can be in tension with the academic freedom of individual faculty members. In fact, lower courts have used institutional academic freedom on occasion as a justification for allowing administrators to limit individual academic freedom—a sometimes disastrous conclusion.

17. *Tinker v. Des Moines Independent Community School District*, 393 U.S. 503 (1969), Section 1, paragraph 2.

18. *Board of Education v. Pico*, 457 U.S. 853, 864, 866 (1982).

19. Tyll Van Geel, *The Courts and American Education Law* (Buffalo: Prometheus, 1987), 222.

20. *Hazelwood School District v. Kuhlmeier*, 484 U.S. 260, 267, 273 (1988). While *Hazelwood* concerned student speech rights, courts have appealed to it in limiting the academic freedom of university faculty members. The most egregious example is when the 11th Circuit Court used *Hazelwood* to justify the administration of the University of Alabama in limiting the academic freedom of one of its professors. See *Bishop*, 926 F.2d at 1066.

21. Stephen Patrina, "Academic Freedom for K–12 Teachers," in *Battleground Schools*, vol. 1, ed. Sandra Mathison and E. Wayne Ross, 1, 6 (Westport: Greenwood, 2008).

22. See, for example, *Mayer v. Monroe County Community School Corporation*, 474 F.3d 477 (7th Cir. 2007); and *Webster v. New Lenox School District*, 917 F.2d 1004 (7th Cir. 1990).

23. See, for example, *Peloza v. Capistrano Unified School District*, 37 F.3d 517 (9th Cir. 1994).

24. Charles Haynes, *Finding Common Ground* (Nashville: First Amendment Center, 2008), 52.

25. Charles C. Haynes and Oliver Thomas, *Finding Common Ground* (Nashville: First Amendment Center, 2001), 7:8.

26. Ibid., 7:6.

27. See Christian Smith, *Christian America: What Evangelicals Really Want* (Berkeley and Los Angeles: University of California Press, 2002), 132.

28. Among major scholars, Martin Marty is the major exception. The National Council of Churches, the organization of mainline and liberal Protestant denominations, has (rightly) been forceful in addressing racial and economic justice issues relating to public schools, has been very critical of the No Child Left Behind legislation for a variety of moral and educational reasons, defended teaching evolution in science courses, and has been concerned about any possible breach of the wall of separation between church and state in public education. But while it perfunctorily endorsed several of the common-ground statements that legitimize "teaching about religion" in public schools, it has done little to actually encourage such teaching or criticize public schools for failing to take religion seriously.

29. Cherry, *Hurrying Toward Zion: Universities, Divinity Schools, and American Protestantism* (Bloomington: Indiana University Press, 1995), 266.

30. See, for example, Gary Dorrien, *The Making of American Liberal Theology*, vol. 3, *Crisis, Irony, and Postmodernity, 1950–2005* (Louisville: Westminster John Knox, 2006), 5.

31. See Dawkins, *The God Delusion* (Boston: Houghton Mifflin, 2006), 340–43.

32. Dennett, *Breaking the Spell* (New York: Penguin, 2006), 327.

33. Some atheists resist being defined in terms of what they oppose—theism (*a-theism*)—and would rather be defined in terms of what they favor, say, naturalism, or perhaps freethinking.

34. It is also important—perhaps even helpful—to discuss atheism in the context of religious liberty (which protects unbelief as well as religious belief).

35. Dennett, *Breaking the Spell*, 327.

36. Some teachers are also wary of controversy and argue that if they are to teach about religion they should stick to the facts and not venture into theology, empathy for people in different religious traditions, or controversial religious interpretations of the subjects of the curriculum. Stephen Prothero has suggested that teaching about religion "is controversial enough without mucking it up in moral or political agendas" (*Religious Literacy: What Every American Needs to Know—and Doesn't* [San Francisco: HarperSanFrancisco, 2007], 142). No doubt teaching about religion shouldn't be *mucked up* in any agenda, but, as I argued in chapter 5, a basic religious literacy isn't sufficient for the purposes of a liberal education, and if we are to take religion seriously we can't avoid the complexities and controversies.

37. Modesto, California, has had a required ninth-grade world religions class that has proved uncontroversial.

38. Styers, "Liberal Values and the Public Classroom: A Response to Stephen H. Webb," *Journal of the American Academy of Religion* 70, no. 1 (March 2002): 164. Styers goes on to argue, "Many religious believers are justifiably skeptical about the capacity of public school teachers to teach central theological issues in a meaningful way in the context of pluralism. I would ask why this form of instruction is the state's prerogative in the first place. Is it not preferable, from a religious point of view, to leave those vital matters to those with greater expertise, who can train our children in a context of faithfulness?"—that is, to religious communities (165–66). From the perspective of religious communities Styers may be right, but from the perspective of liberal education we have no choice, for the many reasons I gave in chapters 5–7. I share Styers's concern about doing the job well.

39. Greenawalt, *Does God Belong in Public Schools?* (Princeton: Princeton University Press, 2004), 80–81.

40. Ibid., 153.

41. Ibid., 144.

## CHAPTER 9

1. While professing attraction to the idea of natural inclusion, Mark Edwards has concluded that even among university teachers the idea is "quixotic." His interviews with faculty members "strongly suggested that proponents of natural inclusion were going to find it extraordinarily difficult, if not impossible, to convince busy and already overworked faculty members that they should venture beyond their disciplinary field and devote sufficient time and energy to gain requisite experience in the appropriate religious and spiritual traditions" (*Religion on Our Campuses: A Professor's Guide to Communities, Conflicts, and Promising Conversations* [New York: Palgrave Macmillan, 2006], 163). I fear that Edwards is right, though we shouldn't lose sight of the ideal. Of course, good textbooks can help with the problems he mentions—though they are a problem in their own right.

2. One yearlong course in universities is, of course, two semester-long courses. I argued in chapter 4 that neutrality (or robust fairness) doesn't require equal time, but it does require adequate time. A one-semester course simply isn't adequate for taking religion seriously in an overwhelmingly secular curriculum.

3. As I suggested in chapter 7, it is wise for a school to assume that a court would use the Sherbert (or "compelling interest") Test if a student challenges a school policy—such as a requirement to take a religion course. Of course, even if a court used the Sherbert Test, it might well find for the school—indeed, I trust that it would in cases of high school students. The Sherbert Test does not guarantee that free exercise rights will be upheld in the face of a compelling governmental interest to ensure a good education.

4. That school system, in Modesto, California, has required a nine-week world religions course for high school freshmen since 2000. It resulted from extensive community discussion and planning in a community feeling the strains of cultural and religious pluralism. Not only has it not proved controversial, there is a great deal

of public support for the course across Modesto's many religious communities. Only one-tenth of 1 percent of students have taken advantage of the opt-out provision. See Emile Lester and Patrick S. Roberts, *Learning about World Religions in Public Schools* (Nashville: First Amendment Center, 2006).

5. See Diane L. Moore, *Overcoming Religious Illiteracy* (New York: Palgrave Macmillan, 2007), 94–97. Moore is the director of the program.

6. Ibid., passim.

7. For a nice summary of the literature on good pedagogy see Barbara E. Walvoord, *Teaching and Learning in College Introductory Religion Courses* (Malden, Mass.: Blackwell, 2008), 82–98.

8. Moore distinguishes between two models, a banking (or instructor) model and a seminar model. She strongly advocates the latter and devotes a good deal of her book to walking the reader through her own experience with seminars, providing a good deal of helpful advice along the way. My own suspicion is that such seminars are unrealistic possibilities at most schools and universities, which require much larger classes and often don't have the thoughtful, motivated students that she has at Philips Academy and Harvard. I don't wish to defend her banking or instructor model, so I have suggested a middle position that would be a reasonable alternative in most high schools and universities.

9. Robert Nash and DeMethra LaSha Bradley explain that in their college classes they "respect the spiritual narratives" of their students: "There are no right and wrong answers here: Each person's life has its own integrity. Our goal in the classroom is simply to invite each person fully into the conversation. To that end, we have found that our students are more likely to talk openly about their spirituality if we structure classroom discussions as mutual, open-ended conversations where we share our meaning-stories rather than as debates intended to convert or convince" ("The Different Spiritualities of the Students We Teach," in *The American University in a Postsecular Age,* ed. Douglas Jacobsen and Rhonda Hustedt Jacobsen, 137 [New York: Oxford University Press, 2008]). I have no doubt that in many contexts this is a wise strategy. In other contexts, however, students can and should debate the merits of various ideas. Perhaps this is done best when students don't speak personally (out of their own spiritual narratives), but address various texts or arguments simply as questioners or advocates or critics.

10. As Walter Capps put it, "Religious studies is a multiform subject-field within which a variety of disciplines are employed to treat a multiplicity of issues, interests, and topics" (*Religious Studies: The Making of a Discipline* [Minneapolis: Fortress, 1995], 331).

11. Ray S. Hart, "Religious and Theological Studies in American Higher Education," *Journal of the American Academy of Religion* 59 (Winter 1991): 716, my emphasis.

12. William Scott Green, "Something Strange, Yet Nothing New: Religion in the Secular Curriculum," *Soundings* 71 (Summer–Fall 1988): 274.

13. This contributes to what Martin Marty has called a "more secular than thou" attitude on the part of many scholars in religious studies ("Half a Life in Religious Studies: Confessions of an 'Historical Historian,'" in *The Craft of Religious Studies,* ed. Jon R. Stone, 153 [New York: St. Martin's, 1998]).

14. AAR, "The Religion Major and Liberal Education—A White Paper," *Religious Studies News* (October 2008): 23. The white paper also emphasizes the importance of intercultural and comparative study, and the multidisciplinarity of the field.

15. "The Religion Major and Liberal Education," 13. I should add that if students are exposed to religious voices, those voices are typically to be found in texts; they are not the voices of their teachers, who typically refrain from taking religious positions at least in their roles as teachers.

16. Capps, *Religious Studies*, 345.

17. John W. Dixon Jr., "What Should Religion Departments Teach?" *Theology Today* 46 (January 1990): 369–70.

18. Here I rely on a superb collection of short and readable essays, written by philosophers in both philosophy and religious studies departments, collected by William J. Wainwright under the title *God, Philosophy and Academic Culture: A Discussion between Scholars in the AAR and the APA* (Atlanta: Scholars Press, 1996). We might distinguish between P-philosophers (found in departments of philosophy) and RS-philosophers (found in departments of religious studies). P-philosophers tend to be interested in theism, in fairly traditional philosophical questions about the God of Christianity and Western religion. RS-philosophers are interested in the many ways in which people and cultures are religious—religion is, after all, much more than belief in God—and in nontheistic religions. P-philosophers typically work within the tradition of Anglo-American analytic philosophy, while RS-philosophers are more likely to draw on Continental philosophy as well as on social science to understand religions not just as philosophical beliefs and systems, but as dimensions of culture. Because of their philosophical bent, P-philosophers are more likely to be concerned with questions of truth, and have some confidence in the power of reason to settle them. RS-philosophers are less interested in such questions. Given their philosophical bent (drawing on Continental traditions and postmodernism) they are more likely to hold that everything is a matter of interpretation.

19. Merold Westphal, "Traditional Theism, the AAR and the APA," in *God, Philosophy and Academic Culture*, 23.

20. C. Stephen Evans, "On Taking God Seriously: Philosophy of Religion in the APA and AAR," in *God, Philosophy, and Academic Culture*, 60.

21. Linell E. Cady and Delwin Brown, eds., introduction to *Religious Studies, Theology, and the University* (Albany: State University of New York Press, 2002), 5. William D. Hart writes that such scholars wish to avoid "guilt by association" with theologians: "These intellectual Victorians (bourgeoisie who are so easily shocked, shocked!) want to guard their chastity. They fear being caught with their pants down, of charges that they consort with the wrong crowd. [To be caught with a theologian] is a mortal sin. . . . What are respectable academics to think? Imagine the gossip, raised eyebrows, and the sardonic laughter" (William D. Hart, "From Theology to *theology*: The Place of 'God-Talk' in Religious Studies," in Cady and Brown, *Religious Studies, Theology, and the University*, 93).

22. Russell McCutcheon, "The Study of Religion as an Anthropology of Credibility," in Cady and Brown, *Religious Studies, Theology, and the University*, 13.

23. Donald Wiebe, *The Politics of Religious Studies* (New York: Palgrave Macmillan, 2000), xiii.

24. Robert Cummings Neville, "Religious Studies and Theological Studies," *Journal of the American Academy of Religion* 61 (Summer 1993): 191.

25. David Ray Griffin, "Professing Theology in a State University," in *Theology and the University: Essays in Honor of John Cobb* (Albany: State University of New York Press, 1991), 7.

26. Ibid., 10.

27. Stephen H. Webb, "The Voice of Theology: Rethinking the Personal and the Objective in Christian Pedagogy," *The Journal of the American Academy of Religion* 65 (Fall 1997): 766–67.

28. George M. Marsden, *The Soul of the University*," 38–39. Also see Marsden, *The Outrageous Idea of Christian Scholarship*, 26–31.

29. It is important to emphasize that in holding that theology must be subject to critical review, I do not mean to hold it hostage to any narrowly scientific conception of criticism. Theological claims often acquire their meanings by being embedded in traditions, in ritual and religious practices, in dense thickets of religious symbolism, in ways of life. Indeed, religious traditions can generate powerful intellectual and cultural critiques of Enlightenment rationalism and postmodern relativism.

30. Brown, "Academic Theology in the University or Why an Ex-Queen's Heir Should Be Made a Subject," in Cady and Brown, 138, my emphasis. Similarly, Ursala King refers "to 'spiritual challenges' as those challenges that raise the question of what the knowledge of and about religion might be for in the twenty-first century. Is the whole discipline of religious studies merely a playing field for philosophical and religious ideas, full of constructions that academics arrange and rearrange on their game boards of knowledge? Or has the study of religions further relevance, substance, and vision beyond the merely arbitrary in a postmodern carnival of ideas? . . . If contemporary society is a society in spiritual crisis, a society in search of a soul, then we need intellectual and spiritual resources" (King, "Is There a Future for Religious Studies as We Know It? Some Postmodern, Feminist, and Spiritual Challenges," in *JAAR* 70, no 2 [June 2002]: 376). And that is a task of the religious studies.

31. David Ray Griffin, *Reenchantment without Supernaturalism* (Ithaca: Cornell University Press, 2001), 14.

32. Linell E. Cady, "Territorial Disputes: Religious Studies and Theology in Transition," in Cady and Brown, *Religious Studies, Theology, and the University*, 111.

33. Ibid., 123.

34. See Griffin, *Reenchantment without Supernaturalism*, 16.

CHAPTER 10

1. I would have high school students take a three-year history sequence: world history to 1500, world and American history from 1500 to 1900, world and American history from 1900 to the present. Each history course would be taught in parallel with courses in world and American literature that cover the same historical periods.

2. David M. Kennedy, Lizabeth Cohen, and Thomas A. Bailey, *The American Pageant: A History of the Republic*, 12th ed. (Boston: Houghton Mifflin, 2002).

3. Moore, *Overcoming Religious Illiteracy: A Cultural Studies Approach to the Study of Religion in Secondary Education* (New York: Palgrave Macmillan, 2007), 63–66.

4. All too crudely I would distinguish among (1) sacred literature that has become canonical within a religious tradition (the New Testament, the Qur'an); (2) religious literature written within a religious tradition but that is not canonical (*Paradise Lost*); (3) spiritual literature that grapples with spiritual and religious themes, perhaps using religious symbols, stories, and metaphors but that it is not orthodox (*The Scarlet Letter, The Satanic Verses*); and (4) secular literature that doesn't raise or explore religious questions and concerns, much less affirm a spiritual or religious understanding of the world.

5. T. S. Eliot, "Religion and Literature," in *Religion and Modern Literature*, ed. G. B. Tennyson and E. E. Ericson, 27 (Grand Rapids: Eerdmans, 1932).

6. Peter Singer, "America's Shame," *The Chronicle Review* 55, no. 27 (March 13, 2009): B6.

7. It is appalling that the problem of religion and economics has been almost totally ignored. I am happy that both Diane Moore and Kent Greenawalt have discussed the relevance of religion to economics, though I find their discussions somewhat tepid at best. They fail to convey a sense of how egregiously inadequate economics texts and courses are.

8. Stephen Prothero finds this neutrality argument "absurd and impractical." The Bible, he argues, "is of sufficient importance in Western civilization to merit its own course" (*Religious Literacy: What Every American Needs to Know—and Doesn't* [San Francisco: HarperSanFrancisco, 2007]), 134.

9. See Mark Chancey's review of these legislative forays in "A Textbook Example of the Christian Right: The National Council on Bible Curriculum in Public Schools," *Journal of the American Academy of Religion* 75, no. 3 (September 2007): 554–81.

10. The quotation is from p. 169 of the 1996 edition. There are a number of editions of the curriculum, none of which is easy to come by. Also see Chancey's review of various editions of the curriculum in ibid.

11. For Catholics, the Bible requires the authoritative interpretation of the church; Jews have long read the Bible through rabbinic commentary; secular scholars draw on research in the humanities and social sciences to make sense of biblical texts; mainline and liberal Protestants (and Jews and Catholics) often draw on that scholarship as well as on centuries of theological interpretation to illuminate their understanding of the Bible. To just read the Bible doesn't avoid sectarian bias; rather, it adopts a particular sectarian approach.

12. Brennan Breed and Kent Harold Richards, "Review of *The Bible in History and Literature*," in *Religion and Education* (Fall 2007): 94, 99.

13. Chancey, "A Textbook Example of the Christian Right," 568–69. Chancey also claims that the various editions of the curriculum "are filled with factual errors, tabloid scholarship, and plagiarism, as well as religious claims and presuppositions that cause them to run afoul of pertinent court rulings" (555).

14. *The Bible and Public Schools: A First Amendment Guide* (Front Royal, Va.: Bible Literacy Project; Nashville: First Amendment Center, 1999), http://www .firstamendmentcenter.org/about.aspx?id=6261. The Society of Biblical Literature's (SBL) "Bible Electives in Public Schools: A Guide from the Society of Biblical Literature," can be found in *Religion and Education* (Spring 2009): 94–112, and online at http://www.sbl-site.org/educational/thebibleinpublicschools.aspx. The SBL promises teachers training workshops and lesson plans that will eventually be incorporated into a textbook.

15. "The Bible in Public Schools," 11 (pdf version without visuals). It is also online at the First Amendment Center's Web site.

16. Or, to take a New Testament example, most scholars agree that the Gospels were written thirty to sixty years after Jesus' death by men who did not know him but drew on various sources to develop somewhat different, perhaps conflicting, portraits of him.

17. Stephen Prothero claims that Bible courses "should not focus on biblical criticism" (*Religious Literacy*, 133). He thinks this would "undermine the convictions of students who believe that the Bible is the Word of God" (133). I take it that both neutrality and liberal education require that students be exposed to various secular as well as religious interpretations of the text. Indeed, both historical and textual criticism are important in understanding mainline and more liberal religious interpretations of the Bible.

18. The SBL statement claims that the academic goals of a good Bible course are "similar to the goals of any literature course. Some include: to teach students about selected books and passages of the Bible; to familiarize students with the themes, characters, plots, narratives and structures of the Bible; to enjoy and appreciate the rewards of reading a biblical text closely, with the aid of secondary materials; [to] teach students about the formation of the Bible, oral tradition, textual transmission and translation, and canon formation; to familiarize students with the social, cultural, and political aspects of life reflected in the biblical writings; to appreciate the diverse interpretations of the Bible; to understand the wide-ranging effects of the Bible on religions, culture, politics, and art; to recognize different literary forms in the Bible; to practice critical thinking skills" ("Bible Electives in Public Schools," 102).

19. Prothero, *Religious Literacy*, 132–37.

20. See Ninian Smart, "Secular Ideologies: How Do They Figure in Religious Studies Courses," in *Teaching the Introductory Course in Religious Studies: A Sourcebook*, ed. Mark Juergensmeyer, 167–73 (Atlanta: Scholars Press, 1991).

CHAPTER 11

1. We might distinguish methodological from *philosophical* naturalism. The former is agnostic about ultimate reality; if the supernatural exists, it simply can't be caught in the methodological nets of science. The latter is a stronger position, according to which there is no God or supernatural dimension to reality. That is, it makes a philosophical, not just a methodological, claim.

2. As I argued above, advanced or upper-level and graduate courses are not bound by the requirements of a liberal education.

3. Nel Noddings, *Educating for Intelligent Belief and Unbelief* (New York: Teachers College Press, 1993), 144, my emphasis.

4. Thomas Kuhn, *The Structure of Scientific Revolutions* (Chicago: University of Chicago Press, 1962), 165.

5. Quoted in Henry Margenau and Roy Abraham Varghese, *Cosmos, Bios, Theos* (La Salle, Ill.: Open Court, 1992), 1.

6. Michael Polanyi, *Science, Faith and Society* (Chicago: University of Chicago, 1964), 45.

7. Edward Shils, *Tradition* (Chicago: University of Chicago Press, 1981), 22.

8. Alfred North Whitehead, *Essays in Science and Philosophy* (New York: Philosophical Library, 1948), 129, my emphasis.

9. Though I don't follow his typology precisely, I am deeply indebted to Ian Barbour for his immensely helpful discussion of the various ways science and religion might relate. See chapter 4 of his *Religion and Science: Historical and Contemporary Issues* (San Francisco: HarperSanFrancisco, 1997), 77–105.

10. Arthur Peacocke, *Intimations of Reality: Critical Realism in Science and Religion* (Notre Dame: University of Notre Dame Press, 1984), 51.

11. National Research Council (NRC), *National Science Education Standards* (Washington, D.C.: National Academy Press, 1996), 59, 23, 107, 197–98, 107, 201, 107.

12. Larry Witham, *Where Darwin Meets the Bible* (New York: Oxford University Press, 2002), 272. The survey results were initially published in *Nature* in 1997 (April 3): 435–36, (July 23): 313. A number of later surveys have confirmed that about 40 percent of biologists believe in God.

13. Michael Ruse, "Science under Siege," *The Christian Century* (November 15, 2005): 31.

14. See John B. Cobb, ed., *Back to Darwin: A Richer Account of Evolution* (Grand Rapids: Eerdmans, 2008), especially the essay by A. Y. Gunter on scientific alternatives to neo-Darwinism ("Six Scientific Alternatives to Neo-Darwinism," 128–44).

15. The National Academy of Sciences, *Science and Creationism* (Washington, D.C.: National Academy Press, 1984), 4–6.

16. According to the National Academy of Sciences (NAS), *Science, Evolution, and Creationism* (Washington, D.C.: National Academies Press, 2008), "Science and religion are separate and address aspects of human understanding in different ways. Attempts to pit science and religion against each other create controversy where none needs to exist" (12). A latter passage says that "science can neither prove nor disprove religion," although "scientific advances have called some religious beliefs into question, such as the ideas that the Earth was created very recently, that the Sun goes around the Earth, and that mental illness is due to possession by spirits or demons." So *sometimes* science calls into question and presumably falsifies religious claims (54).

17. Richard Dawkins, *The God Delusion* (New York: Houghton Mifflin, 2006), 101; and Sam Harris, *Letter to a Christian Nation* (New York: Vintage, 2006), 63.

18. Michael B. Berkman, Julianna Sandell Pacheco, and Eric Plutzer, "Evolution and Creationism in America's Classrooms: A National Portrait," *PLoS Biol* 6(5) (May 20, 2008): e124. doi:10.1371/journal.pbio.0060124. The Berkman survey also found that one in six biology teachers believes that "God created human beings pretty much in their present form at one time within the last 10,000 years or so."

19. Advocates of ID typically claim that as scientists, they are as agnostic as scientists about the cause of design. Critics of ID point out that most advocates of ID are in fact conservative Christians. Still, the concept of design is a fully secular concept, and it can be identified apart from the cause of the design—the designer. Whether the designer is God is conceptually a separate theological or philosophical matter. Regarding falsifiability, most scientists think that neo-Darwinism falsifies ID theory, so that if a plausible neo-Darwinian explanation of a particular phenomenon is forthcoming, then there is evidence that falsifies the design claim. In fact, naturalism would appear to be unfalsifiable, for as neo-Darwinians constantly argue, the absence of a naturalistic explanation now doesn't mean that one isn't forthcoming at some point. That is, a naturalistic explanation can never be ruled out. The archnaturalist Daniel Dennett argues, for example, "When they [scientists] are confronted with a *prima facie* powerful and undismissible objection to natural selection . . . they are driven to reason as follows: I cannot (yet) see how to refute this objection, or overcome this difficulty, but since I cannot imagine how anything other than natural selection could be the cause of the effects, I will have to assume that the objection is spurious; *somehow* natural selection must be sufficient to explain the effects" (Dennett, *Darwin's Dangerous Idea* [New York: Touchstone, 1995], 47).

20. Michael Ruse, "The Argument from Design: A Brief History," in *Debating Design,* ed. William A. Dembski and Michael Ruse, 30 (Cambridge: Cambridge University Press, 2004).

21. Richard Lewontin, "Billions and Billions of Demons," *The New York Review of Books* (January 9, 1997): 31, my emphasis.

22. According to the National Academy of Sciences, "Nothing is wrong with teaching critical thinking. Students need to learn how to reexamine their ideas in light of observations and accepted scientific concepts." That is, critical reasoning takes place within science, not about science. The NAS adds, "The ideas offered by intelligent design creationists are not the products of scientific reasoning. Discussing these ideas in science classes would not be appropriate given their lack of scientific support." In fact, "There is no scientific controversy about the basic facts of evolution [among scientists]. In this sense the intelligent design movement's call to 'teach the controversy' is unwarranted" (NAS, *Science, Evolution, and Creationism,* 52). In my terms, this is critical thinking as rationality not reasonableness.

23. Provine notes that he has taught evolution from middle school to graduate school, and "in every case, students have greatly enjoyed sharing and criticizing ideas

and evidence concerning evidence. . . . The goal is not to fill the student's noggin with what is believed about evolutionary biology now, but to leave the study with an interest in evolution for life." He adds that "students are delighted because they are heard and are taken seriously" (Provine, "Design? Yes! But Is It Intelligent?" in *Darwinism, Design, and Public Education*, ed. John Angus Campbell and Stephen C. Meyer, 510–11 (East Lansing: Michigan State University Press, 2003). While Provine encourages discussion, he does not require students to read critiques of neo-Darwinism or accounts of alternative ways of understanding nature. It is not clear, as a result, how informed, thoughtful, or fair the discussions would be.

24. *Epperson v. Arkansas*, 393 U.S. 97, 104 (1968).

25. Ibid., 109.

26. *Edwards v. Aguillard*, 482 U.S. 578 (1987). Justice Antonin Scalia argued in dissent that the act did have a secular purpose, to prevent indoctrination: the Louisiana legislature "wanted to ensure that students would be free to decide for themselves how life began, based upon a fair and balanced presentation of the scientific evidence" (*Edwards v. Aguillard*, 482 U.S. 578, 637 [1987]). Of course, requiring a *balanced* treatment of "scientific" theories is a misguided and heavy-handed approach; it does not lie within the competence of legislatures to determine what is good or bad science and how many pages each theory should get.

27. Here are a few of the problems: (1) Instead of ruling on narrow grounds, Judge Jones ruled on the broadest possible grounds, a dubious approach in terms of conventional jurisprudence. (2) He naively attempted to settle philosophical issues relying only on testimony given at the trial. (3) He unconstitutionally took theological sides in arguing that the correct view is that evolution is compatible with religion. (4) Jones didn't consider the differences between evolution and neo-Darwinism; indeed, he repeatedly contrasted ID with evolution rather than with neo-Darwinism. (Arguably, ID is compatible with evolution, which might be designed.) (5) Even if advocates of ID are religious this doesn't make ID religious; certainly the concept of design is a secular concept. (6) He repeatedly conflated ID with creation-science, a dubious position. (7) While Jones criticized the "contrived dualism" of ID advocates in arguing that if there isn't a naturalistic explanation for some phenomenon the only alternative is a design explanation, he uncritically adopted his own contrived dualism in concluding that if an explanation isn't naturalistic it must be religious. (8) Jones didn't distinguish between "teaching ID" and "teaching about ID." (9) He wrongly dismissed "teaching the controversy" as "dangerous, and at worst a canard." (10) Perhaps most important, Jones didn't consider the wider role of science courses within a liberal education.

28. According to Francis Crick, "'You,' your joys and your sorrows, your memories and your ambition, your sense of personal identity and free will, are in fact no more than the behavior of a vast assembly of nerve cells and their associated molecules. As Lewis Carroll's Alice might have phrased: 'You're nothing but a pack of neurons'" (Crick, *The Astonishing Hypothesis: The Scientific Search for the Soul* [New York: Touchstone, 1995], 3).

29. Sam Harris, *The End of Faith* (New York: Norton, 2004), 208–9. The philosopher William Lyons concludes his history of twentieth-century attempts to solve the

mind-body problem by writing that there has been in the last several decades, a reaction against the "naturalizing tendency" in the philosophy of mind: "Philosophers, psychologists, as well as those involved in the brain sciences, have all had to admit that, in our attempted explanations of human nature, we are completely confounded by that part of us we call 'consciousness.' No scientists have even begun to make sense, say, of how it is that consciousness has evolved, or how it is that consciousness arises out of and is maintained by certain types of brain processing but not others" (Lyons, *Matters of the Mind* [New York: Routledge, 2001], 230).

30. That is, the distinction between methodological and philosophical naturalism is lost.

## CHAPTER 12

1. Martha Nussbaum has commented that "as children explore stories, rhymes, and songs—especially in the company of the adults they love—they are led to notice the sufferings of other living creatures." Stories confront children "with the uneven fortunes of life, convincing them emotionally of their urgency and importance." By inviting readers (or spectators in the context of drama) to identify with heroes "compassion for suffering seizes the imagination" and "their sympathies are broadened in the process" (Nussbaum, *Cultivating Humanity* [Cambridge, Mass.: Harvard University Press, 1997], 93). Perhaps nothing is so important as developing students' empathy—especially their sensitivity to the suffering of people and animals. Of course, we also need to nurture an appreciation of the causes of suffering and possible response to it, both of which are somewhat more controversial.

2. Theissen, *Teaching for Commitment: Liberal Education, Indoctrination, and Christian Nurture* (Montreal: McGill-Queen's University Press, 1993), 274.

3. Ibid., 235.

4. The literature used in character education programs can be historically and culturally rich—and reveal something of the motivations and traditions that do provide deep justifications for moral virtues and values. Indeed, it might give life to the diverse ways in which people and cultures make sense of their moral virtues and values. Often, however, the history and literature used in character education is cherry-picked to make particular points, to reinforce particular virtues and values, rather than to encourage any deep encounter with traditions in all their richness and complexity.

5. Some religions have required nonviolence, others have called for holy wars; some have emphasized love and mercy, others justice and retribution; some have required chastity and poverty; others have sanctified marriage and wealth. Some religions have understood morality in terms of God's Law, others in terms of love, grace, tradition, or liberating the oppressed. Indeed, these differences can often be found within the same religions, each of which harbors variations of extraordinary richness. Religious liberals and religious conservatives disagree deeply about gay marriage and abortion. At a deeper level, conservatives are often wary of human reason and claims about progress, insisting that people are essentially sinful, and must live by tradition, faith, and God's grace. Liberals are typically more inclined to believe

that God works through social, political, and intellectual movements to further social progress (though they often feel considerable alienation from the kind of technocratic, consumer culture that has become dominant). Some conservatives believe that people are so sinful that only the threat of hell or the experience of divine grace can move them. Liberals often have a somewhat more optimistic view of human nature in which we have at least a significant potential for doing good apart from supernatural intervention.

6. Beginning in the 1960s, and for several decades thereafter, the values clarification movement dominated moral (or values) education in public schools. The core idea was that it was the goal of teachers to help students clarify their existing personal values, typically by encouraging them to confront hard choices and dilemmas, rather than to teach them to be virtuous or that some actions are actually right or wrong. Indeed, we shouldn't think of children as having right or wrong values. A kind of 1960s-style existential authenticity and autonomy was the ideal.

7. L. H. Getchell et. al., *Perspectives on Health* (Lexington, Mass.: D. C. Heath, 1994), 163.

8. Nel Noddings puts this well: "Here is a question central to almost every human life: Do you love me? Do I have that special something that makes your eyes sparkle and your heart sing? Ah, what a topic! Surely this should be a major part of sex education, and it can include biography, fiction, poetry, music, art, and history. Surely this would be the place to read the Brownings, Romeo and Juliet, *The Scarlet Letter*, *Wuthering Heights*, the story of John and Abigail Adams, of Marie and Pierre Currie; to listen to Berlioz's Romeo and Juliet, Wagner's *Tristan and Isolde*, Bernstein's *West Side Story*, Gershwin's *Porgy and Bess* ("Beyond Teacher Wisdom: In Quest of Wisdom," lecture, University of North Carolina, 1993, 12).

9. Terry Eagleton, *Reason, Faith, and Revolution* (New Haven: Yale University Press, 2009), 134.

10. I am not thinking so much here of stem-cell research, but of technologies that are still largely on the drawing boards: the redesign of humanity that germline genetic engineering, artificial intelligence, and robotics may well make possible. See, for example, Bill Joy, "Why the Future Doesn't Need Us" (*Wired*, issue 8.04 [April 2000], http://www.wired.com/wired/archive/8.04/joy.html); Bill McKibben, *Enough* (New York: Henry Holt, 2003); and Roger Shattuck, *Forbidden Knowledge* (New York: St. Martin's, 1996).

## CONCLUSION

1. Charles Haynes and Oliver Thomas, *Finding Common Ground: A Guide to Religious Liberty in Public Schools* (Nashville: First Amendment Center, 2007), provides a wealth of resources for doing this (http://www.firstamendmentcenter.org/about .aspx?id=6276).

2. See the Religion and Public Education Resource Center at California State University, Chico, http://www.csuchico.edu/rs/rperc/index.html.

# Index

AAR. *See* American Academy of
  Religion
AAUP. *See* American Association of
  University Professors
*Abington School District v. Schempp*,
  157, 163, 164–65
abortion, 277–78
academic freedom
  *Declaration of Principles* and,
    170–71, 173
  disciplinary orthodoxies
    regarding, 174
  Establishment Clause and, 172,
    312n9
  faculty body/university
    administration and, 175
  First Amendment and, 172–73
  in higher education, 170–72,
    173–76
  institutional, 175, 313n16
  liberal education and, 169–78
  limitations on, 173–76
  member of disciplinary profession
    and, 173–74, 312n12
  *Observation on Ideology* and, 171
  political points of view and, 175,
    313n15
  public school teachers and,
    176–78
academic theology, 213, 317n21

accommodationism, 161
agnosticism
  college faculty a nd, 22, 296n7
  statistics on, 20, 295n2, 296n7
alternatives, criteria for taking
    seriously, 115–17
*The Ambivalence of the Sacred*
    (Appleby), 28
American Academy of Religion
    (AAR), 58, 136–37, 174, 202,
    299n32, 307n23
American Association of University
    Professors (AAUP), 170–71, 173
American colonies, religious
    liberty in
  church/state and, 148–50, 309n4
  economics and, 149
  Enlightenment and, 150
  evangelicals and, 148–49
  pluralism and, 148
American education, secularization
    of, 61–79
Americanism, 64–65
Americans
  belief statistics on, 20, 21,
    295nn1–3
  institutional secularization and,
    21–22
American standards
  biology and, 53–54